Lecture Notes in Computer Scien

T0238382

Commenced Publication in 1973
Founding and Former Series Editors:
Gerhard Goos, Juris Hartmanis, and Jan van Leeuwen

Norbert Streitz   Achilles Kameas
Irene Mavrommati (Eds.)

The Disappearing Computer

Interaction Design, System Infrastructures
and Applications for Smart Environments

 Springer

Volume Editors

Norbert Streitz
Fraunhofer IPSI
AMBIENTE - Smart Environments of the Future
Dolivostr. 15, 64293 Darmstadt, Germany
E-mail: streitz@ipsi.fraunhofer.de

Achilles Kameas
Hellenic Open University
and
Computer Technology Institute, DAISy group
23 Sahtouri str, 26222 Patras, Greece
E-mail: kameas@eap.gr

Irene Mavrommati
Computer Technology Institute, DAISy group
and
University of the Aegean
N. Kazantzaki str, University Campus, 26500 Patras, Greece
E-mail: Mavrommati@cti.gr

Library of Congress Control Number: 2007927057

CR Subject Classification (1998): H.5.2, H.5.3, H.5, H.4, H.3, D.2, C.2, K.4

LNCS Sublibrary: SL 3 – Information Systems and Application, incl. Internet/Web
and HCI

ISSN   0302-9743
ISBN-10   3-540-72725-6 Springer Berlin Heidelberg New York
ISBN-13   978-3-540-72725-5 Springer Berlin Heidelberg New York

Springer is a part of Springer Science+Business Media

springer.com

© Springer-Verlag Berlin Heidelberg 2007

Typesetting: Camera-ready by author, data conversion by Markus Richter, Heidelberg
Printed on acid-free paper   SPIN: 12068029   06/3180   5 4 3 2 1 0

Preface

It is our position that "the-computer-as-we-know-it" will soon have no role in our future everyday lives and environments. It will be replaced by a new generation of technologies, which will move the computing power off the desktop and ultimately integrate it with real world objects and everyday environments. Computing becomes thus an inseparable part of our everyday activities, while simultaneously *disappearing* into the background. It becomes a *ubiquitous utility* taking on a role similar to electricity – an enabling but invisible and pervasive medium revealing its functionality on request in an unobtrusive way and supporting people in their everyday lives.

The common theme of the research presented in this book is to explore how everyday life can be supported and enhanced by smart environments composed of a collection of interacting artefacts and intelligent services, in which "the-computer-as-we-know-it" has disappeared from our perception. Nevertheless, computing – now distributed, networked, and ubiquitous – is still the supporting backbone of the envisioned environment. The exploration of new concepts and techniques out of which future computing applications can be developed is the common goal and driving force of the *Disappearing Computer* research presented in this book.

The Disappearing Computer

The term *Disappearing Computer* (DC) was coined as the title of a proactive research initiative (www.disappearing-computer.net) planned by the Future and Emerging Technologies (FET) unit and launched in the context of the European Commission's Information Society Technology (IST) research programmes. Some time later, the IST Advisory Group (ISTAG) developed a related vision of the future and called it "Ambient Intelligence" (AmI). Other similar terms used worldwide are: ubiquitous computing, pervasive computing, proactive computing, ambient computing, and smart environments. In general, all these terms imply that the computer as an object will gradually move out of our perception while at the same time becoming ubiquitously available and providing its functionality.

The common goal of these research efforts is to investigate how information and communication technology modules can be embedded into objects or diffused into the environment, in order to support activities in ways beyond those possible with the computer today. Everyday objects with embedded sensing, information processing and communication modules are turned into smart artefacts, capable of interacting with other artefacts through local (wireless) networks and able to adapt and change.

One of the distinguishing features of the *Disappearing Computer* research is that it also investigates how these objects and environments can be designed so as to enhance people's lives and facilitate rich everyday experiences in an engaging and coherent way. This research aims not only to develop computing systems and technology know-how, but also robust methods and tools for creating novel people-friendly environments. It is our belief that the starting point is not technology per se, but technology as an enabler for the people-centred creation of activity-supporting ubiquitous computing applications.

The chapters in this book address, from different perspectives, the design of *Disappearing Computer* technology, tools and applications. They resulted from the research funded within the context of the *Disappearing Computer (DC)* research initiative. Individual research teams started from different backgrounds, including computer science, electronics, material sciences, social sciences, architecture and design. They developed novel concepts, investigated user requirements, employed participatory design, and turned this into the development of smart artefacts and enabling environments, including corresponding middleware and infrastructures. The common denominators were to design technology for people and to implement prototype applications in order to evaluate their outcome.

The collective impact of the research results was multiplied via a mechanism – novel for the European Commission – that was established in parallel to the DC projects: the *Disappearing Computer Network (DC-Net)*. It explicitly encouraged the DC research teams to collaborate, share information and expertise in different formats, exchange people, welcome visitors, explore synergies and tackle issues beyond the scope of each research project via a range of innovative measures and activities. These network activities proved to be very effective and were widely subscribed to.

In this book, we have collected the different perspectives and findings of various research teams that were involved in the *Disappearing Computer* research initiative. However, this book is intended to present the highlights and to provide an account of these early research efforts towards the realisation of the vision of future smart environments. This includes an overview of the current state of the art in selected areas and aims at providing insight into future research and development efforts.

Structure of the Book

The multidisciplinary research efforts presented in this book address a wide range of topics, including the development of core technology (i.e., system architectures, modules, middleware, tools, protocols, services). Other lines of research are concerned with techniques for integrating IT components with materials, such as paper or fibre. There were also approaches constructing more comprehensive smart environments that augment the boundaries of physical spaces, such as homes, offices, museums, and educational settings. Last but not least, a line of people-centred research is concerned with the design, development and deployment of artefacts and applications to support people's activities within smart environments.

This multidisciplinary perspective is reflected in the content and structure of this book, which contains 13 chapters clustered in 4 parts:

Part 1: Interacting within Smart Spaces
Part 2: Designing for the Home and Social Activities
Part 3: System Architecture and Infrastructures
Part 4: Augmenting Physical Artefacts

Part 1, *Interacting within Smart Spaces*, is concerned with people's relationships and communication within spaces that are augmented by ubiquitous and pervasive technology. The chapters describe applications of technologies developed in the framework of the Disappearing Computer paradigm that provide support for social processes and experiences in local as well as distributed settings. The common theme of the four papers in this Part 1 is the notion of "space and place". Conceptual frameworks and work practises from Architecture (here in its original meaning referring to the real built environment around us) play a central role. The specific environments address office work, exhibitions in museums, learning and educational spaces, and work practices of (landscape) architects. Moving from information design to experience design, it is described how experiences can be shared when they are mediated via ambient displays and mobile devices constituting examples of smart artefacts populating augmented spaces. Starting from observations of people and confronting them with mock-ups sparked ideas of alternative and unexplored directions for technology. New routes of development were found based on observations retrieved in real-world human-centric experiments. While "interactivity" is mostly in the foreground, the work in these chapters also required development of a substantial infrastructure to address the problems of coupling multiple devices and to make things happen as they were.

The first chapter describes design, development, and evaluation of a smart office environment that enables awareness of distributed teams using ambient displays in combination with mobile identification devices. As a starting point, the design approach exploits the affordances of real-world artefacts and also succeeds in creating aesthetically pleasing results. The second chapter addresses how innovations in mixed and augmented reality can publicly be deployed in less controlled settings as, e.g., in living exhibitions at different museums. It also shows what is needed in terms of combining technology development with social science studies and close collaboration with museum personnel. The third chapter suggests that concepts like embodiment and performative elements of space, mixed objects, configuring and place making together form interesting challenges for the design of inspirational learning environments. It describes the study of design education and trials with prototypes in real-use settings of design and architecture classes. The final chapter in this part addresses the extension of experimental participatory design methods and ethnographic methods to spatial computing solutions based on a 3-D collaborative virtual environment.

The following **Part 2, *Designing for the Home and Social Activities***, focuses on investigating peoples' needs and desires in inhabiting augmented spaces that are very close to their daily activities. Participatory design and responsiveness to ethnographic studies are key elements here, while the emphasis is placed on empowering end users to create applications within the home environment. This cluster of research started from the identification and understanding of actual human needs expressed within specific usage contexts (rather than needs originating from technological requirements). An open ended nature is often promoted in many of the resulting prototypes. Applications coming from this research angle can be characterized by their openness to manipulation and to being shaped; they are open for people to explore ubiquitous technology and to live with it. Observing people's actual requirements as well as the co-existence of people and Disappearing Computer technology, this research unveils a list of requirements pertaining to the human aspects of Disappearing Computer research.

The three chapters in this part address the following applications in particular. The first chapter investigates families' needs for intergenerational communication for living together by using a combination of cultural probes, video prototypes and technology probes working closely with exemplary families in two different countries. The second chapter addresses the development of a lightweight component model that allows users to manage the introduction and arrangement of new interactive services and devices in the home. The model is responsive to ethnographic studies of the interior layout and use of equipment in different spaces of the home. The third chapter in this part investigates the well-known intrusiveness problem when technology is too dominating and disturbing. Based on usability studies of meetings in local work contexts, design principles were identified and applied to the development of a system that allows handling a variety of intrusive communication technologies like incoming phone calls, SMS, instant messaging, and e-mail. While it has its origin in work situations, it can be extended to situations outside work.

Subsequently, **Part 3, *System Architecture and Infrastructures***, comprises three chapters that describe different architectural approaches to building systems from communicating components. Due to their "digital self", artefacts can now publicize in the digital space their properties (what the object is), capabilities (what the object knows to do) and services (what the object can offer to others). Until now, the ways that an object could be used and the tasks it could be used for were always determined by and depended on its shape, as a direct consequence of the anticipated uses that object designers "embedded" into the object's physical properties. Artefacts have also the compose-ability affordance, that is, the ability to be used as building blocks of larger Disappearing Computer applications and the changeability affordance, that is, the ability to change or adapt their functionality. Consequently, the Disappearing Computer paradigm introduces several challenges for people, as their existing task models become inadequate or obsolete. The technology to be developed must ensure that people will be enabled, with user friendly tools, and supported, with efficient middleware platforms, in discovering the necessary services and in combining them into Disappearing Computer applications intended to optimally suit their needs.

The first chapter presents a conceptual and technological framework for describing and manipulating ubiquitous computing applications. This framework, referred to as the Gadgetware Architectural Style, extends component-based architectures to the realm of tangible objects and provides the tools and middleware that support the composition of ubiquitous computing applications from functionally autonomous artefacts. The second chapter explores the issues that arise when building a system in an ad hoc fashion from communicating wearable, portable and infrastructure devices, when the number and type of resources that are available at any point in time may change constantly. The chapter describes an approach towards handling and exploiting the varying resource availability in such a system, giving an overview of the application support which was developed in terms of resource discovery and remote access, distributed and adaptive user interfaces, and cooperative file management. In the third chapter an attention-based model is presented, inspired from the human brain, for identifying context switches through sensory information. Context-based adaptation is achieved by focusing on irregular patterns, so as to verify possible context switches, and adapting the behaviour goals accordingly.

Finally, **Part 4, *Augmenting Physical Artefacts***, groups together three chapters that describe efforts to create novel artefacts from physical objects or materials. Every new technology is manifested with objects that realize it. These objects may be new or improved versions of existing objects, which by using the new technology, allow people to carry out new tasks or old tasks in new and better ways. An important characteristic of Disappearing Computer environments is the merging of physical and digital space: as the computer disappears in the environments surrounding our activities, the objects therein become augmented with information and communication technology (ICT) components and acquire new affordances. Artefacts, in addition to their physical presence, publish representations of their properties and services in the digital space. At the same time, they differ from traditional objects in their ability to process and store information, to perceive and adapt to the context of operation, and to communicate and collaborate with other artefacts and the environment.

The three chapters of the fourth part describe research efforts to create novel forms of widely used materials, such as fibres and paper, which will have augmented functionality. The first chapter argues that non-speech sounds will be important in information exchange between artefacts and humans. It presents versatile and efficient sound models that are based on the physics of sound-generating phenomena, which have been integrated within artefacts and appliances that interact with humans. The second chapter is representative of an approach to make information processing an intrinsic capability of artefacts, which will be a result not of embedding ICT components, but of the material used to fabricate them. The material that was investigated was textile fibres; the term "fibre computing" was used to describe the concept of turning objects into artefacts by building them from augmented fibres. Two approaches for the development of fibre technology are presented. The last chapter presents research efforts to augment paper – the ubiquitous artefact – so that it will support practical activities like reading and writing, and discusses one particular solution that enables people to create dynamic associations between paper and digital resources, which does not rest upon replacing paper with technology, nor with transforming the character of paper, but rather with augmenting paper to support systematic links with digital content.

Impact and Conclusion

The impact of the *Disappearing Computer* research was significant in that it proved the feasibility of the visions that were proposed under different terminologies such as Calm Technology, Ambient Intelligence, etc. and, at the same time, evaluated different science and technology approaches. It has contributed in formulating concise requirements, efficient methodologies and elaborate theories. At the same time, it made clear that a key factor of the success of this new paradigm is to involve people in all stages of the design and deployment process of smart artefacts and applications. Based on the studies conducted by several projects, we are now starting to apprehend how to ensure that people's experiences in these new environments can be coherent and engaging. Besides its impact within the scientific community, a very important outcome was the contribution in charting the research dimensions of this new complex technology territory, which resulted in follow-up research initiatives funded by the European Commission. Some of these explored ways to enhance people's presence through technology; others attempted to solve the complexity problems that arise due to the huge number of artefact interactions. An independent line of research is using inspiration from biological systems to investigate ways to design more natural settings and experiences, even to directly interface living and artificial systems.

The design and development of novel global computing paradigms as well as of autonomous systems is another research dimension. All these are tackled in close relation to human-centred issues, such as social intelligence, universal access, privacy and dependability.

However, these are still the early days. It will take a few more years before the results of the *Disappearing Computer* research find their way into people's everyday lives and homes and become commonplace. The novel ideas and concepts born within this initiative will play a catalytic role in shaping research agendas and roadmaps as well as product lines. In the future, we shall look back at the concepts and prototypes described in the chapters of this book with some pride: although they will (hopefully) appear simple, they are a first glimpse into the shape of things to come.

Before moving on to the following three forewords and then the chapters, we would like to acknowledge the support and help of several people who were instrumental in getting this book published. There is, of course, the support from Springer: Alfred Hofmann and Ursula Barth who believed in the book and supported us also in difficult phases of the process as well as Christine Günther, Anna Kramer, and Markus Richter accommodating a tight schedule in the final phase. We especially would like to thank Gérard Schwarz in Darmstadt who helped to transform all incoming material into a common format, aligning reference styles, and improving pictures and diagrams. Special thanks are due to the European Commission, in particular Jakub Wejchert, Thomas Skordas and Thierry van der Pyl, for launching and supporting the Disappearing Computer initiative as well as the publication of this book as an activity of the DC-Network. Last but not least, we would like to thank the many Disappearing Computer researchers who contributed with their work to the research results published here, and the chapter authors who made this book possible.

Enjoy reading!

April 2007   Norbert Streitz
                                          Fraunhofer IPSI, Darmstadt, Germany

                                                              Achilles Kameas
                                                Hellenic Open University and
                          Computer Technology Institute, Patras, Greece

                                                         Irene Mavrommati
                          Computer Technology Institute, Patras, Greece

Foreword
The European Commission's View

The Internet and other digital networks have now become an integral part of our economy and society and support vital parts of our activities. In the coming years, with further miniaturisation and commoditisation of computing and networking, we expect to see smart devices such as sensors, tags or other artefacts being integrated into everyday objects. The move towards such smart embedded devices that interconnect and interact through digital networks has now clearly started with technologies such as sensor systems, RFID tags or biometrics. These, together with other emerging technologies, are only the beginning of what could become the *Internet of Things* and a smart *Ambient Intelligence*, paving the way to a ubiquitous Information Society permeating all aspects of our lives.

We thus see the often quoted visionary observation of Mark Weiser in 1991 that "The most profound technologies are those that disappear; they weave themselves into the fabric of everyday life until they are indistinguishable from it" is now progressively turning itself into reality. It takes, however, a lot of science to move technology from the foreground to the background. Since 1991, this has been an ongoing endeavour in a series of international research programmes and initiatives.

One prominent example of such an early programme is *The Disappearing Computer* (DC) research initiative. DC was launched and funded under the 'Future and Emerging Technologies' action of the European Commission's IST programme, which is one of the EU's research framework programmes. The DC initiative comprised a set of 17 research projects that ran from 2000 to 2004, with a total budget of around 40 million Euros.

The Disappearing Computer initiative anticipated and pioneered the concept of ambient intelligence. Projects in this initiative have allowed researchers to advance the boundaries of what is possible with the computer today. They have investigated how new, human-centred approaches for designing collections of artefacts in everyday settings can support people's experience in these environments. In doing so, they have achieved many outstanding research and engineering accomplishments in sensing, computing and networking, digital design, user interfaces and machine learning. Examples of landmark results are the creation of many new gadgets and artefacts and their communication protocols, novel software and hardware architectures for such artefacts, ambient surfaces and interactive displays, innovative mobile services and new functionalities for home and business environments. DC projects have also developed several technology use scenarios for assessing the impact of these new interaction paradigms on peoples' lives.

The DC initiative has managed to mobilise most of the key representative European research groups in computing and communication, architecture and interaction design, psychology and sociology, to work closely together. The results clearly show the benefits of multidisciplinary collaborative research in well-defined and pioneering research areas. The above would not have been possible without DC-Net, a pioneering network mechanism, chaired by Norbert Streitz and organized together with the other members of the DC-Net Steering Group (Paddy Nixon, Achilles Kameas, Irene

Mavrommati, Lars Holmquist, Allan MacLean, Alan Munro), that defined an inter-disciplinary framework encouraging DC projects to collaborate and acting as leverage for sharing insights across the entire initiative.

We welcome the edition of this book, motivated by the progress and results achieved by the DC projects, which lays out the design, research and engineering foundations that will underpin the development of future forms of ambient computing systems.

We hope that the book will become a flagship publication, serving as a fundamental knowledge base and also providing further inspiration for any new development in the area.

April 2007

Thierry Van der Pyl
Head of Unit

Thomas Skordas
Coordinator of the DC initiative

Future and Emerging Technologies,
DG Information Society and Media, European Commission

Foreword by Emile Aarts

For more than a decade computer scientists from all over the world have been inspired by a strikingly consistent view on the future of computing, which is given by the belief that the future world will consist of a large network of distributed computing devices that surround people in an unobtrusive way. This common view, which was first broadly articulated at the occasion of the 50th anniversary of the Association of Computing Machinery in 1997, builds on the early ideas of Mark Weiser published in 1991, who used the notion Ubiquitous Computing to refer to a novel computing infrastructure that would replace the current mobile computing infrastructure by a network of interconnected embedded devices that facilitate ubiquitous access to any source of information at any place at any point in time by any person.

Over the past decade these far reaching ideas have been further developed, and one of the more recent novel achievements is the concept of Ambient Intelligence (AmI), which was introduced in the late 1990s as a novel paradigm for digital systems for the years 2010-2020. AmI takes the early ideas of Weiser one step further by embedding computational intelligence into networked smart environments thus moving computing infrastructure to the background and bringing the user to the foreground by supporting him or her with intuitive and natural interaction concepts.

From a computational point of view, these novel computing paradigms are all aimed at replacing the computer, as we currently know it, by smart electronic environments. Consequently, one speaks of the *Disappearing Computer* reflecting the main objective of this major pursuit, which is to get rid of the computer as a single box whilst maintaining its functionality as a service provided by an intelligent integrated computing infrastructure. The user advantage of such an infrastructure would be given by the ability to make it context aware, personalized, adaptive, and anticipatory, thus enhancing and empowering the user from a point of view of productivity, self-expression, and social well being. In its capacity as a disruptive technology the Disappearing Computer carries the potential of providing a basis for new models of technological innovation within a multi-dimensional society, thus opening up unprecedented business options and unforeseen ways of social interaction.

From a technological point of view the Disappearing Computer has become within our reach. There are many recent technological developments that support this statement. First there is the ongoing one-dimensional integration in semiconductor devices resulting in high performance computing, storage, and communication devices. Second, there are many breakthroughs in the design of two-dimensional large-area electronic devices resulting in photonic textiles, electronic paper, flexible displays, and other interaction devices. Finally, there are major novel developments that enable the design of fully integrated three-dimensional electronic systems leading to a wide range of autonomous sensor and actuator devices.

So, we may safely conclude that hardware technologies are not the limiting factor in the development of the Disappearing Computer. Evidently, the major challenge is contained in the development of novel user interface paradigms that support natural and intuitive interaction of users with their smart environments. The major issue in this respect is the requirement that smart environments must meet a number of basic user requirements such as *usefulness* and *simplicity*. Obviously, this statement has a broad endorsement by a wide community of both designers and engineers, but reality reveals that it is hard to achieve in practise, and that novel approaches are needed to make it work.

The ultimate success of the Disappearing Computing paradigm heavily relies on social acceptance of the newly proposed ambient technology, and consequently, we need to gain more insight into the human factors side of the vision to understand the relation between ambient technology and the behavior of people thus revealing the true added value of the Disappearing Computer in the everyday-life of people. To elicitate these insights we need more scientific investigations, and this current volume in the Springer Lecture Notes in Computer Science undoubtedly provides a major contribution to fill up this gap of knowledge. The editors have succeeded in bringing together an interesting and inspiring collection of research contributions reporting on the progress in the development of the Disappearing Computer, both from an application development and a systems engineering point of view. The book provides the reader with a full and comprehensive overview of the state of affairs in this domain, and I am quite confident that the volume will raise excitement about the great progress that has been made in the development of the Disappearing Computer.

Congratulations and well done!

April 2007   Emile Aarts
                                                                   Vice President
                                                    Philips Research Laboratories

Foreword by Gregory Abowd

The *Disappearing Computer* initiative. When I think now about this name for one of the Fifth Framework programs of the European Commission, I have two reactions. My first reaction is that it seems like an odd name, suggesting intentional extinction of the essence of Computer Science, the computer itself. My second, and more serious, reaction is that it is inspirational, simultaneously emphasizing the development of new form factors for computational artefacts and the thoughtful integration of that technology into everyday experiences. The Disappearing Computer initiative resulted in 17 different international projects, a significant chunk of which were driven by human-centered themes. In contrast, in the mid-to-late 1990s, DARPA in the US had attempted a similar program to inspire research in the area of ubiquitous computing, resulting in five different projects, all of which were single or dual-institution efforts and none of which included a significant human-centered research agenda. One of the defining characteristics of the technologies of ubiquitous computing is that they try to bridge the gap between the physical and electronic worlds. It is much wiser to embed the explorations of these technologies in the social experiences of the physical world. From that perspective, the Disappearing Computer initiative got it right from the start.

The visions of the late 1980s by a handful of researchers across the globe —Ken Sakamura in Tokyo, Japan, Andy Hopper, William Newman and Mik Lamming in Cambridge, UK, and Mark Weiser, John Seely Brown and Roy Want in Palo Alto, California, USA — foreshadowed a world of heterogeneous, interconnected computational objects. Each effort resulted in significant computing and engineering advances, but they are most remembered for the inspiration of a proactive, information-rich world that we could aspire to create for ourselves. As a young researcher in the mid 1990s, I aligned myself with the goals of ubiquitous computing because it was a new interactive experience that I could build and use to assist my own everyday life. People resonated with this work because they could see its application in the "ordinary" activities of the classroom, workplace, home, and outdoors. The Disappearing Computer initiative executed on this same inspiration, with a three-fold emphasis on information artefacts created out of everyday objects, new behavior and new functionality emerging from collections of these artefacts, and coherent and engaging user experiences that can be supported. While substantial progress was shown on the creation of information artefacts, it is the new behaviors and user experiences that promise long-term impact.

The individual projects are separately appealing, and this book will offer summary contributions from many of those projects. What should impress the reader even more, in my opinion, is the process for collaboration that intentionally allowed each of these efforts to influence the others. I recall the tremendous energy of the 150+ researchers who assembled for a Disappearing Computer Jamboree collocated with the Fourth International Conference on Ubiquitous Computing (Ubicomp 2002 in Göteborg, Sweden). Jamborees, Research Ateliers, Troubadours, Disappearing Days and other mechanisms were consciously built into this initiative, increasing the likelihood that the whole contribution of this research effort would be greater than the sum of its parts. I encourage all researchers, and in particular research administrators in organizations similar to the European Commission, to not only read the reports from selected projects in this edited book but also to read and reflect on the process for collaboration facilitated by the DC-Network outlined at http://www.disappearing-computer.net and in the preface of this book. This process may end up being at least as influential as the research output reported in this book.

April 2007

Gregory Abowd
College of Computing
Georgia Institute of Technology

Table of Contents

Part I. Interacting within Smart Spaces

Part II. Designing for the Home and Social Activities

Part III. System Architecture and Infrastructures

Part IV. Augmenting Physical Artefacts

Part I

Interacting within Smart Spaces

Smart Artefacts as Affordances for Awareness in Distributed Teams

Norbert Streitz[1], Thorsten Prante[1], Carsten Röcker[2], Daniel van Alphen[3],
Richard Stenzel[1], Carsten Magerkurth[4], Saadi Lahlou[5], Valery Nosulenko[6],
Francois Jegou[7], Frank Sonder[8], and Daniela Plewe[9]

[1] Fraunhofer Institute IPSI, Darmstadt, Germany
[2] now at University of California, San Diego, USA
[3] now at Philips Design, Boston, USA
[4] now at SAP Research CEC, St. Gallen, Switzerland
[5] Electricité de France, Paris, France
[6] Russian Academy of Science, Moscow, Russia
[7] Solutioning Design, Brussels, Belgium
[8] Wilkhahn and Foresee, Bad Münder, Germany
[9] now at National University of Singapore, Singapore

1   Introduction

The manifolds of spaces and places we are entering, populating, transiently crossing and eventually leaving (only to immerse in another subsequent context) as part of our daily activities in our personal, public and professional lives are undergoing a dramatic change. Although this change is taking place we are aware of it only in a limited fashion due to its unobtrusive character as illustrated in the statement by Streitz and Nixon (2005): "It seems like a paradox but it will soon become reality: The rate at which computers disappear will be matched by the rate at which information technology will increasingly permeate our environment and our lives".

Due to the proliferation of information and communication technology we are encountering increasingly spaces that are being transformed into augmented and shared environments. Augmentation takes place via embedded technologies (e.g., sensing, networking) resulting in smart artefacts as the building blocks of smart environments at different levels and scales. While this development takes place in many areas of our daily live, we are focusing in this chapter in particular on office spaces and how to transform them into augmented shared work environments. The office environments we anticipate should be able to support communication and cooperation of individuals and teams, especially also taking into account the issues arising from distributed settings where people are not sharing the same architectural space. The associated problems do not only affect large organizations but also small companies and groups of people forming loose and temporary networks of collaboration.

Originally, "shared environments" denote work situations where people actually share architectural spaces and physical places in an office building. They share the same office; meet each other in the hallway or the cafeteria. These settings provide multiple opportunities for being aware of what is going on in the building and for engaging in spontaneous chance encounters with colleagues. They can be from the same or a different team or organizational unit, from a related or a completely different pro-

N. Streitz, A. Kameas, and I. Mavrommati (Eds.): The Disappearing Computer, LNCS 4500, pp. 3 – 29, 2007.
© Springer-Verlag Berlin Heidelberg 2007

ject. People can gain and extend their knowledge about what is going on in the organization.

Successfully working together involves and requires more than exchanging only data and information. To act as a team, people have to develop commonalities on at least two dimensions. First, they have to develop and experience a common basis of understanding, i.e., a mental model of the task domain and the procedures that is shared by all team members. Second, they have to develop a common feeling as a team, the "corps d'esprit". Establishing the shared mental model and the common feeling is dependent on the type of communication channels and media available. They determine the social cohesion and other group processes. Our thesis is that this process of developing a common understanding can be successfully supported by information and communication technology if the enabling environments are designed and developed in a task-oriented and user-centered way.

In this chapter, we describe an example of enabling environments supporting team work and mobility and the development of smart artefacts as constituents populating what we have called earlier "cooperative buildings" (Streitz et al. 1998). The specific application scenario and the different smart artefacts were developed in the "Ambient Agoras" project (www.ambient-agoras.org) that was part of the EU-funded "Disappearing Computer" initiative.

The chapter is organized as follows. First, we describe the problem domain of supporting team work in the age of increased mobility and its implication for the design of future office buildings. Second, we introduce the Ambient Agoras project. Third, we argue for the notion of people-oriented and empowering smartness keeping the human in the loop. Fourth, we discuss - in the context of the disappearing computer paradigm - the role of affordances for interaction and experience design of smart artefacts constituting a social architectural space. Fifth, a brief characterization of ambient displays and privacy issues provides the basis for the development of the specific artefacts in the next sections. Sixth, after illustrating the specific "connecting remote teams" application scenario, we describe the development and implementation of three smart artefacts (Personal.Aura, Hello.Wall, and View.Port) and their functionalities. Finally, we report about their integration in a concrete test environment between Germany and France as well as its evaluation.

2   Awareness in Distributed Teams

2.1   The Role of Communication

Within the last decades, the role of teamwork has gained significant importance. Besides an immense increase in the use of work groups within companies (Guzzo and Salas 1995; Sundstrom 1999; Utz 2000), also virtual teams, where team members collaborate from remote locations, become increasingly popular (Potter and Balthazard 2002). But successful teamwork involves more than just people working at the same project or in the same room. To act as a team, the team members have to experience a special relationship and attitude (the 'team spirit"), they have to take over responsibilities and work towards a common goal. It is essential to share knowledge, to make decisions and to coordinate the activities of all people working in the team. As a result, the relevance and amount of communication is constantly increasing.

In addition to explicit verbal communication, especially implicit communication in form of mutual awareness is an important requirement for a shared understanding and knowledge about ongoing and past activities within a team (Streitz et al. 2003). Mutual awareness usually leads to informal interactions, spontaneous connections, and the development of shared cultures, all important aspects of maintaining working relationships (Dourish and Bly 1992). Gaver et al. (1992) define awareness as the pervasive experience of knowing who is around, what sorts of things they are doing, whether they are relatively busy or can be engaged, and so on. Especially information about presence and availability of remote colleagues is of high value during the daily work process. This is also confirmed by the findings of Nardi et al. (2000), who evaluated the use of buddy lists. They showed that people found it valuable to simply know who else was "around", as they checked the buddy list, without necessarily planning to interact with anyone.

In a local work environment, information about presence and availability of colleagues is continuously available and picked up by those present. Teams, which are geographically distributed, by their nature, are denied the informal information gathered from a physical shared workspace (Kraut et al. 1990). Hence, it is particular important to support the need of distributed teams for informal interaction, spontaneous conversation and awareness of people and events at other sites (Bly et al. 1993).

In contrast to local work environments, where minimal or no effort is required to maintain awareness, the members of distributed teams have to communicate awareness information explicitly. The amount of information that is communicated is determined by the benefits users gain and efforts for providing the relevant information to their remote team members. This explains why traditional communication tools, like e-mail or telephone, are only of limited appropriateness for supporting awareness in distributed teams. Communicating relevant information requires a comparatively high effort and, therefore, will be used only for things, which are considered to be more important, like scheduling of meetings, task management or other work related subjects (Rohall et al. 2003; Bellotti et al. 2003; Gwizdka 2002).

2.2 Mobility: Local vs. Global

Since the introduction of office work in the beginning of this century, work environments are subject to a constant change towards higher organizational flexibility and personal mobility. Especially within the last decade, a continuous trend towards higher local mobility could be observed in most companies. Even if employees are within the office building, they spend considerable time away from their own desk, working in meeting rooms, other offices or in the hallway (Lamming et al. 2000; Huang et al. 2004). According to some estimates, white-collar workers spend between 25% and 70% of their daily working time in conferences or meetings with colleagues (Panko 1992; Eldridge et al. 1994; Whittaker et al. 1994). Bellotti and Bly (1996) studied local mobility in a design company and observed an even higher level of mobility with people being away from their desk for around 90% of the time.

To get a better understanding of the interdependency between mobility and teamwork, two forms of mobility are distinguished: "local mobility" and "global mobility". The term local mobility refers to the mobility of an individual within a building or organization, which is mainly determined by the organizational structure and the design of the work environment in a specific building. In contrast, global mobility describes the fading linkage of employees to a fixed workplace as a result of globalization trends and technology trends like the availability of networked mobile devices. People are becoming increasingly part of distributed teams working at remote sites.

The advantage of local mobility, regarding the collaboration of team members, has to be seen in an increased awareness about activities and events in the surrounding of their own work place. Findings by Bellotti and Bly (1996) led to the assumption, that the relevant information is received passively, as soon as a team member is in physical proximity to the activity. They come to the conclusion, that local mobility is imperative for communication within teams and, at the same time, supports informal communication and awareness about local colleagues. Based on the work of Kraut et al. (1990), Whittaker et al. (1994) come to similar results and additionally stress the fact that informal communication plays a key role for the collaboration within companies.

Regarding the working methods of many teams, higher mobility seems appropriate and natural: creative processes cannot be initiated on command; they are independent of time and place. As a matter of fact, the most creative and inspiring ideas are usually not born while sitting at the office desk (Sonnentag 2001). Pelizäus-Hoffmeister (2001) argues in the same way, and sees the most important benefits of higher mobility in a broader wealth of experience and the additional opportunities for new relationships. So, there is no doubt that the increase of local mobility in workspaces affects teamwork.

Observing the prevailing developments, one has to assume that future office environments will allow a much higher level of personal mobility as today's office concepts do.

3   Cooperative Buildings

In 1998, we introduced the concept of so called *Cooperative Buildings* (Streitz et al. 1998). Using the term "building" (and not "spaces") was motivated by emphasizing that the starting point of the design of future office buildings should be the real, architectural environment. This was at a time when the discussion was pretty much dominated by the notion of virtual environments as the offices of the future. Calling it a "cooperative" building, we indicate that the building serves the purpose of cooperation and communication. At the same time, it is also "cooperative" towards its users, inhabitants, and visitors by employing active, attentive and adaptive components. This is to say that the building does not only provide facilities but it can also (re)act "on its own" after having identified certain conditions. It was part of our vision that it will be "smart" and be able to adapt to changing situations and provide context-aware information and services. In Streitz et al. (1998, 2001), we identified the following distinctions spanning three dimensions of what has to be taken into account when designing cooperative buildings:

- individual vs. group activities
- local vs. global contexts
- real vs. virtual worlds

In this chapter we report on how to incorporate these design dimensions for one of the application scenarios that were investigated in the Ambient Agoras project.

With respect to the third dimension, one can observe that the use of information technology has caused a significant shift: away from real objects in the physical environment as the sources of information towards computer monitors as *"the"* new interfaces to information and thus an increasing emphasis on virtual environments. Continuing the approach of our previous work, e.g., on Roomware® for cooperative buildings (Streitz et al. 1998, 1999, 2001), we argue also in this context now for returning to the real world as the starting point for designing future information and communication environments. It is our intention to design environments that exploit the affordances provided by real world objects and spaces, at the same time making use of the potential of computer-based support available via the digital or virtual world. Our thesis is to take the best of both worlds by combining and integrating real and virtual worlds resulting in hybrid worlds.

4   Ambient Agoras

The Greek *agora* (market place) was the guiding metaphor for our work in the Ambient Agoras project. We investigated how to turn everyday places into social market places of ideas and information where people can meet and interact. We addressed the office environment as an integrated organization situated in an architectural context and having specific information needs at the collective level of the organization, and at the personal level of the individual team member. The overall goal was to augment the architectural envelope creating a social architectural space to support collaboration, informal communication, and social awareness. This was achieved by providing situated services, place-relevant information, communicating the feeling of a place (*genius loci*) to users, enabling them to communicate for help, guidance, work, or fun. We promoted an approach of designing individual as well as team interaction in physical environments using augmented physical artifacts. In particular, we were interested to go beyond traditional support for productivity-oriented activities and rather focus on providing experiences via "smart" or augmented spaces. The goal was to take a closer look at activities and social processes in lounge areas, hallways, and other transient spaces (see Figure 1).

In order to be able to focus on the needs of potential users, we employed a scenario-based approach, starting out with a large number of so called "bits-of-life" (very short descriptions of functionalities, situations, events, …), aggregated them to scenarios and presented them, e.g., via video mock-ups to focus groups for user-feedback. This served, in combination with extensive conceptual work based on different theories in architecture (e.g., Alexander 1977) as the basis for the development of a wide range of smart artefacts and corresponding software so that their combination provides smart services to the users.

Design, development, and evaluation followed an iterative and rapid prototyping approach. For the Ambient Agoras environment, we addressed several interaction design objectives (disappearance and ubiquity of computing devices) with different sensing technologies (active and passive RFID) which resulted in the development of several smart artefacts.

Fig. 1. Vision scribble of a lounge area in future office environment

In this book chapter, we focus on the specific application scenario of coordination and collaboration between remote sites of distributed teams and the corresponding subset of ambient displays and mobile devices that we developed for it. One important aspect was the combination of more or less static artefacts integrated in the architectural environment with mobile devices carried by people. At the same time, we addressed issues of privacy in sensor-based environments.

5   Smart Environments

The availability of information technology for multiple activities is one important step but it is not sufficient for achieving the objectives indicated above. It is to be followed by the integration of information, communication and sensing technology into everyday objects of our environment in order to create what is called "Smart Environments". Their constituents are smart artefacts that result from augmenting the standard functionality of artefacts thus enabling new quality of interaction and "behaviour" (of artefacts). Work on Ambient Intelligence (ISTAG 2001) addresses similar aspects but we prefer the term "smart" over "intelligent" in order to avoid a too anthropomorphic association. Without entering into the philosophical discussion of when it is justified to call an artefact "smart" or what we consider "smart" or "intelligent" behaviour in general, the following distinction is useful (Streitz et al. 2005b).

5.1   System-Oriented, Importunate Smartness

An environment is to be considered "smart" if it enables certain self-directed (re)actions of individual artefacts (or by the environment in case of an ensemble of artefacts) based on previously and continuously collected information. For example, a space or a place can be "smart" by having and exploiting knowledge about which people and artefacts are currently situated within its area, who and what was there before, when and how long, and what kind of activities took place. In this version of "smartness", the space would be active, (in many cases even proactive) and in control of the situation by making decisions on what to do next and actually take action and execute them without a human in the loop. For example, in a smart home, we have access control to the house and other functions like heating, closing windows and blinds are being done automatically. Some of these actions could be importunate. Take the almost classic example of a smart refrigerator in a home analyzing consumption patterns of the inhabitants and autonomously ordering depleting food. While we might appreciate that the fridge makes suggestions on recipes that are based on the food currently available (that would be still on the supportive side), we might get very upset in case it is autonomously ordering food that we will not consume for reasons beyond its knowledge, such as a sudden vacation, sickness, or a temporal change in taste.

5.2 People-Oriented, Empowering Smartness

In contrast, there is another perspective where the empowering function is in the foreground and which can be summarized as *"smart spaces make people smarter"*. This is achieved by keeping "the human in the loop" thus empowering people to make informed decisions and take actions as mature and responsible people being in control. In this case, the environment will also collect data about what is going on but provides and communicates the resulting information - hopefully in an intuitive way so that ordinary people can comprehend it easily - for guidance and subsequent actions determined by people. In this case, a smart space might also make suggestions based on the information collected but the people are still in the loop and in control of what to do next. Here, the place supports smart, intelligent behaviour of the people present (or in remote interaction scenarios people being away "on the road" but connected to the space). For example in an office scenario, the smart space could make recommendations to the people currently in the room that it would be useful to consult other people that were there before and worked on the same content or to take a look at related documents created in this room before.

There is no doubt that these two points of view will not exist in their pure distinct form. They rather represent the end points of a dimension where we can position weighted combinations of both somewhere in between. What kind of combination will be realized is different for different cases and depends very much on the application domain. It is also obvious that in some cases it might be useful that a system is not asking for user's feedback and confirmation for every single step in an action chain because this would result in an information overload. The challenge is to find the right balance. The position we propagate here is that the overall design rationale should be guided and informed by the objective to aim at having the human in the loop and in control as much as possible and feasible.

6   From Information Worlds to Experience Worlds

An important aspect of our work is to go beyond traditional support for productivity-oriented tasks in the office and focus on designing "experiences" with the help of smart or augmented spaces (Streitz et al. 2005a). The goal is to design smart artefacts that enable us to interact with them and the overall environment in a simple and intuitive way or just being exposed to it and perceive indicators in the environment that indicate events and changes. This includes extending the awareness about our physical and social environment by providing observation data and parameters that - in many cases - are "invisible" to our human senses and therefore enable new experiences.

The general idea of capturing and communicating "invisible" parameters is known, e.g., in physics where radioactivity is indicated via the sound of a Geiger-Müller counter, and can be applied to existing activity contexts as well as for situations and settings that are newly created. Previous examples in the ubiquitous computing domain included pollution data or computer network traffic data (e.g., Wisneski et al. 1998) that are usually not directly noticeably with our standard human senses. Presenting these data in a format that provides new experiences enables people to get a feeling of what is currently going on around them, i.e., the world around us becomes the interface.

In this paper, we present an application of the general idea of designing these experiences via calm technology (Weiser and Brown 1995) and focus on the creation of an augmented social architectural space in office settings.

7   Interaction Design and Affordances

Developing and having the technology (e.g., sensing) and infrastructure (e.g., wireless network) available is an important ingredient of creating smart environments. Designing the interaction with smart artefacts constituting these environments is another challenge. For our design approach, we found the notion of *affordances* very helpful.

7.1   Different Approaches to the Concept of Affordances

The concept of *affordances* was first introduced by Gibson (1979) who also coined the term. His notion of affordances highlights the function of properties of the environment that enable possible actions available in the environment, independent of the individual's ability to perceive this possibility. He concentrated especially on the relationship between actor and environment.

Norman's (1988) initial treatment of the issues, later on revisiting them again (Norman 1999), made the term popular in the HCI community. In his interpretation, affordances are understood as design aspects of an object which suggests how the object should be used. The concept was widely adopted but with the emergence of complex software and the variety of interfaces these definitions were not elaborate enough. It was Gaver (1991) who proposed a catalogue of "technology affordances" and introduced the concepts of nested affordances and sequential affordances. For a detailed history of the affordance concept see McGrenere and Ho (2000).

Alexander (1977) does not explicitly use the term "affordances". Still, we consider part of his work as an approach to classify "affordances of spaces". As an architect, Alexander observed that in all environments archetypical problems occur to which certain solutions have emerged. One can consider these solutions as providing affordances of spaces. Alexander analyzed existing solutions, extracted the underlying principles and organized them in a so called "pattern-language" (Alexander 1977).

The result is a collection of over 250 hierarchically grouped patterns concerning the affordances of spaces.

Similar to our goal of developing a social architectural space (see below) Alexander aims at an "alive space" characterized by various patterns as communicative, lively and offering various opportunities for exchange.

Against the background of the various concepts of affordances, we adopt the following notion for our work:

> *Affordances* are available elements in the perceived environment that trigger, facilitate, and support certain activities, especially when interacting with artefacts. From the perspective of the design process, the notion of affordances is used to constrain the space of possible interactions with an artefact and to suggest intended and/or possible interactions to the user.

Another related assumption is that users are familiar with the "meaning" or "effect" of affordances provided by "classical" interfaces of artefacts and are able to transfer their previous experiences to the new artefact.

7.2   Interacting with Disappearing Computers

With the trend of the "disappearing computer" new challenges arise. Computers used to be primary artefacts, now they become "secondary" artefacts which move in the background in several ways. They disappear from the scene, become invisible and - in consequence - disappear in the perception of the actors. Therefore, new issues with regard to the notion of affordances arise: how can people interact with disappearing computers? How can we design for transparency and make users "understand" the interface? How can people migrate from explicit interactions and interfaces towards implicit interactions and interfaces? And how can we fulfill the occurring needs for privacy?

Our approach is mainly characterized by returning to the real world as the starting point for design and trying to exploit the affordances that real-world objects provide.

7.3   Social Architectural Space

Once we go beyond individual artefacts to collections of artefacts and their placement in space, we have to extend the notion of affordances. Architectural spaces are coupled in our minds with meaning, memories, associations and previous experiences. If one wants to differentiate between spaces and places, one could say "a place is a space with meaning". A "successful" experience of a place is the result of (re)acting "appropriately" on the affordances offered and using the context with appropriate knowledge. People perform better in known and familiar spaces. Therefore, enriching spaces with an additional interpretative layer via appropriate affordances transforms them into places and can result in a better and more comfortable experience.

Collections of artefacts with corresponding affordances constitute what we call "a social architectural space". A social architectural space is an (office) environment, which supports collaboration, social awareness, thereby acknowledging the role of informal communication and social awareness for creativity and innovations in organizations. This is in line with emphasizing activities requiring support that go beyond the PC-based workplace and traditional productivity tools. The social orientation also takes into account the increase of temporary project teams with irregular presence in the office building, possibly leading to a deficit of social coherence. To counter this, transparency of relationships and light-weight means for communication are needed.

The position of an artefact within an environment influences its affordances. Spaces themselves have properties that support or inhibit certain activities. Inspired by Alexander (1977), we introduce some considerations about spaces which support our goal of designing a social architectural space. To this end, we reference certain patterns and use his classification and numbering scheme.

Meeting our emphasis on informal communication, Alexander (1977) states: "No social group - whether a family, a workgroup or a school group – can survive without constant informal contact among its members." (Pattern Number #80 "Self-governing Workshops and Offices", p 398) In his pattern language, Alexander introduces various patterns that enhance this kind of "intensity of action".

From his notion of "Activity Pockets", we adopt that places need to provide shelter and allow frequency at the same time. "Surround public gathering spaces with pockets of activity – small, partly enclosed areas at the edges, which jut forward into the open space between paths, and contain activity pockets which make it natural for people to pause and get involved." (Pattern # 124 "Activity Pockets", p 602).

According to Alexander, in many modern buildings the problem of disorientation causing mental stress is acute. "An environment, that requires that a person pays attention to it constantly, is as bad for a person who knows it, as for a stranger. A good environment is one which is easy to understand, without conscious attention." (Circulation Realms, #98, p 482). Here, especially large scale artefacts can contribute to create landmarks. The locations may be discernable by their varying atmospheres.

This was reflected in our design of the large ambient display Hello.Wall (to be described later on) that meets the landmark aspect as well as the request "to be understood without conscious attention".

7.4 Disappearing Computers and Inherited Affordances

One of Weiser's (1991) central ideas is the notion of the *disappearing computer* being part of designing *calm technology* (Weiser and Brown 1995). It is best captured in his statement "The most profound technologies are those that disappear. They weave themselves into the fabric of everyday life until they are indistinguishable from it." The notion of the disappearing computer gives rise to a new discussion of the role of affordances. In this context, it is helpful to revisit the distinction of two types of disappearance we introduced some time ago (Streitz 2001):

- *Physical disappearance* is achieved by the miniaturization of computer parts that allows convenient and easy integration into other artefacts, mostly into "close-to-the-body" objects, so that the result can fit in your hand, can be integrated in clothing or even implanted in the body, etc. As a result, features usually associated with a computer are not visible anymore and the interaction happens via the compound artefact in which the computer parts disappeared.

- *Mental disappearance* of computers is achieved by becoming "invisible" to the "mental" eye of the users. This can happen by embedding computers or parts of them in the architectural environment (walls, doors) or in furniture (tables, chairs, etc.) or other everyday objects. Then, computers are not perceived as computers anymore – although the artefacts can be quite large – but as adding interactive, communicative, and cooperative aspects to traditional everyday objects (e.g., an interactive wall or an interactive table is a "table", a "wall" that is interactive and not a computer built into a table or the wall).

Based on the notion of mental disappearance, we introduce the concept of "inherited affordances". The affordances of a well established object help to focus on interacting with the hidden affordances of the digital application. An example is to use real world furniture with well-known ways of interaction facilitating the communication of affordances for interacting with the disappeared computer, because users basically know how to interact with a chair or a table. Everyday objects provide simple affordances guiding the user to the nested and/or sequential affordances of the application enabled by the "invisible" computer.

In analogy to the discussion of the pros and cons of natural world metaphors one may argue, that applying metaphors helps the user initially to learn some basic interactions but later on possibly inhibits transcending the functionality of real-world artefacts – which, of course, is the reason for the existence for any new device. This general problem has already been extensively discussed many years ago in the context of introducing the desk-top metaphor for personal computers. (see, e.g., the notion of mental and conceptual models, Streitz 1988).

7.5 Ambient Displays

Inspired by the discussion on affordances (see above) and selected design patterns proposed by Alexander (1977), we found that a calm and ambient technology implementing the ideas of the disappearing computer would be very well suited to support the informal social encounters and communication processes we have in mind in our Ambient Agoras environment. In contrast to mechanism like open video channels (Bly et al. 1993; Fish et al. 1992), we decided to implement "ambient displays" for our approach.

They go beyond the traditional notion of "display" encountered with conventional graphical user interfaces (GUI) found on PCs, notebooks, PDAs. The design of ambient displays is often based on observations in nature or employing corresponding metaphors. They are designed to display information without constantly demanding the user's full attention. Usually, this is achieved in a more "implicit" way by being available in the periphery compared to traditional "explicit" GUIs. Ambient displays are envisioned as being all around us and thereby moving information off the conventional screens into the physical environment. They present information via changes in light, sound, movement of objects, smell, etc. Early examples are described in Ishii et al. (1998), Wisneski et al. (1998), Gellersen et al. (1999), and ways of evaluating them by Mankoff et al. (2003).

Applying the concept of ambient displays for our purposes is in line with our observations that social affiliations can be strengthened via additional awareness of people's activities. Ambient displays can be used to trigger the attention of team members in a subtle and peripheral way by communicating the atmosphere and thus providing a sense of a place.

Ambient displays are one aspect of the implementation, sensing people and collecting parameters relevant for achieving the goal of providing location- and situation-based services are others. They will be discussed in the context of the artefacts and the application scenario. We will describe later on three types of artefacts that were developed for populating the Ambient Agoras environment: Personal Aura, Hello.Wall, and ViewPort.

8   Privacy in Sensor-Based Environments

Smart objects and environments that support us unobtrusively and intelligently have to gather large amounts of information about almost every aspect of our lives—our past preferences, current activities, and future plans—in order to better serve us. Five characteristics make such systems very different from today's data collections (Langheinrich 2001):

- First, the unprecedented coverage of smart environments and objects present in homes, offices, cars, schools, and elderly care facilities.

- Second, the data collection will be practically invisible: no more card swiping or form signing, as sensors in walls, doors, and shirts silently collect information.

- Third, data will be more intimate than ever before: not only what we do, where we do it, and when we do it, but also how we feel while doing so (as expressed by our heart rate, perspiration, or walking pattern).

- A fourth difference concerns the underlying motivation for the data collection—after all, smart objects are dependent on as much information as they can possibly collect in order to best serve us.

- Lastly, the increasing interconnectivity allowing smart devices to cooperatively help us means an unprecedented level of data sharing; making unwanted information flows much more likely.

Together, these characteristics indicate that data collections in the age of ubiquitous computing would not only be a quantitative change from today, but a *qualitative* change: Never before has so much information about us been instantly available to so many others in such a detailed and intimate fashion.

Surveys since the 1970s show that the loss of privacy is associated with the quantity of personal information collected, and that fear of privacy infringements constantly increases with the integration of computers in everyday life (Robbin 2001). When boundaries between public and private spaces blur, users feel uneasy because they do not know what information they actually share with whom, often triggering substantial privacy and security concerns about the technology. Making technology invisible means that sensory borders disappear and common principles like "if I can see you, you can see me" no longer hold. Because collecting and processing of personal information is a core function of smart environments, privacy and ubiquity seem to be in constant conflict.

Within the Ambient Agoras project, we decided to pay considerable attention to the privacy issues and make them part of the overall design rationale. In this context, a subgroup of the project team produced the *European Privacy Design Guidelines for the Disappearing Computer* (Lahlou and Jegou 2003). It is beyond the scope of this chapter to describe them in detail but they provided a conceptual framework within which the smart artefacts were developed; a particular example is the "Personal Aura".

These guidelines are meant to help system designers implement privacy within the core of ubiquitous computing systems. Designing for privacy is difficult because privacy is often a trade-off with usability. The guidelines state nine rules that not only reinterpret some of the well-known fair information practices (OECD 1980) in light of disappearing computers, such as openness and collection limitation, but also add new rules that specifically deal with the privacy challenges introduced by such invisible and comprehensive data collection. For example, applying the "privacy razor" (rule number four) in design means listing everything the system knows about the human user, and cutting out what is not "absolutely necessary" to provide the service; for example, personal identification. The guidelines are available at www.rufae.net/privacy.html. While these rules still require more feedback from real-world deployments, they nevertheless present an important first step for building privacy-aware ubiquitous computing systems that European citizens can trust (Lahlou et al. 2005).

9   The Ambient Agoras Application Scenario

The initial analysis of working conditions for team collaboration and communication and the implications of increased mobility (local as well as global) in the beginning of this chapter defined the overall problem domain for our research. The goal was to develop computer-based support for informal communication, coordination and collaboration at local and between remote sites of distributed teams. A sample setting of the situation is depicted in Figure 2.

In addition, we set us a second complementing goal in terms of the character of implementation. It should correspond to and be compatible with the nature of informal communication, social awareness, team cohesion, etc. In order to explore the user

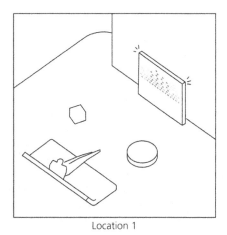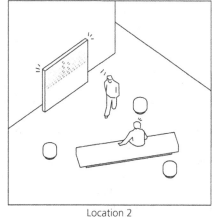

Location 1	Location 2

Fig. 2. Vision scribble of two remote locations connected via an ambient communication channel

requirements, we conducted focus groups and interviews in the project. The combination of our conceptual analysis and these results showed that the traditional ways of communicating information using standard tools and monitors of desktop computer did not achieve this goal and would not meet the expectations of the potential users. Therefore, we took a different route based on the notion of ambient displays and lightweight support with mobile devices to be described in the following sections.

The specific development was guided by three objectives. First, it was aimed to develop "lightweight" awareness devices that help members of a distributed team to communicate in a natural way. As mentioned before, awareness should be provided via a natural communication channel that enables people to be aware of each other, in a subtle, warm and expressive way, which can be easily and intuitively perceived without having to deal very explicitly with technology components.

Second, the interfaces should be adapted to the changing requirements of emerging office concepts as well as to the increased mobility of employees within the work environment. Hence, the conceptual system design aimed to support awareness and informal communication between remote team members through natural interaction in public areas, using intuitive interfaces integrated into an open office landscape implementing the affordances of a social architectural space.

Third, we wanted to integrate a privacy concept that would allow people to be in control of determining if they are being sensed and, if yes, that each person could then select and adopt different roles in such a sensor-augmented smart environment.

Fig. 3. Vision scribble of the artefacts and their integration into the environment

These objectives were achieved by combining various artefacts integrated into a smart office environment (see an example of a lounge area in Figure 3) and tailored to the needs of distributed teams. Ambient displays and sensors are embedded into the physical surrounding to communicate information and support implicit interaction mechanisms. These stationary artefacts are complemented by personal mobile devices, that help users to preserve their privacy in public space and access personalized information.

10   Implementation

Corresponding to the three objectives, the conceptual model was implemented by developing three different artefacts, which use a common communication infrastructure.

10.1 Personal.Aura

To enable user-controlled identification processes as well as personal role management, a mobile control device called *Personal.Aura* was developed (see Figure 4). The *Personal.Aura* is a mobile device enabling users to control their appearance in a smart environment by deciding on their own, whether they want to be "visible" for remote colleagues, and if so, in which "social role" they want to appear. The guiding design principle here was to have a physical artefact and physical actions for providing control to the user.

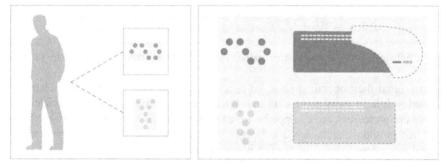

Fig. 4. The Personal.Aura concept for individual identification and role management. Each user has different virtual roles represented by a personal sign. With the Personal.Aura artefact users can activate different roles and thereby control if and how they are identified by the environment. Different patterns (e.g., displayed on the Hello.Wall see Figure 9 below) correspond to different social roles

The *Personal.Aura* is a compound artefact consisting of a *Reader Module* and several complementary *ID Sticks* (see Figures 5 and 6). Every *ID Stick* symbolizes a different social role and contains a unique identification code. Besides the identification information, the *ID Stick* contains additional memory to store personal information or user preferences. The *Reader Module* comprises the power supply, antenna and input/output controls. It decodes the identification stored on an *ID Stick* and transmits the data to a smart environment. More details can be found in Röcker (2006).

To give users the possibility to change their social role or identity, it is important that they have control over the information transmitted to the environment. If people want to signal their presence to remote team members, they can do so by simply connecting a specific *ID Stick* to the *Reader Module*. As soon as both parts are physically connected, the user is identified with the digital profile linked to the specific *ID Stick*. Disconnecting both parts immediately stops the identification process.

To enhance the users' awareness for tracking and identification events, visual and acoustic feedback mechanisms are implemented. While all prototypes use visual feed

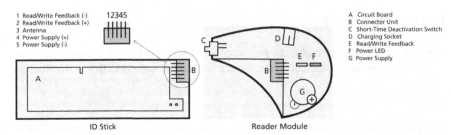

Fig. 5. Technical concept of the Personal.Aura artefact

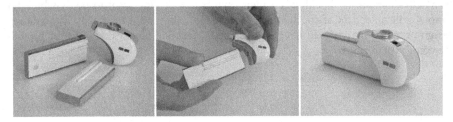

Fig. 6. Activation of the Personal.Aura artefact by connecting an ID Stick to the Reader Module

back to signal their operating state, both, acoustical and visual feedback mechanisms, are tried to inform users about data transfer between the artefact and the environment. Half of the prototypes are equipped with an additional LED to signal data access, the other half provides feedback via a bleeper. Providing acoustic feedback enhances peripheral awareness, even if the artefact is not constantly in the user's field of vision.

To enable users to temporarily interrupt the identification process, the *Personal.Aura* can be switched to a "privacy mode". While in privacy mode, users are invisible for all others. A status change to privacy mode is done via a switch on the side of the artefact. While disassembling the artefact provides intuitively understandable information about its current operating state, a temporary deactivation via a switch might not be as clear. Therefore, the switch was designed to integrate harmoniously into the shape of the artefact when inactive, and to generate a disharmonious perturbation while activated.

In order to clearly identify users and prevent misuse of personal information, it is necessary that *ID Sticks* can only be used by the person they belong to. To guarantee this, a concept of key and lock is applied: only if two matching parts are connected, the *Personal.Aura* is complete and operational. Therefore, a special security profile is engraved into the surfaces of the *Reader Module* and *ID Sticks*, which is unique for each *Personal.Aura* artefact. This security profile works like a key and makes it impossible to connect an *ID Stick* to a wrong *Reader Module*.

10.2 Hello.Wall

In order to represent public awareness information, a large-scale ambient display called *Hello.Wall* was developed. The *Hello.Wall* uses special light patterns to communicate information in an ambient and unobtrusive way (see Figure 7). As the design of the light patterns is independent from the technical realization of the *Hello.Wall*

Fig. 7. Hello.Wall artefact showing different light patterns depending on the social situation

artefact, a broad variety of different patterns can be designed to communicate information. This enables to develop individual "pattern languages", tailored to the specific needs of a distributed team.

To demonstrate the potential of this approach, an exemplary pattern language was developed to visualize information in an ambient and unobtrusive way. The goal was to improve workplace awareness and support opportunities for chance encounters between remote colleagues. Based on the types of information defined in the conceptual approach, patterns for the following information were designed (see Figure 8):

- general mood of the remote team,
- general activity in the remote work space,
- presence and availability of certain team members, and
- interest in communication with a remote team member.

According to the conceptual approach, two groups of patterns are distinguished: ambient patterns that represent general information, like mood and activity, and notification patterns, communicating individual or personalized messages.

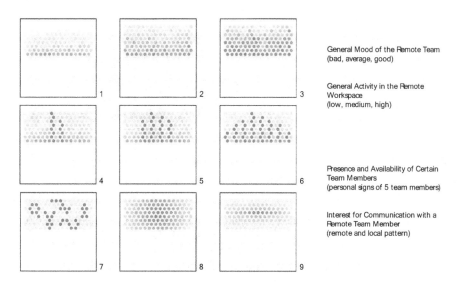

Fig. 8. Visual concept for the design of the different patterns

The *Hello.Wall* continuously displays dynamic ambient patterns overlayed with each other, representing the overall mood and general activity of the remote team members. Churchill et al. (2004) explored different forms of information representation and found that too dynamic visualizations are likely to be distracting, while visualizations with too little variation appear static and unresponsive. Based on these findings, Vogel and Balakrishnan (2004) argue, that the aesthetics of the displayed information, as well as the transitions between different states, are crucial factors for successful system design. In an iterative design process, different types of patterns were created and tested. The final set of patterns is characterized by a rather abstract nature to achieve an aesthetically pleasing and calm appearance. To reduce the complexity and support peripheral perception, each parameter is divided into three levels (low, medium, high) with corresponding patterns.

With the integrated sensing infrastructure of the *Hello.Wall*, it is possible to support context-dependent information representation. This enables several distributed teams to share *Hello.Wall* artefacts available in their local work environment. To support the formation and maintenances of a collective identity, Konradt and Hertel (2002) recommend establishing individual symbols and signs for each team. As the meaning of these codes is known only by the members of each team, it is also possible to "communicate" private and group-relevant information in public spaces.

To visualize individual presence and availability information, a set of abstract personal signs is created. Each team member is represented by one sign (see Figure 9). The different social roles of each user are symbolized through slight variations of the basic form of this sign. These personal signs are displayed as an overlay to the ambient patterns. To ensure better recognizability, the individual signs are displayed at fixed positions on the *Hello.Wall*. Besides the static personal signs, dynamic and attention-catching patterns are used to signal communication requests towards remote team members.

Fig. 9. Identification via the Personal.Aura artefact: Connecting an ID Stick to the Reader Module triggers the identification process, resulting in a personal sign being displayed at the remote Hello.Wall

10.3 View.Port

To provide personalized awareness information and simultaneous multi-user interaction, a mobile device called *View.Port* was developed. The *View.Port* is a portable compound artefact with a touch-sensitive display and sensing technology. Due to its graphical display, it can be used for showing detailed and personalized information stored in the *Information Cells* of the *Hello.Wall*.

The functionality of the *View.Port* is enhanced through the integration of a passive RFID reader that makes it possible to identify tagged people and objects. The information about the spatial surrounding can be used to support direct interaction mechanisms as well as personalized information presentation.

As the integrated sensing technology enables to identify tagged users, the information shown on the *View.Port* can be temporarily personalized for the current user. Depending on the active digital role of the user, the *View.Port* can be used to view personalized information, relevant in the current situation. For example, users can directly access in-depth information about a remote user, by bringing their personalized *View.Port* close to the specific personal sign at the *Hello.Wall*. Depending on their access rights, additional information about the remote user is displayed on the screen of the *View.Port*. In combination with the touch sensitive display, users can "directly" interact with this information.

As smart environments require continuous information exchange, the design of privacy-enhancing interaction metaphors is a major challenge. Especially the mechanisms to disclose private information must be easy and intuitively understandable, to prevent unintended data disclosure. In the current version of the *View.Port*, private and public parts of the display are differentiated by form (see Figure 10). By dragging information objects from the private to the public area, private information can be easily disseminated.

Fig. 10. User interface concept of the View.Port: Public and private display areas for easy information dissemination, and physical buttons for direct access to important functions

To support the interaction between the *Hello.Wall* and the *View.Port*, two independent RFID systems and a wireless LAN network are used. People, entering the *Notification Zone* (see next section) are detected via their *Personal.Aura* artefact, according to the social role currently activated. Once a person is detected, the identification information is sent to a control computer working in the background for further processing. Depending on the kind of application, data can be transmitted to the *View.Port* via a wireless network connection, or personalized information can be displayed on the *Hello.Wall* artefact. Within the *Interaction Zone*, users can access the information "stored" in each *Information Cell* by reading the cell's ID with the integrated short-range reader of the *View.Port*. With the received identification data, the *View.Port* can access the corresponding information stored on the processing computer in the background via wireless LAN. The following figure 11 shows a schematic sketch of the *View.Port* and the *Hello.Wall* coupled via RFID technology and a wireless network.

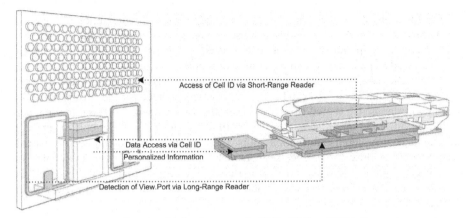

Fig. 11. Communication between the Hello.Wall and View.Port

10.4 Different Zones of Interaction

In order to provide differentiated services, especially for achieving the goal of providing context-aware services, one has to differentiate also the approach for sensing people and collecting relevant parameters. Our objective was that the service provided by the artefact should be location- and situation-based depending on the proximity of people passing by. Therefore, we distinguish between three different "zones of interaction" (see Figure 12) and their respective modes dependent on the distance from the Hello.Wall:

- Ambient Zone
- Notification Zone
- Interaction Zone

The different zones of interaction allows us to introduce a "distance-dependent semantic", implying that the distance of an individual from the smart artefact defines the kind of information shown and the interaction offered. This is realized by integrated sensors covering different ranges. They can be adapted according to the surrounding spatial conditions.

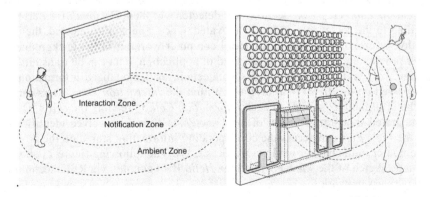

Fig. 12. Three zones of interaction (left and detection of a user (right)

11   Pilot Installation and Evaluation

To evaluate the artefacts under real-world conditions, a test environment was set up at two remote work spaces of a distributed project team. Two remote office environments with dedicated lounge areas for communication were used to evaluate the developed prototypes.

11.1 Test Environment

A symmetrical configuration of two *Hello.Wall* artefacts with additional video-conferencing facilities was installed in the lounge spaces at two sites. The first set of artefacts was installed at Fraunhofer IPSI in Darmstadt (Germany), the second at the Laboratory of Design for Cognition, EDF R&D in Paris (France). See Figure 13 for the spatial setting and Figure 14 for the technical concept.

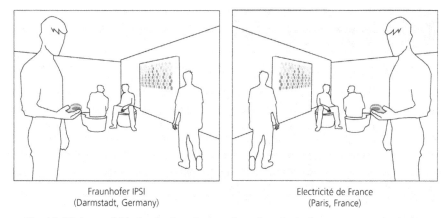

Fraunhofer IPSI
(Darmstadt, Germany)

Electricité de France
(Paris, France)

Fig. 13. Vision scribble for the installation of artefacts in the lounge areas at both sites

This setup draws upon the observation, that people in the lounge spaces are tentatively available for conversations while having their coffee break (Prante et al. 2004).

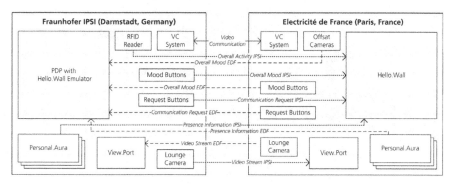

Fig. 14. Technical concept for the test environment.

The "zones of interaction" model, introduced before, was mapped to the floor plans of both office spaces (see Figure 15). While people in the *Ambient Zone* only contribute to the ambient activity patterns, people entering the *Notification Zone* are identified via their *Personal.Aura,* and their personal sign is displayed at the *Hello.Wall* in the remote lounge space. Thus, the *Hello.Wall* continuously presents an intuitively perceivable picture about the atmosphere at the remote site in an ambient and unobtrusive way.

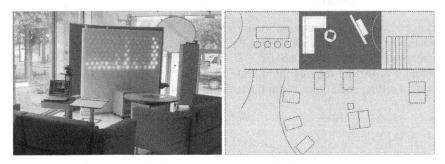

Fig. 15. Lounge area at EDF with the Hello.Wall artefact and the video-conference station (left) and floor plan (right), showing the Ambient Zone (light grey) and the Notification Zone (dark)

To prepare the ground for informal face-to-face communication, the test installation aimed at supporting the team members on both sides in approaching each other by successive signals of agreement, before actually engaging in a conversation. Therefore, special "request buttons" were installed, which could be used to express the interest for a video communication with remote users. Pressing the request button results in an attention-catching pattern to be shown on the *Hello.Wall* at the remote site. The overall mood of each team was captured with an easy, but very effective three-button interface (see Figure 16). After one of the "mood buttons" (bad, average or good) is pressed, its respective value is added to overall mood of the local team, and the updated mood pattern (see Figure 8) appears on the *Hello.Wall* in the remote lounge.

Fig. 16. Request button (left) and mood button (right)

In addition, webcams were installed in both lounge areas, to provide short glances into the remote lounge area. The webcams could be accessed from the remote lounge space using a *View.Port*, which provides users with more detailed information about the current situation in the remote lounge area. To avoid misuse, a special pattern is displayed at the *Hello.Wall*, if a remote colleague is using a *View.Port* to glance into the lounge area.

11.2 Evaluation

To verify the validity of the conceptual approach, and to confirm the added value of the technical prototypes compared to related research results, the developed artefacts were evaluated in a three-step process. To capture subjective as well as performance related aspects, a combination of qualitative and quantitative evaluation techniques was employed.

In a first step, the perception and recognition of the ambient light patterns were tested in a controlled experiment. The evaluation showed, that the ambient light patterns developed for the *Hello.Wall* were easily and intuitively perceptible by all participants. Although the participants were untrained, the recognition rate for both parameters was around 90%. As there might be a learning effect, it is likely, that the recognition will further improve, when users get accustomed to the new representation form.

In a second experimental evaluation, the pattern representation used to visualize information at the *Hello.Wall* was compared to a video representation, which is currently the most-widely used representation form in multi-user awareness systems. Both representation methods were compared regarding their suitability to provide awareness information, their disruptive effects on work as well as privacy concerns that arise during usage. The evaluation showed that the pattern representation used for the *Hello.Wall* significantly reduces distractions. In addition, the privacy concerns, when using the pattern representation, were significantly lower. Hence, the evaluation supported the approach of using ambient patterns to visualize awareness information because it could be shown that using a pattern representation significantly reduces distractions and privacy concerns, without negatively effecting the perception of awareness information.

As standard experimental evaluations are not suitable to test utility aspects of ambient awareness systems, a living-lab evaluation was conducted. All artefacts were tested under real-world conditions for several weeks, in order to investigate their potential for supporting awareness and informal communication in a distributed team. The goal of the evaluation was, to create personal connections between remote team colleagues by establishing awareness moments, and supporting community interactions between both sides. The results of the observation proved the effectiveness of the developed artefacts and confirmed its positive effects on workplace awareness and group communication. The data extracted from the questionnaires showed, that more interactions between both labs took place, and that the video communication system was used more often than before. The test installation was appreciated for providing a feeling for the atmosphere at the remote site and the number of people present, without disturbing the participants' privacy and workflow. Users found it very helpful to see "who is there", and seemed to gain experience of how the remote colleagues work, and the way the lab is organized. The *Hello.Wall* was described as "a good measure to establish an everyday relationship with people, who are not physically present", and to improve the atmosphere in the lab "by taking it from isolation". Besides these more functional aspects, also the design of the artefacts and interaction techniques were considered to be very good and aesthetically pleasing.

It could also be shown, that the *Hello.Wall* can serve as an unobtrusive awareness device in real-world working environments. While the members of the distributed team gained practical benefits using the *Hello.Wall*, the artefact did not attract any attention of people who were not participating in the joint activity, but were just spending some time in the lounge area around the *Hello.Wall*. Details of the evaluation can be found in (Nosulenko et al. 2003).

12   Conclusions

The work reported demonstrates our approach on the role of information and communication technology in future smart buildings for which the notions of the "disappearing computer" and calm technology are of central importance. While in our previous work, e.g., on developing the Roomware components (Streitz et al. 1998, 1999, 2001) the focus was on supporting productivity-related processes of team work and group meetings, the Ambient Agoras environment reported here focused on informal communication and social awareness. In this case, we combined two corresponding design goals: First, to develop a smart environment that supports selected social processes as, e.g., awareness, informal communication, and coordination of team work in local and distributed collaboration settings. Second, the implementation corresponds to and is compatible with the nature and characteristics of the processes addressed by following the objectives of developing a calm technology providing appropriate affordances. Computers move into the background and are not considered or perceived anymore to be computers or computer-related devices.

As part of our subsequent and current work, we exploit the results gained in office environments and transfer our experiences to building intelligent user services for smart home environments with a focus on home information and entertainment. Issues of capturing information about people's activities and transforming them into experiences of awareness exchanged between remote sites reappear here again in the context of scenarios for remote but networked homes. This work is done in the EU-funded project "Amigo – Ambient Intelligence in the Networked Home Environments". Some results on the corresponding work on awareness can be found, e.g., in Röcker and Etter (2007) and Etter and Röcker (2007).

Acknowledgements

The work reported in this chapter was supported by the European Commission as part of the "Disappearing Computer" initiative ("Ambient Agoras" project, contract IST–2000-25134). Furthermore, we like to thank all those project members, not being authors, from the German office manufacturer Wilkhahn and the French electrical power utility provider EDF (Electricité de France) as well as members and students of the Fraunhofer research division AMBIENTE who contributed substantially to realizing the different components and environments.

References

Ambient Agoras website: http://www.ambient-agoras.org

Alexander, C.: A Pattern Language. Oxford University Press, New York (1977)

Bellotti, V., Bly, S.: Walking Away from the Desktop Computer: Distributed Collaboration and Mobility in a Product Design Team. In: Proceedings of the ACM Conference on Computer Supported Cooperative Work (CSCW'96), pp. 209–218. ACM Press, New York (1996)

Bellotti, V., Ducheneaut, N., Howard, M., Smith, I.: Taking Email to Task: The Design and Evaluation of a Task Management Centred Email Tool. In: Proceedings of the Conference on Human Factors in Computing Systems (CHI'03), pp. 345–352 (2003)

Bly, S., Harrison, S.R., Irwin, S.: Media Spaces: Bringing People Together in a Video, Audio, and Computing Environment. Communications of the ACM 36(1), 28–46 (1993)

Churchill, E.F., Nelson, L., Denoue, L., Helfman, J., Murphy, P.: Sharing Multimedia Content with Interactive Public Displays: A Case Study. In: Proceedings of the Conference on Designing Interactive Systems: Processes, Practices, Methods, and Techniques (DIS'04), pp. 7–16 (2004)

Dourish, P., Bly, S.: Portholes: Supporting Awareness in a Distributed Work Group. In: Proceedings of the ACM Conference on Human Factors in Computing Systems (CHI'92), pp. 541–547. ACM Press, New York (1992)

Eldridge, M., Barnard, P., Bekerian, D.: Autobiographical Memory and Daily Schemes at Work. Memory 2(1), 51–74 (1994)

Etter, R., Röcker, C.: A Tangible User Interface for Multi-User Awareness Systems. In: Proceedings of the International Conference on Tangible and Embedded Interaction '07, Baton Rouge, USA, February 15–17 (2007)

Fish, R.S., Kraut, R.E., Root, R.W., Rice, R.E.: Evaluating Video as a Technology for Informal Communication. In: Bauersfeld, P., Bennett, J., Lynch, G. (eds.) Proceedings of the ACM CHI 1992 Conference, pp. 37–48. ACM Press, New York (1992)

Gaver, W.: Technology Affordances. Proceedings of the ACM CHI 1991 Conference, pp. 79–84. ACM Press, New York (1991)

Gaver, W.W., Moran, T., MacLean, A., Lovstrand, L., Dourish, P., Carter, K.A., Buxton, W.: Realizing a Video Environment: EuroPARC's RAVE System. In: Proceedings of the ACM Conference on Human Factors in Computing Systems (CHI'92), pp. 27–35. ACM Press, New York (1992)

Gellersen, H.-W., Schmidt, A., Beigl, M.: Ambient Media for Peripheral Information Display. Personal Technologies 3(4), 199–208 (1999)

Gibson, J.: The Ecological Approach to Visual Perception. Houghton Mifflin, Boston (1979)

Guzzo, R., Salas, E.: Team Effectiveness and Decision Making in Organizations. Jossey-Bass, San Francisco (1995)

Gwizdka, J.: TaskView: Design and Evaluation of a Task-Based Email Interface. In: Proceedings of the Conference of the Centre for Advanced Studies on Collaborative Research, pp. 136–145 (2002)

Huang, E.M., Russell, D.M., Sue, A.E.: IM here: Public Instant Messaging on Large, Shared Displays for Workgroup Interactions. In: Proceedings of the Conference on Human Factors in Computing Systems (CHI'04), pp. 279–286 (2004)

Ishii, H., Wisneski, C., Brave, S., Dahley, A., Gobert, M., Ullmer, B., Paul, Y.: Ambient-ROOM: Integrating Ambient Media with Architectural Space. In: Proceedings of Human Factors in Computing Systems (CHI 1998), pp. 173–174. ACM Press, New York (1998)

ISTAG: Scenarios for Ambient Intelligence in 2010. Final Report by the IST Advisory Group (2001), ftp://ftp.cordis.lu/pub/ist/docs/istagscenarios2010.pdf

Konradt, U., Hertel, G.: Management virtueller Teams - Von der Telearbeit zum virtuellen Unternehmen. Beltz Verlag, Weinheim (2002)

Kraut, R.E., Fish, R.S., Root, R.W., Chalfonte, B.L.: Informal Communication in Organizations: Form, Function, and Technology. In: Oskamp, S., Spacapan, S. (eds.) Human Reactions to Technology: The Claremont Symposium on Applied Social Psychology, pp. 145–199. Sage, Beverly Hills (1990), reprinted in: Baecker, R.M. (ed.) Readings in Groupware and Computer-Supported Cooperative Work. Morgan Kaufmann, San Francisco, pp. 287–314

Lahlou, S., Jegou, F.: European Disappearing Computer Privacy Design Guidelines V1.0. Ambient Agoras Report D15.4, Disappearing Computer Initiative (2003)

Lahlou, L., Langheinrich, M., Röcker, C.: Privacy and trust issues with invisible computers. Communications of the ACM 48(3), 59–60 (2005)

Lamming, M., Eldridge, M., Flynn, M., Jones, C., Pendlebury, D.: Satchel: Providing Access to any Document, any Time, anywhere. ACM Transactions on Computer-Human Interaction 7(3), 322–352 (2000)

Langheinrich, M.: Privacy by Design – Principles of Privacy-Aware Ubiquitous Systems. In: Abowd, G.D., Brumitt, B., Shafer, S. (eds.) Ubicomp 2001: Ubiquitous Computing. LNCS, vol. 2201, pp. 273–291. Springer, Heidelberg (2001)

Mankoff, J., Dey, A., Hsieh, G., Kientz, J., Lederer, S., Ames, M.: Heuristic Evaluation of Ambient Displays. In: Proceedings of ACM Conference CHI 2003, pp. 169–176 (2003)

McGrenere, J., Ho, W.: Affordances: Clarifying an Evolving Concept. In: Proceedings of Graphics Interface 2000 (Montreal, Canada), pp. 179–186 (2000)

Nardi, B.A., Whittaker, S., Bradner, E.: Interaction and Outeraction: Instant Messaging in Action. In: Proceedings of the ACM Conference on Computer Supported Cooperative Work (CSCW'00), pp. 79–88. ACM Press, New York (2000)

Norman, D.: The Psychology of Everyday Things. Basic Books, New York (1988)

Norman, D.: Affordance, Conventions, and Design. ACM Interactions (May and June 1999), pp. 38–42. ACM Press, New York (1999)

Nosulenko, V., Samoylenko, E., Welinski, P.: D12.10 – Hello.Wall and Videomaton User Experience. Deliverable of the 'Ambient Agoras' Project for the Third Disappearing Computer Jamboree, Ivrea, Italy (2003)

OECD - Organization for Economic Co-operation and Development: Guidelines on the Protection of Privacy and Transborder Flows of Personal Data (1980), http://www.junkbusters.com/fip.html

Panko, R.R.: Managerial Communication Patterns. Journal of Organizational Computing 2(1), 95–122 (1992)

Pelizäus-Hoffmeister, H.: Mobilität - Chance oder Risiko? Soziale Netzwerke unter den Bedingungen räumlicher Mobilität - Das Beispiel freie JournalistInnen. Leske und Budrich, Opalden (2001)

Potter, R., Balthazard, P.: Virtual Team Interaction Styles: Assessment and Effects. International Journal for Human-Computer Studies 56(4), 423–443 (2002)

Prante, T., Stenzel, R., Röcker, C., van Alphen, D., Streitz, N., Magerkurth, C., Plewe, D.: Connecting Remote Teams: Cross-Media Integration to Support Remote Informal Encounters. In: Video Track and Adjunct Proceedings of the Sixth International Conference on Ubiquitous Computing (UBICOMP'04), Nottingham, England, September 7-10, 2004 (2004)

Robbin, A.: The Loss of Personal Privacy and its Consequences for Social Research. Journal of Government Information 28(5), 493–527 (2001)

Röcker, C.: Awareness and Informal Communication in Smart Office Environments. Verlag Dr. Driesen, Taunusstein (2006)

Röcker, C., Etter, R.: Social Radio: A Music-Based Approach to Emotional Awareness Mediation. In: Proceedings of the 10th International Conference on Intelligent User Interfaces (Honolulu, USA), pp. 286–289 (2007)

Rohall, S.L., Gruen, D., Moody, P., Wattenberg, M., Stern, M., Kerr, B., Stachel, B., Dave, K., Armes, R., Wilcox, E.: ReMail: A Reinvented Email Prototype. In: Extended Abstracts of the Conference on Human Factors in Computing Systems (CHI'04), pp. 791–792 (2004)

Sonnentag, S.: Work, Recovery Activities, and Individual Well-Being: A Diary Study. Journal of Occupational Health Psychology 6(3), 196–210 (2001)

Streitz, N.: Mental models and metaphors: Implications for the design of adaptive user-system interfaces. In: Mandl, H., Lesgold, A. (eds.) Learning Issues for Intelligent Tutoring Systems. Cognitive Science Series, pp. 164–186. Springer, New York (1988)

Streitz, N.: Augmented Reality and the Disappearing Computer. In: Smith, M., Salvendy, G., Harris, D., Koubek, R. (eds.) Cognitive Engineering, Intelligent Agents and Virtual Reality, pp. 738–742. Lawrence Erlbaum Associates, Mahwah (2001)

Streitz, N., Geißler, J., Holmer, T.: Roomware for Cooperative Buildings: Integrated Design of Architectural Spaces and Information Spaces. In: Streitz, N.A., Konomi, S., Burkhardt, H.-J. (eds.) CoBuild 1998. LNCS, vol. 1370, pp. 4–21. Springer, Heidelberg (1998)

Streitz, N., Geißler, J., Holmer, T., Konomi, S., Müller-Tomfelde, C., Reischl, W., Rexroth, P., Seitz, P., Steinmetz, R.: i-LAND: an Interactive Landscape for Creativity and Innovation. In: Proceedings of ACM Conference CHI'99 (Pittsburgh, USA), pp. 120–127. ACM, New York (1999)

Streitz, N., Magerkurth, C., Prante, T., Röcker, C.: From Information Design to Experience Design: Smart Artefacts and the Disappearing Computer. ACM Interactions, Special Issue on Ambient intelligence (July and August 2005), 12(4), 21–25 (2005a)

Streitz, N., Nixon, P.: The Disappearing Computer. Communications of the ACM 48(3), 33–35 (2005)

Streitz, N., Tandler, P., Müller-Tomfelde, C., Konomi, S.: Roomware: Towards the Next Generation of Human-Computer Interaction based on an Integrated Design of Real and Virtual Worlds. In: Carroll, J. (ed.) Human-Computer Interaction in the New Millennium, pp. 553–578. Addison-Wesley, Reading (2001)

Streitz, N., Prante, T., Röcker, C., van Alphen, D., Magerkurth, C., Stenzel, R., Plewe, D.A.: Plewe~DA Ambient Displays and Mobile Devices for the Creation of Social Architectural Spaces: Supporting informal communication and social awareness in organizations. In: O'Hara, K., Perry, M., Churchill, E., Russell, D. (eds.) Public and Situated Displays: Social and Interactional Aspects of Shared Display Technologies, pp. 387--409. Kluwer Publishers, Dordrecht (2003)

Streitz, N., Röcker, C., Prante, T., van Alphen, D., Stenzel, R., Magerkurth, C.: Designing Smart Artifacts for Smart Environments. IEEE Computer, March 2005, pp. 41-49 (2005b)

Sundstrom, E.: Supporting Work Team Effectiveness. Jossey-Bass, San Francisco (1999)

Utz, S.: Identifikation mit virtuellen Arbeitsgruppen und Organisationen. In: Boos, M., Jonas, K.J., Sassenberg, K. (eds.) Computervermittelte Kommunikation in Organisationen, pp. 41–55. Hogrefe, Göttingen (2000)

Vogel, D., Balakrishnan, R.: Interactive Public Ambient Displays: Transitioning From Implicit to Explicit, Public to Personal, Interaction with Multiple Users. In: Proceedings of the ACM Symposium on User Interface Software and Technology (UIST'04), pp. 137–146. ACM Press, New York (2004)

Weiser M.: The Computer for the 21st Century. Scientific American, September 1991, 66-75 (1991)

Weiser, M., Brown, J.S.: Designing Calm Technology, Xerox PARC report (December 21, 1995)

Whittaker, S., Frohlich, D., Daly-Jones, O.: Informal Workplace Communication What is it Like and How Might we Support it? In: Proceedings of ACM Conference on Human Factors in Computing Science (CHI '95), pp. 131–137. ACM, New York (1994)

Wisneski, C., Ishii, H., Dahley, A., Gorbet, M., Brave, S., Ullmer, B., Yarin, P.: Ambient Displays: Turning Architectural Space into an Interface between people and Digital Information. In: Streitz, N.A., Konomi, S., Burkhardt, H.-J. (eds.) CoBuild 1998. LNCS, vol. 1370, pp. 22–32. Springer, Heidelberg (1998)

From the Disappearing Computer to Living Exhibitions: Shaping Interactivity in Museum Settings

John Bowers[1,2], Liam Bannon[3], Mike Fraser[4], Jon Hindmarsh[5],
Steve Benford[6], Christian Heath[5], Gustav Taxén[1], and Luigina Ciolfi[3]

[1] Centre for User-Oriented IT-Design, Royal Institute of Technology, Stockholm, Sweden
[2] School of Music, University of East Anglia, Norwich, UK
[3] Interaction Design Centre, University of Limerick, Ireland
[4] Department of Computer Science, University of Bristol, UK
[5] Work Interaction and Technology Research Group, Department of Management,
King's College London, UK
[6] Mixed Reality Laboratory, University of Nottingham, UK

1   Introduction

While considerable technical ingenuity is being devoted to making the computer "disappear", comparatively few research endeavours have concertedly explored the issues which arise when innovative artefacts are deployed in public settings. Innovations in "mixed reality", "augmented reality" and "ubiquitous computing" tend to be confined to demonstrations, circumscribed trials or other controlled settings. However, a number of projects have begun to devote themselves to putting such technologies into the hands of the public and reflecting on the design and development issues that are encountered as a result. In particular, the SHAPE project was concerned with deploying innovative technologies in public settings, most notably museums. Over the course of our research, we developed an orientation to design which combines social scientific study, close collaboration with museum personnel and visitors, and a characteristic approach for technology deployment. In this chapter, we describe this orientation, exemplify it through accounts of the exhibitions the project has built at a number of museums in different European countries, and assess its broader implications for research on human-computer interaction, ubiquitous computing, and allied concerns.

Many researchers, following Weiser (1993), suggest that computers are more and more mass-market products with the potential of becoming part of the fabric of everyday life, rather than tools requiring expert skill, used in laboratories or high-tech offices. Our encounters with information technology are less exceptional, more everyday, and increasingly domestic, leisure-related and experienced in public places. Famously, Weiser contrasted this scenario with that typically explored in research on "virtual reality" (VR). While VR envisages future computing scenarios where users are *embodied* within a computer generated environment, research on ubiquitous computing is more concerned with *embedded* computing functionality in a multiplicity of artefacts. For Weiser, "ubicomp" is "VR turned inside out". However, there have been various attempts to articulate combined positions where the hybridisation of the physical and the digital is the research concern. "Augmented reality", "augmented virtuality" and "mixed reality" are all attempts to articulate new opportunities for tech-

N. Streitz, A. Kameas, and I. Mavrommati (Eds.): The Disappearing Computer, LNCS 4500, pp. 30–49, 2007.
© Springer-Verlag Berlin Heidelberg 2007

nological innovation along these lines. Demonstrations of the interplay of physical and digital have been offered in domains such as tele-medicine (Milgram and Colquhoun 1999), education (Rogers et al. 2003), entertainment (Stapleton et al. 2002) and the arts (Bell et al. 2006).

A number of researchers have begun to look at museum settings as a potentially relevant application domain for mixed reality technology while also attempting to help create experiences for the public of genuine cultural worth (Brown et al. 2003; Caulton 1998; Fraser et al. 2003; Grinter et al. 2002; Schnädelbach et al. 2002). The museum setting seems to bring together a number of features which make it most appropriate for study. First, for some time, museums have embraced the use of interactive exhibits alongside more traditional methods of display of the physical objects which make up the museum's collection. Digital solutions have been offered to such well-known curatorial problems as how to make publicly available objects otherwise held in storage or how to bring alive what is known about the use or history of an object which the exhibition of the "mute" object alone does not make possible. In turn, a number of equally well-known problems with "interactives" have emerged. Museum staff express concerns that digital artefacts can detract from a visitor's imaginative appreciation of the actual physical objects (Caulton 1998; Jackson et al. 2002) in much the same way as extensive textual labelling is often held to do. Further, multimedia museum presentations are most commonly built as single-user applications leading to concerns that engagement with them can sometimes disrupt the sociality of the museum visit (vom Lehn et al. 2001). Finally, digital solutions can be controversial if they seem to replace or "de-skill" the role of museum helpers, interpreters or docents (as they are variously called). In all these respects, museums offer us a microcosm of fundamental issues in technology design and deployment, allowing us to address naturally what might otherwise seem abstract matters such as tradition and innovation, skill and automation, the digital and the physical, the social and the individual, and so on.

Research in ubiquitous computing anticipates the mass proliferation of interaction devices and information displays. However, much research is concerned with investigating individual innovative computerized devices, with concomitant reduced concern for how a multiplicity of devices might concertedly combine to fashion a coherent experience. In contrast, SHAPE took construction and management of an "assembly of artefacts" as a primary research topic. An assembly might consist in multiple projections, each presenting a different kind of information, a multi-channel and multi-speaker sound system, a family of manipulable objects used for interactive purposes, a variety of communication media, and so forth. How can such an assembly be organised to fashion a coherent thematic experience for its users? Museums, exploratoria and galleries are relevant areas to study with respect to how artefacts can be assembled, as well as promising domains for evaluating designed solutions. The practical condition many museums find themselves in is one of multiple co-existing displays and presentation technologies of varying age, rationale, design aesthetic and material manifestation. Displays differ in terms of the kinds of activity they support, personalisation, physical scale, cost, portability, commodity or bespoke, and many other factors. This diversity makes museums and related institutions an appropriate case study in managing and integrating assemblies of diverse displays and devices, as well as being a setting in need of genuine practical solutions. The exhibitions developed and installed in the SHAPE project have given us useful information and feedback on the issues involved in crafting scenarios and creating narratives that "hold in" the complexities of multiple artefact assemblies.

2   Studying and Designing with Museums

While there exist many exciting design ideas for embedded devices, there exists much less appraisal of prototypes in genuine use and very little user-study to closely motivate (from the start) how embedded computational artefacts should be developed. A common strategy is to pursue clearly articulated and appealing design concepts, motivating them by theory, by market considerations, or designer-intuition. In common with many creative design traditions, the design ideas tend to stop with their demonstration – a more thoroughgoing reflection upon a designed artefact deployed in a real-world context and encountered by people as part of their everyday lives is somewhat rare in the literature (Gaver et al. 2004, is perhaps an exception to this). While such "design-led" activities are important work, we felt it necessary to complement them with more extensive practical engagement with museum personnel and, where possible, visitors.

Our approach in addressing this challenge was to combine social scientific methods of empirical research (e.g. field studies and interaction analysis) with techniques for facilitating the development of technical systems drawn from the "Scandinavian" participatory design tradition (cf. Greenbaum and Kyng 1991) including envisionment exercises, future workshops, cooperative and low-tech prototyping, and scenario-based design.

2.1   Social Scientific Study

During the lifetime of the project, SHAPE conducted numerous field studies in a range of museums and galleries in several different EU member states. Amongst others sites, studies were undertaken at: Technorama, Technical Museum (Stockholm), King John's Castle (Limerick), Limerick City Museum, the Hunt Museum (Limerick), Castle Museum (Nottingham), The Science Museum (London), @Bristol Science Centre (Bristol), The National Portrait Gallery (London), The Victoria and Albert Museum (V & A, London), The Natural History Museum (London), The Serpentine Gallery (London) and The Transport Museum (London). Data collection was designed to enable us to compare and contrast action and interaction in different types of exhibition space, involving different types of exhibits in different configurations, ranging from "aesthetic" to "applied", from interactive to non-interactive, and involving different types of visitor and visiting arrangement. These field studies included periods of participant observation in which researchers visited museums, used exhibits and information technologies, explored exhibitions and observed people navigating and exploring the museum space.

In many cases this observational research was augmented by the collection of photographic images and, more importantly for analytic purposes, video materials of visitor behaviour. Video recording tended to focus on single exhibits, such as the cabinets of curiosities in the Hunt Museum, which offered people the possibility of closely observing museum objects contained within open drawers in a large cabinet display, or the jumping skeleton in @Bristol, an augmented physical skeletal model allowing participants to interactively explore the connections between different areas of the brain and the limbs they control. However, we were also been able to record hands-on workshops at the Hunt Museum, where groups of visitors are encouraged to feel and manipulate artefacts from the collection, in the presence of a museum docent. Furthermore, we have recordings of sessions at the V & A, where visitors bring artefacts in to have them assessed by curatorial staff. In addition, we conducted informal interviews with museum education officers, curators, content, exhibit and exhibition designers.

Analysis of this diverse and voluminous corpus of empirical data enabled us to address a number of issues. Let us highlight two in particular as these have fundamentally influenced the form that SHAPE's design work in museums has taken: interactivity and assembly.

2.2 Interactivity

"Interactivity" in the design of exhibits in museums and galleries is a very fashionable concern. This notion is key to the proliferation of interactive exhibit technologies and interpretative technologies in the field. However, we argue that "the myth of the individual user" pervades the design of technologies in museums and galleries often at the cost of supporting or facilitating interaction and co-participation. Our observational studies have revealed the significance of co-participation and collaboration to the museum experience and the ways in which the navigation of galleries, the discovery of exhibits, and the conclusions that people draw arise in and through social interaction – interaction not only with those you are with, but with museum guides and docents, and those who just happen to be in the same space (Ciolfi and Bannon 2003; Heath and vom Lehn 2004; vom Lehn et al. 2001). The activities of those others can influence which exhibits an individual or group approach; what they look at; how they touch, manipulate or otherwise interact with the exhibit and so forth. We have also studied some of the issues and problems that arise with and around conventional computer based "interactives" within museums and galleries and in particular the ways in which they delimit interaction with the system, transform co-participants into audiences, fracture the relationship between exhibits, and disregard objects and collections. Accordingly, in our own design work, we sought to make artefacts which were notably "open" for collaborative use (e.g. through the use of an interactive surface that several people could gather around). Furthermore, in considering the disposition of several such artefacts in a whole exhibition layout, we sought to facilitate the degree to which visitors could pick up on the conduct of others and reason on its basis (e.g. by developing artefacts which were interacted with by means of large-scale, and hence noticeable, gestures, and by giving particular artefacts a particular function).

2.3 Assembly

Reflection on our corpus of data encouraged us to expand our sense of "interactivity" to take in many of the practical activities of visitors which are commonly ignored in the design of exhibits – activities which are essentially social, collaborative and contingent to the emerging character of the visit. This naturally led us to an equally expanded sense for "assembly". Our research increasingly manifested an interest in the social and interactional practices of "assembly"; that is, how participants themselves organise and create an assembly of artefacts. Accordingly, the technical work in SHAPE became pre-occupied with the production of assemblies of interconnected technical artefacts, whilst recognising the need to design to support everyday practices of assembling. That is, in SHAPE, "assembly" not merely denotes a set of interlinked artefacts, it also points to a characteristic feature of how people conduct themselves in museum settings. People actively assemble for themselves and display to others a sense of an exhibit which interconnects different aspects of their visit, including comparisons made with other exhibits or between co-visitors' different perceptions. Thus, in our own design work, we were aware of the need to provide a variety of supports for the thematic framing and integration of visitors' activities, while also enabling and encouraging visitors to flexibly engage with our interactive artefacts and formulate their own understandings of exhibition content.

2.4   Cooperative Design in Museums: Living Exhibitions

In addition to conducting social scientific studies with a broad base of museums and allied institutions, we worked very closely with three museums in the production of new exhibits. At Stockholm's Technical Museum, we developed an installation known as *The Well of Inventions* which presents some fundamental mechanical concepts through air and fluid simulations and interactive sound. *The Well of Inventions* is based around a table-top projection and an eight channel sound system allowing multiple participants to engage with the piece. The installation was developed through various iterations. First, a "quick and dirty" prototype demonstration of a number of graphical simulation techniques, sound synthesis and diffusion methods, and interaction principles was developed. This was proposed as providing technical "design responses" to some of the early themes emerging from the social scientific work in SHAPE. Following this, the demonstration was overhauled to more carefully engage with content and themes at the Stockholm Technical Museum, to be more physically robust as an unsupervised public exhibit, and to be of higher quality graphically and sonically. To deal with all these issues, we engaged in extensive collaboration with personnel at the Technical Museum through cooperative design workshops and other forms of collaboration (see Taxén et al. 2004 for details).

The Well of Inventions is a single exhibit. Our subsequent work sought to build on its emphasis for prototyping, iteration and collaboration with museum personnel but to more fully exemplify our concern for constructing assemblies of multiple interactive artefacts in a coherent exhibition. First at Nottingham Castle and then at the Hunt Museum in Limerick, we sought to collaborate with museum personnel at an even earlier stage of design to engage with the existing content and themes of the museums and, in particular, to explore ways in which physical-digital hybrid technology might help address genuine curatorial problems.

The design process that we evolved over the course of these exhibitions became increasingly dependent on the use of "scenarios". Having immersed ourselves in the museum setting, we engaged in initial brainstorming sessions and evolved a number of initial ideas of what the exhibition might entail. Lists of key themes and outline sketches were produced at this stage. These sessions would involve SHAPE personnel as well as museum staff. Initial ideas were developed further in a second round of meetings, where early concepts were fleshed out and discussed, and some rejected. A third set of meetings were held where detailed storyboards of the exhibition concept and realization were produced, walked through, and refined with a wide circle of interested people, not only those in the SHAPE research group. This included, both in the UK and Ireland, working with local schools who typically visit these museums as part of their school education programmes.

Additionally, and again in both cases, we conducted many of our design activities on site at the museum in question. For example, we held cooperative design workshops with schoolchildren and teachers at Nottingham Castle. Our exhibition at the Hunt Museum allowed access to visitors and museum personnel several days before the formal opening, enabling them to comment on the exhibition and in some cases suggest some alterations that we were able to implement, even as it was about to go public.

3   Design Cases: The SHAPE Living Exhibitions

In earlier sections, we have provided some background to the issues of concern to the SHAPE team in the development of novel interactive environments for use in museum settings. Our views on mixed reality technologies, on the ways in which visitors interact with objects, settings and other visitors and guides, on the need for understanding the nature of museums, have all been outlined. Here, we wish to examine in some detail two of our major pieces of work within the SHAPE project, exhibitions designed in close co-operation with the museums in question, in order to give a flavour of the kinds of design decisions that were made, and the experiences visitors had when encountering these exhibits.

3.1   The First Living Exhibition: *Exploring Digital History* at Nottingham Castle, UK

Nottingham Castle was first built in 1067. Over the past millennium, various significant historical events have taken place at different locations around the site. Following the end of the English Civil War, the year 1651 marked the destruction of the castle. Around 20 years later, the Duke of Newcastle built a Renaissance-like "Ducal Palace" on the site of the castle remains. Notably, what is left on the site today bears little relation to the more complex medieval castle. In order to give visitors some sense of the castle, the on-site museum employs various mechanisms and technologies such as slide shows, medieval artefacts with associated text, interactive kiosks, signposts, guides, brochures and textbooks. Nonetheless, museum staff are constantly looking for further ways of helping visitors to understand the castle as it used to be, and the part it played in key historical events.

We designed the exhibition over the course of several months. The research process included consulting museum personnel over exhibit content and requirements. As many visitors are families or groups with children, we also conducted a series of design workshops and staged preliminary trials involving a head teacher and a class of 10 year-old school children.

As a result of these preliminary workshops and discussions, the following exhibition design emerged. Visitors were invited to take part in a "history hunt". On arrival on site, they were given a pack of paper clues and told they were on the trail of a historical character that features in a particular period of the castle's history (either Richard I or Edward III). The visitors used their pack to find clues at various locations around the castle grounds and piece together their character's story. The overall experience was structured as follows:

- **Arrive at the gazebo.** Visitors receive an explanation of their task and pick up a pack of clues to guide their hunt.

- **Search the grounds.** The paper clues guide the visitors to places which feature in the story of their character. These places often only minimally resemble the location's appearance in history. For example, the Castle Green, an open area of grass, was the location for a large castle building called the Great Hall. In these locations they make drawings as instructed by the clue.

- **Back at the gazebo.** RFID tags are attached to the paper clues so that each piece of paper is categorised with a character and a location.

- **At the gatehouse.** The visitors encounter two different displays which they can interact with using their tagged clues. We describe these in detail shortly. The first display is the *StoryTent* which reveals one scene of the story, showing for each clue the event that took place at the location. The second display is the virtual *Sandpit*, at which visitors can dig for pictures that are related to either the character or place for each of their clues.

- **Depart.** Visitors take their paper clues away with them.

3.2   Revealing Scenes in the Storytent

The Storytent occupies one side of the castle gatehouse. It consists of a tarpaulin construction with either side acting as a projection screen (see Green et al. 2002). The projections can be seen from both inside and outside the tent. This provides an intimate projected space inside the tent, and a larger, public space outside.

The tent contains an interaction device, the Turntable, which combines an RFID tag reader and a potentiometer. The reader allows tagged paper to be identified by the tent, whilst the potentiometer allows rotational input around the vertical axis. A UV lamp is positioned over the top section of the Turntable. When a paper clue is placed on top of the Turntable, "invisible writing" is revealed, which is marked in UV ink on the paper. The UV writing describes the historical event related to the particular clue. The tag reader and potentiometer are both connected to a PC running a virtual model of the medieval castle, which is projected onto both sides of the tent. Rotating the top of the Turntable rotates the view of the castle model.

Seven different tag types (four for Richard I and three for Edward III) trigger seven different scenes within the tent. Placing a tagged paper clue onto the Turntable, then, causes a number of simultaneous occurrences.

Fig. 1. The Storytent with close-up of the Turntable interaction device with a clue placed on top (inset)

- The invisible writing on the clue is revealed;
- The tag reader detects the tag and moves the 3D viewpoint projected on the tent to the relevant clue location in the model;
- Sounds associated with the historical event for the clue are played;
- An image selected from the information space is displayed on the public side of the tent.

3.3   Digging for Images in the Sandpit

The virtual Sandpit was positioned in the other side of the gatehouse. The Sandpit was a top-down floor projection enabling groups to gather round it. The Sandpit is a graphical simulation of a volume of sand. Visitors can dig in the sand using one or two video-tracked torches to control animated cursors on the floor projection. Pictures of the castle site, portraits of key historical figures, scanned visitor drawings and other images are "buried" in the sand. When an image is revealed, by "digging" with the torches, it spins up to the top of the projection and then disappears. Nottingham Castle is built atop a sandstone cliff and the metaphor of impressions of the castle's history enduring in the sand seemed suggestive.

There is an RFID tag reader placed under a sandbox on a pedestal next to the Sandpit. Placing a tagged clue onto the sandbox selects the set of images buried in the sand. The images are related either to the character or the place for the particular clue. The Sandpit also includes some sound for ambience and feedback that indicates the tagged clue has been recognised.

Fig. 2. The Sandpit with close-up of the Sandbox device with a clue placed on top (inset)

3.4   Reflections on *Exploring Digital History* at Nottingham Castle, UK

The actual exhibition was "live" for three and a half days in July 2002. In that time, more than 200 visitors experienced the exhibition. Visitors ranged from individuals to groups of seven or eight; and from very young children to elderly citizens. Some participants completed all the clues, some completed only one or two. Generally, visitors found the experience to be extremely engaging and educationally relevant. In terms of the dwell-time metrics which are commonly used to evaluate exhibits, our Storytent and Sandpit were spectacularly "attractive". However, a number of important issues emerged on closer examination. These included:

- The coherence of the experience was critically dependent upon the "scaffolding" provided by the research team itself in explaining to people what was going on, how to use the artefacts, and what the historical events were to which the clues referred.

- The assembly of artefacts enabled people to make a variety of connections as they assembled a sense of the individual clues, of the relationships between displays, and between displays and their activities exploring the castle grounds. However, people rarely combined information across clues to develop an integrated sense of particular historical happenings. The "big picture" did not seem to spontaneously emerge.

- The design of some aspects of our artefacts seemed a little arbitrary. Why exactly use a torch to uncover images from a virtual sandpit? Relatedly, the motivation for some of the exhibition's content seemed a bit unclear. What exactly (e.g. from a pedagogical standpoint) was a visitor supposed to learn of the history of the site through uncovering images or navigating a 3D model?

In sum, we learned a number of things from designing, building and evaluating this exhibition. The sheer scale of the effort involved in marshalling resources, both human and technical, and ensuring that the exhibits worked for the duration of the exhibition was considerable. This is noteworthy in the light of the usual kinds of experimentation teams perform in research projects, where large public demonstrations are rarely attempted. Further, while effort was expended on creating a thematic structure for the visitors, in the sense of the overall conception of the hunt for clues, some features of the design were overly determined by the available technologies that could be deployed.

3.5   The Second Living Exhibition

In our second living exhibition, we sought to address some of these difficulties through having a stronger identity for the overall unifying activity and a more careful selection of appropriate content to be displayed to visitors. One idea that appealed from the first exhibition was the attempt to allow the visitor to add content of their own to the exhibition in the form of a drawing. In *Re-Tracing the Past*, we decided to more thoroughly support visitor-supplied content. As a result we sought to create and assemble a corpus of material, drawings, writings, recordings or thoughts from the visitors about the Hunt collection in order to make our exhibition a truly "living" one, with elements of the exhibition being created daily during the life of the exhibition.

We were also motivated by our strong interest in people's experience of place, and sought to ensure that our augmented space would be sensitive to the specifics of the Museum space and its history and context (Ciolfi and Bannon 2005). In addition, we reflected on the traditional role of docents and interpreters and sought to incorporate them actively in facilitating people's visits. As before, we worked closely with the personnel from the host institution, the Hunt Museum, in formulating the overall design and in working through a number of specific scenarios.

The SHAPE Second Living Exhibition, *Re-Tracing the Past*, was hosted by the Hunt Museum in Limerick, Ireland and remained open to the public from the 9th to the 19th of June 2003. We worked with the museum curators and docents to design an exhibition that supported exploration of the issues related to the interpretation of the museum objects. Visitors were challenged to propose their own interpretation of one or more mysterious objects through interaction with different exhibits. Each element of the exhibition revealed particular evidence about the object that contributed to the visitor's own interpretation. The theme of the exhibition thus had the goal of making people reflect on the way the museum's classification of objects is not something given and unchangeable, but rather the product of investigation, conjectures and discussions among museum docents, art experts and curators. This rationale would also give the visitors the chance to leave a unique trace in the exhibition, thanks to the possibility of recording their opinion about an object and leave it for other visitors to interact with further.

A gallery on the lower ground floor of the museum was reconfigured into two connected spaces for the exhibition. The first space, the Study Room, enabled visitors to explore the backgrounds of the mysterious objects by revealing several kinds of evidence that can be used to interpret them. The second space, the Room of Opinion, contained accurate physical reproductions of the objects, allowing visitors to touch and manipulate the objects, as well as providing a recording station where visitors could leave an opinion on the objects' possible use, contributing new ideas for future visitors.

Fig. 3. Overview of the Living Exhibition space in the Hunt Museum

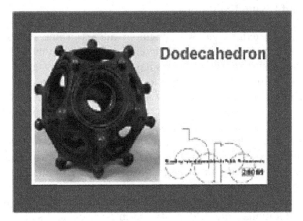

Fig. 4. A laminated keycard for the Dodecahedron object

Fig. 5. The Combination Machine

Groups were met at the entrance by a guide who monitored and supported the visit. Visitors could choose one or more objects to investigate. Each mysterious object had a corresponding keycard. The keycard was a small colour-printed laminated card showing the picture and the original museum label for the object. Each keycard also contained a Radio Frequency Identification (RFID) tag. The embedded tag allowed visitors to control each exhibit, primarily to activate or de-activate each installation and to explore the associated information.

There were four exhibits contained within the Study Room. Each was designed to provide information that visitors could progressively discover, without having to follow a prescribed sequence of actions. These were the Combination Machine, Virtual Touch Machine, Interactive Desk and the Radio.

The Combination Machine (Figure 5). When a card was placed inside the trunk, the visitors were provided some information about the context where the object was found (a burial, a religious site, etc.) If two cards were placed into the trunk together, some fictional and some possible connections between objects were suggested, to prime visitors' imagination about objects and encourage creativity and playfulness when recording their own opinions in the Room of Opinion. This installation was designed to encourage visitors to think about the objects in a playful and creative way using the information gathered at other stations, as a basis for developing their own interpretation of an object.

The Virtual Touch Machine (Figure 6). This installation focused on the material qualities and details of the objects. The Virtual Touch Machine enabled visitors to examine virtual models of the objects in fine detail – zooming in and zooming out to examine traces of the physical workmanship involved in the production of the objects and the patterns on the objects (the raised segments and grooves on the carved stone ball, for example). A "magic wand" was an integral part of the installation and, by handling it and turning it, visitors could manipulate the object model on the screen and reveal details that would otherwise be invisible. The machine also allowed visitors to explore the material qualities of the objects, as the wand allows users to "tap" the 3D objects on the screen in order to hear the sound they would produce if tapped in reality.

The Interactive Desk (Figure 7). The desk enabled visitors to trace the provenance of the objects. Placing a card on specific locations on an overlaid map on the desk displayed information related to the objects' geographical origin and their relationships with other parts of Europe.

The Radio (Figure 8). The radio enabled visitors to listen to the collected opinions, theories and stories of other visitors about the objects. By changing channels on the radio, visitors could browse the myriad of opinions on each object. By tuning within a band, individual opinions were progressively revealed. This installation helped visitors shape their opinions, giving them an opportunity to compare their evolving ideas on the origin of the objects with those left by others. Listening to other people's stories also motivated them and reinforced their involvement in the activity prior to their visit to the Room of Opinion. After recording their opinion in the other room, most visitors returned to the radio installation to listen again to their own and other visitor opinions.

Fig. 6. The Virtual Touch Machine

Fig. 7. The Interactive Desk

Fig. 8. The Radio

Fig. 9. Room of Opinion with plinths and Interactive Painting

Based on their explorations within the Study Room, visitors could then express their own opinions of the objects in the Room of Opinion. Visitors were given a chance to examine exact physical replicas of the objects, each placed on a plinth, before recording their opinion and leaving their own mark on the exhibition. The room contained an ever changing soundscape of voices, some clear, some murmuring, offering fragments and occasionally whole opinions regarding the objects. This soundscape, drawing on visitors' recorded opinions, was diffused through a four channel sound system with a speaker embedded in each plinth.

The visitors could record their opinion by dropping their keycard in a slot speaking into a phone. The recording subsequently became part of the collection of opinions available on the Radio in the Study Room. A new element was also added to the Interactive Painting, a visualisation back-projected into the room to represent the collection of visitors' opinions. After recording an opinion, a visitor could see a graphical brush stroke become part of the painting, contributing to the swirling pool of opinions. The painting was designed to make visitors aware that their contribution had a role in shaping the exhibition and it was now part of the collection.

In attempting to design for social interaction, we ensured that all of our interactives would have an "open" interface that would encourage more than one person to be around the artefact, and allow for people to collaboratively interact, or at the very least, view the interaction. Thus there are no multimedia computer screens and PC keyboards for individual use in the exhibit. Most of the visitors to the space were couples, groups of students, or family groups, and the openness of the exhibits encouraged interesting social interaction around the exhibits. In addition, we wished to support the idea of visitor's interacting with the opinions of others – not just those who might be visiting as part of the same social group. Our concern to record and make available visitor opinions to other visitors is, then, a way of extending the forms of inter-visitor interaction which museums normally support.

Over 900 people visited the exhibition with a similar highly mixed demographic to that observed at Nottingham Castle. As with the First Living Exhibition, we collected an extensive corpus of material to facilitate evaluation of the exhibition. The exhibition was highly valued by museum personnel and visitors for its aesthetic and design quality. Great attention was paid to creating environments of strong aesthetic character and, between the two rooms, contrast. This was strongly appreciated as complementary to the task of exploring mysterious objects. Indeed, we believe that one of the most important features of the Second Living Exhibition was the very powerful effect the designed space had on visitors, in that the space provided a warm, welcoming, yet intriguing environment that encouraged exploration, discussion and interaction, both with artefacts and with other people in the space. Thus, not only does the space literally embody the Disappearing Computer philosophy, in that no computers or keyboards appear anywhere, but, more importantly, it engenders a range of visitor activities such as handling, testing, exploring, discussing, listening, speaking, et cetera. We believe the fact that visitors are not only encouraged to explore and interact with objects, but even more importantly, are asked to reflect, question, and even articulate an opinion on the objects is pedagogically highly relevant (Ferris et al. 2004; Hall and Bannon 2006). Not only are these experiences and behaviours intrinsically valuable, but at another level, they hint to visitors that Museums do not always have "all the answers" and are not simply repositories of undisputable facts. Finally, visitor opinions are not simply requested, but are visibly and audibly encoded and made a part of the experience, and even more importantly, are collected so as to form a continuous, cumulative thread of visitor opinion, thus providing a corpus that can be accessed by other visitors and museum docents during the lifetime of the exhibit itself, as well as being of interest as a permanent record of visitor interest and opinion.

4   Discussion

In the SHAPE project we had very wide ranging concerns from the cultural significance of museums through to the details of exhibition design, from technical issues in mixed reality and ubiquitous computing to the details of interaction design in practical contexts. Let us finish this chapter by discussing a little further just two aspects of our work: the approach to design that we have begun to develop and our orientation to technical issues in contemporary computing research.

4.1   Design

Over the course of our two living exhibitions and in the production of our long term exhibit *The Well of Inventions*, the SHAPE project has evolved a characteristic way of doing design in museum settings. This has involved the varied contribution of four related approaches.

- **Social scientific studies.** These have had manifold influences upon our design work from causing us to reformulate the concept of "interactivity" in museum settings through to specific "groundings" for design details. Essential to the SHAPE approach has been the recognition of the social interactional nature of people's conduct in museum settings at the "exhibit face". We have consistently emphasized the varied ways in which people participate as they and others interact with exhibits and attempted to develop exhibits of our own which are "open" to different forms of engagement and participation. To develop further the impacts of such studies on museum design, we have formulated a set of *design sensitivities* and methods for working with *low-tech prototypes* (for further details, see SHAPE 2002, 2003b).

- **Cooperative, participatory design.** We have extensively consulted with museum personnel to enable various features of our exhibitions to be co-designed with them. Our two living exhibitions contain numerous examples of design details which emerged in collaboration with museum personnel. In addition, where possible we have worked with groups of people who can be taken as exemplary visitors. Most notable is our concern to involve children and their teachers in the First Living Exhibition and the classroom activities associated with the Second Living Exhibition (Hall and Bannon 2005, 2006). Taxén et al. (2004), and SHAPE (2003a) also note how we worked with museum personnel to ensure the durability of an exhibit intended to run unsupervised.

- **Scenario-based design.** Especially in the conduct of the Second Living Exhibition, we found it useful to organise design ideas around scenarios where visitor-interaction with an artefact was envisioned (Ferris et al. 2004). Scenarios also proved valuable in communicating the current state of design with museum personnel without getting bogged down in (potentially changeable) technical details.

- **Constructional workshops.** While we have not had space to discuss these in detail, we kick started the project with a number of constructional workshops. These were project-wide internal workshops where we committed to the construction of functional prototype within a few days' work. This activity proved valuable in demonstrating our competence to potential external collaborators. It also enabled us to explore design concepts which were specifically tailored to provide a response to early social scientific findings (Hall and Bannon 2005). Taxén et al. (2004) describe how some of our earliest demonstration work triggered more extended collaborations with museum personnel and formed the basis for *The Well of Inventions*.

While we have built single exhibits, our most characteristic contributions to museum design have been through our multi-artefact "living exhibitions" at Nottingham and Limerick. Our exhibitions have been "living" in four notable senses.

- **Co-design.** The exhibitions have been co-designed at least in part through living collaborative relations with visitors and museum personnel.

- **Working in public.** Both exhibitions have involved a concerted presence of the SHAPE team on-site. We have participated in numerous "tie-in" activities in relationship to the exhibitions. The exhibits have "lived" through our continued engagement with them.

- **Evolving design.** From time to time, this has involved modifying the design of the exhibition in response to public feedback, even after the exhibition has opened. In both of our main exhibitions, we were on-site (yet available to the public) before the official opening. During this time, visitors were welcome to inspect the work in progress and make design suggestions. The official opening indicated that our designs were intended to be more robust, to be sure, however designs could still be modified.

- **Visitor-supplied content.** Most notably at the Hunt Museum, we developed exhibitions where visitors supply at least some of the content of the exhibition. This is a further sense in which the exhibition can be said to be "living", in that the exhibition itself is changing and growing over the lifetime of the installation.

4.2   Assembling Technologies: Ubiquitous Computing Revisited

We discussed at the outset of this chapter how we were concerned with studying not merely single artefacts but *assemblies* of them – multiple artefacts working in concert. We also argued that museums are ideal settings for pursuing this interest. Our experience in such settings has suggested to us an effective "design schema" for assembling diverse artefacts. Let us posit the following five **Assembly Principles**.

1. Coherence is given to the experience by defining a *unifying overall activity* in which the visitors are to be engaged. At Nottingham Castle, this took the form of a history hunt, while, at the Hunt Museum, visitors identified mysterious objects.

2. An underlying *common information space* is designed which contains a variety of interrelated items that can be revealed as the activity progresses. At Nottingham Castle, we formulated a "time-space matrix" which linked historical events to different parts of the site. Images and views on a virtual model et cetera were linked to cells in this matrix. At the Hunt Museum, different kinds of information about the objects were revealed (e.g. provenance, materials) and a database of opinion was incrementally added to over the lifetime of the exhibition.

3. An *assembly of interactive displays* is used with each display supporting a particular part of the overall activity and revealing a sub-set of the common information space. At Nottingham, there were two artefacts: the Storytent and the Sandpit. At the Hunt Museum, there were two different rooms each containing multiple displays, both visual and sonic.

4. To promote the coherence of the experience *common or related interaction techniques* are provided across different displays. Throughout, we rejected standard desktop multimedia interaction techniques and devices in favour of working with everyday artefacts. Where possible these artefacts were idiomatic for the overall design aesthetic. For example, in the Study Room at the Hunt Museum, all the interactives are based upon traditional artefacts one might expect to find in a scholar's study.

5. To further enhance the overall coherence of the visitor experience, a *portable artefact* is provided to enable visitors to accumulate a record of their visit and/or support their identification as they move around the site. At Nottingham Castle, we worked with tagged paper to "glue" the experience together. At the Hunt Museum, cards with an embedded RFID tag served the same purpose.

Having identified these technical features of our design work, we are in a position to identify what is distinctive in our approach to contemporary computing research. To focus this, let us consider what might be meant by "ubiquitous computing". In common with much work under this rubric, we are concerned to make computing in its traditional manifestations "disappear" into a specifically designed environment. We design hybrid artefacts which typically embed computing and support interaction in and around physical arrangements which do not follow the traditional appearance of a desktop computer. However, our "design schema" makes clear that we can offer a particular sense for "ubiquitous computing". For us ubiquitous computing is *multiply-located computing*. Computing and interaction with computing resources takes place at specific loci with purpose-specific things happening at a particular locus. Computing is made "ubiquitous" by the linkage of these specific loci. This is a very different design image from those which propose an "anything-anyplace-anytime" ubiquity. In our environments, special things are done in special places and, if the sequencing of the experience calls for it, at special times (e.g. the Study Room is worked in before the Room of Opinion, the castle site is explored before one encounters interactives in the gatehouse).

Providing *differentiated* computing environments has been very important for us as it enables, not just a differentiation of forms of participation and engagement with content, but enables different forms of participation to be "readable" by others observing. For example, in the Hunt Museum, it would be possible for a visitor to draw inferences about the conduct of others such as "if you are over there at the desk, you must be finding out about the provenance of something". A ubiquitous computing environment which did not embody the differentiations of activity and purpose that we have designed for would not support such situated inferencing about the conduct of others. To respect and enhance the sociality of the visit, we offer our perspective on ubicomp: ubicomp as multiply-located computing.

We also differ from another image of ubiquitous computing. Some researchers see ubicomp as entailing a "fading away" of devices so that computation is somehow "ambient". Again our image is very different. We see computing as located and visible as such (even if it does not appear in the form of the traditional desktop machine). We have separated digital presentations from encounters with physical museum objects. At the Hunt Museum, one encountered the mysterious objects in a separate room from digitally presented information about them – and this for principled reasons: to retain the specificity of character of each form of experience. We believe that this approach is to be commended for the deployment of advanced interactive technology in museums. However, we can further suggest that, whenever it is important to retain and display a variety of specific forms of interaction (with physical objects versus with digital content) our hybrid approach is viable and sometimes preferable to one where either the computational or the physical/traditional fades away.

Acknowledgement

The work presented in this chapter was funded by the European Union as part of "The Disappearing Computer" initiative in the IST-FET programme (contract number IST-2000-26069). In addition, Liam Bannon and Luigina Ciolfi wish to acknowledge the support of the Science Foundation Ireland (Shared Worlds project 02/IN.1/I230) in the preparation of this chapter.

References

Bell, M., Chalmers, M., Barkhuus, L., Hall, M., Sherwood, S., Tennent, P., Brown, B., Rowland, D., Benford, S.: Interweaving Mobile Games with Everyday Life. In: Proceedings of CHI 2006, pp. 417–426. ACM Press, New York (2006)

Brown, B., MacColl, I., Chalmers, M., Galani, A., Randell, C., Steed, A.: Lessons from the lighthouse: Collaboration in a shared mixed reality system. In: Proceedings of CHI 2003, pp. 577–585. ACM Press, New York (2003)

Caulton, T.: Hands-on exhibitions. Routledge, London (1998)

Ciolfi, L., Bannon, L.: Space, place and the design of technologically enhanced physical environments. In: Turner, P., Davenport, E. (eds.) Space, Spatiality and Technology, pp. 217–232. Springer, London (2005)

Ciolfi, L., Bannon, L.: Learning from Museum Visits: Shaping Design Sensitivities. In: Proceedings of HCI International 2003, Crete, June 2003, pp. 63–67 (2003)

Ferris, K., Bannon, L., Ciolfi, L., Gallagher, P., Hall, T., Lennon, M.: Shaping Experiences in the Hunt Museum: A Design Case Study. In: Proceedings of DIS, Designing Interactive Systems 2004, pp. 205–214 (2004)

Fraser, M., Stanton, D., Ng, K.H., Benford, S., O'Malley, C., Bowers, J., Taxén, G., Ferris, K., Hindmarsh, J.: Assembling History: Achieving coherent experiences with diverse technologies. In: Proceedings of ECSCW, pp. 179–198. Kluwer, Dordrecht (2003)

Gaver, W., Bowers, J., Boucher, A., Gellerson, H., Pennington, S., Schmidt, A., Steed, A., Villars, N., Walker, B.: The drift table: designing for ludic engagement. In: CHI Extended Abstracts, pp. 885–900 (2004)

Green, J., Schnädelbach, H., Koleva, B., Benford, S., Pridmore, T., Medina, K.: Camping in the Digital wilderness: tents and flashlights as interfaces to virtual worlds. In: Proceedings of CHI 2002 Conference Companion, Minneapolis, Minnesota, pp. 780–781. ACM Press, New York (2002)

Greenbaum, J., Kyng, M. (eds.): Design at work: Cooperative design of computer systems. Lawrence Erlbaum Associates, Hillsdale (1991)

Grinter, R.E., Aoki, P.M., Szymanski, M.H., Thornton, J.D., Woodruff, A., Hurst, A.: Revisiting the visit: understanding how technology can shape the museum visit. In: Proceedings of CSCW'02, pp. 146–155. ACM Press, New York (2002)

Hall, T., Bannon, L.: Designing ubiquitous computing to enhance children's learning in museums. Journal of Computer Assisted Learning 22, 231–243 (2006)

Hall, T., Bannon, L.: Co-operative design of children's interaction in museums: a case study in the Hunt Musuem. CoDesign: International Journal of CoCreation in Design and the Arts 1(3), 187–218 (2005)

Heath, C.C., vom Lehn, D: Misconstruing Interaction. In: Hinton, M. (ed.) Interactive Learning in Museums of Art and Design London. Victoria and Albert Museum (2004)

Jackson, A., Johnson, P., Leahy, H.R., Walker, V.: Seeing it for real: An investigation into the effectiveness of theatre techniques in museums and heritage sites. Arts and Humanities Research Board (2002)

Milgram, P., Colquhoun, H.W.: A Framework for Relating Head-mounted Displays to Mixed Reality Displays. In: Proceedings of Human Factors and Ergonomics Society, pp. 1177–1181 (1999)

Rogers, Y., Scaife, M., Gabrielli, S., Smith, H., Harris, E.: A conceptual framework for mixed reality environments: Designing novel learning activities for young children. Presence. MIT 11(6), 677–686 (2002)

Schnädelbach, H., Koleva, B., Flintham, M., Fraser, M., Chandler, P., Foster, M., Benford, S., Greenhalgh, C., Izadi, S., Rodden, T.: The Augurscope: A Mixed Reality Interface for Outdoors. In: Proceedings of CHI 2002, pp. 9–16. ACM Press, New York (2002)

SHAPE Deliverable 4.2 (2002). Available from http://www.shape-dc.org

SHAPE Deliverable 2.1 (2003a). Available from http://www.shape-dc.org

SHAPE Deliverable 2.2 (2003b). Available from http://www.shape-dc.org

Stapleton, C., Hughes, C., Moshell, M., Micikevicius, P., Altman, M.: Applying Mixed Reality to Entertainment. IEEE Computer 35(12), 122–124 (2002)

Taxén, G., Bowers, J., Hellström, S.-H., Tobiasson, H.: Designing Mixed Media Artefacts for Public Settings. COOP 2004, pp. 195–121 (2004)

vom Lehn, D., Heath, C., Hindmarsh, J.: Exhibiting Interaction: Conduct and Collaboration in Museums and Galleries. Symbolic Interaction 24(2), 189–216 (2001)

Weiser, M.: Some Computer Science Issues in Ubiquitous Computing. Communications of the ACM 36(7), 75–84 (1993)

Opening the Digital Box for Design Work: Supporting Performative Interactions, Using Inspirational Materials and Configuring of Place

Pelle Ehn[1], Thomas Binder[2], Mette Agger Eriksen[1], Giulio Jacucci[3], Kari Kuutti[4], Per Linde[1], Giorgio De Michelis[5], Simon Niedenthal[1], Bo Petterson[1], Andreas Rumpfhuber[2], and Ina Wagner[6]

[1]School of Arts and Communication, Malmö University, Sweden
[2]Center for Design Research, Royal Academy of Fine Arts,
School of Architecture, Denmark
[3]Ubiquitous Interaction, Helsinki Institute for Information Technology, Finland
[4]Department of Information Processing Science, University of Oulu, Finland
[5]DISCo, University of Milano - Bicocca, Italy
[6]Institute for Technology Assessment & Design, Vienna University of Technology, Austria

1 Introduction

1.1 Configurable Ubiquitous Technologies and Media

We started the work reported on here with the ambition to create inspirational learning environments for design and architecture students in the spirit of Weiser's vision of taking the computer "out of the box" and making computational resources augment a design studio environment ubiquitously. Computing environments are becoming populated by a rich and diverse set of devices and networks, many of them integrated with the physical landscape of space and artefacts. Early attempts to take the desktop metaphor of graphical interface design back to the real desktops and whiteboards by exploring new semantics of interaction was pioneered by Weiser's group, as well as by Buxton and others (Weiser 1993; Fitzmaurice 1995; Rekimoto 1997). The idea to have a new and more complex set of physical handles to digital media promised a richer interaction between people and technology, and, in line with Engelbart's pioneering work on direct manipulation for graphical user interfaces (Engelbart 1962), a new set of generic interface building blocks would open up a new realm for design of interaction technologies.

In parallel to the work of Weiser, Wellner and colleagues argued for a new and broader interpretation of augmented reality turning computational augmentation into an enhancement of practices well established with the interaction of more mundane artefacts (Wellner 1993). Fuelled by ethnographic studies of work, researchers such as Mackay et al suggested augmented environments where computational resources were brought into play, as extensions of for example the paper flight strips traffic controllers used to control airplanes as they passed through different traffic sectors (Mackay 1998) Such an approach is not in opposition to the development of new interaction modalities but it shifts the balance from a generic interaction scheme to the situated embodiment of interactional possibilities. Ishii and his group forged these two approaches into a wider program for tangible interaction (Ishii 1997). With the ambition

N. Streitz, A. Kameas, and I. Mavrommati (Eds.): The Disappearing Computer, LNCS 4500, pp. 50–76, 2007.

to create seamless interfaces between "people, bits and atoms", Ishii and others have expanded the new field of design to include an integrated re-shaping of desks, board and rooms.

The growing number of experimental ubicom installations has helped shift the focus of interactive systems away from individual work settings and towards larger collaborative environments traditionally the realm of other designers. After some years where automatically generated context information created high hopes for how computational technologies could be made to match the complexity of user behavior (Salber et al. 1999). We are increasingly seeing suggestions for open infrastructures and end-user configurable systems, which may have a lower intensity of computational monitoring, but on the other hand appear more easily extendable to wide spread real life settings. However many of these approaches are technology driven rather than being driven by a concrete practice or setting (Kindberg et al. 2002; Newman et al. 2002). This new type of extendable systems with open boundaries could provide traditional human computer interaction research with important new challenges (Belotti et al. 1992; Grudin 2002). This view is closely related to our experiences within the *Atelier* project and the architectures and technologies in support of inspirational learning that we have explored. The *Atelier* project has been exploring inspirational forms of learning and how to build augmented environments in support of design education. The experiences are related to the general field of ubiquitous and tangible computing and especially to ideas of embodied interaction as a new stance for understanding of both, social and physical, interaction with artefacts and space. It is suggested that concepts like "configuration of mixed objects" and "appropriation of mixed places" together form interesting challenges for the design of architecture and technology for inspirational learning environments.

1.2   Research Approach: Pro-Searching Practice

The two practice settings of inspirational learning environments that formed the basis for observation, design and evaluation were chosen to be complementary. One was a "traditional" master-class environment in architecture in Vienna. It was complemented and contrasted by the setting of a new-media-oriented, interaction design, master program in Malmö.

The approach taken could be seen as design oriented research (Fällman 2003). We have studied design education practice, developed prototypes to enhance such education, introduced prototypes to different real use settings (design and architecture master-classes), hence encountering unintended or unexpected appropriation by the students, and, partly in collaboration with the students, reflected upon the interventions to learn both about how to improve architecture and technology and the learning situation. The idea has not primarily been to examine the past for generalisations or continuous trends, but to generate knowledge by pro-searching (scouting, trailblazing) the present for possible new ways and desirable futures. This pro-searching, as Klaus Krippendorf (Krippendorf 1995) has called this process, is built upon a user-collaborative approach involving users and researchers as reflective co-designers and evolves from early exploring of practice and visions through experiments with gradually more integrated scenarios and prototypes for inspirational learning.

Iteration is a significant aspect of these interventions and reflections. An iterative research and design process for refinement of architecture and technology for inspirational learning environments went through three design cycles: envisioning, prototyping and experiencing. Each design cycle was based on interventions into the everyday practice at two design education sites. The first design cycle was oriented towards ethnographic observations in existing classes, combined with inspiration from art practice, leading to scenarios of enhanced inspirational learning environments and observations of qualities of such environments. The interventions in the second design cycle were stronger: Students were confronted not only with scenarios, technology prototypes and architectural elements, but also with project assignments inviting them to explore ideas and technology for augmenting their design learning environments. The students' appropriation and evaluation of the ideas and the technologies led into the design of more integrated, but also new, technological and architectural components, for the final round of design interventions, again with changed curricula. Experience from this last round of interventions, again led to new technologies for augmenting design learning environments.

"Concurrent design" and "cross-dressing" are other important factors improving the quality of interventions and sensibilities to outcomes. We took the unusual approach of "concurrent" development of technological infrastructure and components, with conceptual development of architecture and technology for inspirational learning environments, and investigations of design practice for architecture and interaction design students. This "concurrent" process was coordinated via workshops in the beginning, middle and end of each design cycle aligning the different actors' activities. There was an important element of "cross-dressing" between interventions and observations from the architecture classes with a stronger focus on materials and space and the interaction design classes more focused on exploring interaction and digital media. The combination of early probings with technology, rapid and flexible development of technological infrastructure and successive hard-edged integrative development efforts resulting in working demonstrators, has managed to stay closely connected with the overall framework of concurrent concept development and participatory pro-searching of practice. In addition to reflections on students' appropriation of architecture and technology for inspirational learning, exhibitions of demonstrators and workshops around central ideas with professional participants outside the student design setting have been important for the assessment of quality of concepts and technologies.

As a result of the initial field trials the project identified particular "atmospheric", material and spatial qualities that should be created and supported. These qualities were: the transient and ephemeral, materiality and the diversity of materials and representations, creative density, re-programming and the "different view", experience of dimensionality and scale, performative interaction, forging connections/multiple travels, configuring, tempo and rhythm. These qualities acted as powerful guidelines throughout the project, for technology design, for developing notions of use, for setting up field trials at the two sites, and for interpreting our observations (see section 2).

1.3 Context: Design Education and Inspirational Learning

The environment for exploring support of design education was the Academy of Fine Arts in Vienna and the school of Arts and Communication at Malmö University. The

Academy of Fine Arts has a history reaching back to 1692. The education of architects at the Academy is based on "project oriented studies". The traditional studio-like learning environment is the place where a diversity of resources - disciplines, people, materials, technologies - are brought together. These resources are multi-medial - their instantiations range from physical objects like CAD plans, sketches and scale models to samples, product catalogues, art books, and everyday objects, as well as immaterial resources such as conversations and emotions. The School of Arts and Communication at Malmö University is on the contrary very young admitting its first students in 1998. A broad perspective on the interaction design field is applied. Interaction design is a multi-disciplinary subject and students have a mixed background including computer science, design, art and music. Besides the computer, they typically work with a mixture of video clips, mock-ups and other physical representations, scale models, prototypes, etc. Our notion of learning in these two environments was strengthened in our first round of field trials, where we carried out ethnographic studies of students' work practice, including the use of cultural probes (Gaver et al. 1999).

- Learning in these environments is stimulated by the presence of inspirational resources – images, music, metaphors, atmospheres, film, samples of materials, and everyday objects, which provide an element of surprise and discovery and help see things differently.

- Learning proceeds by students working with design representations in different media, gradually transforming them into a design in a process which is non-linear, informal, and highly cooperative. The diversity of material and media is an important facilitator of learning. Students work with and produce text, diagrams, comics, video, sketches, sketch models, screenshots, virtual models, and prototypes – material of different degrees of abstraction, different scale and materiality.

- Learning is highly interactive. Students constantly switch between individual and collaborative work. They share knowledge and design material, use collective displays, take turns in working on a specific task to then arrange a spontaneous meeting. While switching mode and tasks, they circulate the space, expanding and concentrating it according to their needs.

- People, co-present and distant, are a crucial part of an inspirational learning environment. Students receive regular feedback from peers, their teachers, and external reviewers, they listen to guest lectures and they meet people when they are cruising the outside world, exploring the city, a particular context or site. There is the need to bring the impressions and the material they collected back to the studio, to make it visible and share it with others.

1.4   Qualities in Action and Emerging Concepts: Opening the Digital Box for Design Education

In the field trials we explored approaches to mixing physical and digital artefacts, experimented with ways of integrating the physical space into the students' learning activities, and investigated the possibilities of configuring the environment. The strategy for these field trials was not to create new and dedicated artefacts and spaces but to motivate students to integrate the prototypes into ongoing project work.

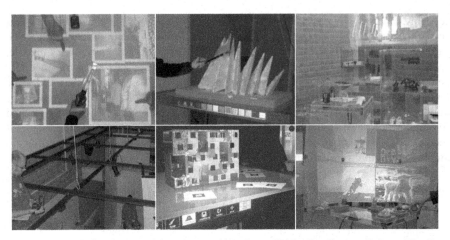

Fig. 1. From top left to bottom right; The Tracking Game Table, The Texture Painter, The Tangible Archive, The Interactive Stage, The Mixed Objects Table and The Physical Building Blocks

This was enabled by what we see as the "open-ended" nature of the prototypes. The major such "open-ended" prototypes or demonstrators included:

- The Tracking Game Table allowing manipulaton of projected frames in which images and videos are displayed
- The Texture Painter for "painting" computer generated visual overlays as texture on physical models using a physical-digital brush
- The Tangible Archive and organizing zone as a place for informal storing, combining and presenting mixed materials,
- The Interactive Stage combining element of a theatrical space with technological augmentation to manipulate media and events,
- The Mixed Object Table including The Texture Painter and other tools and interaction modes for visual overlays on and around physical models
- The Physical Building Blocks for illustrating ideas and concepts in very concrete, interactive full-scale mock-ups and prototypes.

The components of these demonstrators were intergrated via a shared, platform independent, infrastructure and a hypermedia database. In general findings of the research focus on:

- *inspiration* as residing in the diversity of design materials on the one hand, and in the movement of connecting and performing multiple travels on the other hand,
- design work as a process of *transforming design representations* and the role of *mixed objects,*

- the role of *performative interactions* for design work, in particular how spatial features participate in the configuration of mixed media environments and the performative aspects of how people interact in them,

- the importance of supporting students in *configuring* their learning environment of artefacts, technologies and space.

In the later sections we will reflect upon these experiences and emerging concepts, particularly in designing architecture and technology for inspirational learning. In the next section this will be done with a focus on "design qualities in action" and how design practice has been enhanced. The perspective is further broaden into more general conceptual reflections on "performative interaction", "mixed objects", and "configuring of place".

2   Enhanced Design Practice – Qualities in Action

In this section we will conceptually articulate and illustrate some of the explored design qualities in action and their importance for an enhanced design practice: design work as transforming representations, performative interaction, configuring, creative density and multiple travels.

2.1   Design Work as Transforming Representations

An important finding early in the project, as a result of the field trials, was the definition of "diversity of representations" as central to design work at both sites. The phrasing was inspired by Bruno Latour's use of the concept of circulating references to describe how matter gradually moves along a chain before eventually ending up as knowledge (Latour 1999). The references circulate along a series of representational transformations by use of scientific methods and instruments. In that way a sample of soil from the jungle gradually is transformed into formal knowledge representations such as diagrams. The term could well be used to describe how ideas are transformed throughout the design process.

It is a challenge for the designer to handle a multitude of different media and representations. The transference from one media to another without loosing essential qualities is often a crucial issue. Transforming and configuring the design material is in some sense the major part of design work. Clarifying ideas in a sketch in order to explain to others, making a model or enacting with a mock-up are all examples of moving between representations. Experiencing the material from different perspectives or in different scale is important for gaining an open design space where ideas can be stretched in any direction before narrowing down in realization. This means that embodiment or working in full scale is but part of representation and experience, there is no ideal format. The environment must support moving from abstraction to concreteness and we have tried to afford that by including space in design and by letting it be inhabited by mixed objects.

Students' project work proceeds through developing a large number of design representations. These are characterized by the expressive use of a diversity of materials and are sometimes animated and presented dynamically. As an example two students worked on a façade for a furniture house, who sponsored a student project, for their main inner city building. The students envisioned the façade of the building as a threshold between inside and outside. On their table are sketches of the form of the façade, detailed plans, drawings visualizing atmospheres and situations of use, 3D models, diagrams - a collage of visual and tactile material. One reason for this diversity of representations is that changing media and scale adds to the quality of the design process, with different techniques allowing to explore different aspects of the design idea. These heterogeneous representations are often manipulated simultaneously and they evolve in different versions. We can say that design work is creating and manipulating a multiplicity of design representations, jumping between modalities, scales, and materials, thereby transforming them.

These observations convinced us of the need to maintain the diversity of representations and to help students to enhance the representational techniques that are part of their professional practice, providing them with barcodes and scanners, RFID tags, and touch sensors. In the first round of field trials they used these technologies mainly for animating design artefacts through connecting them with multi-media files.

A special aspect of design work as transforming representations is what we called "re-programming". Part of the students" training consists in learning "to see things differently". This implies changing (strangely) familiar images - altering the city, the landscape, objects of everyday life. Students are encouraged to collect and mobilize inspirational material – which is to do with particular qualities of objects, people, ambience, a place – as this plays an important role in seeing things differently. They may vary the context of an object through simple projections, e.g. place a railway station in the midst of a jungle or igloos in the desert (without having to do complex renderings). They may play with dimensionality, scaling up and scaling down, changing familiar objects and thereby arriving at unexpected uses. They may use visual effects for seeing things differently, such as "fuzziness" – views that blur, distort, veil and allow things to remain ill-defined, unfocused and indistinct.

One example observed was how the *Texture painter* (Figure 2) was used by students for performing their models at the final project presentations. Another example is how first semester students used it on their 1:50 and 1:20 scale models of famous architectures made from white styrofoam. They applied different kinds of textures to their models, inserted video material, changed the material of some parts of the model in order to achieve special effects, and systematically varied the context of the buildings. This was done in a playful way and helped them explore the possibilities of seeing – interpreting, analysing, criticising - an architectural object. The students captured these changes with a digital camera and it turned out that this double-digital-processing worked out well - a *Texture painter* layer, photographed by a digital camera – "even better than a life paint"?

2.2 Performative Installations

Students create interactive installations to objectify, present, and discuss their design projects. Installations are inherently different from staged performances, as they engage the spectator bodily, allowing them to turn into co-players (Suderburg 2000). This is evident in some of the installations the architectural students produced, such as the "train ride".

The "train ride" installation consists of a movie of a trip to a stadium in Paris, including the *Atelier* studio space in their performance. Seats were arranged like in the underground and some spectators became passengers. They had to stand and were provided with a handle made from orange plastic. In this configuration they watched the movie, which alternated sequences of travelling the underground (which accelerated, growing noisier and more hectic) with the presentation of stills at a calm and slow pace. The interaction design students have also explored different ways of gaining embodied experience of digital media such as perceiving a situation of use differently by changing light conditions, mimicking use in body pantomimes or interacting with installations with body movements.

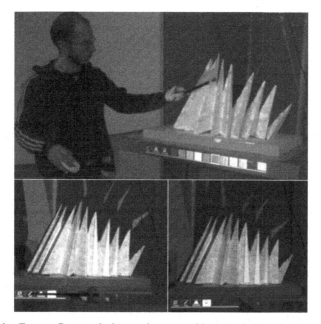

Fig. 2. With the *Texture Painter* design students are able to "paint" various computer generated visual overlays as textures on physical 3D models in real time. Using a brush, which is tracked, this application allows "painting" on objects such as models or parts of the physical space, applying textures, images or video, scaling and rotating them

The "bath room" scenario is another example of how students built a stage for enacting around a paper mock-up of their design of a fire alarm system with capabilities for user to user communication. They had played around with different scenarios trying to stretch their notion of the interplay between everyday settings and the artefact. Using very strong and sterile light coming from behind provoked a discussion on what really was important for the interactional setting. In back projections the interior of a bath-room was displayed. Moving the situation of use from the living-room to the bath-room made the students rethink their notion of what made us comfortable in a situation of communication.

Yet another example is how interaction design students performed an exercise in filming different situations of work or use of technology. Coming back to the studio they played their films in large projections as a backdrop for their enactment. They were supposed to learn the body movements in the film so that they could imitate the situation without talking or commenting to each other. By doing so they experienced just how long time it takes to perform a certain activity, for example how much you actually have time to think while filling the gas into the tank. It is also possible to conceive of how body movements can affect the placing of interface components in a specific setting.

The performative elements of an installation are valuable as they are complementary to working with more abstract mental models of representation. One example is how interaction design students approached the design of an interactive installation at the Central Station in Malmö. Shifting between 3D drawings, sketches and embodied enactment, they gradually narrowed down their concept. Actually starting out from experimenting with different zones of light and ambient sound sources they made a 3D model of a tent. The tent recorded the surrounding environment with a web camera and sound recorder. Inside the tent the user could manipulate sound and vision by computer generated filtering, thus creating a personalized experience of a space. The students" way of working commenced with performing with the body and then got into sketching. Very often traditional working mode is the opposite, starting out with for example sketching.

In the *Interactive stage* (Figure 3) architecture and technologies can be easily configured for experimenting with immersiveness and scale and for using the performative elements of space. Immersiveness can be obtained with simple means, using several projectors and projection screens, "projecting everywhere". Students may use the space for enacting a design concept in performed scenarios, relating to it with the strong presence of the body. 1:1 scale projections of models and other objects may help them to discover new features of a material or a site, experience how a model or texture looks when it is blown up.

As part of an exercise with the aim to create an architectural view of objects, one of the first semester students had chosen a saw for cutting wood. He produced a series of sketches and drawings, took pictures of the saw in movement, build different models, and finally, explored his notion of architectural space in the *Interactive stage*.

The arrangement of projections screens helped the student to have all the different design representations – projections of the hand drawings, of the photographs of the model and the shadows it creates, the model itself - simultaneously present in the space. On a wall he had fixed a series of diagrams, photographs and sketches that explained steps of his investigation. In this installation the student moved beyond the 1:1 scale of a staged performance. Enlarging a small detail, such as the dents of a saw, or scaling a large building down to the size of a person and projecting them in spaces that are "inhabitable".

A physical model that the student had created out of the movement of the saw was placed on the *Mixed objects table* (Figure 4). The student used the *Texture painter* on his model. "Painting" the physical model became a performance and part of the design process; its informality and the imperfections of the product opened a space for associations and spontaneous changes. For the final part of his performance the student configured several sets of three pictures, using three projectors in the *Interactive stage*. Each picture set was assigned to a barcode and could be re-played on the three screens by simply reading the specific barcodes. The pictures enlarged details of models playing

Fig. 3. *The Interactive Stage* combines elements of a theatrical space with technological augmentations that are used to input, manipulate and output design representations, media, and events in the learning environment. The participant in the learning space is thus made a bodily part of the design representation. In practice, the architecture students mainly used the interactive stage for presentations, while the interaction design students used the space to enact use scenarios, engage in design improvisations

Fig. 4. *The Mixed Objects Table* is an artefact that allows students to combine real objects such as architectural models with virtual parts. It consists of a table top formed as a back projection screen. There are outlets for USB-Cameras, RFID-Tag readers and barcode readers integrated into the table frame. With a video camera and special markers virtual 3D objects can be added to the physical model on the table

with scale and immersiveness. Sets of pictures were used to show the relationships between models. A particular set was created out of close-up photo of the physical models and image processing (mirroring, stretching etc.). The three pictures where artfully montaged with the three projectors to create the perception of a space. Finally, while in staged performances the represented places may be imaginary and physical location and features of a site secondary, in everyday use it may be important to convey and re-produce specific qualities or features of a site. Students recreated spatial features of remote physical locations.

2.3   Configuring

For architects configurability is connected to the properties of a space. *Flexibility* connotes the possibility of relatively simple changes to a design so as to adapt it to different or shifting social uses (e.g. moveable walls). *Variability* means that a designed space or artefact, without elaborate transformations, can accommodate a variety of functions. Configuring and re-configuring, although with much more mundane means, is also part of students' practice. Students voice a strong need to adapt their workspace so that they can exhibit, perform, engage in group work or work alone, build models, have a nap, make coffee, interact with material and odd objects, etc.

At the beginning of a project the architecture students set up their workspaces. As the project progresses, they become dense with design material which is exhibited on

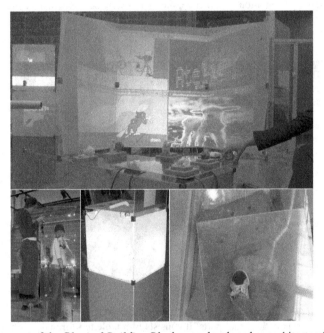

Fig. 5. The concept of the *Physical Building Blocks* was developed as architectural components meeting the need for "Getting out of the box" as well as on the basis of observations about how design students often work, experiment and prototype their ideas and concepts in a variety of places

the surrounding walls and on parts of the desk space. Sketches, plans, model, a panorama print of a site and the computer are all assembled in one desk space. In Malmö it was experienced that a theatre grid fastened to the ceiling in the studio provided a powerful possibility to re-configure the studio as to fit the activities. On the other hand it is a fixed installation that can only be used in the studio. In the workshop we started to explore how the project's technology could be used in assemblies configured by the students themselves. We wanted the students to be able to work in different places outside of the studio such as in the café area of the school or even on places outside the school. This required us to provide some physical building blocks apart from the technological components. The Plexiglas discs (48x48 cm) together with a set of different ready-made joints turned out to be a flexible system for building modules that were associated in different shapes. They have been used for building shelves storing project material, as containers for the technology concealing computers and cables or as mere components for building installations. The interaction design students have used *Atelier* technology in combination with the *Physical Building Blocks* (Figure 5) to mock up situations of use for ubiquitous computing, just like for example *Macromedia Director* has been used for prototyping screen based interfaces.

Fig. 6. *The Tangible Archive* is a "physical database" containing different design artefacts, tagged to carry links to digital media. It is a place for physical exploration and knowledge sharing within an environment of project-based work and learning. The main interaction point is the Organizing Zone. Technically the Organizing Zone is connected to the hypermedia database, a projector, loudspeakers and a printer. It also has a barcode reader and two RFID tag readers. It offers possibilities to view and simply manipulate entered media as well as to create a personal collection of digital media and real things

The *Tangible Archive* is an example of a configurable platform-furniture utilizing the physical building blocks. The furniture can be used as a surface for doing work (with work zones being reserved for particular activities), as shelves for storing materials, or for projections. The interaction design students worked with the *Tangible archive* in a two-week design workshop. During the workshop they worked in groups to explore what we called semi-public places (a public library, a public park and a public square) and they were asked to design an interactive installation that conveyed what they found to be interesting qualities of the places they had studied. They made video, audio and still image recordings of the places they visited and they collected physical items from the area. After an introduction to the *Tangible archive* they build a first version of the archive for the collected material.

The students used the archive frame to set the scene for exploration of their material. The group working with a public park made a table-like archive where collected digital material were connected to tagged leaves gathered in a heap in the middle of the table. Images and videos could be displayed on a sphere mounted above the heap and people where supposed to sit on the floor in a circle around the heap. The group working with the public square created a closed cinema-like space where one could experience the emptiness of the square on an October morning. The group working with the library built a counter-like structure using barcodes and barcode readers in ways similar to the way library staff register books. The barcodes are easy to recognize, but the RFID tags that can be either embedded inside the objects or easily concealed don't signal that they carry links to digital media. The students explored how dedicated zones for interaction could be designed in a way that indicated what could be done and what should be avoided. Those concepts were later refined in other demonstrators. The architecture students used barcode technology for configuring their workspace. They had printed out thumbnails of images and the associated barcodes and they were provided with "system barcodes" for configuring input and output devices – the various projectors/displays on the one hand the *Texture painter* on the other hand – and for saving particular configurations. These print-outs were easy to understand and to handle and the paper format allowed annotations of various kinds.

2.4   Creative Density – Multiple Travels

Inspiration has to do with particular qualities of objects, people, ambience, a place. It always emerges within a context. Objects or a place, for example, are not inspirational as such but may be so in connection with a project, idea, particular task. Fieldwork observations showed a variety of ways to support these inspirational moments. One is connected to what we call "creative density"; the possibility to engage in an immersive mass of material – design representations in different media, inspirational objects, etc. - supports intensity in design situations. "Creative density" offers the chance to encounter surprising or interesting combinations of objects. It also supports "multiple traveling" – students' repeating their journey through design material again and again, with different layers and aspects coming to the surface. One example observed, in a project concerning studies and concept development for football stadiums, is how students after returning from a visit to several stadiums in London, Lille and Paris, spread out the pictures they had taken on the table, arranging and re-arranging them. While looking through the material, together and with by-passers, they started remembering, evoking encounters, telling each other stories. One of the students took a picture of the arrangement, thereby freezing the moment.

Another way to re-experience a site intended for design, that has been used both by students and researchers in the project, is to use collected media in design games. A goal of the games is to set up imaginary situations that complement reflective understanding of practice. The goal is to investigate and negotiate images of what happened. It follows the structure of an ordinary card game, played for fun. The cards were augmented with RFID tags that maintained links to the videos and images. By placing the card on a tag reader the media were displayed in projections on a table (Johansson and Linde 2004).

A special version of the game used the *Tracking Game Table* (Figure 7). In the set up the tracking system used by the *Texture painter* was utilized for tracking the position of the displayed media. Projected from above, the media attached to the playing cards were displayed on a table. As the game continued and more cards were played, the amount of displayed media increased. Films or images were displayed in virtual frames that could be manipulated on the table by a specially designed wireless mouse with a reflector that communicated with the tracking system. This allowed for moving the "media frames" around the table, clustering related stories together and structuring the collection of material into different groups of meaning. By using the mouse, players could also scale the frames, thus focusing on different media by enlarging it or scaling it down. In this way the game continued by collaborative interaction with the images and videos until a set of design narratives had been constructed that the group found to be valid.

3   Performative Interaction, Mixed Objects and Configuring of Place

Experiences such as the ones that we described helped us develop a deeper understanding of what the interplay between architectural elements, artifacts, integrated digital technologies, and performing bodies adds to design work. We express this under-

Fig. 7. *The Tracking Game Table* is a set-up which uses a tracking system, allowing manipulation of virtual frames in which images and videos are displayed. A specially designed wireless mouse communicates with the tracking system by a reflector. The frames can be moved around, scaled to different sizes and videos can be started and paused. Playing cards augmented with RFID tags carry links to media files, and when a selected card is held above a tag reader, the media is displayed in a new frame

standing through a series of concepts: Embodiment and the performative elements of space, mixed objects, configuring and place making.

3.1 Embodiment and Performative Elements of Space

Paul Dourish has introduced the concept of embodied interaction (Dourish 2001). This stance is grounded in the phenomenological tradition, focusing on the phenomenon of *experience*, approaching phenomenon as they appear to the experiencer. Our everyday life-world, just as work practice, consists of concreteness, and calls for collecting the paradoxes and complexity of life worlds rather than unifying them in abstractions. While abstraction seems to be one of the foremost strengths of computation and digital media, it is evident that users are more than information processing systems. The relation between information and knowledge is one example of how meaning is not inherent in information, but rather made meaningful through direct participation in the world. An important facet of Dourish definition is how "embodied interaction is the creation, manipulation, and sharing of meaning through engaged interaction with artefacts" (Dourish 2001). A shift towards embodied interaction is motivated by the recognition that to accommodate a broader understanding of human potential requires moving computation "out of the box" and "into our environments". The notion of embodied interaction addresses how a situation must be considered as a whole. Meaning is created in use of shared objects and social interaction is related to how we engage in spaces and artefacts. In this interplay the body has a central role, in many ways the body can be seen as the medium for having a world. This is a perspective that differs from "disembodied" use of computers and interactive systems.

Our contribution to this line of research has been by investigating the notion of embodied interaction in a real setting. The specific contribution consists in revealing with the *Atelier* trials the *performative* character of interactions involving space, artifacts, digital media and multiple participants (Jacucci et al. 2005; Jacucci 2004). Therefore the use of the adjective *performative* resulted from articulating the concept of embodied interaction further, characterising how it features in a specific setting. This aspect of embodied interaction is gaining relevance in view of attempts of using tangible computing or mixed reality for art and entertainment (Benford et al. 2006; Hämäläinen et al. 2005) but can be relevant in work and educational settings as well (Bannon et al. 2005; Ciolfi and Bannon 2005). The term *performance* can be taken to address everyday life, and can interest a variety of situations beyond theatrical performances and rituals. It is relevant in this discussion as it stresses the event character of action and interaction, as it is about bringing something to completion that has an initiation and a consummation. It indicates an ephemeral and contingent process to particular socio-material-historical circumstances. Moreover performance points to expression and individuality as embedded in people's actions and movements, but also in space and artefacts. It may be considered in the creation of artefacts or architectures, especially in the ways these carry a performative potential that is unleashed through participant's interactions (cf. Acconci's Performative Architecture (Sobel et al. 2001)). *Performance* implies an act of expression directed to others and, dissimilarly to behaviour that is not performance, more efforts in terms of energy, skill and consciousness (thinking) of the acts. Performance proposes a simultaneousness of action and experience, of presence and representation; in Dewey's terms a structural relationship between "doing and undergoing" (Dewey 1934). This in turn points to how expressions can contribute to perception and therefore to new insights, either in their act of creation for the "creator" or as embodied artefacts in their material and immaterial qualities for an "experiencer".

We found different kinds of performative interactions in the field trials:

Performative artefacts. Artefacts augmented with sensors and tags were "scripted", associating images and sounds to different interactions. The artefact in these cases does not unleash its communicative potential by just being observed and scrutinised, but a participant must interact with it activating the playing of digital media. Interactive technology exploited the articulation in material qualities, spatiality (touch sensors in a solid section that becomes an interactive skyline) and affordances (turning the pages of a diary) rendering them more expressive. Artefacts acquire meaning through material qualities, their spatiality, and the way participants interact with them. This is evidence of how physical interfaces, supported performative uses of artefacts, moving beyond the simple tagging or tracking of an artefact.

Fig. 8. Embodiment and performative elements of space – students mimicking a filmed work situation, re-enacting a joint field trip and experimenting with the body as interface to an installation

Staging Spatial Narratives. Performance stresses how meaning is embodied in the careful and expressive arranging of elements in the space. The students played with scale and immersiveness creating inhabitable spaces with multiple projections. In these cases the spatial configuration is not neutral but concurring to narrate the concept; it is a narrative use of the spatiality of projections. The bodily presence of spectators is carefully taken in considerations and in some cases spectators became participants contributing to the representation (becoming the audience of a stadium or passenger in a train).

Staging and performing "mixed objects". "Performance", in this case, refers to how these configurations can be seen as staging and performing objects that are both digital and spatial. These exist for a limited time; they are ephemeral, although they can be saved and reloaded (to some extent). As performances, they are recorded with pictures or through videos or they have to be performed again. Their potential reaches beyond "mere embodiment". *Such "mixed objects"* provide the means for producing configurations that change spatiality, interactivity, and physical landscape in ways that help people experience, explore, present, and perform.

3.2   Mixed Objects

A rethinking of the borders between material and digital is needed. The paradox of *demassification* is an expression introduced by Brown and Duguid several years ago (Brown and Duguid 1994). What they pointed at is how digital technology and new media introduces new material and social conditions for the design of artefacts. Demassification concerns the *physical* or material change - artefacts literary lose mass and can be distributed and accessed globally. Think of a digital book or a library. But there is also a *social* or contextual demassification. This concerns the possibility to customize and make individual copies of digital artefacts - a loss of mass in the meaning of a mass medium. Again think of a personalized version of the book or the digital library. Why is this a design problem? Is it not just great with totally mobile and individualized artefacts? As Brown and Duguid suggest with their paradox of demassification this is achieved at the prize of lost intertwined physical and social *experiences* of the artefacts. The physical demassification deprives the artefact of material "border resources" for shared interpretation. The cover of the book may not be decisive for the content, but its shape, texture, weight and not least "wear and tear" may still be an important aspect of its "bookness" and how we experience it as a book. These "border resources" are lost when every digital copy gets its own form, and hence a relatively established source for interpretation dissolves. Entangled with this, and adding to the problem of lost physical mass, is the social demassification. The individualized versions of a digital artefact, reaching only a few persons, underline the loss of shared "border resources" by jeopardizing a relatively stable contextual resources for shared interpretations within a community. It seems that a feasible design strategy must find ways to counter this loss of mass. This challenge is in line with the perspective of embodied interaction and the understanding that we today have to design digital technology for interaction that is both more tangible and more social.

Embodied interaction does rethink the borders of the digital artefact. Starting from the position that our interaction with artefacts, also digital artefacts, is experiential, we suggest accepting that there is no such thing as an entirely digital artefact. Instead the design materials for digital artefacts are both spatial and temporal. With digital technology we can build digital temporal structures and behaviour. However, to design these temporal structures into artefacts that we can experience and interact with almost any material can be of use in the spatial configuration. Hence, design of digital technologies deals with, what De Michelis (De Michelis 2004) calls a kind of *mixed objects*, including "border resources".

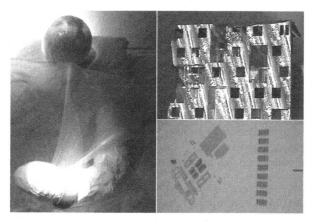

Fig. 9. Mixed Objects – Interactive projections on a physical model, architectural model over-layed with digital textures and CAD plan with barcodes

In preparing a project presentation one of the architectural students plotted out her CAD plans with barcodes on them. In one of her print-outs she had integrated the barcodes into a diagrammatic representation. She presented her work using multiple interactive artefacts that triggered the playing of sound and visual media on a projected screen. Barcodes were integrated into posters, which displayed plans and diagrams. A physical model of the section of the stadium was made interactive with touch sensors. The CAD drawing with barcodes was a first example within the project of *mixed objects*, where integration of the physical and the digital happens within one single object. This notion goes beyond simply enriching a physical artefact by linking it with content in different media. A characteristic of these animated or *mixed objects* is that you have to interact to experience them. By integrating barcodes into her CAD drawing, the student created a new way of engaging with the design artefact. The diagram does not speak for itself - you have to physically interact with it. In the case of the *Texture painter* with which students worked in the second round of field trials the link is such that the properties of the artefact itself can be changed, by applying colour, inserting movement and context, and varying its dimension in relation to other objects in the physical space.

These and the many other *mixed objects* the students created can be characterized by a set of qualities:

- *Openness* refers to how accessible and learnable an artefact is, and to its capability of being combined with other artefacts. Moreover, openness refers to the capability of an artefact (an affordance) to have different, potentially unlimited, ways of being used and perceived. Our experience of providing students with simple prototypes, helping to extend them and furnish them with more complex functionality is an example of openness to appropriation and use. Another crucial aspect of openness is the possibility for an artefact to be combined with other artefacts. Integrating barcodes, tags, and touch sensors in physical models and diagrams helped create interactive and in some cases innovative combinations of physical and digital objects, being perceived and used in many different ways. The *Texture painter* and optical markers, applied in combination with physical objects and projections, resulted in rather intriguing kinds of *mixed objects*.

- *Multiplicity* refers to the capability of a space or artefact of being made of different components having different qualities. Multiplicity can be seen in the combination of input (sensors, tag and barcode readers, scanners, etc.) and output (displays, printers, projectors, etc.) devices characterising the workspace of the students, and/or in the multiplicity of affordances offered by *mixed objects*.

- *Continuity* refers to the capability of moving from one affordance to another, from one representation to another, without changing artefact, without interruption in space and in time. It can be achieved by putting resources on the borders of objects, so that the borders act as both, separators and connectors.

In the design of *mixed objects*, where digital content is integrated in the physical object, there seems to be a vast array of possible levels of integration. While in some cases digital media are just "put on top" of a physical artefact, other examples are more profoundly integrated and digital and physical properties operates within one single object. The difference could be illustrated with the concepts of "collage" as opposed to "sampling". While the older montage form collage is juxtaposition by putting things next to each other, sampling works on a more genetical level and constructs genuine hybrid forms.

An important design strategy for construction of *mixed objects* is to mobilize a great quantity of materials in order to maintain the border resources. Basically any material could be used and different qualities can be supported with different combinations. One example is observed by Redström (Redström 2001) in how LCD displays seems to dominate the overall expression more directly, as opposed to projecting on fabrics. During periods in the project we have pushed this notion one step further, trying not to use any generic displays at all. Integrating space can also be to use whatever surfaces that are available, for projecting upon them, accepting constraints in resolution and light conditions. Freedom in combination of materials will also affect the modalities that will be addressed in perception.

Design objects are also mixed in a social dimension in the sense that they are being shared and the notion of *boundary objects* (Star 1989) is relative to the paradox of demassification. Design artefacts from the Atelier project such as the *Interactive Stage*, the *Tangible archive*, the *Mixed object table*, the *Texture painter* as well as the physical models and project plans enriched with barcodes, or touch sensors, are all examples of boundary objects, or allow the creation of boundary objects. The concept of boundary object can be extended to anything that can help people from different communities to build a shared understanding. Boundary objects will be interpreted differently by the different communities, and it is an acknowledgement and discussion of these differences that enables a shared understanding to be formed. It should be clear why a physical model or a sketch may serve as boundary objects, helping visitors to understand what students do in their projects; whereas the more technical and detailed representations, such as a CAD plan, are only boundary objects for the more specialized professional communities of architects and building specialists (Schmidt and Wagner 2003).

We consider the artefacts we have created to support multimedia representations as boundary objects. They are potential boundary objects, since they allow visitors to share with the students the knowledge about their design space (and the constraints and the opportunities it offers), as well as bring different perspectives onto an object to the forth. Our artefacts support this mixture of commonality and diversity, offering the possibility to move from one representation to another, either changing level of abstraction, or changing supporting medium or, finally, changing viewpoint. Users can access several different representations making reference to one unique thing (the designed building and/or device, the planned territory and/or space, etc.).

In our approach, boundary objects are intrinsically multi-affordance objects, where commonality is supported by the emergence of one unique object, and diversity by the multiplicity of affordance through which users can access and manipulate it. Considering the experiments we have done, some of them deeply adhere to this concept (e.g. the *Texture painter*) while others have not yet fully developed it (in some cases any representation seems to have its own life and its links with other representations of the same object are not highlighted). Our boundary objects, therefore, are often and should always be *mixed objects*, i.e. objects coupling physical and digital qualities. Even the concept of boundary becomes broader than in its original definition by Star, it refers to the contact line not only between different communities, but also between the physical and the digital, and, as a consequence, between the different (spatio-temporal) situations of any user.

3.3   Configuring and Place Making

With the perspective of embodied interaction both the social dimension and our bodily experiences come into focus. As Dourish has argued in his call for embodied interaction *place* reflects the emergence of practice as shared experience of people in space and over time (Dourish 2001). When people share an enriched portion of space and a language to talk about their experience, they transform space into a place. The design challenge is not to design space, but to design for *appropriation* of space according to the activities that take place among a particular set of people inhabiting that place.

Architectural space is not static, it constantly changes with people's activities. The notion of "use-as event" (Lainer and Wagner 1998) emphasizes the changing, evolving, temporary and sometimes performance-like character of activities in space. It is resonant with Tschumi's idea of "architecture not as an object (or work, in structuralist terms), but as an "interaction of space and events". His ideas revolve around choreographed, "cinematic" movement (in time, through space), and through this he arrives at an alternative way of looking at the materiality of architecture as "in its solids and voids, its spatial sequences, its articulations, its collisions" (Tschumi 1981, in Nesbitt 1996). At the same time, a space is not neutral, it is a space for something, being furnished with specific practices, artefacts, symbols, knowledges, and ideologies. It provides actors with a "view from somewhere" (Haraway 1991), a special vision. Smith (Smith 1990) emphasises the possibility to locate and identify positionings as a precondition of knowing. A particular script, she argues, can only be produced at a particular place. This notion of space as shaping social practices on the one hand, being constantly changed by the people who inhabit and use it –"use as event" – on the other hand, needs to be kept in mind when thinking about how to implement particular qualities in the spatial design.

Fig. 10. Configuring and place making – the students appropriating the design studio to different uses

Configuring as a practice is intricately linked to the fact that in evolving environments, such as the architecture class or the interaction design studios, the boundaries of activities are continually moving. Our observations helped identify two meanings of configurability:

- Adapting a space to a diversity of uses and identities – which is achieved through e.g., appropriating a space, personalizing it and configuring it in support of diverse arrangements, such as solitary work, group discussions, performing and presenting, building models.

- Configurations of artefacts within the physical space – with artefacts changing the position in relation to others, and different configurations expressing the conceptual, chronological or narrative links between them.

As to the configurability of a space, we could learn from good architectural design that often plays with an ambiguity in the relationship between spatial configuration and functional program, where

> *"The allocation of functions or uses is malleable, they are fitted into the spatial configuration. While some of them find ample space, others might have to be squeezed in, overlap, extend into neighbouring spaces, thereby creating 'natural' connections or meeting 'fixed' boundaries. This not only allows to suspend or transgress the usual hierarchy of functions and rooms. Also, the boundaries between interior and exterior space are designed as permeable and fluent" (Lainer and Wagner 1998).*

One conclusion to be drawn from this is that a learning space needs not to be perfectly equipped and designed. On the contrary, a certain lack of perfection, the presence of spatial constraints may be important, since they stimulate activities, the creative appropriation of the space, its re-programming for changing events and needs. Hence our approach of designing architectural components that can be assembled and configured for specific purposes on the one hand, our notion of an architecture as augmenting existing spaces on the other hand. Embedding digital media in physical environments cannot be simply understood as an extension of practices we observed in the physical world. Things need to be designed so as to support "the ability to improvisationally combine computational resources and devices in serendipitous ways" (Weiser 1993). Hence our strategy not to create new and dedicated artefacts but to encourage students to embed digital media in the diverse design representations they customarily produce.

At the beginning of our field trials with the students the space was unformed and had to be appropriated. Our pedagogical assumption is that a perfectly furnished space is often not the best solution for creative work. Students need to appropriate the space, struggle with its constraints, and find their own interpretation and set-up. This is why they found the space almost completely empty, apart from an infrastructure of networks, furniture, grids for projections, tag/barcode readers, computers, and other electronic equipment. They were asked to bring their own stuff – pictures, video material, scale models, diagrams, and collages. With these resources at hand, students configured and re-configured space and artefacts to accommodate diverse activities – from browsing through pictures, to discussing a design concept or performing a scenario of use. We can understand these configurations as forming an evolving set of temporary, and, in some ways ephemeral layers onto this neutral, almost empty environment.

We could discern several overlapping strategies in how the students appropriated and configured space, such as: personalizing (equipping it with things that reflect their personal identity and preferences); configuring furniture and technical equipment for a particular task; configuring the space to accommodate visitors, a large number of people, eventually observing a particular ritual of stage/spectators or seating habits; configuring a space for cooperative work, etc. The associated movements of equipment and people reflect the notion of "use as event" and the performative/choreographic elements in how space is integrated into different activities.

As suggested by Dourish in outlining embodied interaction, the philosophy of language-games, as developed by Wittgenstein, is an interesting approach for understanding social and tangible practice (Dourish 2001). This is in line with a position to design as intertwined with *language-games* (or overlapping communities of practice) that has been the basis for much of the research in participatory design during the last twenty years (Ehn 1998). The idea of language-games entails and emphasizes how we discover and construct our world. However, language is understood as our use of it. As we see it, this is not in opposition to how we also come to understand the world by use of physical artefacts. Objects also play a fundamental role in a given language-game. In this view language-games are performed as practice with "embodied" meaning within societal and cultural institutional frameworks. To possess the competence required to participate in a language-game requires a lot of learning within that practice. But in the beginning, all you can understand is what you have already understood in another language-game. You understand because of the *family resemblance* between the language-games. This seems to make us prisoners of language and tradition, which is not really the case. Amongst others, Habermas (Habermas 1968) pointed to the flexibility and reflexivity that is built into our everyday language, as allowing us to learn, to modify, extend and subvert meanings. Being socially created, the rules of language-games, as those of other games, can also be altered.

In participatory design users and designers are fundamentally seen as related via shared experiences in a common design language-game, where the design artefacts like mock-ups, prototypes, scenarios can be seen as boundary objects. This language-game has a family resemblance with the ordinary language-games of both users and designers. A fundamental competence of the designer is the ability to set the stage and make props for this shared design language-game that makes sense to all participants, making the interaction and mediation between different language-games possible.

In a critique of the dualism of virtual reality Hedman comes up with an interesting suggestion along these lines: What if we think of the activities going on in a place as a kind of language-games. He calls them *place making games* and suggests that places allow for multiple place games (Hedman 2003). In studying an exhibition with *mixed objects* in a museum environment within the SHAPE project, exploring an environment with strong similarities to the *Atelier* tangible archive, he observes that visitors may shift between different games during a single visit. Moreover, the kind of place games that can occur constitutes an open ended set of activities where digital elements are joined into an, as he calls it, "esemplastic unity" through the place making games that are played. This concept for moulding diverse ideas or things into unity, borrowed from Coleridge, suggests design for place making uniting corporal and incorporeal spaces rather than adding a virtual reality to the one physical already existing.

The concept of incorporeal places is by no means limited to digital technology and virtual reality. As Hedman writes:

"... humans have always been actively engaged in incorporeal places, whether in art, sleep, through recollection, imagination or fiction. Incorporeal places have always been part of everyday life. Certain disciplines and traditions have put special emphasis on incorporeal places: in religion-heaven and hell, in architecture-the planned building, in art of memory-the information place, in fiction-the place of action and drama" (Hedman 2003). The art of memory, e.g., as practiced by Cicero, rests on the capacity for places to be associated with things to remember. An example of a such public and tangible place was the memory theatre as described in the sixteenth century by Giulio Camillo. This esemplastic place allowed users to enter a cylindrical room where the walls were covered with systematically marked and located little boxes and carvings. From a stage the user was overlooking the totality of human knowledge and it was said that anyone entering the room instantly would be as conversant as Cicero on any scholarly subject. Be that as it may, memory theatre and the art of memory also open up a perspective of story telling and associations relevant to the design for contemporary esemplastic places. We are here reminded about the observation by Ricoeur about narrative time and how the story told not only gives an historical account, but actually also takes place here and now organizing the current activities (Ricoeur 1984).

A good example from the Atelier project of a design for esemplastic unity of place is the tangible archive. The use is informal like in a "Wunderkammer", and it is more associative than in a systematically organized traditional archive. Maybe not an environment that makes the users as conversant as Cicero, but an open environment for appropriation of space in the activities that take place among several people being bodily present, when acting with mixed objects as they make sense to the place. Another example are the semi-immersive spaces created by multiple projections. They allow to mesh times and spaces, presence and distance.

The examples we have provided explore different aspects of configurability of mixed environments: associations of inputs, media, and outputs; spatiality and integration with artefacts; configuring furniture and work zones (Tangible Archive); real time configuration of mixed objects (Mixed objects Table). In all examples configurability and place making includes interventions in the physical landscape of space and artefacts. The complex activity of configuring unfolds, and therefore has to be supported, on different levels and across different aspects of the environment: spatial arrangement (e.g. grid for fixing projection surfaces), furniture (the Tangible Archive with its modules, the table), the landscape of artefacts which can be tagged, furnished with sensors or barcodes, electronic components and devices (scanners, readers, connecting and plugging input and output devices), digital components and their interactions (digital infrastructure, associations of inputs, outputs and media content in the database) (Binder et al. 2005; Ehn and Linde 2004).

This large variety of means can provoke confusion among both users and designers. Users are unable to find a rationale to deal with the new qualities of the space where they act and designers miss the compositional grammar for creating their devices and arrangements. Even the weaknesses of the space offered to users can be attributed to the lack of a conceptualisation shaping the design of tangible computing environments. We were, therefore, somehow forced to enter into a discussion of the qualities the artefacts we were designing had and/or should have. This discussion, on the one hand, has created a deeper understanding of what we were doing in Atelier, on the other, indicates new possibilities for the design for configurability that we have not yet pursued in our research.

4   Out of the Box

We started the *Atelier* project with the ambition to create inspirational learning environments in the spirit of Weiser's vision of taking the computer "out of the box" and making computational resources augment the design studio environment ubiquitously. This led us into design of architecture and technology in support of design qualities in action such as design work as transforming representations, performative interaction, configuring, creative density and multiple travels, and conceptual work in direction of embodiment and the performative elements of space, mixed objects, and configuring as place making.

As a final reflection we could say that in a way this attempt turned out to be too successful. To our surprise we had helped augment the studio environments so well that the students voluntarily got stuck in there, rather than going out exploring practice in the world. We had re-created the computer in a box, only now on the size of a studio. Hence, in rethinking the design studio as a creative environment, portability and flexibility of technology for configuring and making place became central. This required a change of perspective towards regarding whatever space there is available as a potential inspirational learning environment, and *Atelier* technology as a way to configure that space, herby potentially shaping *mixed objects* and esemplastic spaces for meaningful interactions and place making games of design and learning.

Fig. 11. Out of the box…

Acknowledgements

This work would not have been possible without the deep commitment of each person in the *Atelier* research team. From Academy of Fine Arts, Vienna: Andreas Rumpfhuber, Dieter Spath, Rüdiger Lainer, and Yvonne Manfreda. From Consorzio Milano Ricerche: Alessandra Menotti, Giorgio De Michelis, Marco Loregian, Michele Telaro, and Silvia Calegari. From Imagination Computer Services, Vienna: Heimo Kramer, Michael Gervautz, and Thomas Gatschnegg. From Interactive Institute, Malmö: Martin Johansson, Michael Johansson, Nabil Benhadj, Peter Warrén, and Thomas Binder. From Malmö University: Annika Nyström, Bo Peterson, Cecilia Påhlsson, Janna Lindsjö, Mette Agger Eriksen, Pelle Ehn, Per Linde, Simon Niedenthal, and Sofia Dahlgren. From University of Oulu: Antti Juustila, Giulio Jacucci, Kari Kuutti, Pekka Pehkonen, Toni Räisanen, Tuomo Tuikka, and Virtu Halttunen. From University of Technology, Vienna: Ina Wagner, Kresimir Matkovic, and Tomas Psik. Students from the master-class of Architecture at Academy of Fine Arts, Vienna, and from the Interaction Design master program at Arts and Communication, Malmö University, have also played an important role, without whom the project would have been impossible.

The work reported in this chapter was supported by the European Commission as apart of the "Disappearing Computer" initiative under contract number IST-2001-33064.

References

Bannon, L., Benford, S., Bowers, J., Heath, C.: Hybrid design creates innovative museum experiences. Communications of the ACM 48(3), 62–65 (2005)

Bellotti, V., Back, M., Edwards, K., Grinter, R., Henderson, A., Lopes, C.: Making sense of sensing systems: five questions for designers and researchers. In: CHI'02: Proceedings of the SIGCHI conference on Human factors in computing systems, pp. 415–422. ACM Press, New York (2002)

Benford, S., Crabtree, A., Reeves, S., Sheridan, J., Dix, A., Flintham, M., Drozd, A.: Designing for the opportunities and risks of staging digital experiences in public settings. In: CHI'06: Proceedings of the SIGCHI conference on Human Factors in computing systems, pp. 427–436. ACM Press, New York (2006)

Binder, T., De Michelis, G., Gervautz, M., Iacucci, G., Matkovic, K., Psik, T., Wagner, I.: Supporting Configurability in a tangibly augmented environment for design students. Personal and Ubiquitous Computing 8(5), 310–325 (2004)

Brown, J.S., Duguid, P.: Borderline resources: Social and material aspects of design. Human.-Computer Interaction 9(1), 3–36 (1994)

Ciolfi, L., Bannon, L.: Space, place and the design of technologically enhanced physical environments. In: Turner, P., Davenport, E. (eds.) Space, Spatiality and Technology, pp. 217–232. Springer, Heidelberg (2005)

De Michelis, G.: Mixed objects. QD – Quaderni of DISCo, vol. 5. Aracne, Roma (2004)

Dewey, J.: Art as Experience. Perigee Books, New York (1980/1934)

Dourish, P.: Where the action is - The Foundations of Embodied Interaction. The MIT Press, London (2001)

Ehn, P.: Work-oriented design of computer artifacts. Falköping: Arbetslivscentrum/Almqvist & Wiksell International. Lawrence Erlbaum, Hillsdale (1988)

Ehn, P., Linde, P.: Embodied Interaction – designing beyond the physical-digital divide. In: Futureground: Proceedings of Design Research Society International Conference, Melbourne, Australia, pp. 77–89 (2004)

Engelbart, D.: Augmenting the Human Intellect – a conceptual framework. Stanford Research Institute (1962)

Fitzmaurice, G.W., Ishii, H., Buxton, W.: Bricks: laying the foundations for graspable user interfaces. In: CHI'95: Proceedings of the SIGCHI conference on Human factors in computing systems, pp. 442–449. ACM Press/Addison-Wesley, New York (1995)

Fällman D.: In romance with the material of mobile interaction: a phenomenological approach to the design of mobile information technology. Ph.D. thesis, Department of Informatics, Umeå University, Sweden (2003)

Gaver, B., Dunne, A., Pacenti, M.: Cultural Probes. Interactions, January & February, pp. 21–29 (1999)

Grudin, J.: Group dynamics and ubiquitous computing. Communications of the ACM 45(12), 74–78 (2002)

Habermas, J.: Erkenntnis und Interesse. Suhrkamp Verlag, Frankfurt (1968)

Hämäläinen, P., Höysniemi, J., Ilmonen, T., Lindholm, M., Nykänen, A.: Martial Arts in Artificial Reality. In: CHI'05: Proceedings of ACM Conference on Human Factors in Computing Systems, Portland, Oregon, pp. 781–790. ACM Press, New York (2005)

Haraway, D.: Situated Knowledges: the science question in feminism and the privilege of partial perspective. In: Haraway, D. (ed.) Simians, Cyborgs and Women, pp. 183–201. Routledge, New York (1999)

Hedman A.: Visitor Orientation in Context: The historically rooted production of soft places. Ph.D. thesis, Royal Institute of Technology, Stockholm, Sweden (2003)

Ishii, H., Brygg, U.: Tangible bits: towards seamless interfaces between people, bits and atoms. In: CHI'97: Proceedings of the SIGCHI conference on Human factors in computing systems, pp. 234–241. ACM Press, New York (1997)

Jacucci G.: Interaction as Performance. Cases of configuring physical interfaces in mixed media. Doctoral Thesis, University of Oulu, Acta Universitatis Ouluensis (2004)

Jacucci, C., Jacuccui, G., Psik, T., Wagner, I.: A manifesto for the performative development of ubiquitous media. In: Proceedings of the 4th decennial conference on Critical computing: between sense and sensibility, Aarhus, Denmark, pp. 19–28 (2005)

Johansson M., Linde P.: Journal of Research Practice 1(1), Article M5 (2005), published online by ICAAP http://www.icaap.or

Kindberg, T., Barton, J., Morgan, J., Becker, G., Caswell, D., Debaty, P., Gopal, G., Frid, M., Krishnan, V., Morris, H., Schettino, J., Serra, B., Spasojevic, M.: People, places, things: web presence for the real world. Journal of Mobile Networks and Applications 7(5), 3365–3376 (2002)

Krippendorf, K.: Redesigning design. In: Tahkokallio, P., Vihma, S. (eds.) Design – Pleasure or Responsibility? University of Art and Design, Helsinki, Finland, pp. 138–162 (1995)

Lainer, R., Wagner, I.: Connecting Qualities of Social Use with Spatial Qualities. In: Streitz, N.A., Konomi, S., Burkhardt, H.-J. (eds.) CoBuild 1998. LNCS, vol. 1370, pp. 191–203. Springer, Heidelberg (1998)

Latour, B.: Pandora's hope: essays on the reality of science studies. Harvard University Press, Cambridge (1999)

Mackay, W.E., Fayard, A.-L., Frobert, L., Médini, L.: Reinventing the familiar: exploring an augmented reality design space for air traffic control. In: CHI'98: Proceedings of the SIGCHI conference on Human factors in computing systems, pp. 558–565. ACM Press/Addison-Wesley, New York (1998)

Marick, B.: Boundary Object (2001), available at http://www.visibleworkings.com/analogyfest/marick-boundary-objects.pdf

Merleau–Ponty, M.: Phenomenology of Perception (Translated to English by Smith C. Routledge and Kegan Paul Ltd.), London (1962)

Newman, M.W., Sedivy, J.Z., Neuwirth, C., Edwards, K., Hong, J., Izadi, S., Marcelo, K., Smith, T., Sedivy, J., Newman, M.: Designing for serendipity: supporting end-user configuration of ubiquitous computing environments. In: DIS'02: Proceedings of the conference on Designing interactive systems: Processes, practices, methods, and techniques, pp. 147–156. ACM Press, London (2002)

Nesbitt, K.: Theorizing a New Agenda for Architecture - An Anthology of Architectural Theory 1965–1995. Princeton Architectural Press, New York (1996)

Redström J.: Designing Everyday Computational Things. Ph.D. thesis, Studies in Informatics, University of Gothenburg, Sweden (2001)

Rekimoto, J.: Pick-and-drop: a direct manipulation technique for multiple computer environments. In: Proceedings of the 10th annual ACM symposium on User interface software and technology, pp. 31–39. ACM Press, New York (1997)

Ricoeur, P.: Time and Narrative. University of Chicago press, Chicago (1984)

Suderburg, E. (ed.): Space Site Intervention, Situating Installation Art. University of Minnesota Press (2000)

Salber, D., Dey, A.K., Abowd, G.: The context toolkit: aiding the development of context-enabled applications. In: Proceedings of the SIGCHI conference on Human factors in computing systems, pp. 434–441. ACM Press, New York (1999)

Schmidt, K., Wagner, I.: Ordering Systems: Coordinative Practices in Architectural Design and Planning. In: Proceedings Group 2003, November 9 - 12, 2003, Sanibel Island, Florida, USA, pp. 274–283 (2003)

Sobel, D., Andera, M., Kwinter, S., Acconci, V.: Vito Acconci. Acts of Architectures, Milwaukee Art Museum (2001)

Star Leigh, S.: The Structure of Ill-Structured Solutions: Boundary Objects and Heterogeneous Distributed Problem Solving. In: Gasser, L., Huhns, M.N. (eds.) Distributed Artificial Intelligence, vol. 2, pp. 37–54. Pitman, London (1989)

Smith, D.E.: The Social Organization of Textual Reality. The Conceptual Practices of Power. A Feminist Sociology of Knowledge, pp. 61–80. Northeastern University Press, Boston (1990)

Tschumi, B.: The Pleasure of Architecture. Architectural Design 47(3), 214–218 (1977)

Weiser, M.: Some computer science issues in ubiquitous computing. Communications of the ACM 36(7), 75–84 (1993)

Spatial Computing and Spatial Practices

Anders Brodersen[1], Monika Büscher [2], Michael Christensen[1], Mette Agger Eriksen[3],
Kaj Grønbæk [1], Jannie Friis Kristensen[1], Gunnar Kramp[3], Peter Krogh[3],
Martin Ludvigsen[1], Preben Holst Mogensen[1], Michael Bang Nielsen[1], Dan Shapiro[2],
and Peter Ørbæk [4]

[1] Department of Computer Science, University of Aarhus, Denmark
[2] Department of Sociology, Lancaster University, Lancaster, UK
[3] CommunicationDesign, Aarhus School of Architecture, Denmark
[4] 43D ApS, Denmark

1   Introduction

The gathering momentum behind the research agendas of pervasive, ubiquitous and ambient computing, set in motion by Mark Weiser (1991), offer dramatic opportunities for information systems design. They raise the possibility of "putting computation where it belongs" by exploding computing power out of conventional machines and interfaces, and embedding it in myriad large and small communicating devices and everyday objects. Exciting though these developments are, however, they remain "just technology" unless they can be successfully married to things that people really need and want to do. In addressing the "disappearing computer" we have, therefore, carried over from previous research an interdisciplinary perspective, and a focus on the sociality of action (Suchman 1987).

This means that our development of technology is strongly anchored in work practice, with technology and practice evolving together (Büscher et al. 2001a). It leads us to take an interdisciplinary perspective that combines participatory design with ethnographic studies of work, in cooperation with the practitioners in our application domain, who in this case are aesthetic design professionals in architecture and landscape architecture. It means that we seek to understand both work practices and technologies in terms of the support they provide for embodied, material and collaborative activity (Büscher et al. 2001b). One conseque nce is that we give preference to representing action through materials rather than through, for example, avatars, because this acknowledges the qualitative differences between people and things: it accords the appropriate degree of autonomy to people as self-producing and self-materialising entities – who risk, therefore, being fatally diminished through artificial representation – by contrast with materials which may be complex and dynamic but which remain bound by mechanical procedures. Similarly, it leads us to accord as much initiative and organisational capacity as possible to users rather than to automated processes, while acknowledging that it is sometimes necessary and often useful to delegate "decisions" to machines.

Ambient computing creates novel opportunities – and necessities – for the distribution of computing capacity in space, and Weiser saw spatial relationships as a key organising principle for ubiquitous computing (1991). Equally, space is a key organising resource and constraint for human activity. Much work practice is achieved

N. Streitz, A. Kameas, and I. Mavrommati (Eds.): The Disappearing Computer, LNCS 4500, pp. 77–95, 2007.
© Springer-Verlag Berlin Heidelberg 2007

through the dynamic spatial arrangement of materials (Büscher et al. 1999, 2001b) and much collaboration is achieved through the mutual intelligibility of these arrangements when people can overlook each other at work (Heath and Luff 1992a; Anderson et al. 1989).

Within hypermedia research there has also been a focus on spatial structuring of digital material and emerging structures through use (Marshall et al. 1994). Our approach to spatial computing is inspired from spatial hypermedia, and the Topos system can be seen as a novel 3D spatial hypermedia system (Mogensen and Grønbæk 2000).

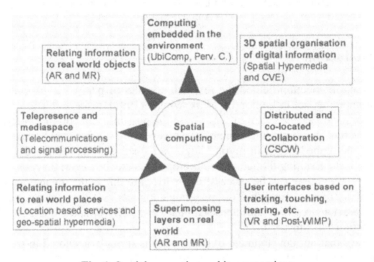

Fig. 1. Spatial computing and its connections

Achieving effective ambient environments is therefore substantially about achieving appropriate connections and mappings between the spatial organisation of activities, materials and technologies. This applies with even greater force when space is the object of work as well as one of its means, as is the case with architecture and landscape architecture. We refer to the design of such technologies as "spatial computing", for which we draw on a range of neighbouring and overlapping technical and analytic research fields, summarised in Fig. 1.

The Disappearing Computer research initiative[1] provided the opportunity to explore spatial computing, and in the WorkSPACE[2] project we applied it by trying to identify the difficulties that landscape architects encounter in their work that would be most amenable to this kind of technical support. Unlike the majority of participatory design projects, this one involved a distant time horizon and advanced technical systems and devices. This has required us to modify our research methods to cope with interim technologies and the difficulties of short-term evaluation and feedback, through techniques such as "future laboratories" (Büscher 2005).

We brought to the WorkSPACE project particular theoretical and methodological orientations, accumulating experience of interdisciplinary collaboration, and familiarity

---

[1]   See www.disappearing-computer.org
[2]   See www.daimi.au.dk/workspace

with the work domain of architecture and landscape architecture. We believe we have emerged with powerful general software for cooperative spatial computing, some useful prototype systems and devices for the architectural design professions, substantial refinement and deepening of techniques, and a basis for ongoing research.

2   Background Research: Collaborative Virtual Environment

In previous research (Büscher et al. 1999, 2000) we created a collaborative virtual environment which is an unbounded three-dimensional space that can contain references and views onto a set of two-dimensional or three-dimensional objects (see Fig. 2). These can be "drag-and-dropped" into the space, e.g. from folders. Double clicking any of the document objects will launch it in its own application – which might be MS Word, Excel, AutoCAD, Photoshop, etc. – and any changes made to a document will be updated in the Topos[3] view in near real time. The objects can be sized, moved and rotated in three dimensions, giving a full 6 degrees of freedom. The viewer/viewpoint can also move freely in the space. Objects can be collected together in sub-workspaces which can be selectively opened and closed, and sub-workspaces can interpenetrate. Objects in a Topos workspace are references to the underlying materials, not those materials themselves, so that workspaces can be composed for particular

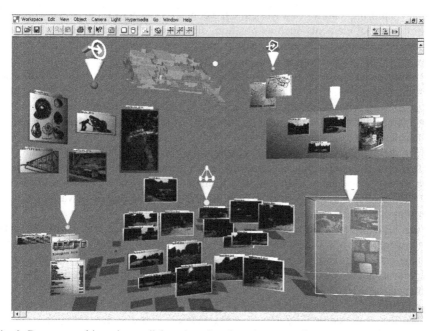

Fig. 2. Document objects in a collaborative virtual environment, Topos. Colour versions of all figures can be seen at: www.daimi.au.dk/workspace/scsp

---

[3]   Topos™ was completely rewritten at the beginning of the WorkSPACE project. It has since been further developed and released as a product, in specialised form, by a spin-off company, 43D ApS, see www.43d.com.

purposes, altered at will, and deleted, without affecting at all the underlying organisation of those materials, e.g. in a directory structure. Workspaces can be shared by distributed users, and objects can exist simultaneously in multiple workspaces. This provides versatile support for cooperative work by allowing people, separately or together, to make meaningful spatial arrangements of their digital materials, to share them, and to "overlook" what is happening in them (Büscher et al. 2001b). Topos has provided a powerful underlying technology for ambient spatial computing, as described in later sections.

3   Towards an Ambient Environment

When analysing the work of landscape architects it is useful for some purposes to distinguish three aspects of their activities, which inform their orientation to the materials and tools available to them and to the various spaces of their work. First, there is the business of "capturing" and "bringing home" the features of a work site, which is especially important for a new job. Second, there are the extended activities of developing and working up a design. And third, there is the process of realising and expressing the design out onto the real world. Though there is an element of temporality to these aspects, they continue and interpenetrate for most of the duration of a design project.

When capturing features of a work site the concern is sometimes to collect straightforwardly factual elements such as position, elevations, soil characteristics, existing planting, etc., and is sometimes to collect more elusive elements such as its atmosphere, character, relationship to its surroundings, potential, etc. This is important both for informing one's own design work, and also because staff may be on site as the one or two representatives of a larger and possibly fluid team which may get drawn into the design work without having the opportunity to visit the site themselves. At present this is mainly done through taking large numbers of photographs, sketching on existing plans and surveys, making notes, etc.

When developing and working up a design, the concern is mainly to assemble and keep track of the appropriate material, to seek relevant advice and reach consensus about the evolving design, and generally to maintain the working division of labour among the probably varying set of people involved with the project at various times. At present this is often achieved with difficulty.

When realising and "expressing" the design back out onto the real world, the concern is mainly to control the construction process, to match the emerging reality with the intended design, and to cope with the inevitable mistakes, clashes and deviations. Here, too, it can at present be difficult to achieve this matching with precision and confidence.

As mentioned, in setting out to support these activities, Topos provided a powerful platform for spatial computing which would underpin many of our subsequent developments. An initial step towards using it to constitute an ambient environment was to make it available on large-scale back-projected displays for co-located teamwork. Thus we have developed various pieces of Roomware components (Streitz et al. 1998) supporting the collaborative use of Topos for architect workspaces, see Fig. 3 and Grønbæk et al. (2001) for further discussion of these components. This is ambient in the preliminary sense that the display becomes a "public" component of the space, and it makes the objects it contains available for public manipulation as "inhabitants" of the space. In order to make it usable with touch or pen based interaction, we developed a gesture interface to manipulate objects in the workspace, such as a downstroke to advance a document front and centre, an upstroke to return it to its default position, a roof-shape "^" to take the user to the home position in the space, and a v-shape to take the user to a selected object (see Fig. 4). These proved so congenial in use that they are often adopted for Topos for all devices (e.g. with a mouse and standard display).

Fig. 3. SpacePanel (left) and stereographic table (right) 3D Topos displays

Sketching toolbar

Gesture interface
left-right strokes toggle between
sketching and normal modes

Fig. 4. Some Topos interaction mechanisms

A further step was to provide a sketching or "doodling" facility so that users could interact with digital documents similarly to how they would do so with physical documents (see Fig. 4). Multiple doodles can be saved as separate layers and users can select doodle colours to aid identification. Users can select either persistent or "fade-away" doodles – the latter approximates, for remote collaboration, the kind of hand gestures that would be visible in, for example, co-located discussion of a plan or drawing.

Distributed Collaboration

With this infrastructure in place we created a prototype environment for "distributed" collaboration, though we simulated some aspects of this in a Future Laboratory by staging it in a single space with two teams separated by a partition, so that they cannot see but they can hear each other directly (see Fig. 5).

Fig. 5. A Future Laboratory for "distributed" collaboration

Each team has a SpacePanel displaying Topos workspaces, a camera, a projector and a projection screen. The projection shows the other team, as illustrated in Fig. 6. Teams of landscape architects undertook a real design job, namely to produce a design for the courtyard and underground car park for some University buildings then under construction, using an appropriate collection of digital plans and documents. This setup has its limitations, for example that it does not provide full reciprocity of perspective (Schutz 1964; Heath and Luff 1992b), but even on the first occasion of use they quickly became accustomed to orienting to the actions of the other team, as reflected in their visible actions on screen such as orientation and gestures, audible talk, and manipulation of shared material in Topos such as moving and sketching on documents.

4   Representational Spaces

The uses of Topos described so far are as a metaphorical, abstract 3D space in which materials can be freely arranged. A further step in connecting with a wider environment of spatial practice was to develop the software to be capable of the highly accurate and efficient 3D representation of real spaces. These may range from a large area, such as an 80km x 85km windfarm terrain (see Fig. 7), through a construction site, to an individual scale model.

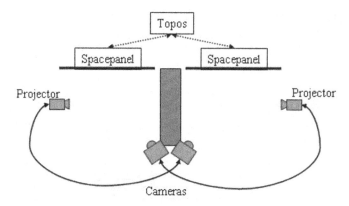

Fig. 6. Supporting remote collaboration

Topos enables users to combine existing features with envisioned changes and allows for a high degree of flexibility, for example supporting on-the-fly change and experimentation with 3D visualizations. Multi-part models (e.g. of windfarms, commercial, housing and other developments, telecommunication masts and pylons in urban or rural areas, etc.) can be placed and manipulated in real time in real-data terrain models. For example, each wind turbine in Fig. 7 can simply be grabbed and moved, and accurate position information is tracked and displayed dynamically. Maps, satellite photographs, and GIS data can be mapped onto the terrain. There is support for creating

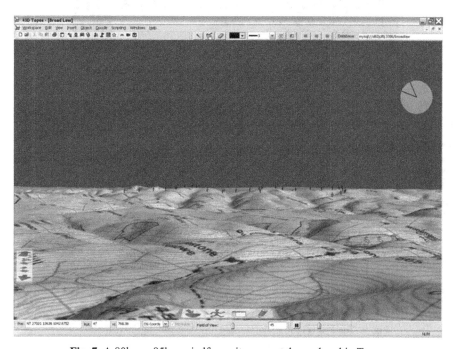

Fig. 7. A 80km x 85km windfarm site accurately rendered in Topos

key viewpoints and paths for animated fly-throughs, rendering realistic impressions of walking, driving or flying through the landscape, with the option of always looking towards the development. Topos provides various tools for free movement – for example, moving at a constant height above the terrain – and for orientation – for example, the "compass rose" at upper right of Fig. 7 shows the compass direction the view is facing, and the field of view. Because this is at the same time a general Topos space, as in the previous section, other documents, e.g. photographs, can be freely placed in the space. Equally, these spaces can be shared for distributed collaboration.

Fig. 8. A tagged document calls up its corresponding workspace

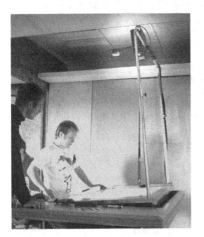

Fig. 9. The ProjectTable: combining physical and digital materials

5   Bridging Digital and Physical Materials

Effecting a bridge between the digital and physical environments is a key objective of ubiquitous and ambient computing (Want et al. 1999). The representational space discussed in the previous section achieves this in one sense, through a direct correspondence between the workspace and a real-world terrain.

Several further techniques for bridging were developed in the project (Grønbæk et al. 2003). In Fig. 8, a physical document has a cheap RFID (radio) tag stuck to it, and bringing it up to a "SpaceTable" display causes the workspace containing the digital version of the document to open. The "ProjectTable" (Fig. 9, left) makes it possible to project digital images onto physical materials on a modified draughtsman's table. The table can also digitally capture (scan) physical materials. Moving a visual tag (Fig. 9, right) manipulates the projection of a 3D model of a building onto the ProjectTable.

6   Working on Site

Topos can be used anywhere with a Notebook computer, and with a fixed or mobile data connection this includes remote collaboration from the site. However, an appropriate assembly of devices enables additional on-site functionality and ways of working.

6.1   The Site Pack

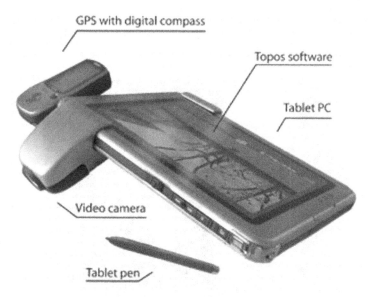

Fig. 10. The SitePack

The prototype Site Pack device in Fig. 10 includes a tablet PC, video camera, GPS, and a digital compass, and it can display the Topos terrain seen from the position, and looking in the direction, where it is located. This is helpful for orientation and – for example – for choosing viewpoints to show the visual impact of a development in what may be a confusing terrain where the constructed objects do not yet exist. The early GPS based version of the Site Pack is discussed in detail in Grønbæk et al. (2002).

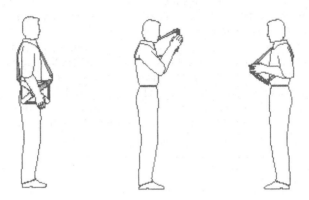

Fig. 11. Carrying and using the SitePack

Another example of the use of the site pack is that the planning and supervision of most architectural development projects involves taking many photographs on site, which must then be referenced to their location and orientation. When a picture is taken using the site pack, it is positioned by the information from the GPS and digital compass on a 2D map or 3D model, thus saving much annotation on site and reconstruction at the office (see Fig. 12). Similarly, sketches can be drawn which are related to the GPS coordinates where the sketch was made.

Fig. 12. Using the site pack for location-referenced photographs or notes

6.2   Feature Tracking and Augmented Reality

Fig. 13. Superimposing a construction in its real-life position on a video stream

Fig. 14. Remote collaboration with the site pack

The Site Pack device in Fig. 10 contains a video camera which can display its live image on the tablet PC screen as the Topos background. Using feature tracking, Topos can place a 3D digital object (e.g. the design of a new building) in its "real life" position in the real time video picture, and thereafter one can move with the camera, while the 3D object stays in its correct "real life" position. It does this by being taught to recognise planar features in the landscape (see Fig. 13). This has obvious value for planning, visual impact assessment, and presentation. As an alternative to feature tracking, determining the position can be supported by visual tags located on the trigonometry points used by site surveyors. These offer a useful supplement to GPS for calibration of position. Further details on the feature tracking mechanisms can be found in Nielsen et al. (2004).

Remote collaboration with the site pack makes it possible to address architectural design issues in direct engagement with the object of design. In Fig. 14, a real life example, the site pack used feature tracking to superimpose the planting design onto live video, to reveal that a planned hedge blocked a key view from the Chief Executive's window. This was discussed live with designers back at the studio, using the sketching facility, and a revised design was agreed.

7   Participatory Design for Emerging Technologies

The complexity and dynamics of situated action that can be drawn into view through participatory and ethnomethodologically informed design create demands that are very hard to meet. The "Disappearing Computer" research initiative is particularly challenging, as it seeks to envisage and design for a future that is quite far away. This requires an imaginative leap and poses particular challenges for the usual repertoire of participatory design techniques, which have tended to focus on the small-scale, local and immediate.

This has required innovation of methods in the project. Some of this is focused on overcoming the fragmentation brought about by teams that are far apart and can only come together occasionally and for limited periods. We have addressed this in part through "Speedays", which involve such activities as experience and video prototyping, animations, instant fieldwork, design interventions, fieldstorms and techstorms, tutorial exercises, breaching experiments, and café-seminars. These methods are discussed in Büscher et al. (2003). They can intensify and accelerate the development of common ground targeted at innovation, and common ownership of data and objectives.

Innovation in methods is also directed at "forcing the future", trying, even for radically experimental designs and prototypes, to maintain a connection with meaningful critical user engagement. This means building partial, but as realistic as possible, future bricolages of prototype technologies, usually in the research laboratory. Practitioners colonise such a prototype design studio of the future and undertake again partial, but as realistic as possible, future bricolages of work practice. These future laboratories help to realise effective co-design involving our principal areas of expertise: landscape architecture (landscape architects, but also ecologists, architects, urban planners); interaction design (architects, communication designers, industrial designers, interaction designers); work analysts (sociologists, ethnomethodologists, participatory designers); and system design (programmers, object oriented designers, software developers).

By no means all user interaction took place in future laboratories, however, and the depth and character of the engagement of the landscape architects with the prototypes varied widely. Broadly, we can distinguish four categories:

- use confined to the "forced environment" of the future laboratories in the Interactive Spaces Lab, largely due to the cost, bulk and/or fragility of the technologies in their current form.

- use in an "experimental bricolage", meaning that prototypes were installed in the landscape architects' own working environment, and were used to work with real materials on live projects, but still required extensive ongoing support from project researchers.

- specialised integration, meaning that a very specific use of the prototypes, and sometimes a specialised variant of a prototype, has almost become self-sustaining in the landscape architects' own working environment.

- "sedimented" use, meaning that a technology has been integrated to the extent that it verges on being a "normal" working tool. Unsurprisingly, not many uses of the prototypes fell in this category.

8   Outline of the Topos Architecture

Very briefly, this version of the distributed Topos architecture can be described as in Fig. 15. Topos applications connect to a collaboration server to coordinate real time distributed collaboration, and they connect to SQL databases to store and retrieve the shared persistent state of workspaces. The Topos application also provides services to the network: for example the ability to display a workspace for another client on a large screen display. Awareness agents monitor changes to databases and enables off-line notifications of changes made since a workspace was last opened.

The circle diagram in Fig. 16 shows a rough picture of the run-time architecture of the Topos application. In the centre is the Business Object Model (BOM) keeping the in-RAM state of the Topos objects (documents, workspaces, links, etc.) and their inter-relations. Object persistence is facilitated through the DB layer interfacing to one or more databases. The 3D graphical interface is manifested through views which present a subset of the BOM via the DScene scene graph library building on OpenGL to implement hardware accelerated 3D graphics.

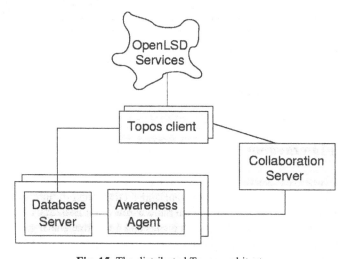

Fig. 15. The distributed Topos architecture

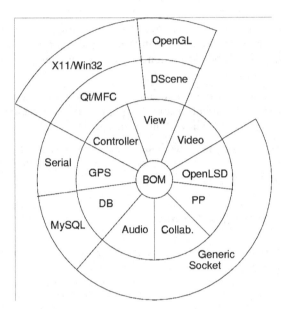

Fig. 16. Topos application run-time architecture

User input is primarily effected through the underlying GUI library (we use Qt on Linux and MFC under Windows). Input events are routed to a Controller which again delegates the events to various sub-controllers implementing different input modalities. Multiple controllers may be associated with a single view to support multiple users collaborating around a shared display.

The GPS subsystem interfaces with GPS receivers through a platform independent serial library. The audio subsystem implements full-duplex network audio communication between workspaces, and the video subsystem interfaces to platform specific video input methods to support augmented reality applications and vision based tracking.

The OpenLSD framework provides various network services based on location-based service discovery. The push-pull (PP) subsystem implements peer-to-peer communication. All the network subsystems build on a platform neutral generic socket library supporting unicast and multicast UDP, TCP/IP, and IrDA/TinyTP as the underlying protocols.

This version of the Topos system is written in C++ and consists of about 200,000 lines of code.

9   Playful Interaction

Studying the work of creative professionals has shown the importance of shifting modes of collaboration, easy access to visual and tactile inspiration, and the spatial organisation of materials. In an effort to push the windows of possibility for interaction, we produced a vision video to address such issues as knowledge sharing, bodily interaction (Ulmer and Ishii 2001) and playfulness (Djajadiningrat et al. 2000). As a metaphor for the exchange of information we came up with an ancient plaything – the ball.

The video *Playful Interaction*[4] is set in a future office for architects, where transitions between selected surfaces (walls, tables, shelves, floors, doors, etc.) can happen through gestures, physical materials and through appliances such as a ball. This is realised through film making and editing techniques rather than through software prototypes. Around the office the ball enables users to "furnish" the environment with different materials, giving colleagues a peripheral awareness of ongoing work. Traditionally many architects organize materials from a project this way, in order to have easy access to drafted materials, plans, maps etc. The ball can pick up or position digital documents on interactive surfaces, so whenever the ball hits a displayed digital document it will pick it up, and when it hits a vacant space, it will release the document that was most recently collected.

Fig. 17. The ball as playful interaction device

The analogue qualities of the ball bring an intrinsic imprecision to the interaction with digital materials. However, being able to create a temporary environment for a meeting by fluently bringing documents forward in a fast and seamless interaction, would often be far more important than the exact positioning of these documents. Between the fingertips, the ball can subsequently be used to roughly adjust the scale, position and rotation of the document. In the central space of the office an interactive floor contains information from a mixture of projects, published for colleagues to draw inspiration and share knowledge. The ball is not a personal object so metaphorically it enables transference of energy from one person to another, giving a very physical dimension to the exchange of information and inspiration, continuously migrating around the office. The ball insists on interaction as a bodily experience.

As a hybrid of a vision video and a video prototype, *Playful Interaction* is also an innovation in the methods of the project. It was a powerful means to communicate design ideas both internally and externally, and to encourage dialogue between the different disciplines. It was also an active design tool.

---

[4] Video available at www.daimi.au.dk/~pkrogh/Videos/Playful_5.avi

Fig. 18. The ball as a shared device for knowledge and inspiration

10   Ambient Environments: Assembling Devices and Functions

The WorkSPACE project addressed issues of ambient, ubiquitous and pervasive computing (Weiser 1991), to do with "exploding" computing and communication power out of the standard processing and interface devices, and embedding them in large or small devices and in the environment where they can be of greatest benefit. However, it did so in a distinctive way that was strongly anchored in the needs of a particular professional domain. The Site Pack discussed above (Fig. 10) was a development in this direction, through making the inputs and outputs of processor, screen, video camera, GPS, compass, and wireless communication available to each other. Similarly with the ProjectTable (Fig. 9), computational power to manipulate objects is "lent" to a small square of paper because the scanning camera can recognise it as a visual tag.

Topos also provides a range of location-based ambient discovery services so that, for example, a portable device can recognise the presence of large wall- or table-size displays and can "colonise" them for its own use.

In our current research[5] with the site pack we are taking this further, investigating how the decomposition and recomposition of devices and services could address problems that are actually encountered in day-to-day work. The example illustrated in Fig. 19 follows our observations of the difficulties and frustrations of driving to and fro across a large terrain trying to identify the best viewpoints for visual impact assessment of a proposed wind farm (that is, those with the worst impact). A video camera on the roof of the car points constantly towards the proposed development, storing GPS location with the image, and taking higher-quality still images when required. Theoretical viewpoint candidates (from Topos) can be compared with actual images to reveal, for example, that it is actually obscured by vegetation or buildings. An audible tone can identify when one is in the "red" (100%) portion of a zone of visual influence (ZVI). The landscape architect might leave the car and walk just with

---

[5] In the Integrated Project 'PalCom: Palpable Computing, A new perspective on ambient computing', in the European Commission Framework Programme 6, Information Society Technology, Future and Emerging Technologies, Disappearing Computer II Programme, www.ist-palcom.org.

the display, with the processing carried out remotely. Most of our prototypes begin with lo-tech mock-ups such as these, with domain practitioners as co-designers. These prototypes are now in a fairly advanced state of development in the PalCom project, as illustrated in Fig. 20.

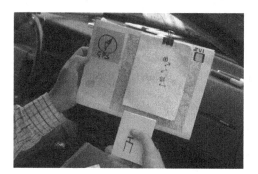

Fig. 19. Lo-tech prototyping for a future Site Pack

Fig. 20. Site Pack prototypes currently in development

11 Conclusions

We believe the results achieved in the WorkSPACE project were considerable, and they have been generously received by those who have seen them – not least by the reviewers for the Disappearing Computer research initiative. Our initial proposal was criticised as over-ambitious, but most of its objectives have been realised, and some of the prototypes have been developed to the point of being launched as products. 43D Topos has all of the functionalities described in the section on "Representational

Spaces" above, and is already in use by most of the major planners and developers of wind farms in the UK. It will soon be marketed for other places and other spatial design applications. We cannot resist seeing this as a vindication of the approach we have pursued, of participatory design with a focus on the specific situation of a user community. By concentrating on the particular, we have arrived at systems with quite general application. For several of us, it also reflects a long term investment in learning how to work together, with the joys and struggles of reconciling different disciplines. This is not the orthodoxy in systems design, but the Disappearing Computer research initiative provided just the right structure and level of resources to explore these ambitions, and an open-minded approach to experimental methods and their evaluation.

Acknowledgements

The research reported here was funded by the European Union under the Information Society Technologies, Future and Emerging Technologies, Disappearing Computer research initiative, project IST-2000-25290 WorkSPACE: Distributed Work support through component based SPAtial Computing Environments. Authors are listed in alphabetic order.

References

Anderson, R.J., Hughes, J.A., Sharrock, W.W.: Working for profit: the social order of calculation in an entrepreneurial firm. Avebury, Aldershot (1989)

Büscher, M.: Social life under the microscope? Sociological Research Online 10(1) (2005), http://www.socresonline.org.uk/10/1/buscher.html

Büscher, M., Agger Eriksen, M.: Grounded Imagination: Challenge, paradox and inspiration. In: Proceedings Tales of the Disappearing Computer, Santorini 1–4 June (2003)

Büscher, M., Mogensen, P., Shapiro, D., Wagner, I.: The Manufaktur: Supporting Work Practice in (Landscape) Architecture. In: Bødker, S., Kyng, M., Schmidt, K. (eds.) Proceedings ECSCW '99 The Sixth European Conference on Computer Supported Cooperative Work, Copenhagen 12–16 September, pp. 21–40. Kluwer Academic Press, Dordrecht (1999)

Büscher, M., Christensen, M., Grønbæk, K., Krogh, P., Mogensen, P., Ørbæk, P., Shapiro, D.: Collaborative Augmented Reality Environments: Integrating VR, working materials, and distributed work spaces. In: Proceedings CVE 2000 The Third International Conference on Collaborative Virtual Environments (San Francisco, 9-12 September), pp. 47–56. ACM Press, New York (2000)

Büscher, M., Gill, S., Mogensen, P., Shapiro, D.: Landscapes of Practice: Bricolage as a Method for Situated Design. Computer-Supported Cooperative Work: The Journal of Collaborative Computing 10, 1–28 (2001a)

Büscher, M., Mogensen, P., Shapiro, D.: Spaces of Practice. In: Prinz, W., Jarke, M., Rogers, Y., Schmidt, K. (eds.) Proceedings ECSCW 2001 The Seventh European Conference on Computer Supported Cooperative Work (Bonn, 16-20 September), pp. 139–158. Kluwer Academic Press, Amsterdam (2001b)

Büscher, M., Kramp, G., Krogh, P.G.: In formation: Support for flexibility, mobility, collaboration, and coherence. Personal and Ubiquitous Computing 7, 136–146 (2003)

Djajadiningrat, J.P., Overbeeke, C.J., Wensveen, S.A.G.: Augmenting Fun and Beauty: A Pamphlet. In: Proceedings DARE 2000 Designing Augmented Reality Environments (Elsinore), pp. 131–134. ACM, New York (2000)

Grønbæk, K., Gundersen, K.K., Mogensen, P., Ørbæk, P.: Interactive room Support for Complex and Distributed Design Projects. In: Hirose, M. (ed.) Proceedings Interact '01 (Tokyo, July), pp. 407–414. IOS Press, Amsterdam (2001)

Grønbæk, K., Vestergaard, P.P., Ørbæk, P.: Towards Geo-Spatial Hypermedia: Concepts and prototype implementation. In: Proceedings 13th ACM Conference on Hypertext and Hypermedia (University of Maryland, 11–15 June), pp. 117–126. ACM, New York (2002)

Grønbæk, K., Ørbæk, P., Kristensen, J.F., Eriksen, M.A.: Physical Hypermedia: Augmenting Physical Material with Hypermedia Structures. New Review of Hypermedia and Multimedia 9, 5–34 (2003)

Heath, C., Luff, P.: Collaboration and Control: Crisis management and multimedia technology in London Underground Line Control Rooms. Computer-Supported Cooperative Work: The Journal of Collaborative Computing 1, 69–94 (1992a)

Heath, C., Luff, P.: Disembodied Interaction: Asymmetries in video mediated communication. In: Button, G. (ed.) Technology in Working Order, pp. 140–176. Routledge, London (1992b)

Marshall, C., Shipman, F., Coombs, J.: VIKI: spatial hypertext supporting emergent structure. In: Proceedings ECHT '94 European Conference on Hypermedia Technologies (Edinburgh, September), pp. 13–23. ACM Press, New York (1994)

Mogensen, P., Grønbæk, K.: Hypermedia in the Virtual Project Room – Toward Open 3D Spatial Hypermedia. In: Proceedings ACM Hypertext 2000 (May 30–June 3, San Antonio, Texas), pp. 113–122. ACM Press, New York (2000)

Nielsen, M.B., Kramp, G., Grønbæk, K.: Mobile Augmented Reality Support for Architects based on Feature Tracking Techniques. In: Bubak, M., van Albada, G.D., Sloot, P.M.A., Dongarra, J.J. (eds.) ICCS 2004. LNCS, vol. 3038, pp. 6–9. Springer, Heidelberg (2004)

Schutz, A.: Collected Papers II. In: Broderson, A. (ed.) Studies in Social Theory, Martinus Nijhoff, The Hague (1964)

Streitz, N.A., Geißler, J., Homer, T.: Roomware for Cooperative Buildings: Integrated design of architectural spaces and information spaces. In: Streitz, N.A., Konomi, S., Burkhardt, H.-J. (eds.) CoBuild 1998. LNCS, vol. 1370, pp. 4–21. Springer, Heidelberg (1998)

Suchman, L.: Plans and situated actions. Cambridge University Press, Cambridge (1987)

Ulmer, B., Ishii, H.: Emerging Frameworks for Tangible User Interfaces. In: Carroll, J.M. (ed.) Human-Computer Interaction in the New Millenium, pp. 579–601. Addison-Wesley, Reading (2001)

Want, R., Fishkin, K., Harrison, B., Gujar, A.: Bridging Real and Virtual Worlds with Electronic Tags. In: Proceedings, CHI 99 Human Factors in Computing Systems (Pittsburgh, 15–20 May), pp. 370–377. ACM Press, New York (1999)

Weiser, M.: The Computer for the 21st Century. Scientific American 265, 66–75 (1991)

Part II

Designing for the Home and Social Activities

Co-designing Communication Technology with and for Families – Methods, Experience, Results and Impact

Sinna Lindquist[1], Bo Westerlund[1], Yngve Sundblad[1], Helena Tobiasson[1],
Michel Beaudouin-Lafon[2], and Wendy Mackay[3]

[1] CID at KTH in Stockholm, Sweden
[2] LRI at Université Paris Sud, France
[3] INRIA in Paris, France

1   Introduction

In academia and in industry there have been many projects focusing on technology in domestic spaces and the Smart home (Hindus 2001; Smith 2000). The focus has been on the place, i.e. the home, and the people living there, rather than the people and the places they inhabit. In this chapter we share experience from using cooperative and novel design methods developed within the project interLiving – Designing Interactive, Intergenerational Interfaces for Living Together. The methods were intended to involve families, both as groups and individuals of all ages, as well as the multidisciplinary research group, in co-design of communication devices for families. We highlight methods, results and impact for future research and development. Research presented here aimed to develop novel and appreciated communication artefacts and to improve design methods within participatory design.

The project research group consisted of a Swedish-French consortium that integrated social science, computer science and design. We established multi-year relationships with six families, three in Greater Stockholm and three in Greater Paris, each with multiple generations in two or three households

Approximately 50 family members in the extended families ranging in age from an infant born at the start of the project to a 76-year-old, have engaged in a wide variety of activities, including home interviews and observations, cultural probes (such as their own use of, diaries and still or video cameras to capture aspects of their home lives) and a series of family workshops (sometimes with individual families, groups of families from one country, or with both French and Swedish families). The photo below, shows the whole interLiving team, researchers and family members from both France and Sweden during a joint workshop (Figure 1).

The families did not only provide us with information about themselves, but also tested novel research methods and prototyped a variety of design ideas and tried some of them in their homes or their whereabouts.

With the methods described here we managed to increase our understanding of multi-household interfamily communication, develop and test innovative communication artefacts, and identify the need for new communication appliances for exchange of personal information within families and other close networks.

We identified the needs for interfamily communication as lightweight ways to stay in touch and facilitate everyday interaction. Although the family members actively

N. Streitz, A. Kameas, and I. Mavrommati (Eds.): The Disappearing Computer, LNCS 4500, pp. 99–119, 2007.
© Springer-Verlag Berlin Heidelberg 2007

Fig. 1. French and Swedish families together with researchers at a joint workshop in Paris

use telephone (and some, electronic mail), it was clear that more subtle, less intrusive, forms of communication were missing. We began with shared surfaces across households and then expanded our designs to incorporate ideas from the families and ourselves. We developed a set of working prototypes, which we installed and evaluated in the families' homes over weeks and months.

In order to spread the interLiving methodology in The Disappearing Computer community and among other large audiences, e.g. at conferences, a specific method, the Interactive Thread, was developed for collecting and sharing design experience,

2   Objectives

The research objectives were to create longitudinal, collaborative relationships with distributed families as the foundation for exploring new methods of collaborative design, and to support the needs of these families by developing and testing a variety of innovative artefacts that disappear into the fabric of everyday family life and are used for a length of time.

Thus one specific aim was to try out, modify and describe different methods for co-designing with persons in private and intimate settings. We wanted to develop methods that let the family members participate and influence the design throughout the whole process.

3   Approaches

Here we describe several approaches used for understanding and gaining information about the problems, needs and desires of the families and their members in intergenerational communication.

3.1   Longitudinal Research; Designing with Real People in a Long-Term Relation

There is, of course, knowledge about family life among all of us. We all belong to a family and we all have relations to our parents and siblings, grandparents and cousins. We all have experience of relations and communication, both good and bad. But we saw the participating families, and the individuals within them, as our experts.

The approach was to try to make us, researchers as well as family members, work as a team sharing research and expert experience.

All families are different and we need methods for obtaining an in-depth understanding of how family members communicate, in order to identify areas for improvement. However, we couldn't simply track them in their daily activities or videotape them at home. This would have been too time-consuming in relation to input gained, as well as intrusive for the observed family members.

In similar household settings videotaping has been used in other research projects. One example is the Equator project where they collected about 6000 hours of video with cameras mounted at fixed locations, which gave a rich understanding of family life in a home, but often missed the fine granularity of interaction between the individuals. Other drawbacks with their method was the time it takes to go through hours and hours of video (approximately 27 years!) and the fact that they couldn't put cameras in certain areas or rooms, like in the bathroom or in the bedrooms (Crabtree 2002).

Instead, we had to find creative ways of gathering information about the family members while ensuring their privacy. We had to mix well-known methods with exploring new ones.

An important element of our research agenda was to identify the design space. As Crabtree et al. (2002) point out; the question is less how to build a particular system, but rather determining what to build. We needed effective ways to interact with the families, in order to generate and explore potential design ideas. We needed all individuals' input, especially ideas that derived from their particular family contexts, relationships and communication needs.

We had to find ways of setting our design space, i.e. possible solutions, together with the families (Westerlund 2005). Although problem setting is a natural part of design, the amount of freedom and uncertainty in interLiving was extreme. The problem setting that usually is done during a design process goes hand in hand with problem solving as a way of learning about aspects of the future situation of use, as discussed by Schön (1993, p 18). The activity of problem setting becomes an inquiry into this situation, in order to understand what it is. Thus, the task of problem setting also makes a contribution to the designer's understanding (Gedenryd 1998, p 83). Our roughly outlined design space was information technology for facilitatating intergenerational communication within families.

Also, we need methods for determining success in the real world. A system, that works technically in the lab or receives a positive response in a user evaluation study, may not be accepted by family members in the context of their daily life. Unlike work settings, in which we often can define goals or metrics for success, in a home setting we must rely on more qualitative forms of evaluation. While there may be some recognizable tasks, such as coordinating appointments among family members, much of family life does not involve goals, and views of success may differ. For example, parents may highly value a system that tracks their teenage son, but he may find it oppressive. We need ways to evaluate systems outside the lab and see how and if they are accepted in the real world.

Through the three years of interLiving we have been more and more convinced that designing in close relation with users is an effective way to generate and ground ideas. One cannot simply ask users just to tell what innovative technologies they want in the future. Instead, one has to provide tools and a creative environment that encourages them, as well as us, to explore novel ideas together.

3.2   Triangulation

From the Scandinavian participatory design tradition (Bødker et al. 2000), from cultural probe ideas (Gaver et al. 1999), and from experience of several other user oriented projects as well as the broad scientific variety of the project members we had the opportunity in interLiving to use and further develop a spectrum of methods. These included observation, interviews, cultural probes and technology probes in the homes, and family workshops with scenarios, film-scripts, design games, mock-ups, video prototyping and presentation of novel technologies.

Thus we got complementary and overlapping information through the use of different methods, which made it possible to triangulate (Mackay and Fayard 1997), broadening the perspective and gaining better understanding of the advantages and disadvantages of the methods themselves.

3.3   Working Closely Together in Synchronous Interdisciplinary Teams

With co-operative design we also mean that the interdisciplinary research group, consisting of industrial designers, computer scientists, ethnographers, psychologists, etc. should work closely together continuously during the whole project.

Both the Swedish and the French research laboratories are multidisciplinary, with expertise in computer science, social science, as well as industrial and graphic design. This proved to be an enormous advantage, providing different perspectives and creative solutions, but was also a risk, due to the potentially large communication gap involved in "handing over" information from one discipline to the other (Lantz et al. 2005). Our solution was to involve everyone in all activities, with at least two researchers from different backgrounds present whenever we worked with the family members. Computer scientists interviewed, and ethnographers prototyped. This naturally gave us a broader perspective on family communication in its context, but also increased the level of shared understanding among the researchers both about the user context but, just as important, about what respective researcher contributes in the collaborative work, with the intention to make better design.

3.4   Problems, Needs or Desires?

What should we try to find in our studies? It could be a problem, it could be a need, i.e. trying to find something that is lacking or something that is important and which can be improved. But family life is not only a unit for physical survival. Thus we also tried to look for potential and actual "desires". Fulfilling needs and desires are concepts that often are used as goals for artefacts. Both concepts are part of the construction of something as meaningful.

"Design concerns itself with the meanings artefacts can acquire by their users" (Krippendorff 1995, p 153). We all create meaning with artefacts and the world around us (Cooper 2003). The concept of meaning and the negotiation between need and desire, was of importance in this project. It is important to notice that meaning, in artefacts for example, is constructed by its user(s). From a design aspect we realise that if something is to be regarded as meaningful, it has to be designed and consciously shaped in order to have an expression and character that will both ease the operation and fit into the existing environments (Ilstedt Hjelm 2004). Therefore it was crucial to get inspiration from as real and concrete situations and environments as possible. It is important to keep in mind that these different concepts let us describe and reflect on the world seen through different models. Models are simplified explanations used for emphasising some aspects and suppressing other aspects. This is very useful and revealing, but we must always be careful because the models do not describe the whole real life situation.

3.5   From No Predefined Technology via Technology Probes to Prototypes

One other important approach was to begin this research strand with no specific solution or technology in mind except a general notion to look for communication surfaces. With communication surface we mean any kind of space, virtual or physical, where communication is taking place. From the initial investigations in the project, focused on understanding the communication needs of the families, we could gradually introduce meaningful technology, starting with technology probes for further understanding, and then introducing, testing and evaluating prototypes.

4   Methodology

In the interLiving project we needed to understand what was considered meaningful to people in their specific context. Several different methods were used in combination, such as cultural probes, interviews, observations, workshops, video brainstorming, prototyping in the homes, technology probes and individual assignments. These are described below and the experience from them in the next main section.

There are of course many different ways to combine methods and no approach can guarantee success. Little is actually known about where, why, when and how the ideas, that lead to successful solutions, are generated (Davis and Talbot 1987).

4.1   Cultural Communication Probes

Cultural probes, a technique developed by Bill Gaver in a team at Royal College of Art (Gaver et al. 1999) was used and developed further in interLiving. The initial thought with cultural probes is to create inspirational artefacts that are handed over to the users for them to use and to collect information about themselves, in order to inspire the design team. In interLiving the gathered data from the cultural probes, containing maps, postcards, disposable cameras, etc., was rather used in the collaborative design process (Figure 2). The first activity with the families after having established contact was for the researchers to send out kits with a variety of cultural probes to each household, with containers aimed for the households to fill with their real life experiences (see Figure 2). Through these we intended to get examples of real communication in real contexts. Another aim was to make the content serve as a basis for common discussions and interviews but also to trigger the joint work.

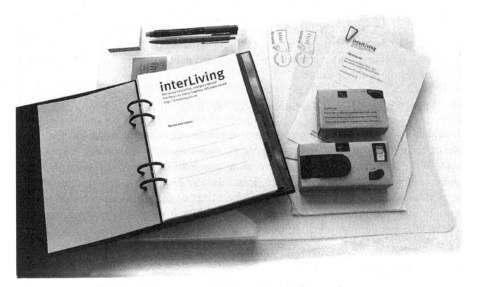

Fig. 2. Cultural communication probe kit: diary and camera

4.2   Family Workshops

The joint family workshops had at least two objectives: to generate design ideas and to get to know one another, both across families and families and researchers. Each workshop activity started with an introduction that framed and focussed the work, such as showing video clips of interviews from the households or displaying photos taken by the families illustrating their environment.

After the introduction the participants express something real and recent that has had some meaning to them, a *use scenario*. It could deal with something problematic, like a breakdown in the internal family communication, or it could be something pleasant, like a family vacation. Typically, a scenario involves some type of communication with others. The concrete, experienced scenario helps to keep the work relevant to and reflecting on real life, expressing real needs and desires. Also, a variety of brainstorming activities and design games were conducted, which helped us and the family members to explore different design ideas.

Far more is revealed and communicated through acting out, instead of only relying on spoken language. Therefore we encouraged the family members to show us how they would like things to work, how they want to interact with artefacts and in what context. The groups developed *design scenarios* and built simple low-tech prototypes with a variety of prototyping materials. The design scenarios were acted out with the help of the low-tech prototypes. The scenarios were often documented as *video prototypes*; the acting out was recorded on video, thus demonstrating novel technologies that they might want to have in their homes.

4.3   Technology Probes

Technology Probes, invented in interLiving, (Hutchinson et al. 2003), combine the social science goal of collecting data about the use of the technology in a real-world setting, the engineering goal of field-testing the technology and the design goal of inspiring users (and designers) to think of new kinds of technology. Technology probes are designed to be extremely simple, usually with a single function, while leaving the interpretation of how to use them as open as possible. The goal is to feed the design process: participants gain experience and new ideas from living with new technologies and researchers obtain data and design ideas from the participants and their use of these technologies in context. Note that technology probes should not be viewed as early prototypes. They must be technically sound and robust enough to be used on a day-to-day basis without technical support. At the same time, they are designed to be thrown away and are not considered technical precursors to later systems. Technology probes should have a single function, with as simple and direct an interface as possible. A probe's single function must be sufficiently attractive for the users to want to interact with it as it is, without training or externally imposed use requirements. A successful technology probe will inspire ideas and should have interpretive flexibility encouraging users to generate unexpected uses (Orlikowski 1992).

The technology probes helped us to address the following three methodological challenges.

1. Providing a non-obtrusive way to learn about a specific family's communication while letting them control their privacy,

2. Letting them use and explore novel communication technologies in their own homes, which provides a much deeper foundation for later collaborative prototyping activities, and

3. Providing a preliminary measure of success, based on the families' patterns and level of use and their reactions over a period of time.

The *videoProbe* is one of two original technology probes (Figure 3). Its function is to take snapshots of daily life of families at home and exchange them with family members living in other households. It is triggered by someone standing still in front of it for a while.

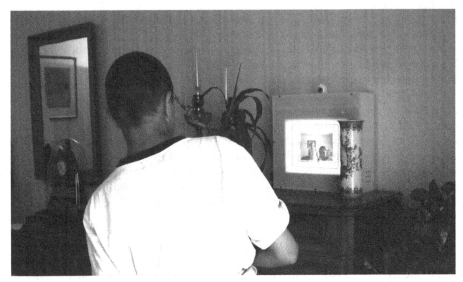

Fig. 3. The videoProbe displays still images taken at a connected remote household

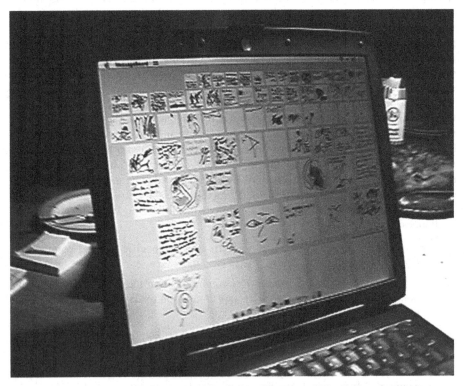

Fig. 4. MessageProbe (on laptop, installed on Wacom and MacCube at families)

Another technology probe, the *messageProbe*, enables family members to draw and write on a shared surface across households (Figure 4). Successive writing pads are generated and shuffled backwards on a display screen with drawing pen. Figure 5 shows examples of usage of the messageProbe.

Both examples combine the goals of gathering data about daily family life, inspiring ideas for new communication technologies and testing them in real-world settings. Family members living in remote households can share pictures, drawings and personal information with each other via a closed, secure network. The probes did not only provide an intimate view of the families and the requirements for a real-world system, but also led us to the novel concept of networked communication appliances.

 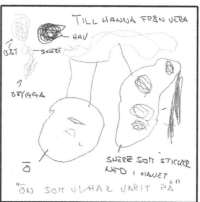

Fig. 5. MessageProbe drawings between two adult sisters and between niece and aunt

Two other technology probes were developed: Mimo and TokiTok. Mimo is a card that allows multiple people, both local and geographically separated, to record and mix video with a tangible interface.

TokiTok is an artefact investigating awareness. When you knock at it in your home it gives away a knock in another connected household. Thus it is a low bandwidth audio channel between two locations that reacts to vibration.

4.4   Prototypes vs Technology Probes

Traditional high-tech prototypes are important for further understanding and reflection of real use situations and usability. They appear later in the design process than technology probes and neither of them can replace the other, they complement each other:

Functionality: Technology probes should be as simple as possible, usually with a single main purpose and two or three easily accessible functions. Prototypes may have many layers of functionality and address a range of needs, not all of which may even be implemented.

Usability: Technology probes are not primarily about usability in the HCI sense, so during the use period, we do not change functions. For prototypes, usability is a primary concern and the design is expected to change during the use period to accommodate input from users.

Logging: Technology probes collect data about relationships within the family and help family members (and researchers) generate ideas for new technology. We should provide ways of visualizing the use of the probes, which can be discussed by both users and designers. Prototypes can collect data as well, but this is not a primary goal.

Flexibility: Although technology probes should not offer many functionality choices, they should be designed to be open-ended with respect to use, and users should be encouraged to reinterpret them and use them in unexpected ways. Prototypes are generally more focused as to purpose and expected manner of use.

Design phase: Technology probes are intended to be introduced early in the design process as a tool for challenging pre-existing ideas and influencing future design. Prototypes appear later in the design process and are improved iteratively, rather than thrown away.

4.5   Interactive Thread

One way of sharing the explored and developed methods among the Disappearing Computer community was the Interactive Thread, a Participatory Design Toolkit in the form of a kit of cards, developed within interLiving, with methods and activities from a variety of disciplines that span the design process (Mackay et al. 2003), It was first used at the DIS2002 conference in London and then at several other such gatherings These special events had several complementary goals: to encourage participants to collaborate with each other in an interactive event, to share and discuss research methods developed by the interLiving project, and to take advantage of the collective design skills of our colleagues to contribute to the development of technologies for a design problem with detail-rich data and design ideas.

Participants receive a Participatory Design Toolkit composed of a set of 12 printed cards. Each describes a participatory design technique, illustrated with a short (15 minute) exercise.

The special sessions can be organised in three parts. The Interactive Thread is introduced in session 1 and the Participatory Design Toolkit is handed out and a specific design problem is described. Participants will then collaborate with each other on two data-gathering exercises: creating a relationship map and using a Polaroid camera as a cultural probe. The results can be assembled into a large poster centrally displayed (Figure 6).

We think that a good way for people to understand participatory design methods is to actively participate in a collaborative design exercise. Thus an enjoyable, educational experience is created for the participants, and, at the same time, it provides new ideas and critical feedback to the design problem.

Summing up, the intention of the Interactive Thread is to meet the following objectives.

- Encourage participants to meet each other and discuss interaction design strategies,

- Teach relevant interactive design techniques

- Test design methods developed by interLiving in new contexts, and

- Gather data and design inspirations about a specific design problem, e.g. family communication.

Fig. 6. Interactive Thread activity at DIS 2002

5   Experience from Activities

5.1   Probing for Understanding

We designed and produced kits of probes. Each of our households got one kit. The kits were produced so that all the contents would have an integrated appearance. It was important that they gave the users a notion of importance and respect. The questions and tasks were very open-ended and we hoped that there would be some unexpected results. We tried to make the probes so that all family members, from one to 76 years old, could contribute. There were plastic pockets to encourage and make it easier for people to collect and send us things. The kit also contained a diary that the family members should write in during a period of two weeks, one work week and one leisure week, and repackaged, disposable cameras with questions printed on them.

We framed the photo probe with three assignments: "Take photos of: places where you leave messages to the others, things that remind you of the others in your family and things that you find pretty or ugly in your home." The purpose of the probe photos was to encourage family members to take pictures of their home environment, emphasizing communication places, artefacts and aesthetics. We wanted the families and their members to reveal to us where and how they find a communication through an artefact meaningful and start a dialogue about aesthetics, Figure 7 and 8 show examples of places where the families leave messages to others in their household.

We wanted spontaneous reactions but we also wanted the people to reflect afterwards on the photos and why they took them. Therefore we had arranged so that the developed photos were sent back to the families for annotating. And after annotation the families sent the photos to us.

The probe photos that were sent to us from the different households had some similarities. Most of the photos of things that were considered "nice" were simply interiors in their homes. People have a hard time making technology fit into their life. Most other things in a household are there because they are experienced as meaningful.

Fig. 7. A shared communication surface. Family members can by a quick overview of the objects see who is home, etc.

Fig. 8. Example of a strategy for getting important messages read. The note lies on the toilet lid

5.2 Probe Diaries

Our probe diaries were interesting for several reasons. We often got several views on the same situation. One Friday Hanna reflected over calling her mother Barbro. But she decided to call the next day instead because she wanted to talk for a long time. Barbro wrote in her own diary that she had thought of calling Hanna the same Friday but decided to wait until Saturday. The reason for this was that she felt that they had a lot to talk about.

The diary probe is a good tool for revealing stories like the one above. This information would be hard to get with other methods because it is about non-communication. The probes gave us insight into the families, but mostly from a few people's view. Head of family = head of probe! We needed a better way of letting all express themselves.

5.3 Probing Different Ages

Different probes help to explore the design space from different perspectives. For the smallest children participating, 3,5 and 1,5 years old, the probes were easy to relate to and simple to handle. The children were given a Polaroid camera and asked to take pictures of things they wanted to show to somebody in their family. The photos were then put into a photo album and their parents annotated them with the children's stories.

The older children, 9 to 14 years old, were lent a simple digital video camera with the assignment to: Describe everyday activities to somebody from outer space that understands your language.

In one of the grandparents' homes it became obvious through observations and interviews that photos of grandchildren, children and events are important in their life. Therefore the grandparents were assigned to make a video describing how they used their collections of photos.

Through these various ways of approaching different age groups we achieved both more interest for the project from these groups and a better understanding of the their everyday life. It is clear that the probes have revealed a lot of information about the complexity and the context seen from the users perspective.

5.4 Workshops

The workshops were carried out on weekends and lasted around five hours including lunch. One objective with the workshops was to help the family members generate and develop design ideas that they experience as meaningful. They were hands-on design exercises in four to five steps.

We started the workshop activities by introducing something that frames or focuses the work. This is not done so much verbally as visually, like showing video clips from interviews with the households. One workshop started with a stack of 17 drawings. Each drawing was inspired by a list of quotes from what the family members had spoken about earlier in the project. The drawings can actually be seen as a form of analysis and synthesises of these quotes. These drawings framed the work into these areas but also opened up for reinterpretations. This feedback gives all participants the opportunity to correct or verify our descriptions. This also gives the different families understandings of the other participating families.

After this introduction the workshops usually continued with a *use scenario* (Figure 9). This is often developed with the help of the *critical incident technique* where the participants express something real and recent that has had some meaning to them. It could have been something problematic, a breakdown or it could be something nice that had happened to them. Usually this should have to do with some type of communication with others. All this helps keeping the work relevant to and reflecting the participants' real life, expressing real needs and desires.

The third step concerned the generation of ideas. Normally a shorter brainstorming sessionwas followed by everybody sharing ideas.

The fourth and longest part was where the groups used one or more of the design ideas to change the use scenario into a better working scenario, a design scenario. Here they did design work, made decisions and contraced the design space. It is important that they show us how they want things to work, how they interact with the artefact and in what context (Westerlund and Lindquist 2006). Therefore the groups were asked to build simple low-tech prototypes of material that we supplied. The members of the group may act out the scenario with the help of the prototype. Sometimes this step was presented as a video prototype. The acting out can be documented on video, other times as a series of photos (Mackay 2000; Ylirisku and Buur 2007).

Fig. 9. A storyboard of a use scenario describing several problems encountered when a daughter tried to have lunch with her mother

Fig. 10. A family workshop discussing low-tech mock-ups

Of course, a lot of exchange of ideas takes place in spoken and written language, but the use of artefacts helps diminishing misinterpretation and negotiation. Figure 10 shows how family members discuss low-tech prototypes. Developing beyond spoken language forces the ideas to be more precisely described (Loi 2004). When a course of events is shown, all the necessary interaction also has to be figured out and the scenarios contain more details. Both the design idea and the contexts are described better. This way of using artefacts also makes it easier to involve people of all ages.

Finally all groups presented their design scenarios and we all reflected on them. It is through that activity that the design is put into other contexts, evaluated, through the other participants. As an example, the fathers and mothers were the most active and suggested family wide control systems. One of the teenage boys built a model of a teleporting device, the "BongoFax", that could be regarded as an escape machine (figure 11). The control that the parents found meaningful to have over their children's location and homework status had very little correspondence in the children's world.

Fig. 11. The BongoFax

5.5   Installation of Technology in Households

Installing new technology into old buildings, in which many of us live, isn't always an easy task. Homes that have had previous inhabitants very often have home made installations and solutions to interior problems. Also, the different technology and service providers do not always communicate.

Installing the videoProbe in the families' households proved more difficult than anticipated. Technology probes must run flawlessly: users will stop using an unreliable system. This is somewhat at odds with the requirement that a technology probe is unfinished and open to interpretation by users, and it requires extra work to make the system robust. For example, we discovered that our ADSL provider shuts down the connection once a day and allocates a new IP number, requiring the router to be reinitialised. In order to make the system as robust as possible, we implemented various watchdogs that check if the videoProbe software is running and responsive and if the network connection is up. If one test fails, the software client is killed and launched again.

The same kinds of problems arouse when installing the messageProbe in some of the households in Stockholm. The families' houses and flats were not newly built, and certainly not with consideration of bringing in tons of new technology equipment that needs electricity and other network connections. This altogether made our installations a continuously ongoing activity of calling different service providers and meetings with families in their homes, which all required a lot of time.

5.6   Prototyping in the Households

In exploratory technology development future use of future artefacts is in focus. In order to tune in the design space both low-tech and high-tech prototypes were installed and used directly in the families' homes. The use of the prototypes was then discussed and evaluated in workshop-like activities in the families' homes. This step naturally gives us a lot of specific information about the use in context. "The practitioner allows himself to experience surprise, puzzlement, or confusion in a situation which he finds uncertain or unique. He reflects on the phenomenon before him, and on the prior understandings, which have been implicit in his behaviour. He carries out an experiment which serves to generate both a new understanding of the phenomenon and a change in the situation." (Schön 1983, p 68)

5.7   Prototypes

Several prototypes considered as innovative distributed communication artefacts were developed and tested using shared surfaces. We describe two such prototypes below: MirrorSapce and InkPad.

MirrorSpace is a proximity-based physical telepresence video appliance. In an empty space, MirrorSpace looks and behaves like an ordinary household mirror (Figure 12). It is in fact augmented with a live-streamed video and is linked to other mirrors that are distributed in remote or local locations.

Fig. 12. & Fig. 13. A MirrorSpace and a superimposed MirrorSpace image

An ultrasonic distance sensor affects the video image rendering in real time. Depending on the physical distance between people and their mirror, the image of themselves and other people will alter. The live video streams from all active places are superimposed onto MirrorSpace, so that two people can make eye contact and merge their portraits into one MirrorSpace with superimposed pictures (Figure 13).

InkPad consists of a shared surface on which the user can draw virtually with time-constrained ink. It is a digital message surface for drawing/writing and sharing notes in real time at a distance, e.g. between households. The ink is supplied by pens handled with interaction device, e.g. mouse, pen or finger, and can have temporal properties such as disappearing after a while, recurring every Monday morning etc. This makes the InkPad useful for messages, reminders and real-time communication both within households and between households. Our intention is to enable communication of both important facts and more informal chatting in a way both youngsters, adults, and elder members of the family, computer literate or not, could find useful and fun.

Fig. 14. The InkPad installed in one of the households

6   Results

The research carried out within the interLiving project has successfully:

- Increased our understanding of multi-household family communication, via a longitudinal study of six families, and of co-adaptation of technology by users;

- Generated novel design methods (specifically, *technology probes* and the *Interactive Thread* as design methods), which have been published and actively shared with other projects;

- Developed and tested innovative distributed communication artefacts using shared surfaces, including four technology probes, all intended for communication between households: VideoProbe (shared video clips), MessageProbe (shared notes), Mimo (shared video mix) and TokiTok (shared knocks), as well as three prototypes: MirrorSpace (proximity-based shared video), FamilyCalendar (paper interface to an on-line calendar), and InkPad (time-constrained shared ink).

- Identified the foundation for a new category of technology devices, called communication appliances, which provide small, secure networks for exchanging personal information within co-located and distributed families.

These innovations in context, process and technology result from our multidisciplinary approach and have served both to define new research problems and to solve them.

7   Lessons Learned - Understanding Design Space

A lot of effort was put into understanding and defining the design space, i.e. possible solutions. This design space is of course constrained by the individual family members' needs and desires but also by the researchers' notion of the project's aim. Not much of this was really known in the beginning of the project except the overall aim of developing "technologies that facilitate communication between generations of family members". The activities that we conducted together with the households gave us answers to what could be interesting but, equally important, what would not fit into the design space. Working with all the different methods gave us over time a clearer view over possible solutions.

To get brilliant design ideas directly from the family members was not really feasible. The ideas they designed and presented were mostly not suitable to go ahead and develop, either because technology isn't there yet to realise them or because it worked against common values and principles of the research team, such as privacy issues and integrity. Instead their ideas proved to be vehicles that enabled us to develop a deep and shared understanding of the families' needs and desires. This knowledge became shared among the researchers and was used to generate design ideas. If you have a common and shared knowledge of your material, the users (here families) and the technology, you as a research group stand on a firmer ground when you decide what to design.

7.1   Problematic Providers and Technology Instead of Problematic Users

In technology development research it is often said that it is time consuming working with users (Blomberg and Henderson 1990). This is true in the sense that you have to spend time with them in the beginning of a project and you need to adjust your methods according to the specific user group.

In interLiving we believed *the users*, distributed over vast areas and in different countries, would be problematic. Instead it turned out to be a real challenge to get *the technology* working. There are many independent factors that can play a decisive role. We would never have guessed that getting broadband to every household and make internet connected applications run smoothly through that would be so complicated and time consuming. We had many technology breakdowns, which were both related to the technology itself, but more alarming, to the companies providing commercial services. Our experience with running technology probes and prototypes in existing homes, dependent on commercial solutions and service providers, was a time consuming activity, probably more time consuming and less awarding than working with the users.

Our pre-understanding of what it could be like to work with families made us carefully choose and use methods, but also to prepare for unforeseen occurrences. So, when the commercial solutions that we paid for and that we assumed would just work, didn't work, we had no good back-up plan.

7.2   Impact for the Future

The design methods described above have already begun to be adopted by other researchers (such as IBM Research, University of Toronto) and have been actively sought by industry (Philips, VTT, Nokia) to help them define requirements for technologies for the home. Longitudinal studies of families provide unique insights into family communication and our published results add to the relevant research literature. The software for some prototypes is currently available via the web under a free software licence. The MirrorSpace has been exhibited in several prestigious exhibitions, including Centre Pompidou.

However, the largest potential long-term impact will derive from our strategy for developing and deploying communication appliances. Although this will require additional research in a future project, the expected impact could be very large, enabling a whole new set of technology artefacts of a style that are currently limited to laboratory research prototypes, but should be usable by a large proportion of the general public.

The research philosophy (multi-disciplinary, collaborative design) of this work, its perspective (families first, not technologies), and a desire to explore a new design space (technologies for distributed, multi-generational families), were achieved via the work with families, development and sharing of innovative design methods and creation of novel communication technologies. We have also been extremely fortunate to identify a new research area of communication appliances and we are now proceeding to the next step, which is to clearly articulate this new type of family network and its associated applications.

The computer industry has repeatedly demonstrated its skill in developing faster, cheaper, smaller, and smarter networked devices. Yet, the most difficult challenge is often truly understanding and satisfying user needs. Just *what* technology makes sense for ordinary people, in the course of their everyday lives? Although general-purpose *information appliances* have been promised for almost 20 years, the vision remains largely unfulfilled. Despite a few notable exceptions, particularly mobile telephones and SMS messaging, many of the promised devices have failed as products (as witnessed by reports from E-Bay of increasing numbers of barely-used e-gadgets for sale) or remained in the labs. Our own research, involving longitudinal, participatory design with families at home, shows that people want *communication appliances*, defined as simple-to-use, single-function devices that let people communicate, passively or actively with one or more remotely-located friends or family. Shared information might include sound, images, video, text or even touch. The desired style of connection may range from focused, synchronous contact to peripheral awareness of one another. Communication can occur over a distance, to other households or places. Communication can also occur over time, including leaving quick messages for oneself and others and preserving and sharing memories over years.

Finally, this experience has been so rewarding not only for the researchers but also for the families and their members that they are most willing to continue as design partners. A continued such relation, in investigating the opportunities mentioned above, will make long-term, longitudinal user studies possible.

Acknowledgements

We extend warm thanks to our approximately 50 family members as design partners in Greater Stockholm and in Greater Paris.

The work presented in this chapter was funded by the European Union as part of the "Disappearing Computer" initiative in the IST-FET programme (contract number IST-2000-26068).

References

Blomberg, J.L., Henderson, A.: Reflections on participatory design: Lessons from the Trillium experience. In: Proceedings of ACM CHI 90 Conference on Human Factors in Computing Systems, pp. 353–359. ACM Press, New York (1990)

Bødker, S., Ehn, P., Sjögren, D., Sundblad, Y.: Co-operative Design - perspectives on 20 years with "the Scandinavian IT Design Model". In: Proceedings of NordiCHI 2000, pp. 1–10 (2000)

Cooper, D.E.: Meaning. Acumen Publishing, Chesham (2003)

Crabtree, A., Rodden, T.: Technology and the Home: Supporting Cooperative Analysis of the Design Space. Position Paper for CHI 2002 New Technologies for Families Workshop (2002) http://www.cs.umd.edu/hcil/interliving/chi02/crabtree.htm

Crabtree, A.: Designing Collaborative systems. A Practical Guide to Ethnography. Springer, London (2003)

Csikszentmihalyi, M., Rochberg-Halton, E.: The meaning of things. Domestic symbols and the self. Cambridge University Press, Cambridge (1981)

Davis, R., Talbot, R.J.: Experiencing ideas. Design Studies 8(1), 17–25 (1987)

Equator Interdisciplinary Research Collaboration, http://www.equator.ac.uk/

Gaver, W., Dunne, A., Pacenti, E.: Projected Realities: Conceptual Design for Cultural Effect. In: Proceedings ACM Human Factors in Computing Systems (CHI '99), pp. 600–608. ACM Press, New York (1999)

Gedenryd, H.: How Designers Work. Making Sense of Authentic Cognitive Activities. Lund University Cognitive Studies, vol. 75. Lund University, Lund (1998)

Gibson, J.: Reasons for realism. Lawrence Erlbaum Associates, Mahwah (1982)

Heskett, J.: Toothpicks and Logos: Design in Everyday Life. Oxford University Press, Oxford (2002)

Hindus, D., Mainwaring, S., Leduc, N., Hagström, A.E., Bayley, O.: Casablanca: designing social communication devices for the home. In: Proceedings of the SIGCHI conference on Human factors in computing, pp. 325–332. ACM Press, Seattle (2001)

Hutchinson, H., Mackay, W., Westerlund, B., Bederson, B., Druin, A., Plaisant, C., Beaudouin-Lafon, M., Conversy, S., Evans, H., Hansen, H., Roussel, N., Eiderbäck, B., Lindquist, S., Sundblad, Y.: Technology Probes: Inspiring Design for and with Families. In: Proceedings of ACM CHI 2003, Fort Lauderdale, Florida, pp. 17–24. ACM Press, New York (2003)

Interliving Project site, http://interliving.kth.se/

Istedt Hjelm S.: Making sense. Design for well-being. Stockholm, KTH, dissertation in Human-Computer Interaction, CID-250 (2004)

Krippendorff, K.: Redesigning Design; Invitation to a Responsible Future. In: Tahkokallio, P., Vihma, S. (eds.) Design - Pleasure or Responsibility? University of Art and Design, Helsinki, pp. 138–162 (1995)

Lantz, A., Räsänen, M., Forstorp, P.A.: Role expectations and relationships in cooperative design projects. TRITA-NA-P0507, IPLab-250. KTH, Stockholm (2005)

Loi D: A suitcase as a PhD? Exploring the potential of travelling containers to articulate the multiple facets of a research thesis. In: Working papers in art and design, vol. 3, the role of the artefact in art & design research. Research Into Practice Conference, Heartfield, London (2004)

Mackay, W.E., Fayard, A.-L.: HCI, Natural Science and Design: A Framework for Triangulation Across Disciplines. In: Proceedings of ACM DIS'97, Designing Interactive Systems, Amsterdam, pp. 223–234. ACM Press, New York (1997)

Mackay, W.E., Ratzer, A.V., Janecek, P.: Video Artefacts for Design: bridging the gap between abstraction and detail. In: Proceedings of ACM DIS'00 (2000)

Mackay, W.E., Evans, H., Hansen, H., Dachary, L., Gaudron, N.: Weaving the Interactive Thread: An Interactive Event for the Tales of the disappearing computer, Santorini, June 2003, pp. 409–415 (2003)

Orlikowski, W.: The Duality of Technology: Rethinking the Concept of Technology in Organizations. Organization Science 3(3), 398–416 (1992)

Schön, D.: The Reflective Practitioner. MIT Press, Cambridge (1983)

Smith, T.: 3Com's first Net appliance - Audrey, in the Register. Posted: 27/09/2000 (2000), http://www.theregister.co.uk/content/1/13558.html

Westerlund, B.: Design space conceptual tool – grasping the design space. In: Proceedings for In the Making, Nordes, the Nordic Design Research Conference, Copenhagen (2005)

Westerlund, B., Lindquist, S.: Case -- How would you phone a deaf person? In: Ylirisku, S., Buur, J. (eds.) Designing with Video, Springer, Heidelberg (2007)

Assembling Connected Cooperative Residential Domains

Tom Rodden[1], Andy Crabtree[1], Terry Hemmings[1], Boriana Koleva[1], Jan Humble[2],
Karl-Petter Åkesson[2], and Pär Hansson[2]

[1] Mixed Reality Lab, University of Nottingham, Nottingham, UK
[2] SICS, Swedish Institute of Computer Science AB, Kista, Sweden

1 Introduction

Between the dazzle of a new building and its eventual corpse ... [lies the] unappreci-
ated, undocumented, awkward-seeming time when it was alive to evolution ... those
are the best years, the time when the building can engage us at our own level of com-
plexity.

– Stewart Brand

Researchers have recently drawn on the work of the architectural historian Stewart
Brand (Brand 1994) to explore the potential of ubiquitous computing for domestic
environments (Rodden and Benford 2003). Of particular relevance is Brand's evolutionary model, characterised by the interplay between the Six S's – Site (where the
home is situated), Structure (the architectural skeleton of the building), Skin (the
cladding of the building; stone, brick, wood, etc.), Services (water, electricity, waste,
etc.), Space-plan (the interior layout of the home, including walls, doors, cupboards,
shelves, etc.) and Stuff (mobilia or artefacts that are located within the Space-plan).
We seek to complement prior research inspired by Brand's model. We focus particularly on the interplay between the Space-plan and Stuff in terms of human interaction.
The supposition underlying this line of inquiry is that computing devices will be situated
within the Space-plan and Stuff of the home and that the effort to develop new technologies for domestic settings may be usefully informed by considering the relationship
between the two from the point of view of use.

We explore the relationship between the Space-plan and the Stuff of the home
firstly by considering the results of a number of ethnographic studies (Crabtree and
Rodden 2002; Crabtree et al. 2002a, 2002b, 2003). These studies draw attention to the
ways in which household members routinely exploit the Space-plan and the Stuff of
the home to meet their practical day-to-day needs. The studies suggest that there is
a need to make interactive devices and associated services available to members
and to allow these to be configured and reconfigured in order that ubiquitous computing might become part and parcel of the "everyday stuff" of the home (Tolmie et
al. 2002). We explore the potential to support the dynamics of interaction through
the development of a lightweight component model that allows household members
to manage the introduction and arrangement of interactive devices. Interaction techniques developed through "mock-up" sessions with end-users enable members to
configure ubiquitous computing in the home via a simple "jigsaw" editor (Humble
et al. 2003).

N. Streitz, A. Kameas, and I. Mavrommati (Eds.): The Disappearing Computer, LNCS 4500, pp. 120–142, 2007.
© Springer-Verlag Berlin Heidelberg 2007

The component model and editor are not only responsive to the findings of ethnographic studies and end-user requirements, but also to one of the major research challenges in the area. With few exceptions (e.g., Gaver et al. 1999; Hindus et al. 2001), the majority of research concerning the potential of ubiquitous computing for the home is currently conducted in "lab houses" (e.g., Kidd et al. 1999; Mozer 1998). As Edwards and Grinter (Edwards and Grinter 2001) point out, however,

> ... while new homes may eventually be purpose-built for smart applications, existing homes are not designed as such. Perhaps homeowners may decide to "upgrade" their homes to support these new technologies. But it seems more likely that new technologies will be brought piecemeal into the home; unlike the "lab houses" that serve as experiments in domestic technology today these homes are not custom designed from the start to accommodate and integrate these technologies.

These real world constraints make it necessary for us to complement lab-based research and consider how users might bring ubiquitous computing into the home in the "piecemeal" fashion predicted. Our component model and editor provide a means of exploring and responding to this challenge and of engaging users with ubiquitous computing at their own level of complexity.

2   Interaction Between Space-Plan and Stuff

A range of ethnographic studies (Crabtree 2003) conducted in the home from the mid-1980s forwards have emphasized the importance of the spatial and temporal nature of technology use in the home (Venkatesh 1985, Mateas et al. 1996; O'Brien et al 1999). More recent studies have examined the "ecological" character of technology use in more detail (Crabtree and Rodden 2002; Crabtree et al. 2002a, 2002b, 2003). These studies show how the Space-plan and Stuff of the home are organizational features of interaction. Specifically, that organization consists of the following features:

- **Ecological[1] Habitats.** These are places where artefacts and media live and where household members go to locate particular resources. They include such places as shelves where phones and address books reside, desks where PCs are situated, tables where mail pending action lives, etc.

- **Activity Centres.** These are places where artefacts and media are manipulated and where information is transformed. They include such things as porches and hallways where mail is organized, sofas where letters are discussed, tables where phone calls are made from, etc.

- **Coordinate Displays.** These are places where media are displayed and made available to residents to coordinate their activities. They include such things as bureaus where mail is displayed for the attention of others, mantelpieces where cards are displayed for social and aesthetic reasons and to remind the recipient to respond, notice boards where appointment cards are displayed, etc.

---

[1] The term 'Ecological' refers here to the physical environment in which work takes place and how that environment and its composite features are integral features of the cooperative accomplishment of work

While discrete, these places often overlap, assuming different functions at different times. For example, the kitchen table may at one time be an ecological habitat where mail pending action lives, at another an activity centre where mail is acted upon (e.g. writing a cheque to pay a bill), and at another time still, it might be a coordinate display where mail is placed for the attention of others. The Space-plan does not simply "contain" action then, but is interwoven with action in various functional ways. In the interweaving it is furthermore apparent that an essential feature of the Space-plans functionality consists of the manipulation of the Stuff of the home.

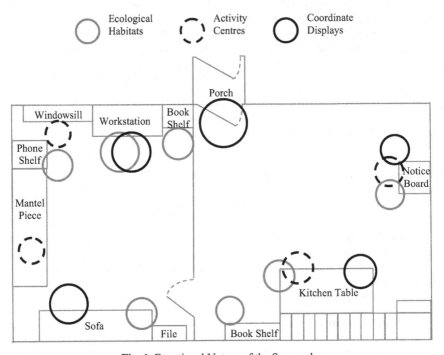

Fig. 1. Functional Nature of the Space-plan

Ethnographic studies inform us that the Stuff of the home is dynamic, coalescing around different sites at different times for the practical purposes of the activities to hand. The places that household members employ to fulfil various functions are places where the Stuff of the home – a range of artefacts and media, such as phones, address books, calendars, letters, emails, etc. – are contingently assembled and used. The Space-plan and the Stuff of the home are tied together in and by interaction and the interplay between the two consists of and relies upon the assembly and manipulation of a bricolage of artefacts and media at various functional sites.

The Space-plan and Stuff of the home are interrelated and tied together then, through the ongoing configuration and reconfiguration of artefacts and media (Crabtree et al. 2002). The functional and configurational character of the interplay between the Space-plan and Stuff of the home draws attention to two basic requirements for the development of ubiquitous computing in domestic settings.

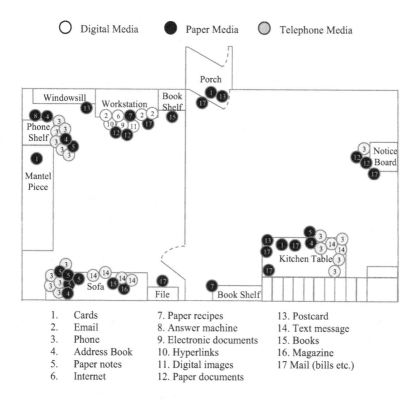

Fig. 2. Bricolage of Stuff at Functional Sites

1. Cards	7. Paper recipes	13. Postcard
2. Email	8. Answer machine	14. Text message
3. Phone	9. Electronic documents	15. Books
4. Address Book	10. Hyperlinks	16. Magazine
5. Paper notes	11. Digital images	17 Mail (bills etc.)
6. Internet	12. Paper documents	

- **Placement.** When designing new technologies for the home there is a need to be sensitive and responsive to the local organization of the Space-plan and enable new technologies to be situated at functional sites within the home.

- **Assembly.** It is not sufficient to simply place new technologies at functional sites in the home, users must be able to configure and reconfigure devices and services across functional sites to meet the day-to-day needs of the household.

We have previously addressed ways in which designers might develop a sensitivity to the local organization of the Space-plan and identify important functional sites for situating ubiquitous computing in the home (Crabtree et al. 2003). We want to concentrate on the second requirement. Enabling users to assemble and manipulate a bricolage of ubiquitous devices is a real challenge for design. If successful, it will not only enable users to manage the introduction of devices in the piecemeal fashion predicted, but also, to dynamically assemble and reassemble arrangements of devices to meet local needs and make ubiquitous computing part and parcel of the "everyday stuff" of the home (Tolmie et al. 2002). In the following section we consider some technical ways in which this might be achieved.

3   Configuring Ubiquitous Stuff

Essentially the challenge here is to enable users to easily place devices in the home, to understand this placement and to rapidly reconfigure those devices. As interactive devices become increasingly ubiquitous the underlying infrastructure supporting them will need to become prominent and available to users. In fact, we would argue that this underlying infrastructure needs to become sufficiently apparent to users to make it part and parcel of their everyday practical reasoning about the nature of their home. Consequently, we need to develop a flexible infrastructure that reduces the cost of introducing new devices and allows users to control and evolve their use within the home. However such an infrastructure need not be intrusive, but form part of the collective of the Space-plan.

A number of existing infrastructures that directly address these challenges include Jini (Waldo 1999), UPnP (www.upnp.org) and the Cooltown infrastructure (http://cooltown.hp.com/cooltownhome/) among others. While these tackle the above challenges directly, they do so for the developer of new devices rather than the eventual inhabitant of a ubiquitous environment. The focus of these infrastructures has by necessity been on the development of appropriate protocols and techniques to allow devices to discover each other and make use of the various facilities they offer. Limited consideration has been given to how inhabitants may see these devices or how they may exploit them to configure novel arrangements meeting particular household demands.

To allow digital devices to be treated as "everyday stuff" we need to open up access to the supporting infrastructure that connects devices and provide users with a simple model that allows them to manage their introduction and arrangement. While existing infrastructures such as Jini provide service and component based abstractions for ubiquitous computing, few researchers have explored how users may be involved within the dynamic configuration of these components. Two notable examples are the Speakeasy system (Newman et al. 2002), which has adopted a composition model based on typed data streams and services, and iStuff (Ballagas et al. 2003) which knits together a number of ubiquitous devices via a state based event heap.

As in the case of iStuff we allow a number of different devices to be composed within a ubiquitous environment. However, our challenge is to allow users to view these compositions and rapidly reconfigure them to meet their changing needs. Below we present a simple user-oriented component model that seeks to allow the rapid composition of devices to meet the everyday interactive arrangement of the home.

3.1   A Compositional Approach to Home Environments

Our starting point has been the development of a component model for ubiquitous devices in home environments. The basis of our component model is the notion of a shadow digital space that acts as a "digital" representation of the physical environment (Fig. 3). Devices can use this shared digital dataspace to become aware of their context, to represent this contextual information to other devices, and to make this manifest in the physical world. The aim of devices within the physical environment is either to make information from the physical available within the digital or to make digital information have a corresponding physical manifestation.

The fundamental aim of components in our arrangement is to ensure the convergence of the physical and the digital environment. There are three main classes of components.

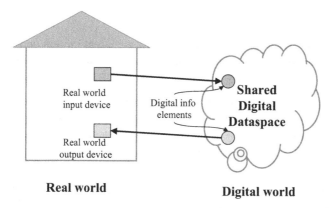

Real world   **Digital world**

Fig. 3. The component model

- **Physical to Digital Transformers**. These take physical effects and transform them into digital effects. Any particular device may make use of a number of transformers. Essentially each transformer measures a physical effect and transforms it into a corresponding digital property that is shared through the data space.

- **Digital to Physical Transformers**. These make digital information physically manifest in the real world. This class of components transforms the values of shared properties to drive some sort of physical device.

- **Digital Transformers**. These act upon digital information and effect digital information. This class of components provides a way to present deeper semantic reactions to changes in the environment to users. For example, data gathered from temperature sensors might be interpreted to herald ambient descriptions, such as warm or cold (see (Humble et al. 2003) for a more detailed description of these component classes).

In the associated toolkit the different transformers are realized as JavaBeans which exposes the properties they wish to share through a distributed digital space or *dataspace*. We exploit our own dataspace called EQUIP (http://www.equator.ac.uk/technology/equip) which provides semantics that are similar to dataspaces such as TSpace. We decided on the Java bean model because of the added benefit of separating individual component development from the infrastructure itself. Our dataspace provides an export facility that introspects the Java software component (i.e. bean) and publishes the relevant component properties associated with the bean. This allows us to incorporate existing and new software components into the infrastructure without the necessity of reengineering the code. Other processes listening to the dataspace can link with the property in the dataspace and be notified when it changes. This model is analogous to the one proposed within iStuff (Ballagas et al. 2003) which provides developers with a set of discrete devices that can be assembled through publication of state information within a dataspace called the event heap.

This project extends this work by focusing on how components – such as the devices in iStuff – and the ways in which they are configured might be exposed to inhabitants for them to reason about and exploit. Consequently, our emphasis is on the development of user-oriented techniques that allow the dynamic composition and assembly of arrangements of devices.

3.2   Interacting with the Component Model

The first issue we had to address concerned how we might present underlying device configurations to users. A number of candidate representations to support practical reasoning within the domestic environment were already available, including variants of electronic wiring diagrams and plumbing schematics currently in use. However, our initial explorations suggested that these were heavily loaded with existing interpretations and their use required a significant degree of technical competence. Consequently, we sought a more neutral approach based on the notion of assembling simple jigsaw-like pieces.

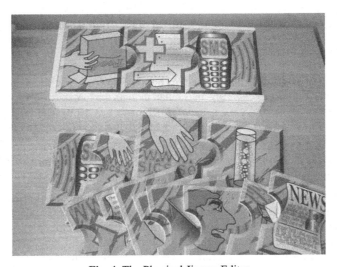

Fig. 4. The Physical Jigsaw Editor

Our choice of the "jigsaw piece" metaphor is based on the familiarity evoked by the notion and the intuitive suggestion of assembly by connecting pieces together. Essentially, we wanted to allow users to connect components and so compose various arrangements through a series of left-to-right couplings of pieces. The "jigsaw" provides a recognizable interaction mechanism for connecting services together. The benefit of this simplified editing mechanism is that inhabitants might more readily understand the environment they are configuring, despite the reduced complexity of assembly.

Our exploration of the applicability of this jigsaw-based approach to reconfiguration was explored through a user-oriented approach. Through a series of focused user workshops we sought to:

- *Understand* the intuitive availability and efficacy of the jigsaw-based approach from inhabitants' point of view.

- *Uncover* inhabitants understanding of abstraction in order that we might keep the level of complexity with in reach of their practical reasoning.

- *Develop* insights into what sorts of devices might fit into real home environments and so inform continued development of new devices and components.

In order to undertake these studies we exploited a paper-based "mock-up" approach (Ehn and Kyng 1991) married to "situated evaluation" (Twidale 1994) where a series of physical jigsaw pieces were made available to users for their practical considerations and recorded on videotape to promote in-depth analysis. We also presented users with a set of initial seed scenarios elaborating various transformers and their potential arrangement. These reflect different levels of abstraction and provide a starting point allowing users to reason about the editor, the complexity of configuration, and the nature of ubiquitous computing in the context of their everyday lives. The seed scenarios were drawn from previous ethnographic studies (Crabtree et al. 2002), and some initial prototype development within a lab based domestic environment. An illustrative selection of scenarios and potential components are presented below.

Seed Scenario #1. A common grocery item is missing from a kitchen cupboard

Using the pieces shown below, **GroceryAlarm** is connected to **AddToList,** which is then connected to **SMSSend**. **GroceryAlarm** reports the missing item after a certain time interval and the missing item is added to an electronic list and then sent via SMS to a mobile phone on request.

GroceryAlarm: Generates names of missing groceries in the cupboard. It detects groceries moving in and out and if one is away more than 30 minutes it is said to be out.

AddToList: Takes an element string and adds it to the list it publishes into the data space.

SMSSend: Takes a message string and sends this as SMS to the given phone.

Seed Scenario #2. A way to access information services from the internet which ties in to common practices, such as reading the newspaper at the breakfast table. Physical icons (Phicons) of various abstract shapes are used to manipulate a web based news feed displayed on the table itself.

Connecting the pieces below, the **TableCommands** receives commands (e.g. "next", "previous") from a physical interaction object (e.g. a "shaker") and controls a **News** service, which in turn is displayed on the **KitchenTableDisplay**.

TableCommands: Reads a physical "shaker" phicon and generates corresponding commands, such as NEXT, PREVIOUS, etc.

News: Takes a command string and outputs a new URL to a news web page.

KitchenTableDisplay: Takes a URL and displays the associated web page.

Seed Scenario #3. Reminders can be directed to a number of outputs

A reminder application lets the user enter textual or auditory reminders (birthdays appointments, schedules, etc.) using a touch display and microphone. This can be connected to a display with speakers, sent to a mobile, etc. The **Reminder** piece can be connected to the either the **KitchenTableDisplay** or **SMSSend** to allow users to receive reminders where they are most appropriate.

Reminder: Corresponds to a reminder application that provides an input GUI, manages the reminder alarms, and publishes reminders as URLs when reminders are due.

KitchenTable Display: Takes a URL and displays the associated web page.

SMSSend: Takes a message string and sends this as SMS to the given phone.

4   Learning from Potential Users

We sought to engage potential users in the development process at an early stage in order that we might establish the veracity of our technological reflections and concepts, and also elaborate future avenues of technical work. Mock-ups provide an opportunity to engage end-users in a formative process of mutual learning. They enable users to get "hands on" experience of potential technological futures, and provide a tangible basis for users to reason about and elaborate technological possibilities. When analysing the mock-up sessions and presenting findings we do so in relation to a number of relevant development criteria (Mogensen 1994) that are concerned to establish whether users can:

- **See the sense of the technology.** On encountering a novel technology, users can rarely see the sense of it. It is not, at first glance, intelligible to them and its potential use must therefore be explained. This involves guiding users through technological functionality and may be accomplished via mockups, prototypes or both. Whatever the medium, the first question is, given that course of explanatory work, will users see the sense of the technology or will it remain unfathomable?

- **Recognise the relevance of the technology to practical activities and practical circumstances.** That users may come to see the sense of the proposed technology does not mean that they will recognize it as relevant to their everyday activities. If users are to engage in any meaningful analysis of the technology's potential utility, and further elaborate functional demands that may be placed on it, then they need to be able to recognize the relevance of the technology to their everyday lives. The question is, will users recognise the relevance of the proposed technology and, if so, in what ways?

- **Determine ways in which the technology might be appropriated.** That a new technology may be recognized as relevant by potential users does not necessarily mean that they wish to appropriate that technology. Naturally there are many reasons for this, though in the early stages of development concerns are likely to be expressed about the available range of functionality. The question is in what ways, if any, will users conceive of appropriating the technology and what will those conceptions be concerned with?

Six mock-up sessions were conducted with eight participants aged from their early twenties to late fifties in six homes. The length of the sessions varied between one and four hours. Below we present a number of session transcripts or *vignettes* conveying the main issues emerging from the mock-up exercise.

4.1   Seeing the Sense of the Technology

Even at this early stage in design it was possible for participants to see the sense of the technology. Although the specific details of participation changed from case to case, the following vignette nevertheless illustrates the way in which our participants generally came to achieve this outcome. It is a transcript excerpt from one of the workshop sessions hosted by Jack, one of our project member ethnographers. We can be sure that participants see the sense of the technology when, as in this case, they make the imaginative leap beyond our initial scenarios to incorporate new elements into the design dialogue. Thus, and by way of example, the vignette shows that Sean makes an imaginative leap from Jack's working of the mock-up, making sense of the technology in the context of his own unique domestic arrangements. Accordingly, Sean speaks of preparing and sending a shopping list to his partner, arriving at concrete sense of the technology by envisioning how it can be incorporated into and tailored to support his life and personal relationships. All our participants came to see the sense of the technology and all did so in similar ways by making the technology relevant to the practical circumstances of their everyday lives. This is of the utmost importance as it in turn moves beyond particular design visions, and the sense others might see in them, to consider ways in which potential users recognise the relevance of the technology to their practical concerns.

Jack is sat at the kitchen table with Sean. The jigsaw pieces are spread out on the table in front of them and Jack is working through the seed scenarios with him.

Jack: OK, so each one of these pieces when they are put together would set up a series of connections (Jack assembles the pieces involved in Seed Scenario #1). So this piece (points to **GroceryAlarm**) connects to this (**AddToList**) and this (**AddToList**) to this (**SMSSend**) and that would then send a message to you, OK?

Sean: So this (pointing to the pieces Jack has connected – see Fig. 5) is configuring it here?

Fig. 5. Mock-up of grocery alarm to SMS service (video frame image)

Jack: Yeah.

Sean: So the computer's in the background somewhere?

Jack: Yeah. Alternatively, you might want a list to be generated and sent to the kitchen table (points to **KitchenTable** jigsaw piece). There could be a display in this table (runs his hand over the table they are sat at) and you could then transfer the list from the table to, say, your PDA. Or you might decide that you want each family member to have an icon (takes an identity card out of his wallet and places on the table). This is you; it's your Identity icon. You could be the administrator for the household - so each person in the house has an Identity icon and they have certain privileges - so you might want to put that down first (puts Identity icon down on table) and that (connects **GroceryAlarm** piece to Identity icon) goes there and that (connects **AddToList** to series – see Fig. 6) goes there and then a list is sent to ...

Sean: Me.

Jack: Yeah, this is your list.

Fig. 6. Mock-up of grocery alarm with identity (video frame image)

Sean: Right, OK. Or you could send it to somebody else, say Charlotte, and make sure she does the shopping instead of me if I'm late home from work.
Jack: Exactly.

4.2 Recognizing the Relevance of the Technology

Recognition of the relevance of the technology follows from the understanding developed of the basic working of the technology – of the assembly of various pieces to produce particular outcomes – and the embedding of that understanding in the participants' practical circumstances. As this vignette makes visible, participants come to recognize and articulate the potential relevance of the technology by continued working of the pieces to meet specific needs, such as the paying of household bills. The vignette, like many others, also instructs us in the participant's grasp of complexity and their ability to handle abstraction, where they take over the assembly of pieces to produce outcomes that are greater than the individual functions of the pieces making up any particular assembly. In other words, in recognizing the relevance of the technology, participants demonstrate the efficacy of the jigsaw metaphor and that reasoning about complexity in this manner is readily intelligible to them. At the same time, and reflexively, in making their own assemblies of pieces, participants articulate areas of activity that they see the technology as being relevant to: paying bills, doing the shopping, organizing the collection of children from school, managing appointments and schedules, monitoring the children, controlling domestic services and appliances, making the home more secure, etc., etc., etc. Participants come to recognise the relevance of the technology by getting their hands on the mock-ups and tailoring their use to address salient issues in their own lives.

Jack has worked through the seed scenarios with another participant, Sam, and she is getting increasingly more curious and articulate about the jigsaw pieces and their potential use. She is starting to "run" with the ideas articulated by Jack, as the following vignette shows:

Sam: What's that? (Points to a piece on the table).
Jack: This is the bubble tower. Say someone's accessed your website – it could be indicated in the water tower with a change in the bubbles or changes of colour.
Sam: Hmmm.
Jack: You can decide what sort information is communicated. So this could be in the corner of the room and its Sunday and
Sam: Actually that's quite a good idea. Let's says you were at work. I know we're talking about home right now but let's say you were at work. Rather than having something like Outlook, you have say a task manager with a list of things (points to the **AddToList** piece then moves her finger, motioning across and down as if to indicate rows and columns). Then say at home, you have bills on your list and you want to be reminded to pay them. So you could have a little sort of nudge in your house, you know, you could see the bubble tower constantly in the corner of the room and you could also be reminded by SMS to your mobile to pay the gas bill or pick the kids up from school.

Fig. 7. Mock-up of grocery alarm to bubble tower (video frame image)

Sam: By the same token you could have your lamp change to blue after that list has been prepared. Effectively you can have your lamp change from amber say to blue when you run out of X number of items of food (connects **GroceryAlarm** to **AddToList** to **BubbleTower** – see Fig. 7). Like that you see.

Jack: Right. Yeah, that's great.

4.3   Appropriating the Technology

In the course of recognizing the potential relevance of the technology participants begin to articulate ways in which the technology might be appropriated. As the sessions unfold, users become more and more familiar with the technological possibilities to-hand and users begin to project the technology into their everyday lives and configure it to meet their particular requirements. These projections go beyond existing design conceptions and engage users and designers in a creative dialogue that conveys participants' practical concerns and reflexively articulates future avenues of work that provide direction for a continued and iterative course of development. User projections elaborated a wide range of practical concerns including being able to survey visitors to the home both from inside and outside the environment, of being connected to family and friends through a variety of devices, of accessing and controlling devices in the home from outside the home. These and a host of other practical concerns elaborate the design domain and real user needs, paramount of which is the ability to configure ubiquitous computing to meet the local, contingent and unique needs of potential users, several of which are articulated in the following vignettes.

4.3.1   The Doorbell

In this sequence of talk we see a specific suggestion emerge that requires the addition of a new component (a doorbell), which the user then exploits to assemble an arrangement of devices to monitor access to the home.

Bill: I might want to see who's coming to the house during the day while I'm at work. So I might want to have this (picks up a blank jigsaw piece) as a door-bell, yes?

Jack: Yes (sketches a Doorbell icon on the blank piece). And when the doorbell is activated it links to?

Bill: A video camera or webcam or something like that.

Jack: Yes a camera, good idea (takes another blank paper jigsaw piece and sketches a Webcam icon).

Bill: Even better. If we have that (points to the newly sketched Webcam icon) and the doorbell rings, OK? Then the image from the webcam goes to

Jack: A web page? (Jack places jigsaw piece showing **WebToText** icon next to jigsaw pieces bearing sketches of Doorbell and Webcam).

Bill: Or even a picture text message. I suppose you could have a picture flashed up on my mobile (points to his Sony Eriksson T300 and then replaces the **Web-ToText** piece with the **SMSRecieve** piece – see Fig. 8) and that shows me just who's at the door!

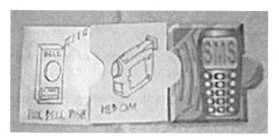

Fig. 8. Mock-up of doorbell-camera-SMS service (video frame image)

Jack: So you'd have an image of who and how many people have been to your home.

Bill: Yeah.

4.3.2 The Office

This sequence of talk suggests the need for more abstracted concepts (in this case the office) to be reflected in the set of components available in the home and for these to be linked with other components to build an arrangement for monitoring the home.

Kate: Let's say you were interested in whose calling at night, as a security measure. If you were in, it could be displayed on your TV screen

Jack: So it goes to your TV at home?

Kate: Yes, or in a little TV monitor that flashes up on your TV, or that's waiting on your TV when you come in from work.

Jack: So you capture pictures with the webcam which sends them to a TV display (sketches a **TVDisplay** icon on a blank jigsaw piece and connects it to the **Webcam** icon).

Kate: You could see the display when you're at home and if you don't want to answer the door you can ignore it. It could come up with a picture of the person at the door automatically in a little insert screen in the corner of the screen while your watching. Or when you come in and turn on your TV you might have a list - a "rogues gallery" of people who have come to your house during the day or night. So when someone says, "I've been and I've tried to deliver this ..." (articulates holding a parcel)

Jack: Yeah, that's a good idea.

Kate: Could you have it sent to work?

Jack: (Sketches an Office icon and then connects the pieces together – see Fig. 9).

Kate: Yeah, that's it.

Fig. 9. Mock-up of home surveillance from the workplace (video frame image)

4.3.3 Main Access Point

In this final sequence the user requests a main point of access to allow her to edit and manipulate the assembly of components.

Jo: Anyway, I don't want to play with your bits anymore (pushes jigsaw pieces away and laughs).

Jack: That's all right.

Jo: You know, my dream is to have one screen which you can access everything through.

Jack: Yeah.

Jo: It's like your main access point - you can access everything through it. That's my thing and I don't think you have a picture of it here?

5   Responding to End-User Projections

Users' projections do not furnish requirements for design – there is not a necessary one-to-one correspondence between user visions and future design work. Rather, users' projections provide inspiration for design. The point might be more readily appreciated if we consider the notion of a "main access point", for example. While intelligible, that notion does not tell us what a main access point might look like, it does not tell us what to build. What it does do is provide a grounded form of inspiration for design which is intimately connected to the development of specific technological concepts through direct user participation. Design work is directed towards developing, in this instance, a single, coherent interface where users can access the technological environment and configure the components therein to meet their particular needs. Below we briefly describe an electronic jigsaw editor and a number of other devices we have developed to articulate the relation between users' projections and design work.

5.1   The Jigsaw Editor Tablet

Responding to the request for a main point of access we constructed the Jigsaw Editor Tablet (Humble et al. 2003). The jigsaw editor (Fig. 10) is made available to users on a tablet PC that uses 802.11 wireless connectivity to communicate with the underlying dataspace. The editor contacts the dataspace through a discovery mechanism of the framework and is initially notified of the components available within the dataspace. The editor is composed of two distinct panels, a list of available components (shown as jigsaw pieces) and an editing canvas. Jigsaw pieces can be dragged and dropped into the editing canvas. The editing canvas serves as the work area for connecting pieces together and visualizing their activities.

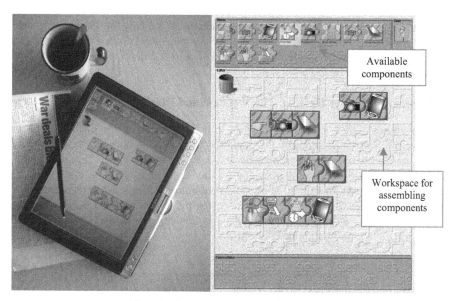

Fig. 10. The Tablet Editor and Editor Screen

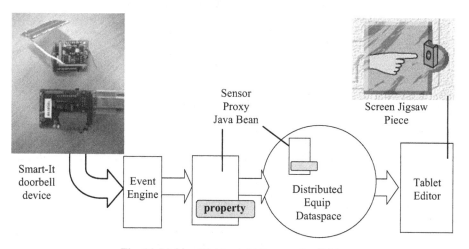

Fig. 11. Making Lightweight Sensors Available

5.2   Adding Simple Sensors: The Doorbell

Responding to the doorbell projection, we extended the set of components to provide a simple touch sensitive component. This component utilizes the Smart-Its toolkit (Smart-Its), a general-purpose hardware toolkit for ubiquitous devices. A component acts as a proxy for the sensor device allowing it to expose the state information in the dataspace (Figure 11).

Once made available to the dataspace the component appears on the jigsaw editor and users can connect the sensor device to other components. For example, the sensor can be used to drive larger scale devices connected to the dataspace. Two such devices are the web camera and a portable display.

5.3   Integrating Larger Devices: The Webcam and Display

The arrangement used to add larger devices to the system is similar to the approach for lightweight sensors. Essentially the device is "wrapped" as a component allowing the associated property to be shared across the dataspace. This means that the device can be combined with the inputs provided by the lightweight sensors. For example, the arrangement shown in Fig. 12 shows the pushbutton being used to signal a webcam to take a picture. Linking the webcam jigsaw piece to a portable display means that this picture is then directed to that display. In this case the display is a driver that sends the image to a mobile phone using MMS.

Fig. 12. The Doorbell, Webcam and Portable Display

5.4   Exploiting Applications: The Blog

Responding to the office projection suggested by users requires us to consider how to ingrate the sensors and devices with more abstract entities. In this case the user suggested that they wanted to be able to monitor the home while at the office. We address this issue by exporting the properties representing larger applications. This allows users to combine these with lightweight sensors and devices.

In order to address the link between the home and the office we see a combination of jigsaw pieces (Fig. 13b) that results in a lightweight sensor (a Smart-It motion sensor (Fig. 13a) triggering a device (a webcam) and making the output from the device available to an application (a blog – Fig. 13c). This configuration means that whenever motion is detected within a space it is used to take a picture that is then automatically added to the blog. Users away from the home can access the blog and view the domestic space remotely, thereby realising the monitoring envisioned by users during the mockup sessions.

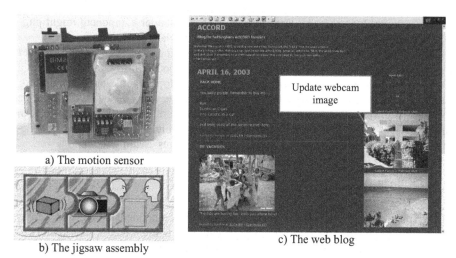

a) The motion sensor

b) The jigsaw assembly

c) The web blog

Fig. 13. Combining a Lightweight Sensor, a Device, and an Application to Monitor a Space

5.5   The Linker Device

The linker device takes an alternative approach to the composition and linking of devices. Rather than provide an overview display that shows the devices and transformations in the home as an abstract graphical representation, the linker device seeks to use physical manipulation within the setting as a means of exploring the properties devices make available to the dataspace and as a means of linking properties on one device with properties on another.

The basic device consists of a PDA which communicates directly with the shared dataspace and a barcode reader that can read barcodes placed on interactive devices (Fig. 14). When the user scans a barcode the linker device queries the dataspace for software properties pertaining to the software component of the physical device (the

Fig. 14. The linking device

physical to digital transformer). For example, an SMS sender component might publish both a phone number and a message property in the dataspace.

The user can select a property through the PDA interface and see what transformer (hence device) the property is linked to. The user can choose to link the property to a property pertaining to another transformer. In order to do this the user can find all of the digital transformers available which have compatible and connectable properties in the system and link the selected property to one of them. Alternatively, the user can scan a second physical device bringing up the compatible properties of the new device. The user can then select the destination property, thus creating the link.

6   Reflections

We have presented the development of a lightweight component model that allows users to manage the introduction and arrangement of new interactive services and devices in the home. The model is responsive to ethnographic studies of the interplay between the Space-plan (interior layout) and Stuff (artefacts) of the home, which emphasize the need to support the dynamic assembly and recombination of ubiquitous Stuff across various functional sites in the home. A tablet-based editor which exploits a jigsaw interaction mechanism has been developed through user-participation and enables household members both to introduce interactive devices in the piecemeal fashion predicted by researchers in the field and to rapidly configure and reconfigure them to meet local needs. In addition to confirming the overall veracity of our design concepts our work with users has also highlighted some broader lessons in designing technologies for domestic settings.

6.1   Inhabitants as Designers and Developers

A key feature of our exploration is that once users became familiar with the broad approach they sought to compose assemblies that met their needs and desires. Essentially, they wished to further refine our existing seed suggestions to interleave them with the practicalities of their everyday lives. For example, users would seek to redirect output to more appropriate devices or even suggest new classes of input and output device. Shifting to consider how we might design for appropriation suggests an interesting relationship between those who seek to design technologies for the home and the inhabitants. Rather than consider design as a problem solving exercise where designers seek to develop a technology to meet a particular need our aim has been to furnish inhabitants with the tools of design. We wish to help users design and develop their own arrangements of technologies just as they design many aspects of their home. We have sought to do this through the provision of a simple editor to allow the direct composition of device assembles.

The jigsaw editor has been improved to allow as much flexibility into the paradigm as possible. For example, among other enhancements it includes features to insert self-authored graphics, images or annotations into the each jigsaw icon, as well as the capability of combining several pieces (or transformers) into a single one to introduce simpler representations of complex behaviours. It is worth stressing that within this approach we are still constraining the potential for development. For example, we do not have the richness of programming expression allowed by iCap (Sohn and Dey 2003).

However, the benefit to be accrued from reducing complexity of assembly is that inhabitants might more readily understand the environment.

6.2 Reasoning with Diverse Elements

It is worth reflecting on the diversity of the components users wished to connect together. It was not unusual to see users develop assemblies that combined lightweight sensors with more traditional computer devices and larger applications and services. For example, users would link something as small as a doorbell with something as complex and varied as "the office". This form of reasoning is somewhat in contrast to how developers might normally consider components where they would seek to understand elements at similar levels of abstraction. It appears from our exploration that inhabitants are less concerned with the variability of the complexity of these components than they are with the interactions between them. We have addressed the need to interconnect components of varying complexity by allowing components to make properties available to a distributed dataspace. This arrangement allows different types of component to offer a very simple state based interface, which can be presented to users to allow them to construct assemblies to meet their particular needs.

6.3 Interleaving the New and the Old

One of the most notable aspects of our sessions with inhabitants was the desire to interleave new devices and facilities with older more established devices and services. For example, users would wish to direct output to their TV or to their mobile phone. Similarly, users would wish to take output from web pages and display this on a local display or to link with their existing alarm systems. Although providing difficult technical challenges links of this form are essential if devices are to be interleaved into the everyday activities of the home. In fact many of our assemblies provided just this function with newer sensors and cameras being connected to more traditional devices such as mobile phones or placing material on the World Wide Web.

6.4 Linking Outside the Home

While the home offers new challenges for designers and developers and suggest new values for design, such as playfulness (Gaver et al. 1999), our explorations also stress that the domestic is interleaved with many activities outside the home. Indeed, these confirm the importance of communication suggested by the Interliving project (Hutchinson et al. 2003) and by Hindus et al. on the Casablanca project (Hindus et al. 2001). Many of the assemblies of devices developed by inhabitants sought to access the outside world from the home or to make the home more accessible from outside. For example, inhabitants sought to send messages to the office or to household members away from the home. We have also aimed to support these through the development of communication facilities including the blog application.

6.5 Future Work

The component model and editor are the product of an ongoing period of interdisciplinary research. Working in cooperation with potential end-users, we continue to iterate and refine the technical infrastructure and toolkit of devices, software, and applications that embed ubiquitous computing in the domestic environment to meet real user needs. Although development is ongoing, our work to date makes a valuable contribution to foundational research in ubiquitous computing for domestic environments, identifying and exploring significant challenges that underpin the migration of ubiquitous computing technology from the research lab into real users homes.

The ACCORD version of the toolkit, including the Jigsaw editor, is publicly available and may be downloaded from the project's website: www.sics.se/accord. This allows developers to wrap their particular sensors, devices or applications as JavaBeans, to provide an iconic representation of the device, and to publish them to our dataspace. Once within the dataspace they become available for use through a number of editors including the Jigsaw editor. Our aim is to allow users more control over the assembly of the ubiquitous devices that share their environment in order that home users can readily situate and exploit ubiquitous technologies within the space they live in.

The ACCORD legacy has provided the launch pad for future home technology research endeavours, such as the Equator Domestic Experience initiative (http://www.equator.ac.uk). It has provided the basic design methodologies and software tools for current ubiquitous technology assemblies. Development is carried on as part of the Equip Component Toolkit ECT (Greenhalgh et al. 2004), which in turn serves as a digital resource for rapid prototyping in academic assignments, design and research collaborations. ECT features vast improvements in the core design of the infrastructure as well as introducing numerous sets of features facilitating third party development and deployment in domestic settings. We are currently in the process of placing a version of the toolkit in a number of domestic environments for prolonged assessment and continued elaboration.

Acknowledgements

This research was funded by the EU Disappearing Computer Initiative, IST-2000-26364 ACCORD (Assembling Connected Cooperative Residential Domains). This article is based on work published in the Proceedings of the 2004 Conference on Designing interactive systems: processes, practices, methods, and techniques.

References

Ballagas, R., Ringel, M., Stone, M., Borchers, J.: iStuff. In: Proceedings of the 2003 CHI Conference on Human Factors in Computing Systems, Florida, pp. 537–544. ACM Press, New York (2003)

Brand, S.: How Buildings Learn. Viking, New York (1994)

Crabtree, A., Rodden, T.: Technology and the home, CHI Workshop. In: Proceedings of the 2002 CHI Conference on Human Factors in Computing Systems, Minneapolis, ACM Press, New York (2002), http://www.cs.umd.edu/hcil/interliving/chi02/

Crabtree, A., Hemmings, T., Rodden, T.: Pattern-based support for interactive design in domestic settings. In: Proceedings of the 2002 Symposium on Designing Interactive Systems, London, pp. 265–276. ACM Press, New York (2002a)

Crabtree, A., Rodden, T., Hemmings, T.: Supporting communication in domestic settings. In: Proceedings of the 2003 Home Oriented Informatics and Telematics Conference, Irvine, California, International Federation for Information Processing (2002b), http://www.crito.uci.edu/noah/HOIT%20Papers/Supporting%20Comm%20Domestic.pdf

Crabtree, A., Rodden, T., Hemmings, T., Benford, S.: Finding a place for UbiComp in the home. In: Dey, A.K., Schmidt, A., McCarthy, J.F. (eds.) UbiComp 2003. LNCS, vol. 2864, pp. 208–226. Springer, Heidelberg (2003)

Crabtree, A.: Designing Collaborative Systems: A Practical Guide to Ethnography. Springer, London (2003)

Edwards, K., Grinter, R.: At home with ubiquitous computing: seven challenges. In: Abowd, G.D., Brumitt, B., Shafer, S. (eds.) Ubicomp 2001: Ubiquitous Computing. LNCS, vol. 2201, pp. 256–272. Springer, Heidelberg (2001)

Ehn, P., Kyng, M.: Cardboard computers: mocking-it-up or hands-on the future. In: Greenbaum, J., Kyng, M. (eds.) Design at Work: Cooperative Design of Computer System, pp. 169–195. Lawrence Erlbaum Associates, Hillsdale (1991)

Gaver, W., Dunne, A., Pacenti, E.: Design: cultural probes. Interactions 6(1), 21–29 (1999)

Greenhalgh, C., Izadi, S., Mathrick, J., Humble, J., Taylor, I.: ECT: A Toolkit to Support Rapid Construction of Ubicomp Environments. In: Proceedings of the Workshop on System Support for Ubiquitous Computing (UbiSys04), Nottingham, England (2004)

Hindus, D., Mainwaring, S.D., Leduc, N., Hagström, A.E., Bayley, O.: Casablanca: designing social communication devices for the home. In: Proceedings of the 2001 CHI Conference on Human Factors in Computing Systems, Seattle, pp. 325–332. ACM Press, New York (2001)

Humble, J., Crabtree, A., Hemmings, T., Åkesson, K.-P., Koleva, B., Rodden, T., Hansson, P.: "Playing with your bits": user-composition of ubiquitous domestic environments. In: Dey, A.K., Schmidt, A., McCarthy, J.F. (eds.) UbiComp 2003. LNCS, vol. 2864, pp. 256–263. Springer, Heidelberg (2003)

Hutchinson, H., Mackay, W., Westerlund, B., Bederson, B.B., Druin, A., Plaisant, C., Beaudouin-Lafon, M., Conversy, S., Evans, H., Hansen, H., Roussel, N., Eiderbäck, B.: Technology probes: inspiring design for and with families. In: Proceedings of the 2003 CHI Conference on Human Factors in Computing Systems, Florida, pp. 17–24. ACM Press, New York (2003)

Kidd, C.D., Orr, R.J., Abowd, G.D., Atkeson, C.G., Essa, I.A., MacIntyre, B., Mynatt, E., Starner, T.E., Newstetter, W.: The aware home: a living laboratory for ubiquitous computing research. In: Streitz, N.A., Hartkopf, V. (eds.) CoBuild 1999. LNCS, vol. 1670, pp. 191–198. Springer, Heidelberg (1999)

Mateas, M., Salvador, T., Scholtz, J., Sorensen, D.: Engineering ethnography in the home. In: Proceedings of the 1996 CHI Conference on Human Factors in Computing Systems, Vancouver, pp. 283–284. ACM Press, New York (1996)

Mogensen P.: Challenging Practice. DAIMI PB 465, Århus University, Dept. of Computer Science (1994)

Mozer, M.: The neural network house. In: Proceedings of the AAAI Symposium on Intelligent Environments, Palo Alto, California, pp. 110–114 (1998)

Newman, M.W., Sedivy, J.Z., Neuwirth, C.M., Edwards, W.K., Hong, J.I., Izadi, S., Marcelo, K., Smith, T.F., Sedivy, J., Newman, M.: Designing for serendipity: supporting end-user configuration of ubiquitous computing environments. In: Proceedings of the 2002 Symposium on Designing Interactive Systems, pp. 147–156. ACM Press, New York (2002)

O'Brien, J., Rodden, T., Rouncefield, M., Hughes, J.A.: At home with the technology. ACM Transactions on Computer-Human. Interaction 6(3), 282–308 (1999)

Rodden, T., Benford, S.: The evolution of buildings and implications for the design of ubiquitous domestic environments. In: Proceedings of the 2003 CHI Conference on Human Factors in Computing Systems, Florida, pp. 9–16. ACM Press, New York (2003)

Smart-Its, http://smart-its.teco.edu

Sohn, T., Dey, A.: iCAP, Interactive Poster. In: Proceedings of the 2003 CHI Conference on Human Factors in Computing, Florida, pp. 974–975. ACM Press, New York (2003)

Tolmie, P., Pycock, J., Diggins, T., Maclean, A., Karsenty, A.: Unremarkable computing. In: Proceedings of the 2002 Conference on Human Factors in Computing Systems, Minneapolis, pp. 399–406. ACM Press, New York (2002)

Twidale, M., Randall, D., Bentley, R.: Situated evaluation for cooperative systems. In: Proceedings of the 1994 ACM Conference on Computer Supported Cooperative Work, Chapel Hill, North Carolina, pp. 441–452. ACM Press, New York (1994)

Venkatesh, A.: A conceptualization of household-technology interaction. Advances in Consumer Research 12, 189–194 (1985)

Waldo, J.: The Jini architecture for network-centric computing. Communications of the ACM 42(7), 76–82 (1999)

Intrusiveness Management for Focused, Efficient, and Enjoyable Activities

Fredrik Espinoza[1], David De Roure[2], Ola Hamfors[1], Lucas Hinz[1], Jesper Holmberg[3],
Carl-Gustaf Jansson[3], Nick Jennings[2], Mike Luck[2], Peter Lönnqvist[3],
Gopal Ramchurn[2], Anna Sandin[1], Mark Thompson[2], and Markus Bylund[1]

[1] Swedish Institute of Computer Science (SICS), Kista, Sweden
[2] Department of Electronics & Computer Science, University
of Southampton, United Kingdom
[3] Department of Computer & Systems Sciences, Stockholm University
and the Royal Institute of Technology, Kista, Sweden

1   Introduction

When technologies for distributed activities develop, in particular the rapidly developing mobile technology, a larger part of our time will be spent connected to our various distributed contexts. When we meet physically we bring technology, both artifacts and services, which enable us to participate in these non-local contexts. Potentially this is a threat to focused and efficient activities due to the intrusiveness of the technology. Our aim is to contribute to the restoration of a number of the desirable properties of traditional local technology-free contexts. The intrusiveness itself is caused by at least four typical phenomena that have influenced current technology:

- Focus-demanding and clearly distinguishable artifacts like phones or PCs explicitly mediate interaction with the distributed context

- The functionality of services is traditionally based upon the assumption that communication is a deterministic flow of passive information, which for example, does not include information of the participants´ current context

- Services in general perform individually and without coordinated communication schemes

- The switches between contexts introduce a high cognitive load as each distributed context typically has its own system of characteristic objects and rules.

In the FEEL project, we have developed a system called "Focused, Efficient and Enjoyable Local Activities with Intrusiveness Management" (FEELIM) that constitutes an intermediate alternative between the technology-dense and technology-free environments, which addresses the problems cited above. This research is based on a collaborative and cooperative setting where problems of intrusiveness management are confounded by several users meeting and cooperating together as opposed to isolated users dealing with similar problems of interruption management (Chen 2004; Ho 2005).

N. Streitz, A. Kameas, and I. Mavrommati (Eds.): The Disappearing Computer, LNCS 4500, pp. 143 – 157, 2007.

2   Objectives

Usability in Physical Spaces

The design of DC environments in the form of physical spaces that support non-intrusive mechanisms for notification, supporting both local and distributed work is important. Usability studies in such physical spaces were conducted, with the following sub-objectives:

- Capturing concrete scenarios for use of integrated local and distributed services
- Making preliminary studies of user needs for the disappearing computer scenario
- Evaluating the usability aspects of concrete disappearing computer environments, in particular the users' experiences of the emergent functionality
- Evaluating the usability of the integrated local and distributed services in the disappearing computer environment (non-intrusive services).

These research issues were thus investigated in interactive environments with multi-modal characteristics, which can enable mechanisms for handling intrusions. This means physical interactive spaces with a rich set of peripherals and computing devices integrated in the interior decoration) and where small wearable/personal devices can interact dynamically with the stationary/public devices to create a total computing and communication DC environment.

3   Principles of Design

We have identified general design principles that can prevent or diminish many of the negative effects of intrusiveness phenomena resulting from work in computer dense environments.

3.1   Creating Adequate Explicit Models of Work Environments

At the core of mechanisms for diminishing intrusiveness phenomena lay good co-ordination strategies. These in turn must rely on adequate models of the tasks being performed in parallel in each work environment (both in large and small scale), the characteristics of the participants, the physical properties of the work environment and the events that occur. We need also explicit and operable representations of these models, such that observations of a variety of contextual factors can be made and mapped onto those representations. One particular problem with the handling of parallel tasks is the cognitive load when switching between tasks. If the services supporting different tasks can minimize the effort in switching between tasks, the effects of intrusions will decrease. The implementation of such functionality in services in turn has to be based on better modelling of tasks and work situations. This also holds for the personalization of work environments, facilitating the configuration or restoration of an appropriate work environment suitable for a particular group.

3.2   Modelling Intrusiveness and Non-intrusiveness

This modelling should cover:

- the social rules valid for a certain situation,
- the normal behavioural and perception patterns within a group, and
- the creation of rough operational initial models.

McFarlane (1999) was the first to dissociate the notion of intrusiveness from the notion of interruption. He defines intrusiveness as the degree of interference with the realization of the main task of a group caused by a number of intrusions. In turn, an intrusion is defined as an occurrence of a process or event that is not intimately related to the current task of a group and that interferes with the realization of that task. It needs to be pointed out that interruptions and intrusions are clearly distinct concepts. According to McFarlane, intrusions are errors where people incorrectly perform actions from a pre-interruption task after task switching while interruptions are methods by which a person shifts his focus of consciousness from one processing stream to another. Whatever the form in which a message is received, according to Clark (1996), people have four possible responses then:

1. take-up with full compliance – handle the interruption immediately.
2. take up with alteration – acknowledge the interruption and agree to handle it later.
3. decline – explicitly refuse to handle the interruption.
4. withdraw – implicitly refuse to handle the interruption by ignoring it.

3.3   Support for Local Collaboration

To remedy the existing imbalance between technology support for shared local tasks and private and often distributed tasks the hardware and software support for local collaboration must be improved with respect to:

- Shared focus by co-use of public devices like interactive walls or tables.
- Simultaneous interaction by co-use of input devices such as mouse and keyboard.
- Transparent interaction in the sense of uniform mechanisms to interact with information elements across physical and virtual boundaries.
- Ad-hoc device integration. The different entities in the room should not be considered as separate artifacts but rather as components in a coherent dynamically configured system. This should also include the personal artifacts being used in the room.
- Personalization of the work space both during and between work sessions.

A lot of work has already been done in order to try and create environments like this, for example in the *Interactive Workspace* project at Stanford University (iwork.stanford.edu) (Johanson et al. 2002) or in the *i-LAND* project at GMD-IPSI (later Fraunhofer), Darmstadt, Germany (www.ipsi.fraunhofer.de/ambiente/) (Streitz et al. 1999, 2001) but none of them has explicitly targeted the issue of intrusiveness.

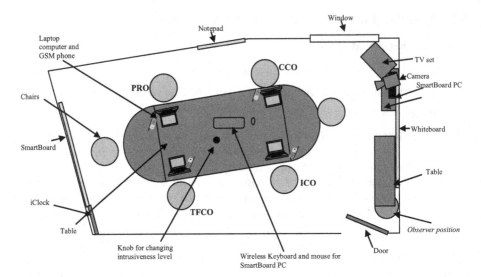

Fig. 1. The physical environment in the 15 square meter room 7517 "Pentagonen" at the IT University in Kista, furnished with chairs and a table catering up to six people. For the shared focus of the experimental groups the room is equipped with a front projected wall-mounted SmartBoard. TFCO, PRO, CCO and ICO represent team members using the room. Specialized hardware devices such as the iClock are described in following sections

4   Implementation

The FEELIM implementation has been build on top of the sView service architecture, see (Bylund 2001; Bylund and Espinoza 2000). The implementation is not a single monolithic component but rather a set of principles and protocols that service modules adhere to as part of their agreement to be FEELIM conformant. The next section describes the sView platform and this is followed by a description of the main FEELIM services.

The sView Service Platform

The sView service platform is an electronic service environment with heavy focus on the individual user. It enables a user to collect, store, and run electronic services, locally, or in a distributed fashion. The whole purpose of sView is to serve as a common area for the services to cooperate amongst themselves and to provide a unified access method to the services for the user. To a developer of services, the sView platform is characterized by openness, modularity, security, and a high degree of flexibility. To a user of the platform, it is accessible in many ways and available continuously.

The system assumes a client/server model, but instead of having a uniform client without service specific functionality for access to all servers (as in the case with the World Wide Web), access to the servers is channelled through a virtual service briefcase. The briefcase in turn supports access from many different types of devices and user interfaces (Nylander and Bylund 2001, 2002). It is also private to an individual

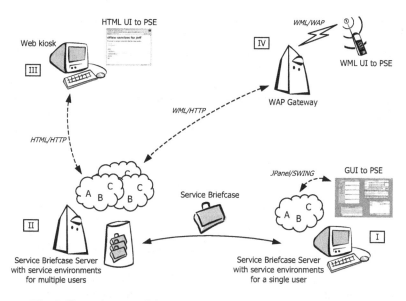

Fig. 2. The main parts of the core sView specification and their relations

user, and it can store service components containing both service logic and data from service providers. This allows the service provider to split the services in two parts. One part provides commonly used functionality and user-specific data that executes and is stored within the virtual briefcase. The other part provides network-based functionality and data that is common between all users. Finally, the service briefcase is mobile and it can follow its user from host to host. This allows local and partially network independent access to the service components in the briefcase.

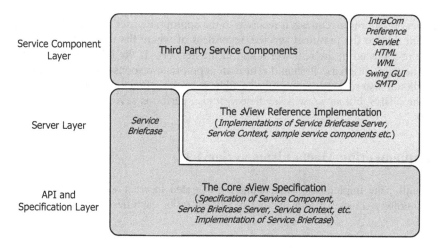

Fig. 3. A schematic overview of the sView system in its three layers

The *core sView specification* provides Application Programming Interfaces (APIs) to developers of service components and service infrastructure that builds on sView technology. Implementing these APIs and adhering to the design guidelines that accompany the APIs, assures compatibility between sView services and service infrastructure of different origin (cf. Figure 1). The *sView reference implementation* provides developers with a development and runtime environment for service components as well as a sample implementation of an sView server. An illustration of how the core specification and the reference implementation are organized in three layers can be seen in Figure 2.

5   The Network Briefcase Lookup Server

The sView platform allows users' service briefcases to move around the network, from server to server (these servers are called sView Enterprise servers and they can house many user's briefcases at once) depending on where in the world and the network the user may be. Since services for a user should always run somewhere, to stand ready in case the use should call, these servers must be situated in the network in computers that are constantly available. This moving around of a user's briefcase of services becomes a problem, however, when someone or something tries to contact the user through one of the services, since it is impossible to know where the briefcase is at the moment. To remedy this problem we have built the Network Briefcase Lookup Server (NBLS).

The NBLS is a server which runs in a well know place in the network. All sView and FEEL sub-systems are aware of its network address and use it to ask for directions when trying to locate a specific user. Users' briefcases all register their own network addresses with the NBLS as soon as they change. Consequently, the NBLS has a constant record of the whereabouts of each user's briefcase, and can forward requests for service or action to the correct one from any incoming request, much like a dynamic DNS provider.

This server can route requests it receives to the appropriate user's service briefcase, and within this, to the pertinent service, regardless of where the user and his or her briefcase are located in the real world and in the network. If the NBLS is unable to contact the user's briefcase it should return an appropriate response and the querying service should also react accordingly. The address tracking function is the main function of the NBLS, but as we will see below, it also performs several other important functions.

6   Implementing Mechanisms as Services

Conceptually, the implemented mechanisms integrated in what we call FEEL software technology consist of four distinct functional tasks, each described in more detail below:

- Filtering
- Routing

- Notification
- File sharing

6.1   Filtering and Scheduling Services

The Sentinel Intrusiveness Controller[1] (Sentinel) is used to establish a common level of agreed upon intrusiveness for an ongoing meeting. The intrusiveness-controlling mechanism is described by the behaviour of the Sentinel in conjunction with the end-user services it controls, as these cooperate to achieve intrusiveness management (see Figure 4). The filtering of notifications relies on the intrusiveness level set in the Sentinel. A high intrusiveness allows for messages to be displayed immediately and in an attention-grabbing manner, whereas a low intrusiveness hinders the message from being immediately displayed, or makes it display less conspicuously.

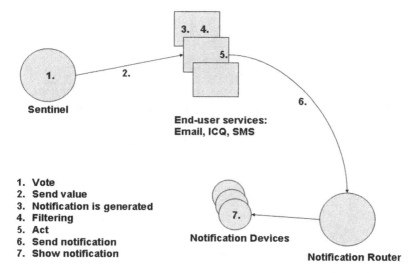

Fig. 4. Sentinel intrusiveness control schema using sView, the Sentinel (in voting mode), and the end-user services, which enable the choice of notification and filtering

6.2   Routing Services

We believe that receiving notifications about messages is less intrusive than receiving real messages. The purpose of the Communication Agent is to act as personal central hub for incoming communications. The Communication Agent does not show the actual content of the incoming messages or phone calls. Instead it decides, based upon the Sentinel value, if the communication is allowed to pass through, or not; if the message is not allowed to pass through the user gets a notification instead (cf. Figure 5). The characteristics of the notification are varying, depending on the current intrusive-

---

[1] One that keeps guard; a sentry. Dictionary.com. The American Heritage Dictionary of the English Language, Fourth Edition. Houghton Mifflin Company, 2004. http://dictionary. reference.com/browse/sentinel (accessed: January 24, 2007).

ness level. If the user is in state A (60-100%, high intrusiveness), a notification is presented in the graphical user interface, and the real communication is let through. The notification contains information about the sender, the message type, and the time it arrived. If the user is in state B (30-60%, medium intrusiveness) the notifications (but no content) are visually presented in the graphical user interface, and on any available public display. The real communication is blocked and queued. Furthermore, the sender receives an auto-reply saying that the message has been queued and will be delivered to the user at later stage. Finally, if the user is in state C (0-30%, low intrusiveness), the communication is blocked and queued, as in the medium state, and auto-replies are sent out. A personal notification is made in the Communication Agent but no public displays are used. The partitioning of three discrete intrusiveness levels was chosen as a reasonable trade-off between an understandable model which would work with users in user tests and a sufficiently interesting span of intrusiveness degrees for demonstrating our findings.

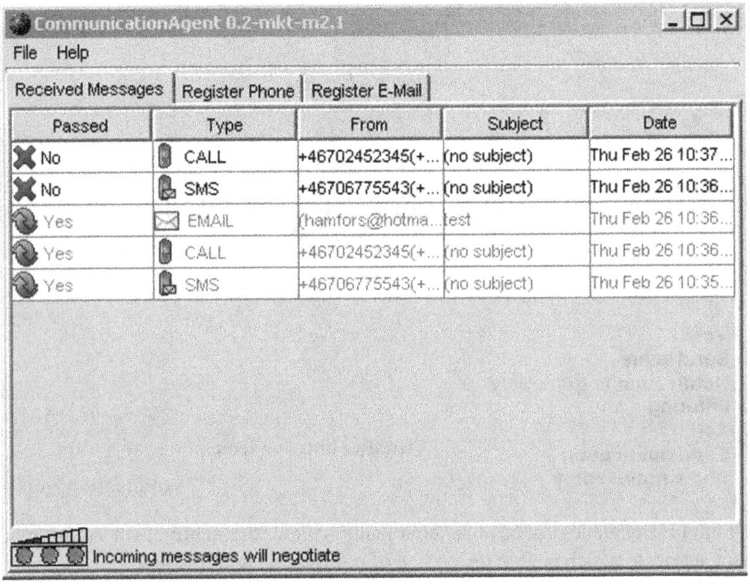

Fig. 5. The Communication Agent, running inside sView in the user's briefcase

6.3   Notification Services and Public Displays

Not all notifications take place within the sView briefcase, which runs on the individual computers of the meeting participants. In some states, notifications are sent to "real world" terminals on public displays. The iClock is implemented as a Java application where the user interface resembles the face of an old-fashioned analogue clock. The clock is publicly displayed on a wall using a small flat screen panel. The iClock is designed to display notifications for incoming messages for all users in its vicinity. When a message is received, the clock display fades out and changes notification mode. In this mode the message is displayed as text. The actual content of the message is not displayed, only, the sender, and the intended recipient and the time stamp, and a notification sound is played. This enables users to notice incoming messages with a minimum of disturbance since the notification sound is very short and the content of the message is withheld. If several notifications arrive at the same time, they are queued by the clock and displayed one after the other in the proper order. In addition to displaying messages, the iClock is aware of the Sentinel states, and the display is coloured in accordance with the state (green for state A, yellow for state B, and red for state C, respectively). The iClock can also be configured to know when messages should be displayed or not, for example only allowing received messages to be displayed in state A.

6.4   File Sharing Services

Zenda is a file-sharing service. It is compatible with sView, but can also run as a stand-alone application. It permits users to start files on each other's computers, using the underlying functionality of the operating system to launch the appropriate application when a file is received. For example, receiving a PDF document will launch Acrobat Reader on the receiving computer. Technically, each running Zenda service instance (running on individual user computers) works as a fileserver, dealing out files, and as a client, receiving files from other Services. Communication between involved users computers for this purpose is enabled by the Jini middleware.

7   The FEEL Intrusiveness Management System

The *FEEL Intrusiveness Management system (FEELIM)* has progressed through iterative development from a set of individual and basic components (the underlying service platform, display devices, negotiation algorithms, etc.) to a fully functioning and demonstrable prototype. Note that FEELIM to a large extent is not visible to the user at all: most of the technology is at work behind the scenes in servers in the network.

The basic intrusiveness management is based on location: where a user is presently located, where a room is located, and so on. An administrator may specify intrusiveness rules for a location, say a meeting room, or the intrusiveness rules may be specified by users themselves when they are in a certain location.

The position of a user is determined by a positioning system based on wireless LAN base station lookup from the SICS *Geonotes* project (Espinoza et al. 2001). This system achieves an accuracy of 10-100 meters since it is based on identifying the position of the closest connected base station, which is registered in a database. The system is further enhanced by allowing users of the system to define arbitrary *place labels* (Espinoza et al. 2001; Fagerberg et al. 2003) tied to any position. These serve to further qualify the position and enables the positioning system to achieve an arbitrary level of accuracy. The position of the user is made available to services in sView through the Position service (see Figure 6). Any other service may subscribe to the Position service for notifications when the user's position changes.

The management of intrusiveness level is based on location, since the location is used by the Sentinel to determine the intrusiveness level. The position or location of a user is of course only one in a probably endlessly large set of possible properties which could be used to influence the intrusiveness management. Location, however,

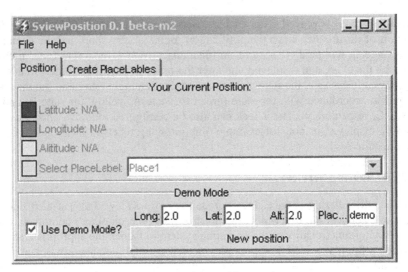

Fig. 6. The sView position service

is easily understood by users and it is often used for conceptual partitioning in real life (stay on this side of the line, park within the parking space, no cell phone use inside the movie theater, borders between countries, etc), and was therefore useful for our user testing purposes.

The intrusiveness level of a location is determined in one of three ways. In the first, there is no pre-set intrusiveness value for the position. This is a very common situation since only a limited set of locations will have been configured by an administrator. In this case any users that happen to meet in this position will have to use local negotiation to determine the appropriate intrusiveness level (local negotiation is explained below). In the second state, the intrusiveness value for the position has been set by an administrator. This situation is straight forward and the rules of the administrator will regulate the intrusiveness levels for any users who meet in that location. In the third state, the intrusiveness value for the position is governed by a hardware knob located in this position. The knob, which is an actual physical device which may be turned left or right to decrease or increase the intrusiveness level, is put in a location to control the intrusiveness rules for that location. Users who meet in the location can turn the knob to regulate the overall intrusiveness management for that spot and the physical properties of the knob make this a tangible experience. Also, since users are in the same location they can discuss, face to face, and agree upon the appropriate turning of the knob. The co-location of users also means that the process of changing the intrusiveness level is apparent to everyone there.

Technically, the knob continuously sends its value to the position database. Any users who are co-located with the knob can query the position database for this value. If the users who are in this position, and by their location are implicitly involved in a common meeting, decide to change the intrusiveness level they can do so using the knob. All users' Sentinel services will find out about this change next time they query the position database for the intrusiveness level. This mode is also characterized by social interaction since it is left up to the meeting participants to discuss how the knob should be set.

Fig. 7. The knob

The hardware knob is a *GriffinTechnologies PowerMate*, a brushed aluminum knob which communicates with a computer through a USB interface. The knob sends events whenever its state is changed; it can be turned in either direction, and addition- ally it works as a button that can be pressed. In our prototype only the turning of the knob is registered. Through low-level drivers the knob communicates with the Linux operating system running on a laptop attached to it, and its events are then forwarded to FEELIM by software running on the computer.

The feedback channels to the users consist of the applications in the sView brief- cases, and the iClock. The sView briefcases of the different users get their intrusion setting events through the NBLS. This means that when a user turns the knob, the knob handling software updates its entry in the NBLS. It then sends a second event to the NBLS, which in turn is forwarded to all sView briefcases, telling them to update their intrusiveness setting. Similarly, when using our Jini architecture, an event is sent through to the NotifyRouter, informing it that a change in the intrusiveness setting has occurred. The NotifyRouter then queries the NBLS, and updates the state of the iClock when a change has occurred. Feedback is then provided to the user through the applications running in the sView briefcases, as well as through the iClock. The ac- tions whenever a user turns the knob are as follows:

1. The user turns the knob

2. Events about the change are sent through USB to the computer to which the knob is attached

3. The events are filtered by low-level drivers, and forwarded to higher-level software

4. The higher-level software updates the intrusiveness entry connected to its loca- tion in the NBLS

5. The higher-level software sends an event to the NBLS that a change has oc- curred

6. The higher-level software sends an event through the Jini middleware to the NotifyRouter, telling it that a change has a occurred

7. The sView briefcases get notified by the NBLS that a change has occurred

8. The sView briefcases query the NBLS to get the new intrusiveness setting for this location

9. The NotifyRouter queries the NBLS to get the new intrusiveness setting

10. Applications, including the IClock, update their interfaces to reflect the change

8   Agent Negotiation

Whenever a message is sent to a user in the meeting room, the user's agent will intercept the message and negotiate for the utility maximizing notification. The utility an agent obtains from a given notification is denoted by its preferences that constitute its utility function. In this work, agents have their preferences specified and fixed a priori. The utility function returns a value between 0 and 1 for a given message received by the agent. The agents can also obtain utility from the "points" that other agents may share with them.

Whenever a message is displayed on a given device, the agent handling that message must pay an appropriate fee to the system agent managing the meeting room. There is no cost to sending notifications to private/non-disturbing devices, but the cost increases the more intrusive the device is. However, the more intrusive the device, the more it will catch other users' attention. Thus other users have an interest in getting certain messages displayed on these devices and will pay a part of the cost, if and only if the contents/recipient/sender of the message brings them some utility. Negotiation (even when there is no need to display on a public device) can then lead to an important message (for other users) being transmitted to a public device (in case it also brings some utility to the direct recipient of that message). The decision making of an agent receiving a message is generally as follows:

- Receive message and parse subject and sender fields to see if matching with preferences of owner (user).

- If message is of no value (i.e. no sender or subject found in the preference list), do not use any arguments in ensuing negotiation.

- Otherwise, negotiate using promises and appeals (to past promises) with other agents.

- If funds received from other agents then choose the public display if sufficient funds are available.

- Else choose the instant messenger if sufficient funds are available.

- else choose the email client (or queue)

- Send confirmation to meeting-room server and update all agents' budgets and commitments accordingly.

The algorithm for the negotiation is as follows.

- Start

- Agent receives the message - parses its contents and determines utility.

- Agent sends out offers to all agents – offer (msg, DeviceX) - for every device available to it. (We assume here that messages do not need to be private but can easily retract that assumption if we simply code the agent to "silently" notify its user).

- Agents respond with their investment given the argument supplied and the message. The offer is not made strategically but in good faith.

- Proponent then pools the investments and determines the device all other agents are willing to invest in according the utility it derives from each.

- Proponent then notifies all agents of its final decision (allowing other agents to store commitments and deduct investments).

- Proponent sends appropriate investment to system agent (keeps the extra for itself) and gets the message displayed.

- End

The choice of which argument to send is dependent on whether the opponent in the negotiation has made promises in the past and whether the proponent is in a position (given its budget) to make a promise of a future reward. In trying to maximize utility, the proponent will go for an appeal if this is enough to cover its needs for funds. Otherwise, the proponent may make a promise of future points.

The above process happens sequentially with all opponents in the environment. In this way, the proponent cumulates points from past negotiations as it is negotiating with each agent. In doing so, the proponent also keeps tracks of promises it is making and appeals it is making and therefore adjusting its cost and budget for that set of negotiation.

9   Potential Impact of Results

We have demonstrated that it is possible to develop a robust prototype, i.e. our FEELIM system, which can handle intrusiveness from standard communication services in a collaborative work setting. The prototype is realistic in the sense that it handles real communication services like phone, SMS, instant messaging and email in a general fashion. The prototype together with demonstration scripts that we developed in the project is an excellent basis for discussions with telecom operators and other service providers on the development of commercial services built upon the same principles as FEELIM.

The commercial development in the area of embedded systems, mobile and hand-held computing is fast and short sighted; little effort is put into usability, considering the usage of the products in a situated usage context. This results in products that might fit an isolated usage scenario, but create problems when introduced en-masse in actual working contexts. This is a potential threat to health and quality of life for such systems' users.

The explicit purpose of the FEEL technology is to increase quality of life in the sense of improving the work environment in collaborative work situations. If intrusions can be diminished in such situations, the level of stress can be lowered and the efficiency and shared focus can be promoted. Even if the FEEL project has studied collaborative work situations, the FEEL technology is applicable also in many other situations of everyday life, where a focused co-located setting has to be protected against potentially intrusive communication requests.

Acknowledgements

The authors acknowledge the funding of the FEEL project by the European Community under the "Information Society Technologies" Programme (project IST-2000-26135).

The authors wish to thank research administrators Gloria Dixon-Svärd (DSV) and Eva Gudmunsson (SICS). Important technical contributions were also made by DSV master students Pelle Carlsson, Jennie Carlstedt, and Oskar Laurin.

References

Bylund, M.: Personal Service Environments - Openness and User Control in User-Service Interaction. Licentiate Thesis, Uppsala University (2001)

Bylund, M., Espinoza, F.: sView – Personalized Service Interaction. In: Bradshaw, J., Arnold, G. (eds.) Proceedings of 5th International Conference on the Practical Application of Intelligent Agents and Multi-Agent Technology (PAAM 2000), pp. 215–218. The Practical Application Company Ltd., Manchester, UK (2000)

Chen, D., Vertegaal, R.: Using mental load for managing interruptions in physiologically attentive user interfaces. In: CHI '04 extended abstracts on Human factors in computing systems, Vienna, Austria, pp. 1513–1516 (2004)

Clark, H.H.: Using Language. Cambridge University Press, UK (1996)

Espinoza, F. et al.: GeoNotes: Social and Navigational Aspects of Location-Based Information Systems. In: Abowd, G.D., Brumitt, B., Shafer, S. (eds.) Ubicomp 2001: Ubiquitous Computing. LNCS, vol. 2201, pp. 2–18. Springer, Heidelberg (2001)

Fagerberg, P., Espinoza, F., Persson, P.: What is a place? Allowing users to name and define places. In: Proceedings of ACM Conference on Human Factors in Computing Systems (CHI 2003), pp. 828–829. ACM Press, New York (2003)

Ho, J., Intille, S.S.: Using context-aware computing to reduce the perceived burden of interruptions from mobile devices. In: Proceedings of the SIGCHI conference on Human factors in computing systems, Portland, Oregon, USA, pp. 909–918 (2005)

Johanson, B., Fox, A., Winograd, T.: The Interactive Workspaces Project: Experiences with Ubiquitous Computing Rooms. In: IEEE Pervasive Computing, pp. 67–74. IEEE Computer Society Press, Los Alamitos (2002)

McFarlane, D.: Coordinating the interruption of people in human-computer interaction. In: Human Computer Interaction - INTERACT'99, Riccarton, Edinburgh, Scotland (1999)

Nylander, S., Bylund, M.: Providing device independence to mobile services. In: Carbonell, N., Stephanidis, C. (eds.) Universal Access. Theoretical Perspectives, Practice, and Experience. LNCS, vol. 2615, pp. 465–473. Springer, Heidelberg (2003)

Nylander, S., Bylund, M.: Device Independent Services. SICS Technical Report T2002:02 (2002)

Ramchurn, S.D.: Multi-Agent Negotiation using Trust and Persuasion. PhD, Electronics and Computer Science, University of Southampton (2004)

Ramchurn, S.D., Deitch, B., Thompson, M.K., de Roure, D.C., Jennings, N.R., Luck, M.: Minimising intrusiveness in pervasive computing environments using multi-agent negotiation. In: Proceedings of 1st Int. Conf. on Mobile and Ubiquitous Systems, Boston, USA, pp. 364–372 (2004)

Ramchurn, S.D., Jennings, N.R., Sierra, C.: Persuasive negotiation for autonomous agents: A rhetorical approach. In: Kurumatani, K., Chen, S.-H., Ohuchi, A. (eds.) IJCAI-WS 2003 and MAMUS 2003. LNCS (LNAI), vol. 3012, pp. 9–17. Springer, Heidelberg (2004)

Streitz, N., Geißler, J., Holmer, T., Konomi, S., Müller-Tomfelde, C., Reischl, W., Rexroth, P., Seitz, P., Steinmetz, R.: i-LAND: An interactive Landscape for Creativity and Innovation. In: ACM Conference on Human Factors in Computing Systems (CHI'99), Pittsburgh, Pennsylvania, USA, pp. 120–127. ACM Press, New York (1999)

Streitz, N., Tandler, P., Müller-Tomfelde, C., Konomi, S.: Roomware: Towards the Next Generation of Human-Computer Interaction based on an Integrated Design of Real and Virtual Worlds. In: Carroll, J. (ed.) Human-Computer Interaction in the New Millennium, pp. 553–578. Addison-Wesley, Reading (2001)

Towards Ubiquitous Computing Applications Composed from Functionally Autonomous Hybrid Artifacts

Nicolas Drossos[1], Irene Mavrommati[1], and Achilles Kameas[1,2]

[1] Computer Technology Institute, Patras, Greece
[2] Hellenic Open University, Greece

1   Introduction

People are an intrinsic part of a Disappearing Computer environment; it is their actions and behavior, their wishes and needs that shape the environment. People have always been building "ecologies" in their living spaces, by selecting objects and then arranging them in ways that best serve their activities and their self-expression. According to the Ambient Intelligence (AmI) vision (ISTAG 2006) people will be able to build more advanced "ecologies", also known as *UbiComp applications*, by configuring and using "augmented" objects; these objects may be totally new ones or updated versions of existing ones. An important new aspect of *AmI environments* is the merging of physical and digital spaces, i.e. tangible objects and physical environments are acquiring digital representations. The traditional computer disappears in the environment, as the everyday objects in it become augmented with Information and Communication Technology (ICT) components (i.e. sensors, actuators, processor, memory, communication modules, etc.) and can receive, store, process and transmit information, thus becoming *AmI objects.*

AmI objects are considered to extend the functionality of physical objects, which nevertheless still maintain their physical properties and natural uses i.e. an "augmented desk" is still a desk that can be used as such without any dependencies from other objects or environmental factors. The artifacts' dependence on a source of power is another factor that determines their autonomy, but it will not be dealt with in this chapter.

When thinking of UbiComp applications for everyday life, it comes out that almost every object, be it physical or software, portable or stationary, resource constrained or not, can potentially become an AmI object and participate in such applications. This means that AmI objects may have to exchange data if combined in the same application, although they may be created by various manufacturers, using various, often proprietary software or hardware technologies or protocols. This heterogeneity factor constitutes a key challenge for systems aiming to support the composition of UbiComp applications.

Another important challenge is the dynamic nature of UbiComp applications deriving both from the dynamic and ad-hoc way that people use UbiComp applications and from the fact that AmI objects are susceptible to failures (e.g. hardware, communication etc.). Thus UbiComp applications need to be *easy-to-use* for a wide range of users, *adaptive* to contextual changes, *robust* enough and *fault-tolerant*. *Scalability* is also a tough issue, since UbiComp applications usually involve a large number of participating AmI objects.

N. Streitz, A. Kameas, and I. Mavrommati (Eds.): The Disappearing Computer, LNCS 4500, pp. 161–181, 2007.

In the end, the human element can be catalytic for the whole system: one of the factors that can cause "emerging" and previously unforeseen functionality is the inherent human creativity and the human capability for problem solving and expression. Nevertheless, this relies on people's willingness to adopt ubiquitous computing technology and their understanding of it, the technology's learnability, flexibility and openness for adaptation.

Adoption depends on understanding, which is a two-way channel between two seemingly distant terrains: technology providers have to understand people's needs and wants; people have to understand the capabilities, limitations and use of the new technology. The research that is described in this chapter aims to create a conceptual framework that will increase the bandwidth of the "understanding channel" and provide the technological platform and tools that will support the development of Ubiquitous computing applications.

2   An Overview of Existing UbiComp Approaches

Building and supporting the operation of UbiComp applications is a demanding task, as it comes up against a number of challenges inherent in distributed systems; more constraints are imposed, new parameters are introduced, a wider user community is targeted, to mention but some. Some of the major requirements a UbiComp system has to confront are: mask the *heterogeneity* of networks, hardware, operating systems etc.; tackle *mobility* and *unavailability* of nodes; support component *composition* into applications; *context awareness*; preserve object *autonomy* even for *resource constraint* devices; be *robust, fault tolerant* and *scalable; adapt* to environmental changes; and *be usable by novice users* via understandable designed models.

In this section, we shall briefly present several different approaches that deal with the open research issues of the UbiComp paradigm. We have grouped them based on a set of broad research areas, which nevertheless covers the UbiComp domain: middleware, architecture, user tools, applications and integration; in this chapter we do not concern ourselves with hardware issues and communication / networking protocols.

Research efforts on *user tools* try to ease the process of development for end-users who have little or no programming experience. The work by Humble *et al.* (Humble 2003) for example, uses a "jigsaw puzzle" metaphor in the Graphical User Interface (GUI). Individual devices and sensors are represented by puzzle piece-shaped icons that the user "snaps" together to build an application. While this metaphor is comprehensible, the interactions are simplified to sequential execution of actions and reactions depending on local properties (e.g. sensor events), which limits the potential to express many of the user's ideas. Similar approaches can be seen in the work of Truong et al (Truong 2004) that provides a pseudo-natural language interface, using a fridge magnet metaphor, and also in the browser approach of Speakeasy (Edwards 2002), where components are connected using a visual editor based on file-system browsers.

In (Jacquet 2005) is presented a clear conceptual model for ambient computing systems together with an architecture that introduces a high-level mechanism to abstract context and allows the rapid construction of ambient computing applications. The model uses a well-defined vocabulary and tries to map the physical and virtual world to elementary component objects, which can be interconnected to form applications. The architecture however, limits the real world's representation to sets of sensors. This restricts the model's scope, while components loose their autonomy.

Other research efforts are emphasizing on the design of ubiquitous computing *architectures*. Project "Smart-Its" (Holmquist 2004) aims at developing small devices, which, when attached to objects, enable their association based on the concept of "context proximity". Objects are usually ordinary ones such as cups, tables, chairs etc., equipped with various sensors, as well as with a wireless communication module such as RF or Bluetooth. While a single Smart-It is able to perceive context information from its integrated sensors, a federation of ad hoc connected Smart-Its can gain collective awareness by sharing this information. However, the "augmentation" of physical objects is not related in any way with their "nature", thus the objects ends up to be just physical containers of the computational modules they host.

Project 2WEAR (Lalis et al. 2007, in this book) explores the concept of a personal system that is formed by putting together computing elements in an ad-hoc fashion using short-range radio. These elements may be embedded into wearable objects, or have the form of more conventional portable computers and mobile phones or are stationary elements that constitute a technological infrastructure. Interactions among objects are based on services, while users can build configurations flexibly using physical proximity as an interaction selection mechanism.

Representative approaches that focus on the development of *middleware* systems are BASE and Proem. BASE (Becker 2003; Weis 2006) presents a micro-kernel based middleware that is structured in multiple components that can be dynamically extended to interact with different existing middleware solutions and different communication technologies. While these approaches provide support for heterogeneity and a uniform abstraction of services the application programming interface requires specific programming capabilities (e.g., proxies as API) to building applications. Proem (Kortuem 2001) is a p2p platform supporting the application developer in creating and deploying applications. The objects managed by Proem are mainly electronic devices, such as PDAs and mobiles, and are abstracted as entities. Connectivity between entities is determined by proximity, while connected entities can form communities. Proem develops communication protocols that define the syntax and semantics of messages exchanged between peers, as well as an application environment including tools, APIs and logical structures. However, Proem does not consider multi-hop mobile ad hoc networks, while proximity poses severe limitations in the formation of UbiComp applications.

A recent research effort, ZUMA (Baker 2006) describes a platform based on a set of clean abstractions for users, content, and devices. The platform enables configuration and organization of content and networked heterogeneous devices in a smart-home environment. The main goals of this work is to achieve interconnection between incompatible devices, resolve conflicting personalization issues according to the users' properties, permissions and preferences, and achieve uniform control and manipulation of the environment. ZUMA employs the notion of multi-user optimal experience and attempts to achieve optimization by migrating applications to different environments. However, the information the system acquires by monitoring the environment via devices and sensor networks is combined with fixed knowledge e.g. regarding a person's permissions or preferences and the produced behaviour is in fact predetermined actions based on simple rules. This results in the system operating without taking into consideration possible current user's feedback, while the user model for building pervasive applications is not very clear.

Finally, there are several approaches trying to establish some kind of *integrated*, preinstalled infrastructure in a physical area, e.g. a room or building, often called an intelligent environment (IE), in which the user and his/her mobile devices are integrated on-the-fly when entering the area. A representative research effort is taken by project Aura (Garlan 2002), which aims to "minimize distractions on user's attention, creating an integrated environment that adapts to the user's context and needs". Aura's goal is to provide each user with an invisible halo of computing and information services that persists regardless of location.

Project iROS (Johanson 2002), considers physically bounded spaces such as offices and meeting rooms that together provide low-level functionality. The system is modeled as an ensemble of entities that interact with each other using message passing. However, iROS does not provide explicit support for application development and management; instead, it relies on service synchronization using an event heap.

Last but not least, project "Ambient Agoras" (Streitz et al. 2005; Streitz et al. 2007, in this book) aims at providing situated services, place-relevant information, and feeling of the place ("genius loci") to the users, so that they feel at home in the office, by using mobile and embedded information technology. "Ambient Agoras" aims at turning every place into a social marketplace (= "agora") of ideas and information where people can interact and communicate.

All these research efforts, together with various research initiatives (i.e. DC 2006) have given us a glimpse of what the UbiComp-enabled future might perhaps bring. As Weiser noted in his seminal paper, we don't really know what's coming (Weiser 1993): *"Neither an explication of the principles of ubiquitous computing nor a list of the technologies involved really gives a sense of what it would be like to live in a world full of invisible widgets. To extrapolate from today's rudimentary fragments of embodied virtuality resembles an attempt to predict the publication of Finnegan's Wake after just having invented writing on clay tablets. Nevertheless the effort is probably worthwhile."*

3   A New Approach for Shaping UbiComp Environments

The ways that we can use an ordinary object are a direct consequence of the anticipated uses that object designers "embed" into the object's physical properties. This association is in fact bi-directional: the objects have been designed to be suitable for certain tasks, but it is also their physical properties that constrain the tasks people use them for. According to D. Norman (Norman 1988) affordances "refer to the perceived and actual properties of the thing, primarily those fundamental properties that determine just how the thing could possibly be used". We therefore say that an object may "afford" some sorts of action, and when it does so, this results in a set of natural or "easy" relations.

Due to their "digital self", AmI objects can now publicize their abilities in the digital space. These include properties (what the object is), capabilities (what the object knows to do) and services (what the object can offer to others). At the same time, they acquire extra capabilities, which during the formation of UbiComp applications, can be combined with capabilities of other AmI objects or adapt to the context of operation. Thus, AmI objects offer two new affordances to their users:

- Composeability: artifacts can be used as building blocks of larger and more complex systems. Composeability is perceived by users through the presentation -via the object's digital self- of the object's connectable capabilities, and thus provide users the possibility to achieve connections and compose applications of two or more objects.

- Changeability: artifacts that possess or have access to digital storage can change the digital services they offer. In other words, the tangible object can be partially disassociated from the artifact's digital services, because the latter result from the execution of stored programs.

Both these affordances are a result of the ability to produce descriptions of properties, abilities and services, which carry information about the artifact in the digital space. This ability improves object / service independence, as an AmI object that acts as a service consumer may seek a service producer based only on a service description. For example, consider the analogy of someone wanting to drive a nail and asking not for the hammer, but for any object that could offer a hammering service (could be a large flat stone). In order to be consistent with the physical world, functional *autonomy* of AmI objects must also be preserved; thus, they must be capable to function without any dependencies from other AmI objects or infrastructure.

Newman states that "Systems should inherently support the ability of users to assemble available resources to accomplish their tasks. ....there will always be particular combinations of functionality for which no application has been expressly written" (Newman 2002). By considering AmI objects as resources, Newman's statement points out that the possible combinations of AmI objects cannot be foreseen, since people –who create and use these objects- are inherently unpredictable.

Instead of trying to predetermine a range of likely UbiComp applications, what seems more familiar to people's way of acting is to make AmI objects *composeable,* that is, make them capable of being easily composed as building blocks into larger and more complex systems. In this way, designing and implementing UbiComp applications could become an apprehensible procedure that even non experts can carry out provided that they are supported by proper end-user tools. Moreover, this approach is also more economically viable, as new applications can be created by sharing or reusing existing AmI objects, thus minimizing the need for acquiring new components.

For the AmI vision to succeed, nobody should be excluded from using UbiComp technology or accessing UbiComp applications or system services. The designers / users dichotomy appears again, only this time it is easier for users to act as designers themselves. People actively participate in shaping UbiComp environments, so the provision of models and metaphors, cognitive or semantic, is necessary to make sure that these environments are coherent and understandable.

The UbiComp paradigm introduces several challenges for people. At first, users will have to update their existing task models, as they will no longer interact with an ordinary object but with a computationally enabled AmI object. Then, people will have to form new models about the everyday objects they use. Finally, as the human-computer interface integrates with the physical world, the prevailing human-computer interaction paradigms (such as the direct manipulation paradigm) will be infused by human-object interaction metaphors, thus becoming more natural.

A similarly large range of challenges are brought forward for the untrained designers. The ones relating to technology have been already discussed. These are complemented by the need to produce designs of controlled obtrusion, handling the new affordances of objects and at the same time minimize disturbance of existing models.

Thus, we assert that on the way to realizing the AmI vision, together with the realization of ubiquitous computing technology, a conceptual framework that will bridge the gap between system design and use is necessary. This framework must be shared both by developers and end users so that the latter are enabled to actively shape the ubiquitous computing environments they live in, without them being hindered by design limitations. Moreover, the visibility of the functionality of the UbiComp system must be transparent and adapting to people; people have to remain informed and aware, in order to build trust on the system. The framework must be complemented with the technological platform and tools that will facilitate users' active participation in the adoption, formation and use of UbiComp applications.

3.1   The Gadgetware Architectural Style (GAS)

We have designed GAS (the Gadgetware Architectural Style), as a conceptual and technological framework for describing and manipulating ubiquitous computing applications (Kameas 2003). It consists of a set of architecture descriptions (syntactic domain) and a set of guidelines for their interpretation (semantic domain). GAS extends component-based architectures to the realm of tangible objects and combines a software architectural style with guidelines on how to physically design and manipulate artefacts (we could call it "a style for tangible objects") (Kameas 2005).

For the end-user, this model can serve as a high level task interface; for the developer, it can serve as a domain model and a methodology. In both cases, it can be used as a communication medium, which people can understand, and by using it they can manipulate the "disappearing computers" within their environment.

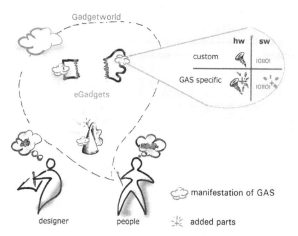

Fig. 1. GAS, an Architectural style that acts as a common referent between people, designers, and artifacts

In our approach, we view the process whereby people configure and use complex collections of interacting artifacts, as having much in common with the process where system builders design software systems out of components. We consider the everyday environment to contain a multitude of artifacts, which people combine and recombine in ad-hoc, dynamic ways. As a consequence, artifacts are treated as reusable "components" of a dynamically changing physical or digital environment; people are given "things" with which to make "new things", rather than only being supplied with fixed and un-changeable tools. The behavior of these "new things" (which are ubiquitous computing applications) is neither static, nor random, as it is guided by how applications are to be used (e-Gadgets 2006).

The underlying hypothesis is that even if an individual artifact has limited functionality, it can have more advanced behavior when grouped with others. Composeability can give rise to new collective functionality as a result of unprecedented but well-defined interactions among artifacts. Then the aim is to look at how collections of artifacts can be configured to work together in order to provide behavior or functionality that exceeds the sum of their parts.

GAS defines a vocabulary of entities and functions, a set of configuration rules (for interactively establishing associations between artifacts), and a technical infrastructure, the GAS-OS middleware (algorithms, protocols, interfaces, etc). It is conceived so as to be compatible with the mental models of ubiquitous applications that are maintained by artifact manufacturers (i.e. in the form of design guidelines and APIs) or people acting as application composers (i.e. in the form of configuration rules and constraints for composing artifact societies); it can also be represented in the collaboration logic of artifacts, in the form of communication protocol semantics and algorithms (Figure 1.).

GAS aims to serve as a consistent conceptual and technical referent among artefact designers and application designers, by allowing the former to provide the building blocks and rules for the latter to compose functional applications. It also serves as conveyor of design semantics from design experts to application designers. Design options and compositional constraints can be embedded in artifacts in the form of configuration rules which guide and inform the composition and use of applications. GAS plays the role of a vehicle that enables people to become creative shapers of their environment - rather than passive consumers - by enabling them to create new and emerging functionalities by composing pre-fabricated artifacts.

3.2   Harnessing the Challenges of UbiComp Environments

In this section, we shall discuss the extent to which GAS-compatible UbiComp applications meet the UbiComp system design challenges.

Heterogeneity results from the fact that components of a UbiComp system have to be implemented using different hardware (e.g. computational boards, sensors/actuators, etc.), operating systems, programming languages and have to communicate with other nodes through different networks (e.g. 802.11, Bluetooth, Ethernet, infrared, etc.). GAS confronts the heterogeneity issues with the help of GAS middleware (GAS-OS) running on a Java virtual machine. The use of Java as the underlying platform for the middleware facilitates its deployment on a wide range of devices from mobile phones and PDAs to specialized Java processors, hiding the underlying computational units and operating systems. GAS-OS also implements a driver-based mechanism to mask the heterogeneity of sensors and actuators, while the development of a modular JXTA-like communication module makes GAS-OS capable of working over the most known standards, such as 802.11, Bluetooth, infrared, and Ethernet, while easily extendible to support other communication technologies as well. Thus the combination of the Java platform and the GAS-OS middleware, solve to a certain extent the heterogeneity issues that may arise when different GAS enabled artifacts need to collaborate.

The need to support mobility is very frequent in UbiComp environments, as many of the nodes that constitute an application may be portable or even wearable devices. As a consequence the structure of the distributed system is changing dynamically which may also lead to service unavailability in cases where a node offering a certain service gets out of the application's range. GAS-OS faces this challenge by using short or long range wireless networking protocols depending on the application's requirements. Furthermore using hybrid routing protocols reduces the probability to loose a moving node. Even in the case where a service eventually becomes unavailable GAS-OS offers service replacement functionality discovering nodes offering the same service in order to replace the missing one.

Designing a UbiComp system to be composeable allows the nodes of the system (e.g. artifacts) to be used as building blocks of larger and more complex systems. GAS builds on the foundations of established software development approaches such as object oriented design and component frameworks, and extends these concepts by exposing them to the end-user. To achieve this, GAS defines the Plug/Synapse model (Figure 2) which provides a high-level abstraction of the component interfaces and the composition procedure.

Using the Plug/Synapse model GAS also achieves context awareness. Context is collected independently by each artifact via its sensors, is semantically interpreted using its stored ontology and manifested via its plugs. Synapses are the means to propagate each artifact's context to other components, resulting in context aware applications.

A further challenge in UbiComp systems is to preserve each object's autonomy, according to which artifacts must function independently of the existence of other artifacts. Taking into consideration the ad-hoc nature of UbiComp environments and the fact that service unavailability is a frequent phenomenon rather than an exception, object autonomy seems to be a prominent factor for keeping an application functional. Furthermore, object autonomy makes applications more flexible and portable as their operation does not depend on any kind of infrastructure. Preserving object autonomy implies that even resource constraint devices would have to be self contained. GAS-OS copes with this challenge by adapting ideas from the microkernel design where only minimal functionality is located in the kernel, while extra services can be added as plug-ins. This way all objects, even resource constraint ones, are capable of executing the kernel which allows them to be autonomous and participate in applications.

Preserving object autonomy is also a way to make UbiComp applications robust and fault tolerant as the failure of one node does not necessarily mean that the whole system fails. Other ways GAS uses to increase the system's credibility is the provision of reliable p2p communication protocols, the replacement of services in case of unavailability, the provision of routing protocols to increase node accessibility, etc.

A very important challenge in UbiComp systems is scalability. Systems must be scalable in terms of numbers of users and services, volume data stored and manipulated, rates of processing, numbers of nodes and sizes of networks and storage devices. Scalability means not just the ability to operate, but to operate efficiently and with the adequate quality of service over the given range of configurations. GAS-OS is designed to support a large number of nodes by encompassing a lightweight communication module supporting p2p asynchronous communication. In order to avoid large messages and the resulting traffic congestion in the network, XML-based messages are used to wrap the information required for each protocol. Furthermore, polling techniques that usually cause message flooding and bandwidth reduction are avoided. Routing is also designed as a hybrid protocol that combines a proactive and a reactive part, trying to minimize the sum of their respective overheads.

Up to now, the ways that an object could be used and the tasks it could participate in have usually been determined by it's physical affordances, that are, in turn, determined by its shape, material, and physical properties. GAS enabled artifacts overcome this limitation by producing descriptions of their properties, abilities and services in the digital space using ontologies, thus becoming able to improve their functionality by participating in compositions, learning from usage, thus becoming adaptive.

3.3 Plug/Synapse: The GAS Conceptual Framework

The basic concepts encapsulated in the Plug/Synapse model are:

eGadget: eGadgets are everyday physical objects enhanced with sensing, acting, processing and communication abilities. eGadgets can be regarded as artifacts that can be used as building blocks to form GadgetWorlds.

Plugs: From a user's perspective, they provide for the possibility of connectivity, as they make visible the artifacts' properties, capabilities and services to people and to other artifacts; they are implemented as software classes.

Synapses: They are associations between two compatible plugs, which make use of value mappings; they are implemented using a message-oriented set of protocols.

GadgetWorld: A GadgetWorld is a dynamic distinguishable, functional configuration of associated eGadgets, which communicate and / or collaborate in order to realize a collective function. GadgetWorlds are formed purposefully by an actor (user or other).

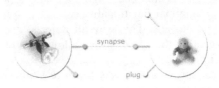

Fig. 2. The Plug Synapse model: The artifacts' capabilities (Plugs) can be inter-associated with invisible links (Synapses) to form ubiquitous computing applications

To achieve the desired collective functionality, one forms synapses by associating compatible plugs, thus composing applications using artifacts as components. Two levels of plug compatibility exist: direction and data type compatibility. According to direction compatibility output or I/O plugs can only be connected to input or I/O plugs. According to data type compatibility, plugs must have the same data type to be connected via a synapse. However, this is a restriction that can be bypassed using value mappings in a synapse (Figure 2). No other limitation exists in making a synapse. Although this may mean that seemingly meaningless synapses are allowed, it has the advantage of letting the user create associations and cause the emergence of new behaviours that the artifact manufacturer may have never thought of. Meaningless synapses could be regarded as analogous to "logical errors" in a program (i.e. a program may be compiled correctly but does not manifest the desired by the programmer behavior).

3.4 Methodology

According to AmI vision, people live in an environment populated with artifacts; they have a certain need or task, which they think can be met or carried out by (using) a combination of services and capabilities. Then, in this approach, they search for artifacts offering these services and capabilities as plugs; they select the most appropriate ones and combine the respective plugs into functioning synapses; if necessary, they manually adapt or optimize the collective functionality. Note that we are referring to the selection of plugs, not artifacts, thus preserving physical independence; this selection is task-based.

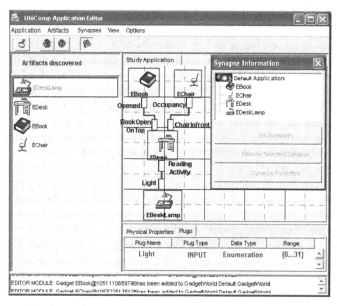

Fig. 3. Combined artifacts in the UbiComp application editor

The use of high-level abstractions, for expressing artifact associations, allows the flexible configuration and reconfiguration of UbiComp applications. It only requires that they are able to communicate. Moreover, they have to run the GAS-OS middleware in order to "comprehend" each-other, so that people can access their services, properties and capabilities in a uniform way. To support people in this process and to hide the complexity of artifact interactions, appropriate tools were developed that implement the conceptual framework (Mavrommati 2004) (Figures 3 and 4). People in that way do not need to be engaged in any type of formal "programming" in order to achieve the desired functions.

Because synapses are formed by end-users, who are not programmers, they can only be debugged by "trial and error" approach. In this case however, what, from a programmer's standpoint, may seem as erroneous behaviour, or inappropriate synapse "programming", from the end user's standpoint and in certain occasions, may simply cause the manifestation of unexpected, unprecedented, but still interesting and desirable system behaviour.

4   Building a Home Application

These concepts can be better illustrated if we consider the Study application example, adopted from (Drossos 2006), which we'll follow throughout this chapter. Let's take a look at the life of Pat, a 27-year old single woman, who lives in a small apartment near the city centre and studies Spanish literature at the Open University. A few days ago she passed by a store, where she saw an advertisement about these new augmented artifacts. Pat decided to enter. Half an hour later she had given herself a very unusual present: a few furniture pieces and other devices that would turn her apartment into a smart one! On the next day, she was anxiously waiting for the delivery of an eDesk (it could sense objects on top, proximity of a chair), an eChair (it could tell whether someone was sitting on it), a couple of eLamps (one could remotely turn them on and off), and some eBook tags (they could be attached to a book, tell whether a book is open or closed). Pat had asked the seller to pre-configure some of the artifacts, so that she could create a smart studying corner in her living room. Her idea was simple: when she sat on the chair and she would draw it near the desk and then open a book on it, then the study lamp would be switched on automatically. If she would close the book or stand up, then the light would go off.

The behavior requested by Pat requires the combined operation of the following set of artifacts: eDesk, eChair, eDeskLamp and eBook. The properties and plugs of these artifacts are shown in Table 1 and are manifested to Pat via the UbiComp Application Editor tool (Mavrommati 2004), an end-user tool that acts as the mediator between the plug/synapse conceptual model and the actual system. Using this tool Pat can combine the most appropriate plugs into functioning synapses as shown in Figure 3.

In the case of the synapse between eDesk.ReadingActivity and eDeskLamp.Light plugs, a data type compatibility issue arises. To make the synapse work, Pat can use the UbiComp Editor to define mappings that will make the two plugs collaborate, as shown in Figure 4.

Table 1. Analyzing the UbiComp Application

Artifact	Properties	Plugs	Functional Schemas
eChair	Sensing chair occupancy capability (C_1) Transmitting object type capability (C_2)	Occupancy: {OUT | Boolean}	eChair.C_1 ← read(pressure-sensor) eChair.C2 is an attribute Occupancy ← {eChair.C_1, eChair.C2}
eBook	Sensing open/close capability (C_1) Transmitting object type capability (C_2)	Opened {OUT | Boolean}	eBook.C1 ← read(bend-sensor) eBook.C2 is an attribute Opened ← {eBook.C_1, eBook.C2}
eDesk	Sensing objects on top capability (C_1) Sensing proximity of objects capability (C_2)	BookOpenOnTop: {IN | Boolean} ChairInFront: {IN | Boolean} ReadingActivity: {OUT | Boolean}	eDesk.C1 ← read(RFID-sensor) eDesk.C2 ← read(proximity-sensor) IF eDesk.C1 = eBook.C2 AND eBook.C1 = TRUE THEN BookOpenOnTop ← TRUE ELSE BookOpenOnTop ← FALSE IF eDesk.C2 = TRUE AND eChair.C_1 = TRUE THEN ChairInFront ← TRUE ELSE ChairInFront ← FALSE IF BookOpenOnTop = TRUE AND ChairInFront = TRUE THEN ReadingActivity ← TRUE ELSE ReadingActivity ← FALSE
eDesk-Lamp	Light service (S_1)	Light: {IN | Enumeration}	IF eDesk.ReadingActivity THEN S1(on) ELSE S1(off)

The definition of the functional schemas of the artifacts, that is the internal logic that governs the behaviour of each artifact either when its state changes or when a synapse is activated are predefined by the artifact developer (for our example, they are shown in Table I). Rules that require identification of the remote artifact can be specified using the property schema information, which is available in the representation of each of the two artifacts that participate in a synapse.

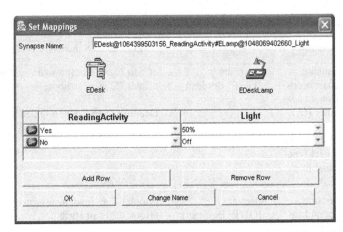

Fig. 4. Setting mappings between the eDesk.ReadingActivity and eDeskLamp.Light plugs

The eBook, eChair and eDesk comprise an artifact composition (GadgetWorld) whose composite property is manifested via the ReadingActivity plug. This plug allows the participation of this composition, in a way similar to any artifact, in other compositions. In this way, there's no conceptual upper limit in the structural complexity of GAS enabled UbiComp applications. Any GadgetWorld can be edited to extend the functionality of the application. For example, consider that Pat also buys an eClock and wants to use it as a 2 hour reading notification. The eClock owns an Alarm plug that when activated, via a synapse, counts the number of hours (which can be configured) and then rings the alarm. To implement her idea, what Pat has to do is to use the UbiComp Application editor to create a synapse between the ReadingActivity plug of the eDesk and the Alarm plug of the eClock and specify the number of hours in the Properties dialog box of the eClock.

5   GAS-OS: The GAS Middleware

To cope with heterogeneity and provide a uniform abstraction of artifact services and capabilities we have introduced the GAS-OS middleware that abstracts the underlying data communications and sensor/actuator access components of each part of a distributed system, so that a UbiComp application appears as an integrated system. GAS-OS follows the Message-Oriented Middleware (MOM) approach, by providing non-blocking message passing and queuing services. Furthermore, to handle the need to adapt to a broad range of devices, we have adapted ideas from micro-kernel design (Tanenbaum 1991) where only minimal functionality is located in the kernel, while extra services can be added as plug-ins.

We assume that no specific networking infrastructure exists, thus ad-hoc networks are formed. The physical layer networking protocols used are highly heterogeneous ranging from infrared communication over radio links to wired connections. Since every node serves both as a client and as a server (devices can either provide or request services at the same time), communication between artifacts can be considered as Peer-to-Peer (P2P) (Schollmeier 2001).

The prototype of GAS-OS is implemented in Java but relies only on features available in the Java personal edition, compatible with the Sun J2ME Personal Profile. This allows the deployment on a wide range of devices from mobile phones and PDAs to specialized Java processors. The proliferation of systems besides classical computers capable of executing Java, make it a suitable underlying layer providing a uniform abstraction for our middleware.

The use of Java as the underlying platform of the middleware decouples GAS-OS from typical operations like memory management, networking, etc. Furthermore, it facilitates the deployment on a wide range of devices from mobile phones and PDAs to specialized Java processors.

The combination of the Java platform and the GAS-OS middleware, hide the heterogeneity of the underlying artifacts, sensors, networks etc. and provides the means to create large scale systems based on simple building blocks.

5.1   Design

The key idea behind GAS-OS is the uniform abstraction of artifact services and capabilities via the plug/synapse high-level programming model that abstracts the underlying data communications and access components of each part of a distributed system (Figure 5). It isolates clients from back-end processes and decouples the application from the network layer. Messaging and queuing allow nodes to communicate across a network without being linked by a private, dedicated, logical connection. The clients and servers can run at different times. Every node communicates by putting messages on queues and by getting messages from queues.

Our approach is inspired by micro-kernels. Only minimal functionality is located in the kernel, while extra services can be added as plug-ins. One issue in the design

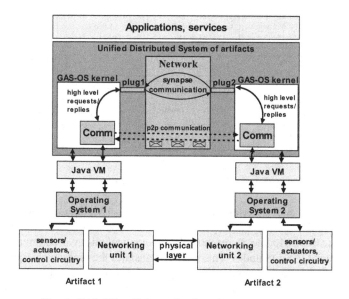

Fig. 5. GAS-OS unifying a distributed system of artifacts

of GAS-OS was to decide on the set of minimal functionalities. The policy that was adopted was to maintain the autonomous nature of artifacts but at the same time make even the more resource constraint ones capable of participating to ubiquitous applications. As a consequence, the kernel of GAS-OS accepts and dispatches messages and manages local hardware resources and the Plug/synapse interoperability protocols.

The GAS-OS kernel implements plugs in order to manifest the artifact's services and capabilities and can initiate or participate in a synapsing process using the Plug/synapse interoperability protocol. The communication module, translates the high-level requests/replies into messages and using low-level peer-to-peer networking protocols, dispatches them to the corresponding remote service or device capability (Figure 5). The kernel is also capable of handling service and resource discovery messages in order to facilitate the formation of synapses.

5.2   Architecture

The outline of the GAS-OS architecture is shown in Figure 6 (adopted from (Drossos 2006), where it is presented in more detail). The GAS-OS kernel is designed to accept and dispatch messages, manage local hardware resources (sensors/actuators), and implement the plug/synapse interaction mechanism. The kernel is also capable of managing service and artifact discovery messages in order to facilitate the formation of the proper synapses.

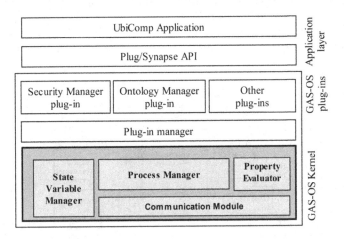

Fig. 6. GAS-OS modular architecture

The GAS-OS kernel encompasses a P2P Communication Module, a Process Manager, a State Variable Manager, and a Property Evaluator module as shown in Figure 6. The P2P Communication Module is responsible for application-level communication between the various GAS-OS nodes. This module translates the high-level requests/replies into messages and by using low-level networking protocols it dispatches them to the corresponding remote peers. The Process Manager is the coordinator module of GAS-OS. Some of its most important tasks are to manage the processing policies, to accept and serve requests set by the other modules of the kernel or to initiate reactions in collaboration with other modules, tasks which collectively serve the realization of the Plug/Synapse model. Furthermore, it is responsible for handling the memory resources of an artifact and caching information of other artifacts to improve communication performance when service discovery is required. The State Variable Manager handles the runtime storage of artifact's state variable values, reflecting both the hardware environment (sensors/actuators) at each particular moment (primitive properties), and properties that are evaluated based on sensory data and P2P communicated data (composite properties). The Property Evaluator is responsible for the evaluation of artifact's composite properties according to its Functional Schema. In its typical form the Property Evaluator is based on a set of rules that govern artifact transition from one state to another. The rule management can be separated from the evaluation logic by using a high-level rule language and a mechanism that translates high-level rule specifications to XML that can be exploited then by the evaluation logic.

The adoption of a layered modular architecture allows the replacement of a module without affecting the functionality of the rest provided that the APIs between them remain consistent. This principle holds for the different layers of the architecture as well as within each layer. The modular design of GAS-OS, for example, allows the integration of up-to-date algorithms and protocols in the form of plug-in modules. Extending the functionality of the GAS-OS kernel can be achieved through plug-ins, which can be easily incorporated to an artifact running GAS-OS, via the plug-in manager.

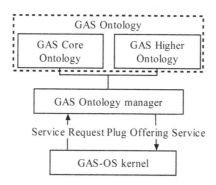

Fig. 7. The GAS Ontology manager

GAS Ontology (Christopoulou 2005) describes the semantics of the basic terms of our model for UbiComp applications and their interrelations. It contains a service classification, since the AmI objects offer various services and the demand for a semantic service discovery mechanism in UbiComp applications is evident. Due to the facts that AmI objects acquire different knowledge and may have limited capabilities, the GAS Ontology was divided into two layers: the GAS Core Ontology (GAS-CO) and the GAS Higher Ontology (GAS-HO). The GAS-CO is fairly small and provides AmI objects with the necessary common language that they need in order to describe their acquired knowledge represented by the GAS-HO. In that way, high-level descriptions of services and resources independent of the context of a specific application are possible, facilitating the exchange of information between heterogeneous artifacts as well as the discovery of services.

Figure 7 demonstrates the interaction among the ontology manager and the GAS-OS kernel. An important feature of the ontology manager is that it adds a level of abstraction between GAS-OS and the GAS ontology, because only the ontology manager can manipulate the ontology; GAS-OS can simply query this module for information stored into the ontology without having any knowledge about the ontology language or its structure. GAS-OS receives from the ontology manager the necessary knowledge stored in an AmI object's ontology relevant to its services, in order to implement a service discovery mechanism. The GAS Ontology manager using this mechanism and the service classification can identify AmI objects that offer similar semantically services and propose objects that can replace damaged ones.

The security manager plug-in on the other hand, when developed, will be responsible for realizing the security policies of each artifact. These policies will be encoded as rules in the ontology, thus becoming directly available to the Process Manager. The security manager will mediate information exchange via synapses in order to ensure that security policies are respected.

6   The Evolution of GAS

GAS is an architectural style which represents a worldview of everyday living that directly descends from the AmI vision. In a world where all objects in our living spaces are built according to this style, a whole new way of interacting with our environment can emerge. The success of this vision depends both on technological advancements that need to be made, as well as on future research on GAS-like components, such as the conceptual framework, the middleware, the ontology, and the user editing tools.

Advancements that have to be achieved involve first of all hardware miniaturization. If we want to consider computers "disappearing", then it is crucial that hardware units like processors, sensors, networking boards etc. become small enough so that their actual embedding in all kinds of objects, no matter their size or shape, is possible. Furthermore, low power consumption is essential especially for mobile and wearable objects as it is closely related to longer battery life and object autonomy. This can also be promoted by the use of low power networking technologies like short range RF or low-frequency RF, without sacrificing the quality of communication. Advancements must also be made regarding sensors not only with respect to their size but also to their precision, fault tolerance etc. Finally, since the hardware part of the eGadget is the most expensive one, efforts have to be made to reduce the overall cost. This will make these "augmented objects" affordable for everyday people, thus achieve their intended purpose, to be used widely in everyday applications.

In addition, a number of enhancements in software must also be taken into consideration. Software systems must target more on the human's perspective rather than technology itself. To achieve this, software must become adaptive to people's needs making UbiComp applications as usable by people as possible, reducing the required time and effort in learning how to interact with the system. User oriented tools must also be developed to facilitate people's intervention in their living environments, while keeping it simple to actually live in such environments.

Along these lines the design and development of a security/privacy module on top of the middleware (e.g. as a plug-in) would definitely extend the functionality of GAS-OS to realizing the security policies of each artifact as well as handle privacy issues in applications, which are proved to be of utmost importance. Especially, when envisaging a world composed of UbiComp applications executing all together, the provision of ways to prohibit violations and undesirable interactions among them is prominent. This module must also implement mechanisms to set digital boundaries to the otherwise unlimited access in computational environments, in order to ensure that as private spaces are limited by "walls" in the physical world, they will also be restricted via privacy algorithms and techniques in the digital world.

Further research is also required for the development of a resource management module, capable of dealing with physical resources scarcities by providing resource mapping and mediation services. This module has to keep track of the available resources and arbitrate among conflicting requests for those resources. Local management of those resources is already undertaken by the local operating system of each node, thus the role of the resource management module is to globally manage resources at the application level. Examples are allowing eGadgets lending their resources under certain circumstances (e.g. certain time interval, certain QoS, etc.) to other eGadgets which do not have the adequate resources to execute a task with the required performance, searching for eGadgets with adequate resources before assigning a task, etc..

Achieving an acceptable level of quality of services is also very important in UbiComp applications, thus a separate module ensuring that the provided services will meet certain requirements is needed. QoS affects all layers in a UbiComp application, from the application layer ensuring real-time system responses, stability, constant service provision for a certain time interval, down to the networking layer ensuring reliable communication, high data transmission rates, etc.. Dynamically supporting QoS also contributes to adaptation, as the system dynamically changes its parameters to maintain the required QoS level. QoS parameters vary depending on the application, thus the QoS module should be able to receive requirements, probably by the developer of the application, while automatic determination has to be investigated.

Furthermore, as ecologies of collaborating artifacts are dynamically reconfigured aiming at the accomplishment of tasks, their formation heavily depends not only on space and time but also on the context of previous local interactions, previous configured teams, successfully achieved goals or possible failures. This means that in order to initially create, manage, communicate with, and reason about, such kinds of emergent ecologies, we need to model and embed to these entities social memory, enhanced context memory, models of self and shared experiences. One way to achieve this is to design and implement evolving multidimensional ontologies that will include both nonfunctional descriptions, goals, rules and constraints of application, as well as aspects of dynamic behaviour and interactions. A core ontology will be open and universally available and accessible; however, during the ecology lifetime the core ontology is evolved into higher goal, application and context specific one. Hence, ontologies describing specific application domains can be proprietary.

In order to make UbiComp applications as usable by people as possible, the use of intelligent agents is an option that could possibly reduce people's time and effort in learning how to interact with the system. The idea is to have software agents monitoring and learning how people actually want to use their augmented environments. Based on monitored data, agents are capable, using either rule-based or even fuzzy logic, of inferring or even predicting the ways people expect their environment to behave.

Finally, the improvement of the existing UbiComp application editing tools aimed at end users as well as the development of new ones is a step forward towards the closest and easiest people's involvement into shaping their living spaces. The UbiComp Application Editor is a prototype that realizes the people's requirements from GAS using the plug/synapse model (Figure 8). The experiences reported after expert and user trials suggest that an architectural approach where users act as composers of predefined components is worthwhile (Markopoulos 2004). However, these sessions have also pointed out that further improvement is necessary in the design and interaction of such tools. Providing for adaptive interfaces, to cater for a variety of user profiles as well as augmented reality and speech interfaces, pose a number of challenges on the design of editing tools

Fig. 8. Test subjects using the GAS Application Editor, during a user trial session

Additional tools are also required to harness the ubiquity and the logic governing this new type of environments. Such tools are addressed more to the developer or the advanced user rather to an everyday end-user. The purpose of these tools is to configure certain aspects of the system's behavior that need user intervention. Decision making is one such aspect according to which the developer or advanced user may want to dynamically define or change the rules determining an individual eGadget's or even an application's behavior in a high level manner. Dynamically defining QoS parameters for an application is another aspect that can be defined or altered using tools.

All in all, there are many achievements waiting to be realized and paths to be explored in order to make computers ubiquitous and well accepted by people in their everyday living. As Weiser noted in his article "The computer for the 21st century" (Weiser 1991), "There is more information available at our fingertips during a walk in the woods than in any computer system, yet people find walk among trees relaxing and computers frustrating. Machines that fit the human environment instead of forcing humans to enter theirs, will make using a computer as refreshing as taking a walk in the woods."

Acknowledgements

Part of the research described in this chapter was conducted in the "extrovert Gadgets" project (funded under project number IST-2000-25240 in the context of the European funded IST-FET "Disappearing Computer" initiative). The authors would like to thank fellow e-Gadgets researchers at CTI, Tyndall and University of Essex as well as the TU/e experts and all the experts involved in our research and studies.

References

Accord project website (2006): http://www.sics.se/accord/ (last accessed on 11/22/2006)

Baker, C.R., Markovsky, Y., van Greunen, J., Rabaey, J., Wawrzynek, J., Wolisz, A.: ZUMA: A Platform for Smart-Home Environments. In: Proceedings of the 2nd IET Conference on Intelligent Environments, Athens, Greece (2006)

Becker, C. et al.: BASE - A Micro-broker-based Middleware For Pervasive Computing. In: Proceedings of the 1st IEEE International Conference on Pervasive Computing and Communication (PerCom03), Fort Worth, USA (2003)

Lalis, S., Savidis, A., Karypidis, A., Gutknecht, J., Stephanides, C.: Towards Dynamic and Cooperative Multi-Device Personal Computing. In: Streitz, N., Kameas, A., Mavrommati, I. (eds.) The Disappearing Computer. LNCS, vol. 4500, Springer, Heidelberg (2007)

Christopoulou, E., Kameas, A.: GAS Ontology: an ontology for collaboration among ubiquitous computing devices. International Journal of Human – Computer Studies 62(5), 664–685 (2005)

Disappearing Computer initiative (2006): http://www.disappearing-computer.net (last accessed on 11/22/2006)

Drossos, N., Goumopoulos, C., Kameas, A.: A Conceptual Model and The Supporting Middleware For Composing Ubiquitous Computing Applications. Special Issue in the Journal of Ubiquitous Computing and Intelligence (JUCI), entitled Ubiquitous Intelligence in Real Worlds, American Scientific Publishers (ASP) 1(2), 1–13 (2006)

e-Gadgets project website (2006): http://www.extrovert-gadgets.net (last accessed on 11/22/2006)

Edwards, W.K., Newman, M.W., Sedivy, J., Smith, T., Izadi, S.: Challenge: Recombinant Computing and the Speakeasy Approach. In: Proceedings of the Eighth Annual International Conference on Mobile Computing and Networking (MobiCom 2002), pp. 279–286. ACM Press, New York (2002)

Garlan, D., Siewiorek, D.P., Smailagic, A., Steenkistie, P.: Project Aura: Toward Distraction-Free Pervasive Computing. IEEE Pervasive Computing Magazine 1(2), 22–31 (2002)

Holmquist, L.E., Gellersen, H.-W., Schmidt, A., Strohbach, M., Kortuem, G., Antifakos, S., Michahelles, F., Schiele, B., Beigl, M., Mazé, R.: Building Intelligent Environments with Smart-Its. IEEE Computer Graphics & Applications 24(1), 56–64 (2004)

Humble, J. et al.: Playing with the Bits: User-Configuration of Ubiquitous Domestic Environments. In: Dey, A.K., Schmidt, A., McCarthy, J.F. (eds.) UbiComp 2003. LNCS, vol. 2864, pp. 256–263. Springer, Heidelberg (2003)

ISTAG ISTAG in FP6: Working Group 1, IST Research Content, Final Report, available at http://www.cordis.lu/ist/istag.htm (last accessed on 11/22/2006)

Jacquet, C., Bourda, Y., Bellik, Y.: An Architecture for Ambient Computing. In: Proceedings of the 1st IEE International Workshop on Intelligent Environments, Colchester, UK, pp. 47–54 (2005)

Johanson, B., Fox, A., Winograd, T.: Experiences with Ubiquitous Computing Rooms. IEEE Pervasive Computing Magazine 1(2), 67–74 (2002)

Kameas, A. et al.: An Architecture that Treats Everyday Objects as Communicating Tangible Components. In: Proceedings of the 1st IEEE International Conference on Pervasive Computing and Communications (PerCom03), Fort Worth, USA, pp. 115–122. IEEE Computer Society Press, Los Alamitos (2003)

Kameas, A., Mavrommati, I.: Configuring the e-Gadgets. Communications of the ACM (CACM) 48(3), 69 (2005)

Kortuem, G., Schneider, J.: An Application Platform for Mobile Ad-hoc Networks. In: Abowd, G.D., Brumitt, B., Shafer, S. (eds.) Ubicomp 2001: Ubiquitous Computing. LNCS, vol. 2201, Springer, Heidelberg (2001)

Markopoulos, P., Mavrommati, I., Kameas, A.: End-User Configuration of Ambient Intelligence Environments: Feasibility from a User Perspective. In: Markopoulos, P., Eggen, B., Aarts, E., Crowley, J.L. (eds.) EUSAI 2004. LNCS, vol. 3295, pp. 243–254. Springer, Heidelberg (2004)

Mavrommati, I., Kameas, A., Markopoulos, P.: An Editing tool that manages the devices associations. Personal and Ubiquitous Computing 8(3-4), 255–263 (2004)

Newman, M., Sedivy, J., Neuwirth, C.M., Edwards, W.K., Hong, J.I., Izadi, S., Marcelo, K., Smith, T.: Designing for serendipity. In: Serious Reflection on Designing Interactive Systems (ACM SIGCHI DIS2002), London, England, pp. 147–156. ACM, New York (2002)

Norman, D.A.: The Psychology of Everyday Things. Basic books, New York (1988)

Schollmeier, R.: A Definition of Peer-to-Peer Networking for the Classification of Peer-to-Peer Architectures and Applications. In: Proceedings of the IEEE 2001 International Conference on Peer-to-Peer Computing (P2P'01), Linköping, Sweden (2001), IEEE, Los Alamitos (2001)

Streitz, N., Röcker, C., Prante, T., van Alphen, D., Stenzel, R., Magerkurth, C.: Designing Smart Artefacts for Smart Environments. IEEE Computer March 2005, 41–49 (2005)

Streitz, N., Prante, T., Röcker, C., van Alphen, D., Stenzel, R., Magerkurth, C., Lahlou, S., Nosulenko, V., Jegou, F., Sonder, F., Plewe, D.: Smart Artefacts as Affordances for Awareness in Distributed Teams. In: Streitz, N., Kameas, A., Mavrommati, I. (eds.) The Disappearing Computer. LNCS, vol. 4500, Springer, Heidelberg (2007)

Tanenbaum, A.S. et al.: The Amoeba Distributed Operating System-A Status Report. Computer Communications 14(6), 324–335 (1991)

Truong, K.N., Huang, E.M., Abowd, G.D., CAMP,: A Magnetic Poetry Interface for End-User Programming of Capture Applications for the Home. In: Davies, N., Mynatt, E.D., Siio, I. (eds.) UbiComp 2004. LNCS, vol. 3205, pp. 143–160. Springer, Heidelberg (2004)

Weis, T., Handte, M., Knoll, M., Becker, C.: Customizable Pervasive Applications. In: International Conference on Pervasive Computing and Communications (PERCOM) 2006, Pisa, Italy (2006)

Weiser, M.: The computer for the 21st century. Scientific American 265(3), 94–104 (1991)

Weiser, M.: Some computer science issues in ubiquitous computing. Communications of the ACM 36(7), 75–84 (1993)

Towards Dynamic and Cooperative Multi-device Personal Computing

Spyros Lalis[1], Anthony Savidis[2], Alexandros Karypidis[1], Jurg Gutknecht[3], and Constantine Stephanides[2]

[1] Computer and Communications Engineering Department, University of Thessaly, Volos, Greece
[2] Institute of Computer Science, Foundation for Research and Technology Hellas, Heraklion, Crete, Greece
[3] Computer Science Department, Swiss Federal Institute of Technology, Zürich, Switzerland

1 Introduction

The significant technological advances in hardware miniaturisation and data communications change the landscape of computing in a profound way. A rich variety of sensing, storage and processing nodes will soon be embedded in artefacts and clothes worn by people. Numerous computing elements will be integrated in appliances, furniture, buildings, public spaces and vehicles. It now becomes possible to move beyond the physical but also mental boundaries of the desktop, and to develop novel forms of computing that will efficiently support people in their daily activities without constantly being in the center of their attention.

In the 2WEAR project[1], we have explored the concept of a system that can be formed in an ad-hoc fashion by putting together several wearable, portable and infrastructure devices that communicate via short-range radio. This setting deviates from the desktop paradigm in significant ways. What we usually refer to as "the" computer becomes a collection of different autonomous elements that co-operate in a dynamic fashion without relying on a pre-arranged setup. Various applications and units of functionality reside on separate devices that can be widely heterogeneous in terms of computing and user interaction resources. Moreover, the number and type of elements comprising the personal system can change at any point in time. Using proximity as a natural form of control, the user may produce a wide range of system configurations, leading to different device interactions and application functionality. As a step towards this vision, we have worked towards advanced mechanisms for dealing with yet at the same time exploiting the heterogeneous and dynamic nature of such a system, with minimal programmer and user intervention.

In the following, we put our work in perspective of the research done in the area of ubiquitous computing. We continue by giving a motivating scenario and an overview of our system architecture. Then, we present in more detail the most important elements of the 2WEAR system: (i) an open and flexible communication framework; (ii) support for distributed user interfaces; and (iii) seamless distributed storage management. Finally, we revisit our scenario, indicating how it can be actually implemented using our system.

---

[1] http://2wear.ics.forth.gr

N. Streitz, A. Kameas, and I. Mavrommati (Eds.): The Disappearing Computer, LNCS 4500, pp. 182–204, 2007.
© Springer-Verlag Berlin Heidelberg 2007

2   Background and Related Work

The vision of ubiquitous or invisible computing, formulated several years ago by Marc Weiser (Weiser 1991), has inspired numerous research efforts during the last years. Work covers a broad spectrum of technical and scientific areas, including wireless networks, special purpose devices, embedded sensors, distributed and mobile computing, runtime and middleware systems, activity recognition, application composition frameworks, human computer interaction, and security and privacy. It also crosscuts many application sectors, like the professional and business domain, classroom and home environments, mission critical computing and healthcare. In the following we put our work in perspective and briefly discuss related work[2].

A distinguishing characteristic of the 2WEAR project is its focus on the ad-hoc combination of several wearable and portable devices to form a single personal computing system. Unlike some major research efforts on mobile, ubiquitous and pervasive computing systems (Brumitt et al. 2001; Garlan et al. 2002; Johanson et al. 2002; Kunito et al. 2006; Roman and Cambell 2000), in our work there is no strong reliance on a smart infrastructure. By design, applications may reside on different devices, and devices providing auxiliary resources can be replaced by others to continue operation, with degraded or enhanced functionality. Infrastructure-based resources found in the environment can also be exploited in an opportunistic fashion.

Most work on mobile and wearable computing focuses on context acquisition and activity recognition, ergonomic design or investigates new forms of user interaction based on special sensors and input/output devices (Amft et al. 2004; Bang et al. 2003; Gellersen et al. 2002; Krause et al. 2003; Ogris et al. 2005; De Vaul et al. 2003). However, system configuration is typically fixed, based on a single wearable or portable computer, and several peripherals wired to it. 2WEAR takes a largely complementary approach, targeting a multi-device ad-hoc personal computing environment whose configuration may change at any point in time. The Spartan Bodynet (Fishkin et al. 2002) follows a similar approach, letting embedded applications interact with different wireless peripheral components, but there seems to be little advanced support in terms of handling a changing device configuration during application execution. The SoapBox system (Tuulari and Ylisaukko-Oja 2002) employs short-range radio for the special case of letting wearable sensors communicate in a flexible way with a central processing node, typically a personal computer or laptop. Pursuing a somewhat extreme model, the Personal Server system (Want et al. 2002) advocates a single portable device holding all data and applications, which can be accessed over wireless via PC-based terminals found in the environment using a web-based protocol. However, applications residing on the Personal Server cannot exploit the resources of other wearable and portable devices. The wearIT@work project (Kuladinithi et al. 2004) investigates wearable computing in conjunction with many wireless devices which may belong to different persons, but focus is mainly on mesh networking issues rather than higher-level forms of application support. Contrary to 2WEAR and the aforementioned systems, which use radio-based communication, there is also

---

[2] Even though we try to provide indicative references, we most certainly do not give a comprehensive survey of work on ubiquitous and wearable computing, which is well beyond the scope of this article.

significant work on intra-body communication and corresponding user interaction metaphors, such as "touch and play" (Park et al. 2006).

In terms of service / resource discovery and invocation, our work has common characteristics with other architectures designed for ad-hoc distributed computing systems, such as MEX (Lehikoinen et al. 1999) or MOCA (Beck et al. 1999). The main difference is that we do not commit to a specific programming language, middleware API or application model. Interoperability is achieved via an open and platform neutral communication protocol and encoding, which can be easily supported in different languages and runtime environments. Location and distribution (programming) transparency, if indeed desired, is achieved by introducing language- and runtime-specific libraries and/or proxy objects. Our approach is thus more in the spirit of web technologies, but we do not use HTTP or XML which introduce considerable overhead. Some middleware systems, such as PCOM (Becker et al. 2004), provide considerable support for dynamic service (component) selection and binding at runtime. Our system provides similar functionality, but this is specifically tuned for the purpose of user interface management.

The user interface framework developed in 2WEAR, named Voyager, offers to the application programmer a library of abstract interactive components that utilize distributed user interface services hosted by proximate wearable, portable and ambient devices. Dynamic service discovery, negotiation, synthesis and adaptation occurs in a transparent fashion to application programmers, hiding all underlying user interface management details, while ensuring state persistence and automatic dialogue recovery upon disconnection or device failure. Related work in the area of ubiquitous and wearable computing is mostly concerned with the design and implementation of ambient dialogues, context awareness and adaptive interfaces. For instance, the work reported in (Banget al. 2003) investigates new types of interaction devices suited for traditional static wearable interactions. The notion of context awareness is related to ways of sensing information from the physical and computational environment (Abowd and Mynatt 2000) making a system aware of the context in which it is engaged. However, there are no propositions on how to address the situation where the context can be the interface as well; like in Voyager. The need to effectively reflect such awareness in interaction is discussed under the concept of plasticity in (Calvary et al. 2001), emphasizing the requirement for distributed applications to "withstand variations of context of use while preserving usability", but no full-scale development framework is proposed. There has been work regarding the engineering of context-aware applications based on re-usable higher-level software elements, called widgets (Salber et al. 1999). These are responsible to notify the run-time application of various types of events occurring in the environment, such as particular activities, or the presence of persons. The Voyager framework adopts a similar toolkit-based approach in order to support distributed and adaptive user interfaces. Dynamic adaptation is also provided in the SUPPLE system (Gajos et al. 2005), but in this case focus is on the rendering / placement of graphical user interface components on a single display as a function of its size and user input statistics.

Storage management in 2WEAR is based on a peer-to-peer model where individual wearable and portable storage devices are viewed as autonomously collaborating and self-organizing elements. This makes it possible to perform several file management tasks such as backup, offloading and replication in an automated and asynchronous fashion, requiring little or no explicit user input. Traditional network file systems like Coda (Satyanarayanan 2002) focus on more conventional client-server interactions. They support mobile clients and disconnected operation, but assume a single device per user, typically a laptop. Other ad-hoc file systems (Yasuda and Hagino 2001) allow users to flexibly share their data without relying on any infrastructure. The difference with our approach is that we do not support direct file access over the network. Programs wishing to read or write a remote file must explicitly create a local copy. Autonomous data exchange between portable devices is supported in the Proem system (Kortuem et al. 2001), by plugging into the system application-specific tasks, called peerlets. The main difference is that we introduce the basic file transfer functionality at the system level, via asynchronous operations to tolerate slow and intermittent connectivity.

3   Motivating Scenario and System Overview

We begin by giving an example of the envisioned system in operation: *"Mary arrives in City-X. At the airport she is given a city-guide application card, which she activates and puts in her pocket. She takes a bus downtown to explore the old city center. The application tracks her position using a GPS integrated in her backpack. Each time she is close to a site of general interest, a message appears on her wristwatch. At the click of a button, more information about the site is shown on the display of her camera, if turned on. She takes pictures using her camera, which are annotated with the GPS coordinates. When the camera starts running out of space, old images are offloaded on her wallet. Mary bumps into Jane who also happens to be visiting the city. They sit at a café and Mary takes out her camera to show Jane the pictures she took during the day. Meanwhile, the photos are being backed up at her home computer via a nearby access point. Jane expresses her interest in several of them. Mary marks them for access by Jane who switches on her data wallet. Feeling a bit hungry they decide to have a bite at a cozy restaurant suggested by the city-guide. Mary pinpoints its location on a map, using the café's table-display to view a large part of the map in detail. As they walk down the road, Jane's wallet silently copies the selected pictures from Mary's camera."* This short scenario already illustrates the potential wealth of interactions between devices that are carried by persons or encountered in the surrounding environment. It also suggests that such a computing system exhibits several key properties, briefly listed below:

The system is inherently distributed and heterogeneous. Different functions and resources are provided by various devices and artifacts. For instance, the city-guide application uses resources provided by other devices such as the GPS, the wristwatch and the table-display of the café, and the camera uses the GPS to annotate pictures and the wallet to store them.

The system is extensible and adaptive. New devices can be dynamically added or removed, and applications adapt their behavior as a function of resource availability. For example, the city-guide can be controlled via the wristwatch or the camera controls, and can display the map on the camera or table-display. Also, applications exploit the storage capacity of nearby devices and file backup is performed when close to an access point.

The system is largely autonomous. Most system-level interactions remain invisible and adaptation seldom requires explicit input. For example, the city-guide application automatically adapts to changing user interface resource availability (wristwatch vs camera resources), and data transfers between the camera, Mary's wallet, Mary's home computer and Jane's wallet are performed behind the scenes.

In pursuit of this vision, we have implemented our system according to the architecture, shown in Figure 1. At the low level, basic communication and discovery functionality is provided so that programs may access the resources that are available at any point in time; contributed to the system by the nearby devices and infrastructure. On top of it, more advanced functionality is provided in the form of a "vertical" exploitation of particular resources to relieve the application from having to deal with the details of a (changing) underlying system configuration. We have investigated two separate aspects which we felt were of particular importance, namely distributed user interface and storage management, which are actively supported via corresponding mechanisms. No attempt was made to implement this functionality in the form of a common middleware or API. Instead, project partners were free to choose their own level and flavor of support, depending on the characteristics of their development platform.

Our system prototype includes custom hardware (Majoe 2003), such as an embedded GPS, a wristwatch with a small display and four buttons, and a small wearable computer with no user interface elements (see Figure 2). The latter is used as a generic data and computation "brick", which may host a variety of subsystems and applications;

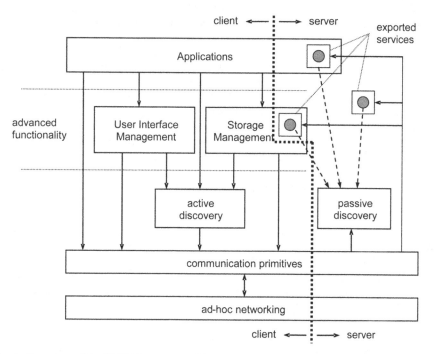

Fig. 1. Overview of the 2WEAR system architecture: arrows show the main control flow (invocation direction) between the various subsystems; the dotted line separates between client- and server-related functionality

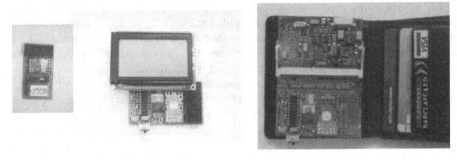

Fig. 2. Custom-made prototype devices

a personal system may include several such bricks, e.g. with different functionality assigned to each one of them. PDAs and laptops are also used to emulate other devices, such as a digital camera or a large public display and keyboard. Ad-hoc communication is implemented using Bluetooth radio (Bhagwat 2001)[3]

We note that the runtime setup is not necessarily the same for all devices. Special-purpose peripheral devices, such as the GPS and the wristwatch, have a minimal discovery and communication functionality installed in order to make their resources available to the system. On the other hand, the wearable computer (brick) or a PDA may be equipped with the full-fledged 2WEAR functionality to support local applications. Between these extremes, a device may only feature the storage management or user interface management subsystem, depending on its role and application requirements.

4   Open and Flexible Communication Framework

The envisioned system includes many heterogeneous devices which interact with each other in an ad-hoc fashion. Thus a key problem is to implement interoperable discovery and access, while catering for the significant differences in the computing resources of the various embedded, portable and infrastructure-based platforms. This is achieved via an open and flexible communication framework, described in the following.

4.1   Remotely Accessible Resources as Services

Interaction between devices follows a service-oriented approach. The concept of a service is used to denote a distinct resource or functionality that is accessible to remote clients over the (wireless) network. Any device may *export* a service to its environment and, conversely, *invoke* services being provided by other devices. The notion of a service in no way predetermines its implementation, and in this sense is orthogonal to the notion of a hardware or software component. Applications can, but do not have to, use services exported by devices, and may also provide services themselves.

---

[3] Bluetooth was chosen primarily because (at that time) it was the only mature short-range ad-hoc radio technology, with rudimentary support for most operating systems, including Windows and Linux.

Services are categorized using an open type system. Each service type is identified via a unique name, associated to: (i) a set of attributes; (ii) an access protocol; and (iii) a description document, which gives the semantics of the service attributes and access protocol. Attributes have as values ASCII strings. If it is desired to constrain an attribute value, the allowed expressions must be specified in the corresponding service description document. Service providers must supply a value for each attribute, i.e. specify a concrete service descriptor, and adhere to the respective access protocol. This concept is illustrated in Figure 3.

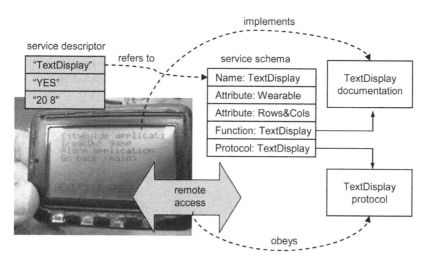

Fig. 3. A wristwatch device providing a TextDisplay service

4.2   Syntax-Based Protocols

Service access protocols are defined as *formal languages* that govern the data exchange between an entity invoking a service (client) and an entity implementing it (provider). The corresponding grammar is given using the Extended Backus-Naur Formalism (EBNF) (Wirth 1977) with some modifications.

Each protocol is specified as a set of productions that take the form <name> "=" <expression> ".", where <name> is the label of the production, and <expression> is an expression built out of labels, operators and tokens. There are five operators: (1) concatenation, denoted by a space character; (2) alternative, denoted by "|"; (3) grouping, denoted by "(" ")"; (4) option, denoted by "[" "]"; and (5) repetition, denoted by "{" "}". Labels occurring in expressions refer to productions whereas tokens refer to elements of the underlying alphabet[4]. To capture the bidirectional nature of communication, we augment the symbols appearing in expressions by a *direction* mode, denoted by normal and underlined text, indicating whether tokens travel from the client towards the provider or vice versa.

---

[4] Although tokens are the *atoms* that any production can finally be resolved into, their values need not be single bytes or characters; see token types.

The basic set of token types is listed in Table 1. Constants are given in the form of literals with an optional type cast to alleviate ambiguities. As we found that the extensive use of constants severely compromises the readability of protocol definitions, we introduce special symbols referred to as *keywords*. These are defined using an enumeration-like production, and are (per definition) mapped to consecutive natural numbers starting from zero. Since tokens are issued over a network, a corresponding type-safe serial encoding was also specified.

Table 1. The token types of the 2WEAR protocol syntax

Token name	Description
CHAR	ASCII character
STRING	Sequence of ASCII characters (zero terminated)
INTEGER	Integer (variable value-based length encoding)
BOOLEAN	Boolean
UUID	Universal unique identifier
BBLOCK	Byte block (length is specified as a prefix)
KEYWORD	Symbolic names

Listing 1 gives a few indicative examples. The TextDisplay protocol defines a transaction for writing an ASCII character at a given column and row, and receiving a failure/success feedback. The Alarm protocol describes a notification transaction, for setting a threshold and then continuously receiving (several) values. The RequestReply protocol defines a generic exchange of STRING tokens whose contents are left "open", thus can be used as a tunnel for higher-level scripting protocols. The Teller protocol specifies a simple e-banking dialog.

```
TextDisplay = {WriteChar}.
WriteChar = CHAR Column Row BOOLEAN.
Column = INTEGER.
Row = INTEGER.

Alarm = Threshold {Value}.
Threshold = INTEGER.
Value = INTEGER.

RequestReply = STRING STRING.

Teller = Login Password (OK {Action} | NOK).
Action = Balance | Deposit | Withdraw.
Balance = BALANCE INTEGER.
Deposit = DEPOSIT INTEGER (OK | NOK).
Withdraw = WITHDRAW INTEGER (OK | NOK).
Login = UUID.
Password = INTEGER.
Keywords = BALANCE DEPOSIT WITHDRAW OK NOK.
```

Listing 1. Indicative syntax-based protocol definitions

This formal approach enables a protocol specification to be used as a syntactic contract between developers who implement service clients and providers in a decoupled fashion. In addition, a wide range of interaction schemes, which go well beyond a simple request-reply pattern, can be expressed in a straightforward manner. Note however that the service-related semantics associated with a protocol cannot be inferred from its syntax and must be specified in the corresponding description document.

Protocol definitions are independent from programming languages and runtime systems, so that developers are free to design and implement the primitives that are most suitable for their system. Indeed, the flavour and level of application programming support in 2WEAR varied significantly, ranging from simple templates used to produce efficient monolithic code for embedded devices, to libraries providing general-purpose communication facilities (and protocol parsers) for different operating systems and languages. The minimal requirement for the transport layer on top of which such communication mechanisms can be developed is the ability to exchange bytes in a semi-duplex and reliable fashion. In our prototype implementations, Bluetooth L2CAP was used as the underlying transport mechanism[5].

4.3   Service Discovery

We advocate a multi-device personal computing system whose configuration can be changed at *any point in time* and in an *out-of-the-loop* fashion, i.e. without devices being explicitly notified about it by the user. Programs wishing to exploit the services provided by remote devices must therefore be able to detect them at runtime.

Service discovery is implemented as a two-step procedure. In the first step, the wireless ad-hoc network is searched for new devices. This is done by employing the native Bluetooth discovery (inquiry) mechanism. When a device is detected, in a second step, it is queried about the services it provides via the so-called Home protocol, which allows a client to specify the desired service types and / or attribute value(s) in order to receive the respective contact (port) information. The Home protocol is quite similar to other client-driven discovery protocols, like Salutation (Pascoe 2001). The main difference is that it is defined as a proper syntax-based protocol, hence can be invoked using the standard 2WEAR communication facilities.

Just like any service-level access, the Home protocol requires the establishment of a (L2CAP) transport connection, which consumes energy and network resources. This is done in vain if the target device does not provide any service of interest to the querying party. As an optimization, we exploit the class-of-device (CoD) field of Bluetooth inquiry packets to encode service provision hints. This makes it possible to infer which types of services *are not* provided by a discovered device, without employing the Home protocol; which seemed to considerably enhance service discovery as well as the overall network connectivity, especially in the presence of many devices. Finally, device and service discovery information is cached locally to eliminate frequent querying over the network. Entries have an expiration time which is renewed whenever the remote device shows signs of existence. It is nevertheless possible for a

---

[5]   We also developed a TCP/IP "adapter" in order to perform initial interoperability tests between the programs of different partners over the Internet, before deploying code on the various portable and wearable devices.

program to receive outdated information. This can be explicitly invalidated upon an unsuccessful attempt to contact the service.

5   Dynamically Distributed User Interfaces

The ad-hoc nature of the envisioned system leads to an unusually dynamic and heterogeneous environment in terms of user interaction resources. In general, as illustrated in Figure 4, it is possible to differentiate among two layers of interaction-capable devices: inner layer wearable devices, which the user may or may not carry, depending on the situation; outer layer environment devices that fall inside the communication range of the user's portable / wearable computing system. Wearable devices are typically owned by the user and do not vary significantly while on-the-move. On the contrary, environment devices are part of the physical infrastructure, thus their availability is expected to vary as the user changes location.

Ideally, applications should be constructed in a way that facilitates the dynamic exploitation of the proximate interaction-specific devices which are available at any point in time, without requiring extensive programming effort. Research and development work towards accomplishing this goal has resulted in the delivery of the *Voyager* framework, which provides considerable development support for dynamically distributed user interfaces, built on top of the discussed communication framework.

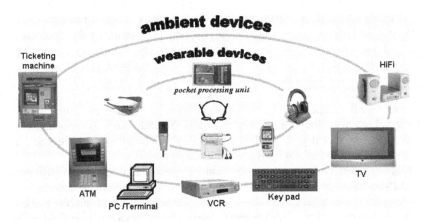

Fig. 4. Dynamically engaged ambient computing resources in mobile interactions

5.1   The UI Service Protocols

Due to the large diversity of user interface resources that can be provided by the various devices, it was mandatory to prescribe a common protocol that would be applicable to all possible UI service classes. Additionally, the protocol should allow programmers to detect and exploit on-the-fly any particular non-standard features offered by discovered devices. To this end, interaction with UI services occurs via three basic protocols: (i) the control protocol, (ii) the input protocol, and (iii) the output protocol. Slightly simplified definitions of these protocols are given in Listing 2.

```
Control = {GetP} [ACQ (OK {Main} RLS | NOK)].
Main = GetP | SetP.
GetP = GETP PropId PropVal.
SetP = SETP PropId PropVal BOOLEAN.
PropId = STRING. /* scripting */
PropVal = STRING. /* scripting */
Keywords = ACQ RLS GETP SETP ACK OK NOK.

Input = INPUT {InEventId InEventVal}.
InEventId = STRING. /* scripting */
InEventVal = STRING. /* scripting */
Keywords = INPUT.

Output = OUTPUT {OutEventId OutEventVal BOOLEAN}.
OutEventId = STRING. /* scripting */
OutEventVal = STRING. /* scripting */
Keywords = OUTPUT.
```

Listing. 2. The basic UI protocols

The control protocol describes the communication for acquiring, releasing and checking the availability of a UI resource. It also allows clients to determine, query and modify the so-called properties of a resource. The input and output protocols dictate the reception of user input events from a UI resource and the issuing of user output events towards a UI resource, respectively. Every distinct UI resource is expected to support the control protocol, as well as the input and/or output protocol, depending on its type.

It is important to note that property / event identifiers and values are defined as STRING tokens, hence are open to definition and interpretation by service providers and application programmers. This makes it possible to accommodate extended introspection and parameterization functionality as well as to exploit the special UI capabilities of devices in a flexible way, without breaking the basic UI protocols. Of course, this introduces an additional level (or dimension) of service meta-information that must be appropriately documented by service providers and consulted by application developers. Some sort of coordination is also needed to ensure that identical STRING identifiers of properties and event classes actually imply identical semantics and compatible corresponding content-value expressions across all UI service implementations.

5.2   Primitive UI Services

Several UI resources, exported as corresponding UI services, were developed to provide rudimentary distributed input / output functionality: Button (input); Keyboard (input); TextDisplay (output); TextLine (output); GraphicsDisplay (output); Menu (input and output); TextEditor (input and output). Their functionality is summarized in Table 2. The access protocol for each UI service is defined by refining the basic UI protocols in a suitable way. In addition, to simplify programming, appropriate client-side APIs were implemented that hide the underlying discovery and communication process. For certain UI services several alternative implementations were provided on different wearable and portable platforms, while others had to be emulated[6] on laptops and PCs.

Most of the UI service abstractions correspond to primitive input or output functionality, which are likely to be found in small wearable and embedded devices. However, services such as the Menu and the TextEditor encapsulate both input and output functions in a single unit. This reflects the situation where a device may provide advanced interactive behavior as a built-in feature. For instance, home appliances such as TVs employ menu-based dialogues, using their screen for output and their remote control unit for input. Thus it would be possible to export this UI functionality in the form of a distinct UI service, such as the Menu, which can be discovered and exploited by remote applications.

Table 2. The UI services

UI service type	UI mode	Functionality
Button	Input	receive button events
Keyboard	Input	receive key press events with key code
TextDisplay	Output	display a character at a given column & row
TextLine	Output	display a character at a given position
GraphicsDisplay	Output	display a bitmap
Menu	Input/Output	display list of textual options and receive as a result the choice of the user as a number
TextEditor	Input/Output	display text for (offline) editing and receive as a result a new text

5.3   Higher Level UI Management Support

Primitive UI services provide the basic functionality which can be used to implement a wide range of user interfaces. However, the application programmer is responsible for discovering the available services and combining them together to form meaningful interaction styles. Also, failure to communicate with a remote UI service must be handled, e.g. by replacing it with another available service of equivalent or similar functionality. Due to the inherently dynamic nature of the system, this becomes a commonly expected case rather than an exceptional situation, reflecting the need to accommodate dynamic UI re-configuration and deliver a persistent interaction throughout application execution.

To effectively provide such functionality at the application level, high-level *dialogue abstractions* were developed, taking into account the characteristics of small devices with restricted UI capability and relatively slow wireless communication. The adopted technique is based on virtual interaction objects supporting polymorphic platform bindings (Savidis 2005). For the purpose of the 2WEAR project, two generic dialogue object classes were introduced: (i) the Selector, allowing the user to select from an explicit list of displayed textual options; (ii) the TextEntry, enabling the user to enter / edit textual input. The application may employ an arbitrary number of such instances, but only one dialogue object instance may own the focus of user interaction at any point in time (i.e. a single focus object policy).

---

[6]   All primitive UI services were emulated on a desktop environment to perform initial tests of the framework without relying on wearable / portable hardware.

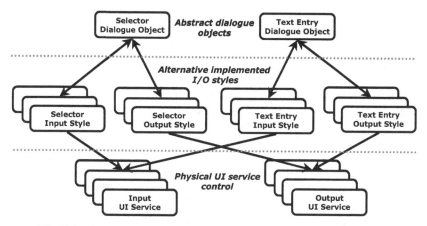

Fig. 5. Implementation structure for abstract (distributed) dialogue objects

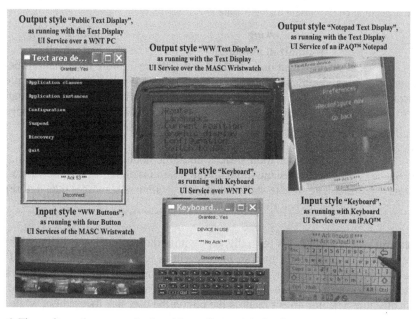

Fig. 6. Three alternative output (top) and input (bottom) styles for the Selector, based on different implementations of primitive UI services on various devices

These object classes encapsulate appropriate runtime control logic for the dynamic handling of UI services to achieve dynamic UI reconfiguration. This is accomplished through the implementation of alternative dialogue input and output control policies, also referred to as instantiation styles, as illustrated in Figure 5. Each style relies on a specific combination of UI services, and encompasses the code for managing its basic input / output functionality. Different input and output styles can be orthogonally combined to produce a large number of plausible physical instantiations for a given dialogue object class. As an example, Figure 6 shows various styles that have been implemented for the Selector dialogue.

At runtime, the application may interact with the user as long as there are adequate UI services to support at least one input and one output style for the focus dialogue object. Else, the dialogue enters a stalled state, where it is attempted to discover new UI services in order to make at least one input and output style of the focus dialogue viable. In this case, the dialog reverts back to working state and user interaction is resumed.

UI service discovery is also possible when the application is in working state. This may enable additional I/O styles for the focus dialogue object, thus creating the opportunity to reconfigure a dialogue *in the midst* of user interaction. In order to control system behavior, the user can specify whether such on-the-fly optimization is desirable and introduce priorities between dialog instantiation options (different preferences can be given for each application). Table 3 summarizes the UI reconfiguration logic.

Table 3. Outline of the algorithms for UI re-configuration behavior, upon UI service discovery or loss, depending on the current dialogue state

	working	*stalled*
UI service discovery	(optimization round) if UI optimization is enabled and a preferable instantiation became viable, deactivate the current instantiation and activate the new one	(revival round) if one or more instantiations became viable, select the most preferred one, set the dialogue state to running and activate the new instantiation
UI service loss	if the lost service is used by the current instantiation, deactivate the current instantiation, set the dialogue state to stalled and perform a revival round	do nothing (it is impossible that an instantiation became viable with less resources than before)

The state of user interaction is centrally kept within the application's dialogue object instances. It is updated each time an input event is received from a remote UI resource, associated to its current input style, before communicating the effects back to the user via the respective the UI output resource of its current output style. More specifically, the Selector object records the option the user has focused on, while the TextEntry object records the text entered by the user and the current cursor position. This separation between remote input / output and application-resident processing with support for state maintenance is illustrated in Figure 7.

Since the dialogue objects and styles reside within the application, this state is preserved locally even if the communication with the dynamically employed (remote) UI services fails. As a consequence, when a dialogue object instance is resumed / reconfigured using a new input / output style and / or new corresponding UI services, these can be properly initialized to reflect the last state of the dialogue.

A special application, called the Application Manager, is used to initiate, terminate and give focus to other applications. Even though several applications may be running concurrently to each other, only one may own the application focus (i.e. a single focus

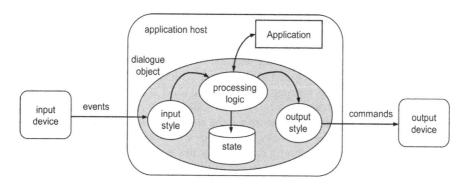

Fig. 7. Input / output processing of abstract dialogue objects; arrows indicate typical

application policy). Newly started applications are initialized in a suspended state, where no attempt is made to discover or allocate UI resources on their behalf. This is done only when an application receives focus, in which case a revival round is performed for its focus dialog object (see Table 2). The application then enters a working or stalled state, depending on the current availability of UI services. Conversely, when an application gives away the focus, it falls back to the suspended state, and the UI services allocated to its dialogue objects are released so that they can be used for the application that will receive the focus next.

6   Seamless Distributed Data Management

Data management becomes a key issue in a personal system that comprises many wearable and portable devices. Already today, the data that can be generated on the move, at the click of a button, can grow to exorbitant numbers. This imminent data explosion along with the fact that the number of personal devices used to generate, store and access data is most likely to increase in the future, aggravates the problem of data management. It quickly becomes clear that the conventional and *already* awkward model of moving data between devices via explicit and synchronous user commands does not scale. Even less so for embedded and mobile computing environments where devices have a limited user interface and user attention should be preserved.

With this motivation we developed a file-based[7] data management facility which turns storage devices into proactive self-organizing elements. This approach makes it possible to support several tasks in a largely automated way, requiring little or no explicit user input. For instance, we let wearable and portable devices collaborate with each other in an ad-hoc manner to copy or exchange files. Also, files generated on portable devices are forwarded via the Internet to a reliable storage service, referred to as the repository.

---

[7]   This work focuses on (data) files generated by the user, rather than binaries and internal system and application-specific configuration files. We also assume, even though this is not enforced by our implementation, that files are immutable (Schroeder et al. 1985), i.e. files with the same name are guaranteed to have identical contents.

6.1 Architecture and Implementation Overview

The storage facility is implemented as a set of components which reside on personal and infrastructure devices and interact with each other to achieve the desired functionality. Figure 8 depicts a personal area network with two personal devices, a camera and a wearable brick (as a storage wallet), close to an access point through which the repository can be reached.

Portable and wearable storage devices run the *storage daemon*, a process that is responsible for performing the necessary interactions with other devices as well as with the repository. Applications running on portables use the *storage library* API to invoke the storage daemon[8]. The functionality of the repository is implemented via the *repository daemon* that handles requests received from remote storage daemons.

Finally, the *gateway daemon* acts as a network and protocol gateway, allowing portable devices to communicate with services that reside in the Internet, such as the storage daemon. The gateway daemon can be installed on any device (e.g. our wearable computer equipped with a GPRS modem) or infrastructure element (e.g. a PC plugged on an Ethernet network) that features a network interface through which Internet connectivity can be provided. The communication between the storage, repository and Internet access daemons is implemented using the basic 2WEAR communication mechanisms.

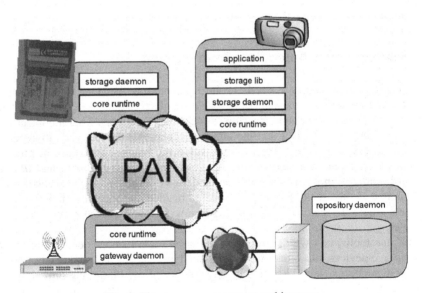

Fig. 8. The storage management architecture

6.2 Archival

The backup process is performed asynchronously behind the scenes with minimal effort on behalf of the application programmer. The storage library provides a *backup*

---

[8]   Some devices may act as "pure" storage data carriers, in which case they feature the device daemon without the device library or any local application.

operation to initiate backup for a given file. The backup status of a file can then be examined via the *isbackedup* operation.

The storage daemon maintains internally a queue of references to local files that need to be transferred to the repository. As long as this list is not empty, it periodically attempts to discover a gateway through which it can contact the repository daemon. When such a connection is eventually established, the storage daemon commences data transfer until all files have been successfully backed up at the repository.

Each entry of the backup queue is processed as follows. First, the file identifier (name) and size is sent to the repository daemon, which records this information and replies with a list of offset-length pairs indicating the missing file fragments. The storage daemon proceeds by sending the requested parts to the repository daemon. This is repeated until the repository replies with an empty fragment list, indicating that the entire file is safely stored, in which case backup proceeds with the next entry.

The transfer protocol is designed to support incremental data transfer on top intermittent connectivity, which is typical for mobile and ad-hoc computing environments[9]. As a result, if the connection with the repository breaks and is later re-established, backup continues from the last fragment that was successfully received by the repository. Notably, an interrupted backup process can be resumed via another device holding a copy of the same file. If several devices concurrently attempt to backup the same file, the repository daemon will request different file fragments from each one of them, thereby achieving parallel backup.

6.3   File Collection, Offloading, and Replication

The storage daemon automatically creates free space on devices when storage is filling up. Reclamation is driven by two parameters[10]: the minimum free ratio (MFR) and the desired free ratio (DFR). When free space drops below the MFR, the device daemon attempts to remove local files. Candidates for deletion are the least recently accessed files that have been successfully backed up in the repository. Garbage collection stops when the DFR is reached.

It is however possible that the DFR cannot be met given the above restrictions. As a last resort option, the storage daemon attempts to offload a file on another device, which will assume responsibility for backing it up to the repository. When such a device is found, data transfer between the two storage daemons occurs employing a protocol that is almost identical to the backup protocol; making it possible to tolerate frequent disconnections. Notably, the receiving daemon is free to collect file fragments of an interrupted transfer at any point in time. The sending daemon may remove the file only if it was successfully received by another device.

As a special case of offloading, the storage daemon may copy a file on another device without removing it locally. Replication is meaningful if it is desirable to increase the availability of a file within the personal area network. Applications can specify the number of copies that should be created on different devices via the *setreplicas* operation.

---

[9]   This is even more likely to occur in our system, since communication is implemented using a short-range radio technology.

[10]   We assume these values as given. In practice, these could be set using a configuration tool or adjusted automatically using a meaningful system policy.

6.4   PAN-Wide File Access and Dissemination

The storage facility does not automatically provide a unified and up-to-date file system view for all neighboring devices. To implement this, it would have been required to frequently exchange file information between co-located storage daemons, consuming a significant amount of CPU time, bandwidth and energy. Instead, we decided to provide basic primitives that can be combined under application control to achieve similar functionality.

Local files that are to be made visible to applications residing on remote devices need to be specified in an explicit way. This is done using the *setexport* operation, which marks a file so that its existence can be determined by remote storage daemons. Export entries can be given a lifetime and are removed by the storage daemon upon expiration. If no lifetime is specified, the export status of a file must be revoked via *setexport*. To declare its interest in remote files, a program registers with the storage library a lookup expression and notification handler. As a result, the storage daemon starts to periodically query nearby devices for exported files that match this expression. In case of a match, the corresponding programs are notified by invoking their registered handler routine.

Programs access local files via the standard *open, read, write* and *close* operations. Direct access is not supported for remote files (that have been discovered via the via the lookup mechanism). If a program wishes to access a remote file, it must create a local copy via the *fetch* operation of the storage library. The corresponding data transfer over the network is performed in the background by the storage daemon, following the same protocol as for file replication, in the reverse direction. If the connection breaks, data transfer may be resumed, also by redirecting the request to another device that has a copy. Fetch operations are given an allowable silence period, indicating the maximum amount of time for establishing contact with a device that can provide the target file. If the storage daemon fails to commence or resume transfer within this period, it aborts the fetch operation and deletes the corresponding file fragments.

Listing 3 gives sample code for fetching all .jpg images found on nearby devices with a silence threshold of 5 minutes. The same mechanism is used to disseminate files of public / common interest to other people, e.g. family, friends and colleagues. The difference is that the interacting devices do not belong to the same person. Rather than introducing yet another operation, the existing *setexport* operation was extended to take an additional (optional) parameter, indicating the persons for which the file should be made visible. In our prototype implementation people are identified via unique UUID values, and devices provide the UUID of their owner via the Home protocol[11]. A special value is reserved to indicate "any person"; files exported using this value become accessible to all devices. Fully automated yet controlled file dissemination can thus be easily achieved between devices that belong to different people: the provider needs to export the desired files, and the receiver must run in the background a simple program in the spirit of Listing 3.

---

[11] This work does not address the various security issues that arise in this context.

```
void notifier( char *fname, char *location ) {
 printf( "file %s was found\n", fname );
 printf( "let's copy it locally!\n" );
 fetch( location, fname, "/mypicts/" , 60*5);
}

int ld;

ld = registerLookup( "*.jpg", notifier );
...
unregisterLookup( ld );
```

Listing 3. Registering a lookup task for fetching remote .jpg files found

7   Putting the Pieces Together

Returning to the scenario given in the beginning of this article, we outline how it can
be realized using the features of the 2WEAR system. Figure 9 depicts the corresponding interactions that (may) take place between the various devices, applications, sub-
systems and services. The communication and discovery subsystem is not shown to
avoid cluttering the picture.

Peripheral devices, like the GPS, the wristwatch and the table-display (emulated on
a laptop), make their particular resources available to other devices in the form of corresponding services, such as GPSLocation, TextDisplay, Button and GraphicsDisplay.

Similarly, the camera (emulated on a PDA) exports a GraphicsDisplay and Menu
service. In addition, it features a local photo application that exploits the storage management subsystem to back up new images on the repository, offload old images on

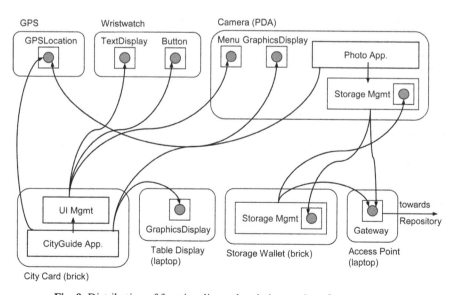

Fig. 9. Distribution of functionality and main interactions for our scenario

the user's storage wallet (brick), or let images be transferred to a storage wallet (brick) of another person. The application also periodically searches for a GPSLocation service which, if found, is used to annotate the photos taken with geographical coordinates.

The city-guide card (brick) comes with an embedded application that takes advantage of the user interface management subsystem. As a consequence, the application can be controlled via the wristwatch and/or camera user interface elements. It is possible to switch between the two configurations at runtime, via user selection or automatic adaptation (when a device is switched off or goes out of range). The map of the city can be optionally rendered on any available GraphicsDisplay service, under user control. Finally, the city-guide application employs a GPSLocation service to track user movement and issue a notification when approaching a landmark.Of course, this scenario and proposed functional arrangement is merely indicative; and by no means optimal in terms of device affordances or user interaction. We nevertheless believe that it illustrates the potential of the envisioned system as well as the level of application support that has been implemented to simplify development in such a setting.

8   Summary

In the 2WEAR project we have explored the paradigm of cooperative multi-device personal computing, where different wearable, portable and infrastructure elements communicate with each other in an ad-hoc fashion. The physical decoupling of the elements that form the system results in great flexibility, making it possible for the user to change its configuration in a simple way and at any point in time. However, it is precisely due to this dynamic nature of the system that makes the exploitation of the distributed available resources difficult. An additional challenge is to achieve this without forcing the user to (continuously) provide input to the various devices of the system in an explicit manner. Towards this objective, advanced mechanisms were developed on top of an open communication and discovery framework, which address key issues of distributed user interface and storage management on behalf of the application programmer.

For the interested reader, a more elaborate introduction of the syntax-based protocols is given in (Gutknecht 2003). The UI framework is described in detail in (Savidis and Stephanidis 2005a; Savidis and Stephanidis 2005b). Finally, work on different aspects of core runtime support for personal area network computing and a more updated version of the storage management facility is reported in (Karypidis and Lalis 2005) and (Karypidis and Lalis 2006), respectively.

Acknowledgements

This work was funded in part through the IST/FET program of the EU, contract nr. IST-2000-25286.

References

Amft, O., Lauffer, M., Ossevoort, S., Macaluso, F., Lukowicz, P., Troester, G.: Design of the QBIC wearable computing platform. In: Proceedings 15th IEEE International Conference on Application-Specific Systems, Architectures and Processors, Texas, USA, IEEE, Los Alamitos (2004)

Abowd, G., Mynatt, E.: Charting Past, Present, and Future Research in Ubiquitous Computing. ACM Transactions on Computer-Human. Interaction 7(1), 29–58 (2000)

Bang, W., Chang, W., Kang, K., Choi, W., Potanin, A., Kim, D.: Self-contained Spatial Input Device for Wearable Computers. In: Proceedings7th IEEE International Symposium on Wearable Computers, NY, USA, pp. 26–34. IEEE Computer Society Press, Los Alamitos (2003)

Bhagwat, P.: Bluetooth: Technology for Short-Range Wireless Applications. IEEE Internet Computing 5(3), 96–103 (2001)

Beck, J., Gefflaut, A., Islam, N.: MOCA: A Service Framework for Mobile Computing Devices. In: Proceedings 1st ACM International Workshop on Data Engineering for Wireless and Mobile Access, Seattle, USA, pp. 62–68. ACM Press, New York (1999)

Becker, C., Handte, M., Schiele, G., Rothermel, K.: PCOM - A Component System for Pervasive Computing. In: Proceedings 2nd IEEE International Conference on Pervasive Computing and Communications, Florida, USA, pp. 67–76. IEEE Computer Society Press, Los Alamitos (2004)

Brumitt, B., Meyers, B., Krumm, J., Kern, A., Shafer, S.: EasyLiving: Technologies for Intelligent Environments. In: Thomas, P., Gellersen, H.-W. (eds.) HUC 2000. LNCS, vol. 1927, pp. 12–29. Springer, Heidelberg (2000)

Calvary, G., Coutaz, J., Thevenin, D., Rey, G.: Context and Continuity for Plastic User Interfaces. In: Proceedings I3 Spring Days Workshop on Continuity in Future Computing Systems, Porto, Portugal, CLRC, pp. 51–69 (2001)

Fishkin, K.P., Partridge, K., Chatterjee, S.: Wireless User Interface Components for Personal Area Networks. IEEE Pervasive Computing 1(4), 49–55 (2002)

Gajos, K., Christianson, D., Hoffmann, R., Shaked, T., Henning, K., Long, J.J., Weld, D.: Fast And Robust Interface Generation for Ubiquitous Applications. In: Proceedings 7th International Conference on Ubiquitous Computing, Tokyo, Japan, pp. 37–55 (2005)

Garlan, G., Siewiorek, D., Smailagic, A., Steenkiste, P.: Project Aura: Toward Distraction-Free Pervasive Computing. IEEE Pervasive Computing 1(2), 22–31 (2002)

Gellersen, H.G., Schmidt, A., Beigl, M.: Multi-Sensor Context Awareness in Mobile Devices and Smart Artifacts. Mobile Networks and Applications 7(5), 341–351 (2002)

Gutknecht, J.: A New Approach to Interoperability of Distributed Devices. In: Stephanidis, C. (ed.) Universal access in HCI: inclusive design in the information society, pp. 384–388. Lawrence Erlbaum, Mahwah (2003)

Johanson, B., Fox, A., Winograd, T.: The Interactive Workspaces Project: Experiences with Ubiquitous Computing Rooms. IEEE Pervasive Computing 1(2), 67–74 (2002)

Karypidis, A., Lalis, S.: Exploiting co-location history for efficient service selection in ubiquitous computing systems. In: Proceedings 2nd International Conference on Mobile and Ubiquitous Systems, San Diego, USA, pp. 202–209. IEEE Computer Society Press, Los Alamitos (2005)

Karypidis, A., Lalis, S.: Omnistore: A system for ubiquitous personal storage management. In: Proceedings 4th IEEE International Conference on Pervasive Computing and Communications, Pisa, Italy, pp. 136–146. IEEE Computer Society Press, Los Alamitos (2006)

Kortuem, G., Schneider, J., Preuitt, D., Thompson, T.G.C., Fickas, S., Segall, Z.: When Peer-to-Peer comes Face-to-Face: Collaborative Peer-to-Peer Computing in Mobile Ad-Hoc Networks. In: Proceedings 1st International Conference on Peer-to-Peer Computing, Linkoping, Sweden, pp. 75–94 (2001)

Krause, A., Siewiorek, D., Smailagic, A., Farrington, J.: Unsupervised, Dynamic Identification of Physiological and Activity Context in Wearable Computing. In: Proceedings 7th IEEE International Symposium on Wearable Computers, NY, USA, pp. 88–97. IEEE Computer Society Press, Los Alamitos (2003)

Kuladinithi, K., Timm-Giel, A., Goerg, C.: Mobile Ad-hoc Communications in AEC Industry. ITcon 9(Special Issue on Mobile Computing in Construction), 313–323 (2004)

Kunito, G., Sakamoto, K., Yamada, N., Takakashi, T.: Architecture for Providing Services in the Ubiquitous Computing Environment. In: Proceedings 6th International Workshop on Smart Appliances and Wearable Computing, Lisbon, Portugal (2006)

Lehikoinen, J., Holopainen, J., Salmimaa, M., Aldrovandi, A.: MEX: A Distributed Software Architecture for Wearable Computers. In: Proceedings 3rd International Symposium on Wearable Computers, Victoria, Canada, pp. 52–57. IEEE Computer Society Press, Los Alamitos (1999)

Majoe, D.: Ubiquitous-computing enabled wireless devices. In: Stephanidis, C. (ed.) Universal access in HCI: inclusive design in the information society, pp. 444–448. Lawrence Erlbaum, Mahwah (2003)

Ogris, G., Stiefmeier, T., Junker, H., Lukowicz, P., Troester, G.: Using Ultrasonic Hand Tracking to Augment Motion Analysis Based Recognition of Manipulative Gestures. In: Proceedings 9th IEEE International Symposium on Wearable Computers, Osaka, Japan, pp. 152–159. IEEE Computer Society Press, Los Alamitos (2005)

Park, D.G., Kim, J.K., Bong, S.J., Hwang, J.H., Hyung, C.H., Kang, S.W.: Context Aware Service Using Intra-body Communication. In: Proceedings 4th IEEE International Conference on Pervasive Computing and Communications, Pisa, Italy, pp. 84–91. IEEE Computer Society Press, Los Alamitos (2006)

Pascoe, R.: Building Networks on the Fly. IEEE Spectrum 38(3), 61–65 (2001)

Roman, M., Cambell, R.H.: Gaia: Enabling Active Spaces. In: Proceedings 9th ACM SIGOPS European Workshop, Kolding, Denmark (2000)

Salber, D., Dey, A., Abowd, G.: The Context Toolkit: Aiding the Development of Context-Enabled Applications. In: Proceedings ACM SIGCHI 99 Conference on Human Factors in Computing Systems, Pittsburgh, USA, pp. 434–441. ACM Press, New York (1999)

Satyanarayanan, M.: The Evolution of Coda. ACM Transactions on Computer Systems 20(2), 85–124 (2002)

Savidis, A.: Supporting Virtual Interaction Objects with Polymorphic Platform Bindings in a User Interface Programming Language. In: Guelfi, N. (ed.) RISE 2004. LNCS, vol. 3475, pp. 11–22. Springer, Heidelberg (2005)

Savidis, A., Stephanidis, C.: Dynamic deployment of remote graphical toolkits over Bluetooth from wearable devices. In: Proceedings 11th International Conference on Human-Computer Interaction, Las Vegas, USA (2005a)

Savidis, A., Stephanidis, C.: Distributed interface bits: dynamic dialogue composition from ambient computing resources. Personal Ubiquitous Computing 9, 142–168 (2005b)

Schroeder, M.D., Gifford, D.K., Needham, R.M.: A caching file system for a programmer's workstation. SIGOPS Operating Systems Review 19(5), 25–34 (1985)

Tuulari, E., Ylisaukko-Oja, A.: SoapBox: A Platform for Ubiquitous Computing Research and Applications. In: Proceedings International Conference on Pervasive Computing, Zurich, Switzerland, pp. 125–138 (2002)

DeVaul, R., Sung, M., Gips, J., Pentland, A.: MIThril 2003: Applications and Architecture. In: Proceedings 7th IEEE International Symposium on Wearable Computers, NY, USA, IEEE Computer Society Press, pp. 4–11. IEEE Computer Society Press, Los Alamitos (2003)

Want, R., Pering, T., Danneels, G., Kumar, M., Sundar, M., Light, J.: The Personal Server: Changing the Way We Think About Ubiquitous Computing. In: Borriello, G., Holmquist, L.E. (eds.) UbiComp 2002. LNCS, vol. 2498, pp. 194–209. Springer, Heidelberg (2002)

Weiser, M.: The Computer for the 21st Century. Scientific American 265(3), 94–104, reprinted in IEEE Pervasive Computing 1(1), 19–25 (1991)

Wirth, N.: What can we do about the unnecessary diversity of notation for syntactic definitions? Communications of the ACM 20(11), 822–823 (1977)

Yasuda, K., Hagino, T.: Ad-Hoc Filesystem: A Novel Network Filesystem for Ad-hoc Wireless Networks. In: Lorenz, P. (ed.) ICN 2001. LNCS, vol. 2094, pp. 177–185. Springer, Heidelberg (2001)

An Attention-Based Architecture for Context Switch Detection

Nicolas Tsapatsoulis[1], Stathis Kasderidis[2], and John G. Taylor[2]

[1] Department of Telecommunications Science and Technology,
University of Peloponnese, Tripolis, Greece,
[2] Department of Mathematics, King's College London, London, UK

1 Introduction

In the era of Ubiquitous Computing (Weiser 1991), software applications, hidden in information appliances (Birnbaum 1997), will be continuously running, in an invisible manner (Weiser 1993), aiming at the best fulfilment of human users' needs. These applications should be characterized by interaction transparency and context-awareness (Abowd 1999). *Interaction transparency* means that the human users are not aware that there is a computing module embedded in a tool or device that they are using. It contrasts with the actual transparency of current interactions with computers: both traditional input-output devices such as mice and keyboards and manipulations such as launching browsers and entering authentication information (by using a login and a password) are purely computer oriented. *Context awareness* refers to adaptation of the behaviour of an application depending on its current environment. This environment can be characterized as a physical location, an orientation or a user profile. A context-aware application can sense the environment and interpret the events that occur within it. Sensing the environment is very important for adapting the provided to the user services.

In this work we present an attention control architecture which shows how sensory control can be used for sensor based context capturing. The principal idea behind such an approach is that user context switches correlate with higher probability with important changes in the user's state. A context switch is a concept that indicates a transition from a previous equilibrium state to a new equilibrium. This concept is specialized further as it is applied in specific domains. However, this transition is the core property of detecting context switches.

There are two principle ways in which such a state transition could take place. It is either a slow, gradual process ("*adiabatic*") or a "*sudden*" jump to the new state. So, the rate of transition is the actual criterion for classification of the proper approach. Typically a fast (with respect to time) change (deviation from the current equilibrium point) indicates an increased uncertainty and as such is a prudent strategy to deal with it first. On the other hand slow changes are more easily captured by observation in the macro-scale, i.e. by considering general statistical characteristics of an appropriate population.

Human beings, as well as many other species, detect sudden changes in their environment through the mechanism of attention. Attention based processes and models

N. Streitz, A. Kameas, and I. Mavrommati (Eds.): The Disappearing Computer, LNCS 4500, pp. 205–229, 2007.
© Springer-Verlag Berlin Heidelberg 2007

have been applied so far in two main application areas: Systems' control (Taylor 2001), (Bonasso 1996) and human assistance (Moccia 2002). In the first case the proposed models are either in an abstract level aiming at the explanation of brain processes (Taylor 2001) and it is, therefore, difficult to implement and use them in practical situations, or they are driven by programming issues (Levinson 2005, 1995) and they have, therefore, limited generalization abilities. In assisting humans, the proposed applications of attention are mainly lacking coherence with the corresponding brain processes (Moccia 2002).

The basic aim of our work is to provide a complete view of how attention models that combine modelling and applicability of abstract concepts can be used in practice. The flow of information in this chapter is as follows: We begin by introducing the ubiquitous health scenario through which the added value of the proposed model should be made clear. The proposed architecture for context switch detection is then thoroughly discussed, followed by a demonstration to a real life problem: the health monitoring problem. Finally conclusions are drawn and suggestions for further work are given.

2   The Ubiquitous Health Scenario

Prevention of medical incidents that endanger vulnerable groups of patients, e.g. individuals with chronic diseases, special needs, etc., is considered one of the key applications of ubiquitous computing. Despite the extended research and development activity of tele-care in such cases (Jovanov 1999; Martin 2000), most approaches assume that the patient is permanently situated in a particular location (e.g. at home) and that all biosignals are transmitted in a raw form to the medical center. Both assumptions degrade significantly the patients' quality of living, since they have to choose between the sense of security and the freedom of movement outside their home. In addition to that, they increase the related costs, due to continuous usage of telecommunication channels and numerous processing units, for either patients or medical centers.

Ubiquitous health monitoring can be achieved through a different concept: Instead of continuously transmitting raw signals to the medical center this can happen only in attention seeking or emergency incidents. Technological evolution in the fields of microelectronics and telecommunications provide the required technology and know-how to build systems serving this concept. Biosignals can be collected and transmitted by comfortably worn wireless microsensors (Roth 2002) to programmable portable devices (Abowd 1999), capable of intelligent processing, e.g. PDAs and cutting-edge cellular phones. As a result, biosignals are not transmitted in raw form to the medical center, but are collected from the intelligent devices via Bluetooth networks and utilized to evaluate the patient's status. Communicating the biosignals to the medical center is then triggered by the estimated health status. Health status estimation, however, should be done in context aware manner taking into account the physical location of the patient and its profile.

A general setup of the ubiquitous health scenario is illustrated in Figure 1. It includes a set of sensors that are attached on the patient's body, and a mobile computing unit (e.g. a PDA) responsible for processing and analyzing the data provided by the

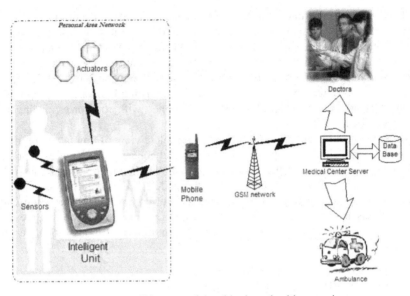

Fig. 1. A possible setup of the ubiquitous health scenario

sensors, reaching meaningful conclusions and, if needed, dynamic decisions. The sensors together with the intelligent unit (mobile computing device) form a personal area network that monitors the patient's health status, gives advice to the patient, adjusts the environmental conditions according to the patient's needs, and, in the case of an emergency, notifies the patient's doctor or the corresponding medical center.

2.1 Sensors and Actuators

Sensor sub-system consists of special non-perceptible and non-obtrusive intelligent sensors for capturing and measuring biosignals (Lei 2000) such as ECG, blood pressure, heart rate, breath rate, and perspiration, and extracting-evaluating on-line diagnostic information such as ECG QS detection (Kunzmann 2002). These sensors are autonomous (as far as energy issues are concerned), able to self-evaluate their operation, and include built-in RF transceivers compatible with the Bluetooth and IEEE 802.11b protocols for wireless communication.

Actuators are distinguished in: (a) ambient actuators (e.g., air-conditioning units) that perform adjustments on the environmental conditions according to the patient's state, based on the instructions of the intelligent unit (for example the intelligent unit may request a lower room temperature if sensor data indicate that this will be relieving for the patient), and (b) integrated actuators built in the intelligent unit software (that connects to information bases for providing consultation to the patient, and notifies the patient's doctor and the corresponding medical center in the case of an emergency). Additionally, software actuators can perform service discovery (Goland 1999) in the nearby area. Finding a doctor (through his own intelligent unit) for providing first aid could be one such service.

2.2   Intelligent Unit

The inputs of the intelligent unit are the wirelessly transmitted signals captured by the sensors. Incoming signals are processed[1] with respect to the patient's history record and other peculiarities, as well as environmental information, in order to reach conclusions about the patient's health status, take simple actions such as adjusting the environmental conditions or giving certain advice to the patient, and notify specialized personnel (e.g., doctors) that can handle emergency cases (providing as well justified estimation of the patient's health status together with the data used to reach this conclusion)[2]. The connection to the medical centre is achieved via a GSM line so as to notify the caregiver doctor, transmitting at the same time the latest measures of the bio-signals obtained by the sensors.

The intelligence of such a unit lies in the following: (a) There exist distinct modes of operation that are automatically activated according to the current external state of the patient, i.e. whether he is asleep, working, walking, or even exercising, (b) The system is context aware. This means that on the one hand the environmental conditions are taken into account when processing the data, while on the other the system has the possibility to adjust them as well. For example it can collect data concerning ambient temperature and humidity and adjust them according to the patient's needs when possible (e.g., at home or at the office).

(a) It identifies problems in the operation of the sensors (e.g., low batteries) so as to notify the patient and realize whether the conclusions it has reached are valid.

In the following Sections we present an attention-based architecture for the intelligent unit which allows it to operate in a context aware fashion.

3   The Architecture of the Intelligent Unit

An architecture which tries to model the sensory role of attention process found in humans and animals in a system level perspective is shown in Figure 2[3]. We argue that through this architecture context switch detection, required for the functionalities of the intelligent unit mentioned earlier, is feasible. Boxes, in Figure 2, represent processing components while arrows represent signals and information flow. Explanation of the processing components follows immediately while a clear example, of what the signals might be, is given through the User Monitoring problem use case, discussed in section "Demonstration: The User Monitoring Problem".

---

[1] The term "Processing" is used, in this paper, in a broad sense. Processing, in general, refers to digital signal processing accomplished mainly through time series processing, signal transformations and mapping through Neural Network models. However, the kind of processing that is employed is different from module to module and is implied by the description of the corresponding modules. In the Implementation section is given a concrete example clarifying this issue.

[2] The functionality of the various architectural components is supported either by software routines (implemented in whatever way one wishes) or even through hardware implementation with the aid of a Digital Signal Processor. In our implementation modeling was done using the SIMULINK model libraries (see *The Mathworks http://www.mathworks.com*) and a prototype was built using the Texas Instruments TMS320C6713 Digital Signal Processor.

[3] Figures 2 -6 in this paper are visual representations of the corresponding modules that have been implemented using the SIMULINK platform (The Mathworks 2005).

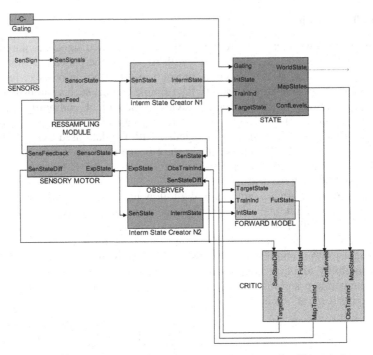

Fig. 2. The overall attention-driven architecture for an intelligent unit

Attention refers to two forms of control: sensory and motor response (Rush-worth 1997). In the proposed model emphasis is given to sensory response. Sensory response is based on lower level data (down to the input sensors, so as to change sampling rate, for example) monitoring and feedback is given in response to an attention signal. In the particular situation of the above mentioned intelligent unit the *attention process* may refer to user monitoring; that is detecting irregular patterns as far as the state of the user is concerned. The attention control process, accommodated mainly by the Observer and Sensory Motor modules, "looks" into the data stream for any un-usual patterns of behaviour. In the sensory role of the attention, therefore, the focus is to catch unexpected events that possibly indicate a user transition (possibly context switch) or other non-stationery behaviour. A possible action in such an event may be a change in the sampling rates (accommodated by the Resampling module) of the corresponding sensors (these sensors are identified by the Observer module) and/or changing the type of feature analysis that takes place in the Intermediate State Module. In the latter case more demanding analysis could be activated that would enable the identification of special features that are ignored by the default analysis. This in turn could give further information to the decision-making systems (State module) to better evaluate the current user state.

Table 1 indicates how the basic modules of the architecture, shown in Figure 2, are further decomposed into sub-modules. Brief description of these modules follows. Some of them are discussed in more detail in subsequent sections because they relate to the way the learnable components (see sub-section "Learning mode", in section "Operational modes of the Intelligent Unit") of the architecture are trained.

Table 1. Sub-modules in the architecture of the intelligent unit

S/N	Module	Sub-module 1	Sub-module 2	Sub-module 3	Sub-module 4
1	State	Maps	Self-Evaluators	Committee Machine	
2	Observer				
3	Critic	Credit As-sign	Target State Creator		
4	Forward Models	Action-State Map	State Reward Model		
5	Sensory Motor	Monitor	Attention Con-troller	Goals	Rules

4 Sensory Motor

This module accommodates the sensory role of Attention (mentioned as Attention Controller: Role 2 in the Figure[4] that follows).

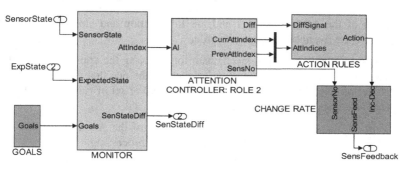

Fig. 3. The Sensory Motor module

In its full form the Sensory Motor includes the *Rules*, *Goals*, *Monitor*, and *Attention Controller* sub-modules, the functionality of which is explained briefly below:

Rules: This module serves as an elementary action planner determining the feedback that is given back to sensors. In the Figure 3 above it is shown the simple action "CHANGE RATE".

Goals: This module is responsible for representing the various goals ("programs") that the intelligent unit executes or tries to achieve. It also contains appropriate parameterizations both for the User and the Goals. It is further decomposed into the following:

---

[4] The numbers in the ellipsoid objects in Figure 3 (near *SensorState*, *ExpState*, *SensFeedback* and *SenStateDiff* labels) indicate the numbering of inputs (that is *SensorState* is input number one, and *ExpState* is input number two) and outputs (*SensFeedback*, *SenStateDiff*) of this particular module (Sensory Motor module). They appear inherently in every Simulink model.

- *Values*: This part represents the Base component of the User Profile. The Base component is a set of values for all the parameters present in the Maps (see description of State module) and other modules that model the User. These values are statistical averages of appropriate population groups (clusters), i.e. middle-aged black male, young woman, etc. They are used as centers of reference for the learning algorithms present on the Maps and they are invariant.

- *User Profile*: This part represents the Delta component of the User Profile. These are deviations ("deltas") added to the corresponding Base values above. Deltas are changeable through learning. While the Base Values represent the general context, the Deltas represent the specific individual differences.

Monitor: The module is responsible for comparing expected (created by the Observer module) with realized sensor states. In case of a deviation it produces an Attention Event (characterized by its Index).

Attention Controller: It implements a structure that imposes an order in the space of Attention Events and provides a selection mechanism based on this order. It is further decomposed into the following:

- *Priority Function*: This component implements a mapping for inducing a priority order in the space of Attention Events. In general the mechanism uses the values of the Attention Index and the Information and Context attributes describing the Event and assigns the order.

- *Dispatch Function*: This is mechanism for selecting the appropriate event to be executed. In general the highest order event is the one that is selected. The dispatcher produces a feedback signal that selects the set of rules that will be executed as a response to the event.

- *Attention Stack*: This is a conceptual container of the Attention Events. There, all the generated events are stored and await for processing.

5   State Module

This module is responsible for transforming, in a robust way, *Intermediate states* being in subsymbolic form (features derived based on sensor measurements) to *World state representations* of symbolic form (being interpretable by humans). It includes the following sub-modules:

- *Maps*: These are classifier systems. Maps produce the appropriate World Representations from the Intermediate Representation.

- *Self Evaluators*: They support monitoring of the performance of their associated Maps providing confidence level of their mappings.

- *Committee Machine*: This module combines the Maps in the best possible way, according to a given context and taking into account the confidence levels that are provided by Self-Evaluators.

In this paragraph we focus on the signals and sub-modules present in State module as well as on modules interconnection. Furthermore, we explain how the difference in the two different methods that we use for mapping (CAM/SPM (Raouzaiou 2002) and PAC/MED (Apolloni 2002) is gracefully incorporated in the architecture through gating.

Figure 4 presents an overall view of the State module while Figure 5 looks into a Map. The basic concepts that govern the design of State module are: (a) Multiple Maps combined provide better classification performance than a single Map (see Section referring to Committee Machines), (b) Self-evaluation of Maps provides a fair indication on which Maps should Committee Machine rely on to take the right decision, (c) Gating can be used to provide information about which of the CAM/SPM or PAC/MED methods is more appropriate in a particular context.

The Maps, in addition to the intermediate state vector, are fed with two other inputs which are related with retraining / parameter adaptation. Both stem from the *Critic*

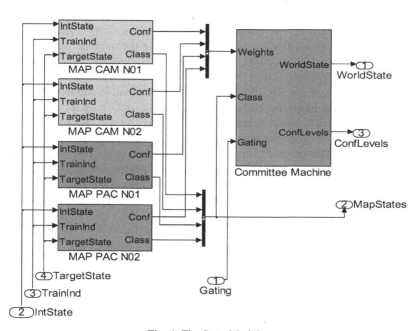

Fig. 4. The State Module

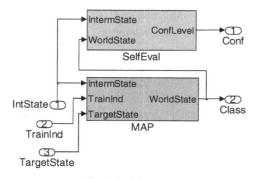

Fig. 5. Inside Maps

module; the first (*TrainInd* in the diagram) is an indication as to whether or not the particular Map requires retraining or parameter tuning. The other (*TargetState* in the diagram) provides target output for the transformation of the current intermediate state. In the case of parameter tuning (online adaptation) this target output can be used to compute the Mean Square Error and back-propagate it so as to alter Maps weights on a sequential basis. In the case of re-training (offline adaptation) target outputs along with the corresponding input vectors are collected and stored in order to create a new training set.

Self-Evaluators are correlated to Maps on a one-to-one basis. That is every Map is accompanied with a self-evaluator. The purpose of self-evaluators is to provide confidence levels for the mapping, performed by the Maps, of input vectors (intermediate states) to output classes (world states). Self-evaluators are fed by both intermediate and world states while having stored either the initial training set, used for the training of the corresponding Maps, or parameters that model the distribution of the initial training set. The methods that are used for estimating the outputs' confidence level can be found at (ORESTEIA 2003b).

The *Committee Machine* (Tresp 2001) combines the classifications of the individual Maps to achieve a final classification taking into account, in addition to the classification results of the Maps, the current context and the confidence levels provided by the Self-Evaluators. The input named *Gating*, models the current context in a very simple way. In closed problems (like medical ones) where prior knowledge and rules may be available, these guide the Committee Machine to rely mainly on the CAM/SPM method while in open problems (like the problem of psychological state estimation of drivers) priority is given to the PAC/MED method. This is typically accomplished through the following procedure:

In every context only three Maps are considered by the Committee machine. The two Maps of the favored method are always attending the committee while the MAP that is left out is the one that has the lowest confidence level among the not-favored method. This means that gating allows the favored method to have the majority of votes while the Map that is not attending the committee is always from the part of the non-favored method but changes with the input vector depending on which Map classifies that vector with the lowest confidence level.

A formal definition of Committee Machine's functionality is as follows: Let the input signal (intermediate state) noted as $\bar{x}$, and $\bar{y}_i = f_i(\bar{x})$ be the output vector of the i-th Map. We denote with $f_i^{(j)}(\bar{x})$ the output value of i-th Map regarding the j-th class. Let also $c_i(\bar{x})$ to be the confidence level of the i-th Map, provided by the corresponding Self-Evaluator, for the input vector $\bar{x}$. Then the final classification of the Committee Machine is given by:

$$class(\bar{x}) = \arg\max_j \sum_{i \in G(C, c_i(\bar{x}))} c_i(\bar{x}) \cdot f_i^{(j)}(\bar{x}) \tag{2.1}$$

where by $G(C, c_i(\bar{x}))$ we denote the set of Maps that are attending the committee, according to gating.

6   Other Modules

In addition to Sensory Motor and State modules which consist the core of the attention-based architecture there are three other modules (see Figure 2) whose role is auxiliary:

Observer: The module is responsible for implementing a map that predicts the current observed sensor state. In this way we can detect discrepancies between what should be happening and what actually occurred. In this way we can detect change in the User/Environment state in the fast timescale. Classifiers (Maps) capture discrepancies in the slow timescale.

Forward Models: Typically Forward models transform the current selected action (coming through Rules or the Action module) into a future state. However, in the real implementation future states are obtained through a Map that transforms intermediate states that are based on Observer predictions to expected world states. Therefore, no *State Reward Model* is considered while the *Action-State Map* is basically realized as a Prediction-State Map.

Critic: This module is the heart of the overall learning process of the intelligent unit. It defines which of the Observer or State module is malfunctioning (if any) through the *Credit Assignment* module. Moreover, in the case of State malfunctioning it identifies which of the Maps require re-training or parameter updating by issuing the *MapTrainInd* signal. Since all the Maps are based on supervised training, the Critic creates also target states to be considered by the Maps. This is done through the *Target State Creator* signal.

7   Operational Modes of the Intelligent Unit

While in the previous section we presented the structural decomposition of the attention-driven model by enumerating the various modules and their function, in this section we focus on the functional aspects of it and we outline its learning strategy. Therefore the discussion that follows refers to the processing and learning operation modes.

7.1   Processing Mode

In the most of the time the intelligent unit operates in the normal processing mode. In this mode all modules shown in Figure 2 participate. However, their operation is grouped in two sub-systems. The first is the State Evaluation which is implemented mainly by the State module, while the other modules participate in the second major sub-system that of Attention Control.

7.1.1   State Evaluation
State evaluation is performed within the State module, with the help of the structure shown in Figure 4. Here we briefly describe the state evaluation process and not the structure.

The State module is connected by several communication links to a number of sensors (through the *Intermediate State Module* which pre-processes sensor measurements). Through each communication it is recorded a particular sensor's response, which in general we consider it as a vector of real numbers. For now the semantics of this response vector is not important being either a sensor providing raw data or an Intermediate State Module providing symbolic information (including the case of the user feedback). What is important is that we concatenate all response vectors in a new one, which is the Cartesian product of all these information sources. Obviously different sections of this Cartesian vector have different interpretation but this does not need to concern us for now. We call this representation the *Native Representation*. Related directly to this Cartesian vector is another vector, which keeps its history. This history can either be only the "previous" time step (at time $t-1$) or can include a number of past time steps. For our discussion we can assume that we can have access to values up to a maximum lag time $t-T$. It is mainly a matter of system modelling if more than one historical value is kept in this Historic Cartesian vector or not. In the simplest case the Cartesian vector is used directly by the decision-making methods (*Maps*). The application of the Maps in the Native Representation produces an output that is another type of representation of the world around us, which we call the *World Representation*. Typically this form is more compact and as such is closer to reasoning with symbols than subsymbolic features. After a Map has produced a new World Representation (pre-decision), its output is used in two distinct ways:

In one hand is forwarded to another part inside the State Module, which is called *Self-Evaluator*. The purpose of this part is to monitor in run time the performance achieved by its (corresponding) Map. If this performance at times is judged as poor, the evaluator sends a signal to its Map so as to indicate the need for further (off-line usually) training and starts collecting appropriate data for this purpose. Assuming that this operation is performed successfully one should have at the end of a service cycle (typically the end of day for a user) appropriate data so as to re-estimate the models that implement the Map with off-line training in a server. After the re-training session finishes the new model parameters are upload to the artefact. These parameters are part of the User's Profile. The operation that is described above is the simplest possible from the part of Self-Evaluator. The following situations could be identified by the Self-Evaluator:

(a) The Map's operation is correct given the current input and output vectors.

(b) The operation is less than satisfactory. Further training will be needed.

(c) A first time case has been encountered. The probability of correct response is minimal (generalisation performance very poor). Further training is needed.

(d) A disruption on the data stream occurred and/or we receive missing values. The Map operated on this data stream and as a result it is questionable its output.

On the other hand the Map's output is used for evaluating the current response of the intelligent unit. In the simplest case this involves the production of an action by the Rules module. Of course in the set of possible actions it is included the case of *No operation* (if it is appropriate). An Attention Process, which performs a more complex evaluation of the User's environment, can also use the output of the Map. This aspect is discussed in the following sub-section.

As we stated in the start of our explanation a number of decision-making systems (Maps) can be present. In this case we adopt a strategy for fusing the individual World Representations of each Map into a new one by using committee-type algorithms or otherwise. Of course a requirement for this type of operation is the compatibility in a semantic level of the specific representations. This is the case for the intelligent unit as the two methods that implement the Maps are compatible with each other and can be mixed together. The CAM/SPM Method uses rules from a knowledge base while the PAC/MED system can create itself its own rules from the data. In the above sense they are complimentary and augment the functionality of the intelligent unit.

7.1.2 Attention Control Process

A clarification is required before we proceed with our main discussion regarding the attention control process. The *User Profile* contains both model parameter values that represent a Map and suitable threshold values that indicate the acceptable deviation level from the model predictions.

One assumes that at any given time a *State Representation* is available. For now we are purposefully vague if this is a Native or a World Representation. It could be either. We also assume that the past history of this State is known up to some given lag time *t-T*. Then the following general sequence of events takes place. Not all steps are present in every different case.

The *Observer Module* produces an *Expected State* from the known *Historical State* (using usually the contemporaneous State information as well). In essence this component models the "System" Transition function from state S_t to S_{t+1}, i.e. $S_{t+1}=\delta(S_t)$. The *system* here could be the *User*, or the Environment of the intelligent unit. Hopefully if the model is good enough it can capture some essential aspects of the data generation process. In a first approach this module can have a very simple implementation using a moving average process or otherwise. The Observer Module produces the Expected State itself based on some statistical characteristic of the Historical State (such as a mean, a variance, etc). The Expected and Actual States are forwarded to the *Monitor Module*. There a measure of difference is calculated. The calculation is of course depended on the role of the *Goal* that is been serviced. The third input to the Monitor comes from the Goal Module, which provides (at a minimal level) some "threshold" values as measures of convergence to the specified goal. Alternatively the Goal Module could provide the Expected State. In such a case the Monitor module could collect the result of the goal evaluation function and the threshold values.

The *Monitor* then using the above information calculates an *Attention Index*. The index is a function of the difference: $||Expected-Actual||-Threshold$, formally defined as (Kasderidis 2003):

$$AttentionIndex = 1 - \Pr(E > \delta) \qquad (3.1)$$

where E is the Monitor error measure and δ is a threshold coming from the *User Profile*. *Pr* is the probability that the *Error* is larger than the threshold. We assume that a suitable error distribution has been selected, e.g. the Normal distribution. This definition implies that the more "improbable" is an event the higher is the index that it creates. This is consistent with the fact that sudden changes in the user state imply in turn a rather large error deviation between the prediction and the current state. As a result higher priority should be given to such events.

Once an Attention Index it has been created it is forwarded to the *Attention Controller Module*. Therefore, the larger the difference between expected and actual state is the larger the probability to be picked up by the Attention Controller.

The *Attention Controller*'s structure is conceptually simple. It consists of an event stack (*Attention Stack*) and a policy for selecting events and dispatching jobs, related to the selected event, to the *Action Rules* module. On receipt of a new Attention Index (i.e. Event) the Controller places it into the Event Stack ("Attention Stack"). Then a selection process takes place, which sets the priority of the event using its Attention Index. The *Priority Function* takes as argument the Attention Index and produces a *Priority Index*, which indicates the event's place in a priority event queue. In the trivial case the Priority Function can be the Identity Transformation. Once the event has been entered in the appropriate place in the queue a dispatch process takes place. This process indicates which event will be handled next.

Typically we start with default behaviours for the above strategies. For example the largest attention index (if any) is recorded in any given time and then priority is given in the handling of the event that caused this. However, there is not in principle a reason why the policy could not handle a number of events in parallel at the same cycle and dispatch appropriate jobs for their handling. This processing could be done up to some given maximum number of events per cycle and under the condition that the events are independent from each other. Still in practice caution is needed for implementing such a strategy; scheduling considerations and statistical independence constrains exist. Assuming now that the highest priority event is dispatched to the *Action Rules* for further processing then a *Feedback Signal* is produced as the end result from the Attention Controller. This signal classifies the type of strategy/action plan that needs to be executed as a response to this event. The processing that needs to take place could be either simple or more complex.

Some comments are due for the "Attention" character of the control mechanism we use:

- It uses a *Priority Policy* instead of sequential event processing in a first-come-first-served basis. In this sense it induces a hierarchical structure of priorities and focusing of system resources.

- It uses an explicit *Dispatch Policy* that could potentially service weakly dependent events. In this aspect resembles the processing that takes place in Human Attention Division. This is not the default mode of operation for a typical control system. In addition the Feedback Signal carries instructions on which system resources should be freed by other executing process for use from the current Attention Event.

- Finally to complete the argument we make explicit the fact that what activates this control system is the deviation of the expected state from the actual one. Typically one sets a goal state in a control system and lets the controller perform essentially the first Role of a Goal. Here the key word is "Expected". This implies that the system should be able to look ahead in time in order to perform better in a complex environment.

Further information about the Attention Process and the Attention Roles of the proposed model can be found at (ORESTEIA 2003a).

7.2   Learning Mode

The second basic mode of operation of the intelligent unit is the learning mode. There are three modules in the proposed model that are learnable or include learnable sub-modules: *State*, *Observer* and *Forward Models*. As already mentioned, State includes Maps and Committee Machine, both requiring learning for performing classification. The Observer acts as a predictor while in the Forward Models we have another Map, called the Action-State Map that also performs classification tasks. Basically the discussion that follows in subsequent sections is concentrated on three categories of training:

- *Maps training*, realized through CAM/SPM and PAC/MED methods and referring to all Maps, being either in State or in Forward Models

- *Committee Machine* training, realized through a typical boosting by filtering method (Tresp 2001)

- *Observer training*, realized as a function approximation problem.

7.2.1   Learning Phases
In general three learning phases are considered for the learnable modules stated above:

- *Initial Training* (typical user case). This is a typical supervised training procedure performed on a domain D from which the learner has access to a representative example set E of pairs $\{\bar{x}, \bar{t}(\bar{x})\}$. Without loss of generality we consider that the domain D refers to the behavior of a set of human users in a particular context C and that this behavior is recorded through signal vectors $\bar{x} \in \Re^n$. Then by the end of learning, performed on set E, a set of parameters W_I (typically represented as a matrix) that model the function $g : \Re^n \to \Re^m$ is available so that $\|W_I \cdot \bar{x} - g(\bar{x})\| < \varepsilon$, $\varepsilon\Theta$. With initial training we consider that the basic principles of any typical user's behaviour are identified. Initial training is performed offline.

- *Adaptation to a particular user* (specific user profiles). In this phase further training is performed so as to make the appropriate adjustments to the parameter set W_I in order to meet any user peculiarities and optimise the performance of learnable modules w.r.t. a particular user. This training phase is supervised and performed offline.

- *Adaptation to a slowly changing context* (online adaptation). In this phase the parameters of learnable modules are adapted in an online mode so as to meet slow changes in the context. Changes in the context may be identified as an increased frequency on the number of outlier vectors or by exploiting possible user feedback (through reinforcement signals). If the environment being encountered is changeable in a manner that requires large modifications of the parameters or even modifications of the architectures of the models (such as increasing or decreasing the number of hidden nodes in the Forward predictor) then it will also be necessary to create such new models for the particular context that has changed in the environment. These new models will then be brought on-stream when the context is appropriate. Such model switching is known to occur in humans, in respect of motor control models in varying environments (such as learning "sea-legs" to automatically handle the pitching and tossing of a ship at sea, with switching back to the land model of gait control when on land). The most appropriate model for a given environment (in terms of parameters specifying the architecture) can be obtained by model order selection, using a criterion such as AIC.

7.2.2 Overall Self-Evaluation and Credit Assignment

The need for training for the intelligent unit is identified through an overall evaluation which is realized through:

- Identification of possible mismatches in the functionality of *State* and *Observer* modules.

- Recognition of which module (*State* or *Observer*) is malfunctioning (if any)

- Identification of mismatches between *Maps* and corresponding credit assignment

- Identification of context drifting. This could activate online retraining to account for dynamic changes in the operating environment.

- Confidence level estimation on the output of Maps.

The basic module that is responsible for intelligent unit's self-evaluation is the *Critic* while confidence level estimation is accommodated within the *State* module through the *Self-Evaluators*.

The learning process of the various modules of the proposed model is described in detail in (ORESTEIA 2003b).

8   Demonstration: The User Monitoring Problem

In order to better understand the architecture and the processing mode of the attention-driven model for context switch detection is described in the previous Sections we include here a demonstration dealing with the user monitoring problem.

8.1   The User Monitoring Problem

In many circumstances intelligent units would have to monitor their users and decide on behalf of them for their welfare. To facilitate intelligent decision-making the intelligent units should be able to adapt their monitoring strategy according to the context of the user. Due to (mainly) power and communication limitations sensors could not be continually polled in their highest sampling rate. This leads to the problem of limited information for effective decision-making. The controlling unit then have to adaptively monitor their users by increasing or decreasing the sampling rates of the various sensors involved. This is the *User Monitoring Problem*. It is an optimization problem in the sense that one has to balance energy and communication overhead against higher resolution information about the user and his environment. A possible strategy for achieving such a balance is attention control.

Let us now expand a little on the Ubiquitous Health Scenario introduced earlier. We suppose that we have a chronic patient user that needs to regularly monitor his health condition. There are three (non-obtrusive) sensors attached to his body, monitoring Heart Rate, Blood Pressure and Chest Volume. A software application, residing in his PDA, polls the sensors, controls their sampling rate, estimates user's health status and informs the user for warning health states or calls the health monitoring service provider in case of an emergency (serving as *actuator*).

A number of events can take place, which induce a change in the state of the user. We use the variable of Alert Level to distinguish the user states. The resting state is labeled *Normal*. Additionally two more states are considered: An *Attention Seeking* and a *Dangerous* one. If an event of interest takes place (e.g., Heart Attack or another major stress) we assume that the following cycle of events takes place:

1. Rest state 1 — Initial Steady State.

2. Pre-cursor state — indicating the onset of the event

3. Onset of event — say with duration of 1 min.

4. Rest state 2 — Final Steady State.

The first Rest State is the current equilibrium state where the system uses a default *monitoring level* for the user. All sensors are sampled on the default sampling rate. The second state is a pre-cursor signal which in many phenomena is present and for this reason useful to be exploited for expectation of system change. We make the assumption here that indeed this signal exists in order to simplify the presentation. The

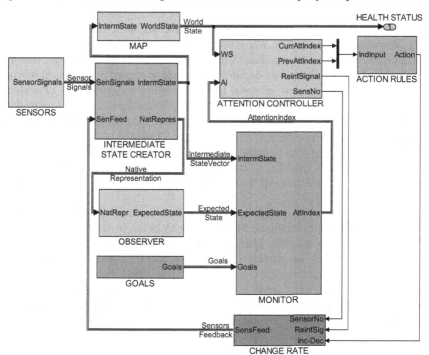

Fig. 6. The Attention-driven Architecture in the Health Monitoring Scenario

existence of a pre-cursor could be exploited by using appropriate rules for the sampling rate setting of the sensors. In a typical setting the sampling rate would be increased on expectation of the main event. In our case the sampling rate of the sensor that identifies the pre-cursor event is doubled (although doubling the sampling rates of all sensors could be also adopted). The onset of the event is manifested by the increase in the mean level of measures in (at least) one sensor. At the end of the event the rate returns to another resting state. During the main event the sampling rate for the sensor that captures the event is doubled again.

The attention-driven architecture shown in Figure 6 is used for the health monitoring problem in a manner described in the following paragraphs. This architecture is based on the general architecture shown in Figure 2 but it is focused on the particular problem. Therefore, the Sensory Motor module shown as a single entity in Figure 2 has been expanded to show the Goals, Attention Controller, Monitor and Action Rules sub-modules. On the other hand, the Intermediate State Creator N2, Forward Model and Critic modules are not shown because the emphasis is given in sensory feedback and not in state evaluation and Map re-design. Furthermore, for the simplicity of presentation the State module includes a single MAP and, as a consequence, both the Committee Machine sub-module and Gating input are missing. Finally, the Resampling module in Figure 2 is named Change Rate in Figure 6 to emphasize on the action that is undertaken as a result of an attention-requiring event.

8.2 Analysis

The sensor module is employed to capture data from biosignals generated by the user. In the current scenario, these signals include time series of the user's *Heart Rate (HR)*, *Respiration Rate (RSP)*, *Chest Volume (CHV)*, *Systolic* and *Diastolic Blood Pressure (PS, PD)*. The *Intermediate State Creator* collects the signals digitises them using appropriate sampling rates. Sampling rates are increased or decreased whenever a corresponding command is received from the *Action Rules* module. Obviously if one increases the sampling rate she/he will observe better the microstructure of the series. At this point, certain features that have diagnostic value in medicine are extracted and form the *Intermediate State Vector,* which is forwarded to the *MAP* module. At the same time, the sampled signals, referred to as *Native Representation*, are forwarded to the *Observer* module. This module includes a model for predicting the current state and future Intermediate States given the history Native Representations up to some lag time T.

At the next step, the predicted Intermediate State coming from the Observer, together with the actual Intermediate State coming from the Intermediate State creator, are fed to the *Monitor* module. There they are compared and if their difference exceeds some thresholds, an *Attention Event* is created for the responsible sensor. Thresholds are obtained from the *Goals* module. The main function of this module in the overall system is to indicate to the system the type of goals we try to achieve as well as to help in the creation and processing of new goals. In our case however its use is restricted in providing the abovementioned thresholds, which are user and context specific values. Attention Events are represented by corresponding *Attention Indices* (the strength of which is analogous to the inconsistency between the real Intermediate State and the predicted one).

In the MAP the Intermediate State Vector is transformed to the *World State Vector*; in our scenario the World State Vector corresponds to *Alert Level* classifications of user's health state. Therefore, the MAP is a classifier system. In our implementation the MAP corresponds to a hybrid intelligence system combining neural and neuro-fuzzy networks; the former provides the means for learning from numerical data and can be adapted to the peculiarities of a particular user while the latter provides the means for including a priori knowledge, in the form of rules, into the MAP.

The Attention Index together with the World State Vector is then forwarded to the Attention Controller. This module identifies the sensor to which attention should be given and decides which job will be dispatched in the next processing stage. Furthermore, it identifies mismatches between the results obtained from the MAP and the Monitor, and creates a reinforcement signal to the Observer. Finally, the Action Rules module defines the actions that should be undertaken in order to achieve the required Goals, thus, in our case, sends commands to the Intermediate State Creator regarding the adjustment of the sampling rate.

8.3   Implementation

The architecture of Figure 6 has been implemented in SIMULINK to address the health-monitoring problem described earlier (the code and installation guidelines can be found at (Oresteia 2005, 2005).

Real sensor signals are emulated in the *Sensors* module. This module creates sensor values based on time series mechanisms. Adjustable parameters are the mean value of each signal, its standard deviation as well as the power of additive noise that may affect the sensor. Interrelations among signals are taken into account: Systolic and diastolic blood pressures are mutually dependent as well as heart rate and respiration rate. Moreover, respiration rate is actually derived from chest volume signal.

The Intermediate State Creator consists of two modules: the *Sampling* and the *Feature Extraction* module. Increase or decrease in the sampling rate is performed whenever a corresponding command by the Action Rules module is received. Feature extraction aims at the derivation of measures that have *diagnostic* value in medicine. Currently the majority of features that are used are statistical ones obtained by using sliding time windows. Most of them correspond to features that medical experts use in their everyday practice. Output variables include:

(a) Three state vectors *HR_SV*, *RSP_SV*, *Press_SV*. The following features are included in the state vectors:

- *HR_SV* ≠ *HRinValue, HRmax-HRmin, HRmean, HRStd}*
- *RSP_SV*≠ *RSPinValue, RSPmax-RSPmin, RSPmean, RSPStd, CHVmean, CHVStd}*
- *Press_SV*≠ *PSinValue, PSmean, PDStd, PDinValue, PDmean, PDStd}*

(b) Native Representation which is forwarded to the Observer.

The Observer module uses prediction models so as to forecast future Intermediate States. In its current implementation it predicts one sample ahead (the next Intermediate State) by using simple moving averages. The Goals module indicates the goals pursued by the Attention Controller in its current process. Currently, it just provides threshold values about the allowable deviation between real and predicted Intermediate State. These may depend on the particular user or context. All threshold values are adjustable.

The Monitor module identifies irregular patterns in the input space and produces Attention Indices for all sensors. It computes the Attention Index for *each one* of the sensors using the following relations (in the example below we consider only the blood pressure sensor). The feature vectors for the actual, the predicted, and the goal values for the blood pressure are:

- Press_SV{PSinValue, PSmean, PDStd, PDinValue, PDmean, PDStd}
- Press_SVpred{PSinValuePred   , PSmeanPred, PDStdPred, PDinValuePred, PDmeanPred, PDStdPred}
- Press_SVgoal{PSinValueGoal,   PSmeanGoal, PDStdGoal, PDinValueGoal, PDmeanGoal, PDStdGoal}

The Attention Index for this sensor is given by:

Press_AI=max{PSinValueAI, PSmeanAI, PDStdAI,   (4.1)
PDinValueAI, PDmeanAI, PDStdAI}
where:

$$PSinValueAI = 1 - \exp\left\{-0.5 \cdot \left(\frac{X_{PSinValueAI}}{2\pi}\right)^2\right\} \qquad (4.2)$$

and

$$X_{PSinValueAI} = \begin{cases} 0, & \text{if } PSinValueDev < PSinValueGoal \\ \\ PSinValueDev - PSinValueGoal, & \text{otherwise} \end{cases} \qquad (4.3)$$

where:
PSinValueDev=|PSinValue - PSinValuePred| (4.4)

PSmeanAI, PDStdAI, PDinValueAI, PDmeanAI, PDStdAI are computed in a similar manner.

The Attention Controller is the most critical component of the architecture. It serves a variety of purposes: (a) Identifies the sensor to which attention should be paid, (b) It has a dispatch policy for deciding which jobs will be dispatched in the next processing stage, (c) Identifies mismatches between the results obtained from the MAP and the Monitor, (d) Creates a reinforcement signal, to be used by the Observer, in cases where the mismatch between MAP and Monitor is due to Observer's malfunction. In more detail, in cases where anyone of the *Attention Indices* is greater than a given value (typically zero) it computes the highest and identifies the corresponding sensor. It forwards the current and the previous value of the Attention Index of this sensor to the Action Rules module. At the same time stores the value of the Attention Index, for any other sensor that requires attention, in the *priority stack*. If all attention indices are null then forwards the current and the previous value of the Attention Index of the sensor found first (if any) in the *priority stack*. It checks the consistency between the World State and the Attention Index. For example if the World State shows *Normal* state while the Attention Index for a particular sensor is high for a long time this indicates a possible problem either to the MAP or to the Observer (bad prediction). If the inconsistency between MAP and Monitor is due to fault operation of the Observer a reinforcement signal is created. In its current form the Attention Controller is not able to identify which module to blame (Observer or MAP).

The Action Rules module defines the actions that should be undertaken in order to achieve the required Goals. In the case of a mismatch between the *current* and *previous* value of the Attention Index it creates an Alert Level which causes commands for increasing or decreasing the sampling rate of the attended sensor to be activated. Although in cases where the current value of the Attention Index is significantly higher than the previous one the command is indeed to increase the sampling rate, the opposite is not that simple. Decreasing the sampling rate might be ordered only if power consumption needs to be reduced.

The MAP module maps the Intermediate State to the World State. MAP is currently implemented using the CAM/SPM model presented in (Raouzaiou 2002). The CAM module partitions the Intermediate State space so as to produce linguistic terms (like *HR_high*). Linguistic terms are then used in the SPM module to activate the rules that have been modeled. Only rules corresponding to *Dangerous* and *Attention Seeking* states are included in SPM. This conforms to the medicine practice where *healthy* means *not ill*. Currently 16 rules have been modeled; nine correspond to *Attention Seeking* and seven to *Dangerous*.

9   Simulation and Results

In this section we present results from the SIMULINK (The Mathworks 2005) implementation of the proposed attention-driven architecture shown in Figure 6. The following assumptions have been made:

1. A User Profile exists for guiding the system, i.e. providing the thresholds for the specific user.

2. Three time series are used, those of the Heart Rate, Blood Pressure and Chest Volume. Features extracted from all are fused in the MAP module, where rules are activated in order to reach useful decisions.

3. A State Classifier (MAP) has been implemented using the CAM/SPM model (Raouzaiou 2002) that distinguishes the classes of events described above.

4. All signals that are used are synthetic.

During the simulation we are able to provide the system with data from a variety of cases, from normal to simulated heart attacks so as to check and evaluate its operation. We have found that in the majority of the cases the system responds rapidly and reaches accurate decisions regarding the user's health status.

Figure 7 illustrates the context switch in the case where the predicted value of the signal is significantly different from the actual value. It should be noted that there are two possibilities for such deviations to occur. On one hand either the model is correct in its prediction and indeed the actual state is different from what was expected, or the model prediction is simply wrong and nothing out of the ordinary has happened. The first case is distinguished from the second by using the classification history trace of the State Classifier. If the history indicates that we do have a change in the state classification we probably deal with the former case. Otherwise the *Observer* model has failed and needs further estimation. This incremental improvement can be implemented as either a supervised learning scheme (off-line) or as a reinforcement scheme (on-line) using the *Monitor Error* level. In the case of Figure 7 an event of interest has actually happened and therefore when the actual value of the heart rate (blue line at the upper plot of Figure 7) starts to divert from the one predicted by the Observer (red line), the sampling rate is increased to correspond to the warning state (lower plot of Figure 7). It can be observed that the response of the system is quite fast. As the difference is further increased, the sampling rate is accordingly increased to the attention state. The increase in the sampling rate is essential for capturing crucial details in the heart rate time series in order to reach more accurate decisions regarding the user's health status. As the heart rate drops and approaches the predicted values, the sampling rate decreases accordingly.

Figure 8 is an example of how the system handles possibly dangerous situations. In this case, the user's blood pressure increases significantly above normal. The system responds by activating the Attention Index for the blood pressure sensor as well as changing the Alert Level. The first results in increased attention to the blood pressure time series, i.e. sampling it at higher sampling rates, while the latter may lead to issuing warnings to the user or taking other actions in the case of an emergency. More specifically, in the upper plot of Figure 8 we can see the time series of the Systolic Blood Pressure. As soon as the blood pressure starts to increase, the MAP module fires a *Warning* as it can be seen at the middle plot of Figure 8 (blue line). When the blood pressure exceeds 150 mbars the Alert Level changes to *Danger* (red line). As blood pressure drops to 150 mbars again the Alert Level changes again to *Warning*. It

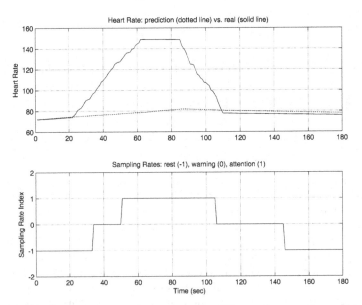

Fig. 7. The sampling rate changes as a response to the difference between the predicted and the actual values of the heart rate

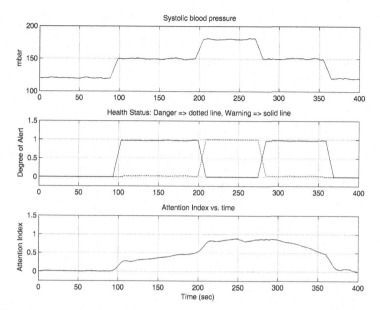

Fig. 8. The Alert Level changes between *Warning* and *Danger* as the blood pressure time series evolves in time

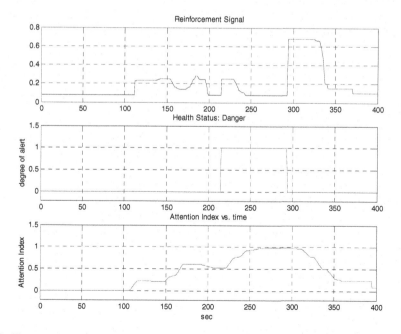

Fig. 9. The system responds with a reinforcement signal in the case of inconsistency between the MAP module and the Attention Index

can be observed that the system reaches timely and accurate decisions regarding the user's health status. The Attention Index for the blood pressure sensor shown at the lower plot of Figure 8 instantly captures the potentially dangerous increase in the blood pressure values and returns smoothly to normal level (zero) as the blood pressure drops back to normal. This ensures that attention continues to be paid to the blood pressure sensor for some time so as to keep on capturing details in the time series in case the blood pressure increases again above normal.

Figure 9 illustrates the response of the system in the case of inconsistency between the MAP module and the Attention Index. The fact that the values of the Attention Index remain at relatively high values (lower plot of Figure 9) although the danger has passed according to the MAP module (middle plot of Figure 9) results in the reinforcement signal of the upper plot in Figure 9. This could be an indication that either the MAP module or the Observer needs retraining. At this point we haven't developed a way of distinguishing which module should be retrained.

10   Conclusion and Discussion

The attention-driven architecture for context switch detection presented in this chapter is part of the ORESTEIA Architecture for attention-based agents (ORESTEIA 2000). There we consider a multi-level environment that is composed by a number of inter-communicating agents. The agents are partitioned in four levels (categories). At the first level the sensors and actuators exist. In the second one pre-processing facilities are provided. The third level involves local decision makers and the fourth one has global decision makers. The architecture presented here is for the most part the architecture of the level 3 ORESTEIA agent.

The system's response to the changes in the time series of the user's biosignals is very fast and the decisions regarding the user's health status are accurate. Improvements in the Goals module so that it indicates to the system a range of goals to be achieved instead of just providing thresholds, a better implementation of the Observer, as well as a mechanism for distinguishing whether it is the MAP module or the Observer the one that needs retraining in the case of inconsistencies were also developed. Additionally, the collection and processing or real biosignals and physiological data has been performed in order to provide the system with real data instead of simulated ones and test its behavior in that case.

Finally, learning it is also present (ORESTEIA 2003b) to enable the system to adapt better to its environment. Adaptation can be achieved by improving the classification power of the MAP module and the prediction ability of the Observer. The latter can be used to predict further into the future so that the system demonstrates a more proactive behavior.

Acknowledgement

The work presented in this chapter has been undertaken in the framework of the ORESTEIA project (Modular Hybrid Artefacts with Adaptive Functionality, IST-2000-26091) (ORESTEIA 2000).

References

Abowd, G.: Software engineering issues for ubiquitous computing. In: Proceedings of the International Conference on Software Engineering, Los Angeles, CA, USA, pp. 5–84 (1999)

Apolloni, B., Malchiodi, D., Orovas, C., Palmas, G.: From synapses to rules. Cognitive Systems Research 3(2), 167–201 (2002)

Birnbaum, J.: Pervasive information systems. Communications of the ACM 40(2), 40–41 (1997)

Bonasso, R., Kortenkamp, D., Miller, D.: Experiences with an Architecture for Intelligent, Reactive Agents. In: Tambe, M., Müller, J., Wooldridge, M.J. (eds.) Intelligent Agents II - Agent Theories, Architectures, and Languages. LNCS, vol. 1037, Springer, Heidelberg (1996)

Goland, Y., Cai, T., Leach, P., Gu, Y., Albright, S.: Simple Service Discovery Protocol. Internet Draft, draft-cai-ssdp-v1-03.txt (1999)

Jovanov, E., Gelabert, P., Adhami, R., Wheelock, B., Adams, R.: Real Time Holter Monitoring of Biomedical Signals. In: Proceedings of DSP Technology and Education Conference, DSPS'99, Houston, Texas (1999)

Kasderidis, S., Taylor, J.G., Tsapatsoulis, N., Malchiodi, D.: Drawing Attention to the Dangerous. In: Kaynak, O., Alpaydın, E., Oja, E., Xu, L. (eds.) ICANN 2003 and ICONIP 2003. LNCS, vol. 2714, pp. 909–916. Springer, Heidelberg (2003)

Kunzmann, U., von Wagner, G., Schöchlin, J., Bolz, A.: Parameter Extraction of the ECG-Signal in Real-Time. Biomedizinische Technik 47(2), 875–878 (2002)

Lei, W., Tong, B.T., Johannessen, E., Astaras, A., Murray, A.F., Cooper, J.M., Beaumont, S.P., Cumming, D.R.S.: An integrated sensor microsystem for industrial and biomedical applications. In: Proceedings of 19th IEEE Instrumentation and Measurement Technology Conference, vol. 2, pp. 1717–1720. IEEE Press, Los Alamitos (2000)

Levinson, R.: Unified Planning and Execution for Autonomous Software Repair. In: Proceedings of International Conference on Automatic Planning Systems (ICAPS-05), AAAI Press, Menlo Park (2005)

Levinson, R.: Computer Model of Prefrontal Cortex Function. In: Annals of the New York Academy of Sciences, vol. 769: Structure and Function of Human Prefrontal Cortex (1995)

Martin, T., Jovanov, E., Raskovic, D.: Issues in wearable computing for medical monitoring applications: a case study of a wearable ECG monitoring device. In: Proceedings of the 4th International Symposium on Wearable Computers, pp. 43–49 (2000)

Moccia, K.: A Pocketful of Miracles: How Pocket PCs Help People with Special Needs. Pocket PC Magazine 5(5), 3–18 (2002)

ORESTEIA: FET DC ORESTEIA Project (2000), http://manolito.image.ece.ntua.gr/oresteia/

ORESTEIA: Deliverable ND1.2: Overall Level 3 architecture and Demos up to Level 3 (Jan. 2003a), http://www.image.ece.ntua.gr/oresteia/deliverables/ORESTEIA-IST-2000-26091-ND1.2.pdf

ORESTEIA: Deliverable ND2.1: Learning for single user in Level 3 artefacts (Oct. 2003b), http://www.image.ece.ntua.gr/oresteia/deliverables/ORESTEIA-IST-2000-26091-ND1.2.pdf

ORESTEIA: Demo for Level. 3 architecture (updated October 2005), http://www.image.ntua.gr/oresteia/present/agent.zip

Raouzaiou, A., Tsapatsoulis, N., Tzouvaras, V., Stamou, G., Kollias, S.: A Hybrid Intelligence System for Facial Expression Recognition. In: Proceedings of EUNITE 2002, on CD-ROM, Albufeira, Portugal (2002)

Roth, H., Schwaibold, M., Moor, C., Schöchlin, J., Bolz, A.: Miniturized module for the wireless transmission of measurements with Bluetooth. Biomedizinische Technik 47(2), 854–856 (2002)

Rushworth, M.F.S., Nixon, P.D., Renowden, S., Wade, D.T., Passingham, R.E.: The left parietal cortex and motor attention. Neuropsychologia 33, 1261–1273 (1997)

Taylor, J.G.: Attention as a neural control system. In: Proceedings of the IEEE International Joint Conference on Neural Networks (IJCNN '01), vol.1, pp. 273–277. IEEE Computer Society Press, Los Alamitos (2001)

SIMULINK Simulation and Mode l-Based Design, Version 6.0. The Mathworks Inc. (2005), Online at http://www.mathworks.com/products/simulink/

Tresp, V.: Committee Machines. In: Hen Hu, Y., Hwang, J.N. (eds.) Handbook for Neural Network Signal Processing, CRC Press (2001)

Weiser, M.: The computer of the 21st century. Scientific American 265(3), 66–75 (1991)

Weiser, M.: Some computer science issues in ubiquitous computing. Communications of the ACM 36(7), 75–84 (1993)

Emerging Sounds for Disappearing Computers

Davide Rocchesso[1] and Roberto Bresin[2]

[1] Department of Computer Science, Università di Verona, Verona, Italy
[2] Department of Speech Music and Hearing, KTH Royal Institute of Technology,
Stockholm, Sweden

1 Introduction

Try this simple experiment one day: wear a couple of earplugs and try to conduct your
regular everyday activities, for a couple of hours. How would you describe your feel-
ings in that deafened state? You would probably feel a sense of isolation, from the
world and from other people. So, absence of sound induces perceived isolation which
may turn into felt oppression in some environments, such as an anechoic chamber.
One may think that if silence induces isolation, sound induces presence, but unfortunately this is not the case. We know sensitive souls that have difficulties falling asleep
because they live in noisy neighborhoods. One solution that may work in this case is
to play loud noise through the hi-fi loudspeakers to mask the noise from the environment. Again, isolation (e.g. from street noise) is the result, but the means to achieve it
is loud noise, the opposite of silence. And how would you describe all those people
that experience modern city life being shielded by earphones that play music from
their walkmans or mp3 players? They look rather isolated from each other, don't
they? In some circumstances there might be a need of concentration (e.g., in studying), or people want to tune their mood (Brodsky 2002). In all those cases sounds may
be the appropriate mean, as it was well known even to Thomas Edison, who used to
accompany commercialization of his phonograph with a "mood change chart" aimed
at surveying users reactions to that new technology. So, it seems that sounds have the
potential to modulate human engagement (from isolation to arousal) in everyday environments, and this is an aspect that should be seriously considered when designing the
artefacts that will populate the environments of the future, likely to be pervaded by
Ambient Intelligence (AmI) in its various facets.

1.1 Soundscapes

Murray Schafer and the school of acoustic ecologists taught us to appreciate the sonic
quality of different environments, the HiFi soundscapes of rural villages or the LoFi
massive noises of industrial plants (Schafer 1977). HiFi environments are characterized by clearly separable sound stimuli, with no prevalent masking effect due to loud
noise sources. These are the places where sounds are mostly informative about the objects, the actions that the objects are engaged in, the possibly animated and expressive
character of those actions, the environmental conditions where those actions are taking place. In HiFi places, sounds are not only useful, they are essential to trigger sensations of comfort, presence, and belongingness to the place.

N. Streitz, A. Kameas, and I. Mavrommati (Eds.): The Disappearing Computer, LNCS 4500, pp. 233–254, 2007.

If sounds have such an important part in the overall aesthetic experience of the spaces we live in, it is clear that in the process of designing new spaces, sound design and control can not be less important than architecture, decoration, and illumination. This was sharply clear to Royal Philips Electronics in 1958, when they set up a team of architects, composers, filmmakers, engineers, and designers to build the company pavilion at the World Expo in Brussels. With the help of sound geniuses Edgard Varèse and Iannis Xenakis, architect Le Corbusier realized a space where the visitors could experience, for the first time, an embracing example of multimedia. In that space, technology was ubiquitous and transparent, and the HiFi artificial soundscape was a key aspect of the experience. That realization was so important that nowadays Emile Aarts, scientific program director at Philips Research, considers it a prelude to Ambient Intelligence[1].

1.2   Designing Soundscapes of the Future

As designers of technological artefacts aimed at improving our lives, we should strive to achieve better working and living places, where objects do not corrupt but rather improve the soundscape. One way to do that is to move away from schizophonia (Schafer 1977), that is the physical separation between the acoustic source and the medium, being it a compact disc, a radio broadcast, or sample playback. Sounds should be tightly attached to physical objects as dynamic entities, that naturally follow the actions and give substance to manipulations. Especially for computer-based artefacts, where the computer is loosing its visual identity to become invisible, embedded into everyday objects, sounds become crucial to communicate information about events and processes. If the interface is embodied into the objects themselves (Dourish 2001), meanings will eventually emerge as experienced phenomena, as a result of actions between people, objects, and the environment. So there is no space for schizophonic sound reproduction anymore. In order to be useful, sounds have to be properly-designed dynamic, reactive entities. In this way they take a key role in defining the identity of these new technological artefacts.

1.3   An Everyday Experience

What we have just described are not far-to-come auspices. In subtle ways, it is already occurring. For example, in some sporty cars that are being produced nowadays, the car-radio loudspeaker system is being used to diffuse the processed sound of the car engine (Scheuren et al. 2004). This may sound paradoxical if one expects that users would prefer silence to the engine noise. Indeed, users want to hear the engine responding to their actions on gears and foot-pedals, and they have clear aesthetic concerns about the quality of engine sounds. On the other end, a car is required to be silent for reducing the environmental noise pollution. If the mechanics is not sufficient to meet the expectations, real-time audio signal processing is used to reinforce and beautify those sounds, thus contributing to defining the acoustic identity of the car. Moreover, those same loudspeakers can be used to signal dangerous situations or other kinds of events.

---

[1] http://www.research.philips.com/technologies/syst_softw/poeme/pe.html

For many people, sitting in a car is a significant portion of everyday experience, and they look for comfort through all the senses. Among these, audition can convey a lot of useful information with minimal distraction from the main task. As far as musical signals are concerned, it has been observed that the car is the concert hall of the 21st century, as people spend longer time listening to music in the car than in other places. Music can even change the driver behavior in the traffic. Fast and aggressive music induces faster driving style; slower and more relaxing music makes the driver drive slower (Brodsky 2002).

In Sect. 2, we provide a historical introduction to the main terms and methods that are currently used in the sounds-for-artefacts research agenda. In Sect. 3, we show how interdisciplinary is such research effort, as it is the result of a tight interchange between diverse domains of expertise. In Sect. 4 we illustrate a few research products that are designed around salient sonic concepts.

2   Terms, Contexts, and Methods

What Schafer calls the schizophonic age is more than one century old, dating back to the invention and diffusion of the telephone, the phonograph, and radio broadcasting. It took some time, however, before these new technologies started to be extensively used as means to investigate the nature of sounds.

After the Second World War, some researchers started using tape recorders, oscillators, and filters to make observations about sounds and their qualities. For instance, the simple action of reversing a piano tone recorded on tape spurred a series of observations about the subjective perception of time and duration. The main figure of this time is Pierre Schaeffer, who practiced and theorized an approach to the study of sound based on direct observations and exemplary demonstrations. In other words, he was doing experimental phenomenology (Vicario 1993). Schaeffer coined the term "sound object" to indicate acoustic events and processes that manifest themselves as coherent phenomena, or gestalts. The fifties were also the time when Karlheinz Stockhausen and other musicians experimented with the new electronic technologies to extend their palette of sonic materials. Paradoxically, early electronic music sounds overly pure nowadays, in sharp contrast with the thick textures of Schaeffer's musique concrete. The latter was indeed facing the complexity of acoustic sources, whose sounds were captured and manipulated. The former was using simple and controllable basic elements (oscillators, filters, modulators) to achieve complexity at a higher scale, through the temporal organization of those elements in concurrent streams. Some time later, Al Bregman conducted a systematic program of investigation of the phenomenal properties of streams, following the indications of gestalt psychology (Bregman 1990).

The seventies and eighties may be considered the golden age of computer music. At that time, computers and programming languages became widespread. Analysis and synthesis techniques were introduced and made available to researchers, so that curious ears such as those of Jean-Claude Risset could explore the sound matter in deconstructed form, at the level of elementary attributes of signals. A century of research in psychoacoustics was already available to guide such exploration providing explanations and directions.

In the nineties, with the advent of fast computer processors, the analysis and synthesis techniques could make remarkable progress, and two main paradigms became the playfield for many scientists and artists: physical models and spectral models. These new techniques, together with new interfaces for computer programming and sound manipulation, allowed the systematic exploration of different levels of complexity, ranging from physics to phenomenology and semantics.

With the new millennium there are a few emerging facts that are conditioning our present approaches to the study of sound. Sensors of many different kinds are available at low cost and they can be organized into networks. Computing power is generously available even in tiny and low-power processors that can be easily embedded into artefacts of different nature and size. New design strategies that take advantage of these technological opportunities are emerging: physical computing, natural interaction, calm technologies are some of the many buzzwords that are being proposed as labels for these new trends in design. For the purpose of sound-based communication, the concept of embodied interaction (Dourish 2001) is particularly significant. Embodiment is considered a property of how actions are performed with or through artefacts, thus embracing the position that treats meanings as inextricably present in the actions between people, objects, and the environment. The designer has a phenomenological attitude: she lets the meanings and structures emerge as experienced phenomena in interaction tasks. A key observation that emerges from embodied interaction examples is that human interaction in the world is essentially continuous and it relies on a complex network of continuous feedback signals. This is dramatically important if one considers that most interfaces to technological artefacts that are currently being produced are developed around switches, menus, buttons, and other discrete devices.

The design of graphical user interfaces has been largely inspired by ecological psychology and concepts such as direct perception and affordances (Gibson 1979). When designing embodied interfaces, we call for a reconciliation of ecological psychology and phenomenology that looks, with equal emphasis, at the objects and at the experiences. By means of physical modelling we can represent and understand the objects. By direct observation we can tell what are the relevant phenomena, which physical components are crucial for perception, what degree of simplification can be perceptually tolerated when modelling the physical reality. Specifically, sound designers are shifting their attention from sound objects to sounding objects, in some way getting back to the sources of acoustic vibrations, in a sort of ideal continuity with the experimenters of the early twentieth century, especially futurists such as Luigi Russolo and his intonarumori. In the contemporary world, sounding objects should be defined as sounds in action, intimately attached to artefacts, and dynamically responsive to continuous manipulations. As opposed to this embodied notion of sound, consider an instrument that came shortly after the intonarumori, the theremin invented 1919 by Lev Termen. It is played by moving the hands in space, near two antennae controlling amplitude and frequency of an oscillator. Its sound is ethereal and seems to come from the outer space. This is probably why it has been chosen in the soundtracks of some science-fiction movies (Martin 2001). Even though relying on continuous control and display, the lack of physical contact may still qualify the theremin as a schizophonic artefact, and it is not by coincidence that it is the only musical instrument invented in the twentieth century (the schizophonic age) that was used by several composers and virtuosi. Indeed, nephews of the theremin can be found in several recent works of art and technology making use of sophisticated sensors and displays, where physical causality is not mediated by physical objects, and the resulting interaction is pervaded by a sense of disembodiment.

An essential precursor of sounding objects in human-computer and human-artefact interaction has been the concept of auditory icon (Gaver 1994). In their simplest form, auditory icons are prerecorded sounds capable of evoking events or processes occurring in the "real" world. In their most sophisticated form, auditory icons are made of a sound synthesis algorithm and an association with events or processes. Sounds can be imitative or evocative of actual sources, but the association has to be ecologically founded. The introduction of synthetic auditory icons to the human-computer interaction community had the merit to highlight the severe limitations of pre-recorded (sampled) sounds. Playing back sampled sounds easily turns acoustic information into undesirable noise, thus leading to silent interfaces. Repeated playback of short recorded sounds may even change the nature of the perceived source, thus altering the message that they are supposed to convey. The situation is similar to a damaged vinyl record that locks into repeating the same musical phrase, thus eliciting a perceptual switch from hearing the music to hearing the apparatus. As far as continuous control is concerned, sampled sounds offer limited possibilities, unless a very complicated control and signal-processing super-structure is constructed, as it is found in sample-based musical keyboards. In the nineties it became clear that interfaces need sound models, i.e. audio synthesis procedures whose parameters humans can make sense of. This is the most genuine interpretation of auditory icons.

From research in sound objects (Schaeffer 1966), in acoustic ecology (Schafer 1977), and in gestalt psychoacoustics (Bregman 1990), we learned that sounds can be organized in soundscapes, and that humans are able to extract figures from backgrounds, to follow streams, and to extract multivariate information from such streams. Ecological acoustics (Gaver 1993a, 1993b) give us a further guideline to design meaningful and pleasant soundscapes as a composition of auditory icons or sounding objects: start looking at the sources to see what are the terms of representation. These terms are called invariants and they can be structural (e.g., wooden objects produce rapidly decaying sounds) or transformational (e.g., a bouncing object produces an increasing density of impacts, and a breaking object produces a decreasing density of impacts and bounces). When the invariants have been extracted, it is possible to devise models of sound sources, where some peculiar features are simplified or exaggerated for aesthetic, perceptual, or feasibility reasons. Such deformed sound models would be called cartoon sounds.

3   Contributions from Different Disciplines

Interdisciplinarity was important in the realization of the Philips pavilion in 1958, and it is well represented by Iannis Xenakis, whose roles in the project were both assisting Le Corbusier in the architectural design and composing a textural soundscape called "Concrete PH". The sonification of artefacts of the future also calls for interdisciplinarity, and in the following we present some of the fields of expertise that get easily involved in the design process.

3.1   Perception

Anyone willing to use sounds in embodied interfaces should consider how the auditory stimuli co-exist with visual or tactile sensations conveyed by the artefacts. In particular, one is easily tempted to use sounds to deliver spatial information, but this may lead to remarkable failures. One example is the ring tone in mobile phones. When a mobile phone is ringing in a reverberant space, as in an underground station, more than one person checks if it is her mobile that is ringing. In fact the frequency range in mobile phone ring tones (usually 1-2.5 kHz), the quasi-sinusoidal waves they produce, and the reverberant environment are conditions where sound localization is difficult (Franssen 1963). It has recently been demonstrated that the same difficulty, in a different frequency range, is manifested in cats (Dent et al. 2004), thus indicating a fundamental limitation of auditory spatial perception in a class of mammals. However, with properly designed stimuli, the ears-lead-eyes design pattern (Barrass 2003) could be applied to any situation where visual attention can not afford switching between different tasks and displays. According to the theory of indispensable attributes (Kubovy and Valkenburg 2001), space is the principal dimension of visual perception because it is a prerequisite of perceptual numerosity. On the other hand, it is on the time-frequency plane that the indispensable attributes of auditory perception can be found. That is the principal domain of sound objects. Location and other spatial features of sound are only secondary, they are often in service of visual perception, and they are easily fooled by inter-modal illusions (e.g., the ventriloquist effect). The sense of belongingness of a sound to an artefact derives mainly from attributes related to the nature of the source and its mechanical properties, and especially from responsiveness to human actions.

Sounds are intimately related to motion, as they are usually the result of actions, such as body gestures (e.g. the singing voice) or mechanical movements (e.g. the sound of train wheels on rails). In the same way as we are very accurate in recognizing the animate character of visual motion only from a few light points corresponding to the head and the major limb-joints of a moving person (Johansson 1973), we are very sensitive to the fluctuations of auditory events in the time-frequency plane, so that we can easily discriminate walking from running (Bresin and Dahl 2003) or even successfully recognize gender, size, and emotional intention of a person walking (Li et al. 1991; Giordano and Bresin 2006). Other expressive characters of objects such as mutual relations of domination or causality are also conveyed either visually via motion (Michotte 1963) or aurally via sound patterns. It is not a surprise that gestures are so tightly related with sound and music communication. A paradigmatic case is that of the singing voice, which is directly produced by body movements. In general, gestures allow expressive control in sound production. Another example is DJ scratching, where complex gestures on the vinyl and on the cross-fader are used for achieving expressive transformation of pre-recorded sounds (Hansen and Bresin 2004).

In the context of embodied interfaces, where manipulation is mostly continuous, it is therefore important to build a gesture interpretation layer, capable to extract the expressive content of human continuous actions, such as those occurring as preparatory movements for strokes (Dahl 2004). Body movements preceding the sound production give information about the intentions of the user, smoother and slower movements produce softer sounds, while faster and sudden movements are associated to louder sounds.

Gestures and their corresponding sounds usually occur in time sequences, and it is their particular time organization that helps in classifying their nature. Indeed, if properly organized in time, sound events can communicate a particular meaning. Let us consider the case of walking sounds. The sound of a step in isolation is difficult to identify, while it gives the idea of walking if repeated a number of times. If the time sequence is organized according to equations resembling biological motion, than walking sounds can be perceived as more natural (Bresin and Dahl 2003). In addition, if sound level and timing are varied, it is possible to communicate different emotional intentions with walking sounds. In fact, the organization in time and sound level of structurally organized events, such as notes in music performance or phonemes in speech, can be controlled for communicating different emotional expressions. For instance in hyper- and hypoarticulated speech (Lindblom 1990) and in enhanced performance of musical structure (Bresin and Friberg 2000) the listener recognizes the meaning being conveyed as well as the expressive intention on top of it. Research results show that not only we are able to recognize different emotional intentions used by musicians or speakers (Juslin and Laukka 2003) but also we feel these emotions. It has been demonstrated by psychophysical experiments that people listening to music evoking emotions experience a change in biophysical cues (such as blood pressure, etc.) that correspond to the feeling of that specific emotion and not only to the recognition. Krumhansl (1997) observed that sad music produced largest changes in heart rate, blood pressure, skin conductance and temperature, while happy music produced largest changes in measures of respiration. Music and sound in general have therefore the power to effect the variation of many physiological parameters in our body. These results could be taken into account in the design of more engaging applications where sound plays an active role.

3.2   Sound Modelling

A sound model may be thought of as a synthesis algorithm plus a control strategy driven by a representation. For instance, additive synthesis relies on the Fourier time-frequency representation, and control parameters can be amplitudes and frequencies of spectral components. What sound models are suitable for embodiment in interfaces? Ideally, they should have a few parameters that are continuously controllable and that can be easily mapped to physical variables that are subject to direct manipulation. Physical models, whose synthesis algorithm is the numerical simulation of a physical system, offer the most straightforward mapping, since the internal physical variables can be the same as the variables that are linked to external sensors and displays. In a sense, physical models are inherently ecological. There are a few problems though. Some physical models (e.g., friction of rigid bodies) have dozens of possible physical parameters. In order to manage and control them, they have to be grouped, organized in a hierarchy, or associated with a phenomenological description of their contribution to the perceived sound. For example, Table 1 provides such description for the parameters of a model of friction which is used to synthesize sounds of brakes, squeaky doors, etc. In some other cases, the physical parameters are not very meaningful and they have to be translated in order to ease the task of sound design. Figure 1 shows how resonance frequency and decay time of a simple mechanical resonator (like a small bar) could be mapped to a categorical attribute called material (steel, glass, wood, plastic). This kind of associations can be assessed using identification tests (as in Figure 1).

There are also cases when strict physical modelling is not suitable, either because a detailed model is not easily derived, or because it is too demanding in terms of computations. In such cases, cartoonification may help. Simplifications in the physical description are introduced in such a way that the principal sound characteristics are kept or possibly highlighted. This is the approach taken, for example, in the model of rolling used in the embodied interface called the Ballancer (Rath and Rocchesso 2005). In that case, the small impacts between the ball and the surface are carefully modelled, but the trajectory of the center of mass as it rolls over an irregular surface is drastically simplified into a sequence of constant-slope segments. Finally, the modulations due to deviation from perfect roundness are synthesized and used to provide slow variations to the model. With this strategy, detailed physical models are reserved to the low-level phenomena (e.g., impacts) and more abstract signal-based models are used for high-level phenomena (e.g., rolling, crumpling, sliding, etc.).

Table 1. Parameters of a friction model and their phenomenological interpretation (Reproduced from Avanzini et al. 2003)

Physical Description	Phenomenological Description
contact stiffness	evolution of mode lock-in
contact dissipation	sound bandwidth
viscous friction	timbre evolution and pitch
noise coefficient	perceived surface roughness
dynamic friction coefficient	high values reduce bandwidth
static friction coefficient	smoothness of sound attack
Stribeck velocity	smoothness of sound attack
normal force	higher values rougher sounds
velocity	higher values louder sounds

3.3   Auditory Display and Interaction Design

Sound can be indeed used as a multidimensional information carrier. Humans are able to extract size, shape, material, distance, speed, and emotional expression from sonic information. Therefore, sound can be used as a powerful channel of communication for displaying complex data. Interactive sonification (Hunt and Hermann 2005) is a new emerging field that will definitely benefit and push further the research on Sounding Objects. The first workshop on this theme organized in 2004 by the COST Action ConGAS[2] showed the use of sound feedback in a variety of applications including sport, medicine, manufacturing, and computer games. There are many issues that have been raised in such applications, and answers are expected to come from interaction design, perception, aesthetics, sound modelling. For instance, how do we achieve pleasant and effective navigation, browsing, or sorting of large amount of data with sounds? In the framework of the Sounding Object project[3], the concept of

---

[2] http://www.cost287.org
[3] http://www.soundobject.org

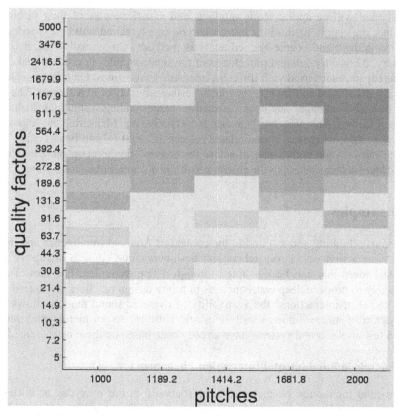

Fig. 1. Results of a material categorization experiment: the four hues correspond to material categories (rubber, wood, metal, glass) and saturation is proportional to the measured agreement in judgments (Reproduced from Avanzini and Rocchesso 2001).

sound cartoonification has been embraced in its wider sense and applied to the construction of engaging everyday sound models. Simplified and exaggerated models have been proved to be efficient in communicating the properties of objects in actions, thus being excellent vehicles for informative feedback in human-artefact communication. For instance, it has been shown that temporal control of sound events helps in communicating the nature of the sound source (e.g. a footstep) and the action that is being performed (walking/running).

The possibility of using continuous interaction with sounding objects allows for expressive control of the sound production and, as a result, to higher engagement, deeper sense of presence, and experiential satisfaction. Low-cost sensors and recent studies in artificial emotions enable new forms of interaction using previously underexploited human abilities and sensibilities. For instance, a cheap webcam is sufficient to capture expressive gesture nuances that, if appropriately interpreted, can be converted into non-visual emotional cues. These new systems, albeit inexpensive and simple in their components, provide new challenges to the designer who is called to handle a palette of technologies spanning diverse interaction modalities. In the future, the field of interaction design is expected to provide some guidelines and evaluation methods that will be applicable to artefacts and experiences in all their facets. It is likely that the classic methods of human-computer interaction will be expanded with both fine-grained and coarse-grained analysis methods. On a small scale, it is often necessary to consider detailed trajectories of physical variables in order to make sense of different strategies used with different interaction modalities. On a large scale, it is necessary to measure and analyze the global aesthetic quality of experiences. The emergence of such challenges has been detected by large funding institutions such as the European Commission, who has launched the initiative on "Measuring the Impossible" in the year 2005, where two sound-related projects (CLOSED[4] and BrainTuning[5]) have been financed. In the community of sound researchers, similar concerns are being addressed and are contributing to the emergence of the discipline of sound design.

4   Examples

By seriously thinking about sound in the context of Ambient Intelligence and human-artefact interaction, some researchers and designers came up with disruptive or incremental ideas that can be illustrated through a few examples. The ideas that are more likely to produce deep consequences in future design practices are indeed found at the kernel of interactions: the availability of dynamic sound models allows better exploitation of innate human sensibilities and abilities. As an incremental development, a few artefacts and systems have already been based on these new sonic ideas.

4.1   Sounds in Fundamental Interaction Phenomena

Fundamental interaction phenomena occur routinely in our everyday activities. For instance, when carrying wine glasses on a tray we exploit our sense of equilibrium, when handling and breaking an egg we exploit our sense of effort, when we repeatedly glue stamps on a stack of letters we exploit our sense of pace. Sounds can be used to enhance many human activities if good auditory displays are found for basic phenomena.

4.1.1   Equilibrium

Consider the complex control actions that we seamlessly exert when riding a bicycle, including steering curves and braking before hitting obstacles. Those tasks are inherently continuous and rely on a mixture of visual, kinesthetic, and auditory cues. It has been shown that continuous auditory feedback can enhance the somatosensory perception of the state of an artefact and be used as a substitute (Massimino and Sheridan 1993) of haptic or visual feedback. Since several complex tasks and interactions can be recast in terms of reaching or keeping an equilibrium point, it makes sense to look for ways of modeling the "sound of equilibrium". As an example, a virtual ball rolling on different surface textures may provide visual, auditory, or haptic feedback in selection by tilting, as required in devices such as the Hikari handheld computer (Fishkin et al. 2000) or in some embodied user interfaces (Fallman 2002).

---

[4] http://closed.ircam.fr
[5] http://www.braintuning.fi

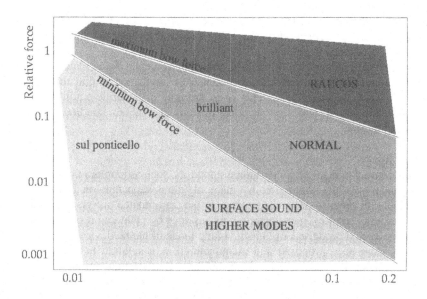

Fig. 2. The Schelleng diagram for string bowing (Adapted from Schelleng 1973). The relative distance of the bow from the bridge is plotted against the relative bow force

Even the action of steering a path within a corridor, deeply investigated in human-computer interaction (Accot and Zhai 1999), can be interpreted as a dynamic equilibrium task around an ideal middle line. According to some theories of perception and action, any task of steering or avoiding obstacles can be modelled in differential form as (Fajen and Warren 2003; Wilkie and Wann 2003)

$$\ddot{\theta} = k(\theta - \theta_0) - b\dot{\theta} \tag{1}$$

which resembles the equation of a damped spring with natural rest length of θ_0. In activities such as bicycle riding the variable θ is the instantaneous heading. This equation can be readily converted into the equation describing a tilt-and-roll situation, which can be interactively sonified (Rath and Rocchesso 2005).

But rolling is just one of the possible metaphors that can be used to provide sonic feedback in equilibrium tasks. Friction is another such metaphor. Indeed, violinists achieve a "balanced" sound by dosing the appropriate amount of bow pressure given a certain transversal bow velocity. When the force increases too much the sound becomes rough, and when the force is too little, a so-called surface sound is produced. This situation is illustrated by the classic "Schelleng diagram" (Schelleng 1973) in the force-position plane.

The Schelleng diagram was originally formulated to find the playability region of bowed string instruments, i.e. the region of the model parameter space where a "good" tone (as opposed to a raucous tone or tones dominated by higher modes) is achieved. Figure 2 shows the original Schelleng diagram, which indicates the theoretical minimum and maximum bow force as a function of the relative bow position b along the string. Between the bow-force limits, "Helmholtz motion" is established.

Helmholtz motion arises from the stick-slip interaction between bow and string, and is characterized by a single "corner" travelling back and forth on the string under an approximately parabolic envelope.

A similar diagram can be redrawn in the velocity versus force plane. Equilibrium in continuous interaction can be reformulated as navigation within the corridor of playability in Schelleng's plots. This is an example of dynamic equilibrium, as opposed to static equilibrium, since it refers to stationary motion conditions rather than absence of motion.

4.1.2 Effort

In many routine human-computer interaction tasks, such as icon dragging, typical visual feedback gives the impression that manipulation is happening on a surrogate, fictitious object. In order to provide substance to the manipulated objects, physical reality must be mimicked or even exaggerated, for instance by including resistance to motion due to the inertial properties of objects. Many kinds of haptic devices providing force feedback have been proposed and manufactured as a solution to this requirement. However, there are many practical cases where it is desirable to substitute haptic feedback with other modalities. One possible reason is that these devices are in most cases cumbersome and expensive, another is that they provide a strictly personal display (e.g., a user cannot share a sensation of effort with an audience). A number of alternatives have been proposed. Approaches based on purely visual feedback have been demonstrated to be effective in some cases. Cartoon animation techniques applied to widget components and graphical object manipulation do enhance the interaction (Thomas and Calder 2001). Force-feedback has also been visually simulated via cursor displacement (Mensvoort 2002) and pseudo-haptic feedback (Lécuyer et al. 2000).

However, in many applications the visual display does not appear to be the best choice as a replacement of kinesthetic feedback. While vision emphasizes properties related to geometry and space, touch is more effective in conveying information about "intensive" properties (material, weight, texture) (Klatzky and Lederman 2002). Since intensive properties strongly affect the temporal behavior of objects in motion and interaction, the accuracy of the auditory system in perceiving temporal events can be exploited for sensory substitution.

For example, continuous contact sounds can be used to give back a sensation of resistance to motion when objects are manipulated. For such purpose, a physical model of friction proved to be suitable (Avanzini et al. 2004). In general, physically-based sound models are suited for interactive sonification settings, since gesture-based control is easily mapped into physical parameters of the model (e.g., normal force and sliding velocity). The situation is well illustrated in the sound-augmented book depicted in Figure 3 and described in Sect. 4.2.1, where the user experiences the door resistance through the friction sound produced by the hinges.

4.1.3 Pace

In many applications, auditory feedback can be used for informing users about their actions. The sound of a clicked button is a typical example, e.g. in mobile phones. But, what happens when the auditory feedback corresponding to a gesture is delayed in time? Is the auditory feedback prevailing over the haptic one, or the opposite? Moreover, actions have often to be repeated and a steady pace has to be kept. This poses further interesting questions about the interplay between different feedback modalities.

Musicians can be considered a special class of users and they can be used as limiting-case testers of new ideas about sound and technology. They are very skilled in playing by adapting to the feedback from their instrument and from other musicians. Feedback can be auditory (the sound from the instrument), visual (instructions from the conductor) and haptic (vibrations from the body of the instrument, such as in the violin). Drummers in particular, are very good in synchronizing with other people playing and they do it either by listening or by watching the other members in an ensemble or both. In normal situations musicians in an ensemble play with an average asynchronicity of about 36 ms (Rasch 1988). But if the audio feedback from their own instrument has a time delay relative to the haptic feedback than problems start to arise. In a recent experiment it was investigated how drummers could cope with a delayed auditory feedback (DAF) (Bresin and Dahl 2003). Subjects were asked to play a single stroke on an electronic drum. They did it at two constant tempi, 92 and 120 beats per minute. The sound resulting from their playing action was delayed to their ears. When the DAF reached values between 20-55 ms and between 80-130 ms, players struggled keeping the beat and they had problems synchronizing the haptic feedback with the acoustic one. In that experiment it was noticed that, in those DAF ranges, players started to play louder (corresponding to faster impact velocities) as an attempt to keep the beat.

These results can be interpreted as follows. Users rely on tactile feedback once the DAF has exceeded a certain critical value. For DAFs below this value users have problems in choosing between the haptic or the acoustic channel as feedback for their actions.

4.2   Sound-Augmented Artefacts

In order to get gradually out of the schizophonic age and have multisensory embodied interaction, sounds should be embedded in the artefacts and controlled by continuous interaction. In some cases the actual sound diffusion could be displaced elsewhere, but the tight coupling between gestures on the artefacts and sound models should give the illusion of embodied sounds. Interactive books and handheld devices are two possible fields of application of this design attitude.

4.2.1   Sound-Augmented Books

Pull-the-tab and lift-the-flap books play a central role in the education and entertainment of most children all over the world. Most of these books are inherently cross-cultural and appropriate for diverse social contexts. By interacting with books, small children learn to name objects and characters, they understand the relations between objects, and develop a sense of causality by direct manipulation and feedback. The importance of sound as a powerful medium has been largely recognized, up to the point that there are books on the market that reproduce pre-recorded sounds upon pushing certain buttons or touching certain areas. However, such triggered sounds are extremely unnatural, repetitive, and annoying. The key for a successful exploitation of sounds in books is to have models that respond continuously to continuous action, just in the same way as children do when manipulating rattles or other physical sounding objects. In other words, books have to become an embodied interface (Dourish 2001) in all respects, including sound. As an example, Figure 3 shows a sensed flap door that is used to control a physical model of friction at the hinges. As side effects we can have visual motion of a door in a virtual environment and a continuously changing squeak.

4.2.2 Handhelds

The increasing computing power available in portable devices, and their high degree of diffusion among the population, make them ideal candidates for the exploitation of sounding objects. In fact, portable devices such as mobile phones are operated with direct manipulation. It would therefore be natural to have an audio feedback as a direct response to user's gestures.

Fig. 3. Moving a squeaky door in a lift-the-flap book

For example, if embedded sensors are available, it is possible to identify typical gestures when using a little portable device such as a mobile phone (Eriksson et al. 2003). Gestures used in menu navigation, such as shaking for deleting information in a device, could be identified and sonified for providing a non-visual feedback to the user. Acoustic feedback in gestures with small devices is important since the display is usually very little and it requires focused attention from the user. We can rely on auditory information in many cases: for instance, we do not need to look towards a bottle that has crashed to the floor to understand that it is broken. There are also situations in which we handle a device without having the possibility to look at it. Also in cases like these an acoustic feedback, i.e. an interactive sonification of the device, can help the user in the control of the portable device (Fernström et al. 2005).

Recent research has demonstrated that it is possible to control expressivity, such as emotions, in the automatic reproduction of music and sounds, and that listeners are able to recognize different emotions independently from their culture. People may not recognize the meaning of a piece of music or of a spoken phrase, what they can recognize is the expressive message (Scherer et al. 2001), i.e. the hyper-articulation of a given structure. For example, most people would not understand what a mother is saying to a child in a foreign language, but they will recognize that she is speaking to her child[6]. As described in Sect. 3.1, listeners will also experience physiological changes when listening to sounds with different emotional intentions. These observations could be used to control in an expressive way the sonification of portable devices according to the context and to the user's mood. For instance, with the help of automatic text analysis techniques, one could sonify the text messages in mobile phones so that users could understand the humor of the sender before actually reading the message. Already available on the consumer market are expressive ring tones, allowing users to associate different emotions to different user groups and people (Bresin and Friberg 2001). The mobile phone, with its MIDI synthesizer, allowing polyphonic ring tones, is probably the most widespread electronic instrument in the world. One could also think of going further and turning the mobile phone into an expressive musical instrument and/or a game machine with gesture control. The embedded sensors could be used for interpreting user gestures and control sound production. New games could be developed based only on audio feedback, instead of using visual display on very small size screen (Hermann et al. 2006). Gesture analysis could also give information about the expressive intention of the user and could be used for personalizing the sound profile of the mobile device. There are already examples of mobile phone orchestras, where either each member of the orchestra plays a different melodic line or all the members play the same polyphonic ring tone at the same time (the latter happened at a rock concert in Estonia in 2004).

4.3   Sound-Mediated Cooperative Work

Acoustic signals carry part of the information in human-to-human communication, and non-linguistic acoustic cues are extensively interpreted by humans. Similarly, computer-mediated cooperative work should make use of the acoustic channel, for example by proper auditory displays associated with interactive screens or tabletops.

4.3.1   Large Displays

Some research groups have developed large interactive displays that can be used for cooperative work as a sort of extended blackboards. Interacting with one such device immediately reveals some inherent problems with visual displays. The limited human field of view and the possible simultaneous occurrence of events at the board calls for non-visual display modes.

---

[6] These phenomena, indeed, are at the root of trans-linguistic communication systems, such as the *grammelot*, used by medieval comedians and revitalized in modern times by playwright Dario Fo and filmmaker Jacques Tati.

Fig. 4. Zizi the Affectionate Couch

In the context of roomware components (Prante et al. 2004), Christian Müller-Tomfelde developed interactive sound models aimed at providing both local feedback and inter-partner communication for teams cooperating in front of a large display (Müller-Tomfelde et al. 2003). For example, a throwing mechanism can be used to move objects across the large board, and an aeolic sound can be used to communicate direction and speed of arrival to the receiving agent. The receiver's visual attention may be momentarily directed somewhere else, but the sound will provide rapid information about the incoming object.

In the interpretation of input gestures, sounds provide a robust form of feedback, especially when gesture recognition is incremental (Müller-Tomfelde et al. 2003). For instance, when a "delete" gesture is recognized by the system a special sound is played so that the user, if the gesture was erroneous, has a chance to undo it in a continuous fashion without even interrupting the gesture flow. For this purpose, the haptic quality of low-frequency sounds become useful: If sounds are played through a sub-woofer that is in contact with the board, the low-frequency components become haptically perceptible, and the resulting interaction experience becomes much stronger.

The interaction between haptics and sound deserves some further comments. Especially when groups of people are sharing interactive experiences there is a subtle border between the public and the private, or the shared and the intimate. This border can be crossed back and forth by cross-fading between modalities. In fact, audition is inherently in the public domain, while haptics is usually a private experience. These properties can be used, for example, to let an audience share a sense of effort by re-placing haptic feedback with auditory display. Or, conversely, the degree of intimacy of an interface can be increased by converting audio into haptics in a certain extent. For leisure and entertainment the exploitation of the border between sound and hap-tics can be the actual key for the acceptance of a product. An example is ZiZi, the Af-fectionate Couch designed by Stephen Barrass, Linda Davy, and Kerry Richens, and displayed in many fairs and trade shows (see Gye 2004 for a review). Large sub-woofers embedded in the couch provide sonic/haptic feedback to the persons moving around and sitting on it. The contact with the piece of furniture becomes a source of intimate sensorial pleasure (see Figure 4).

Another important point, well exemplified in large interactive displays, is the rela-tion between sound and space. In the multimedia and home-theater marketing much emphasis is put into systems for moving sound sources around in space. However, experiences with sound-augmented interactive systems show that the perceived em-bodiment of sound is really more a function of its time-frequency continuous behavior rather than of its illusory spatial qualities. The best of the embodiment is obtained when the actual sound sources (loudspeakers) are embedded in the artefacts. For in-stance, in the DynaWall (Prante et al. 2004) three loudspeakers are placed behind the interactive screens and in physical contact with them. A sound source can not be pre-cisely located on a wall with just three loudspeakers and without a prescribed position for the listener, but the interactive and continuous nature of sounds makes the need of a precise location largely irrelevant, as the other senses (vision and/or haptics) coop-erate with audition to form coherent percepts.

4.3.2 Tabletops

Another active application field for research in human-computer interaction and com-puter-supported cooperative work is that of interactive tabletops. Here the interaction is

Fig. 5. The Virtual Touch machine at the Hunt Museum in Limerick

usually more local as compared with large interactive boards, but there is also the need to trade between individual work and peripheral awareness (Gutwin and Greenberg 2002). There are compelling examples of tabletops where sound plays a crucial role for expressing the self while coordinating in an ensemble, especially those crafted for playing music collectively. Among these, consider the ReacTable under development at the Audiovisual Institute of the University Pompeu Fabra (Kaltenbrunner et al. 2004). In this example the players collaborate at creating and modifying patches for real-time sound synthesis by disposition of tangible objects. It is really the continuous, real-time sound generation that drives composition of the spatial layout and gives collective awareness. As opposed to most conventional interfaces, visual display by projection is not the main output channel, but it is rather used to visualize the sound and control flows among objects, and to highlight activated objects or links. In other words, the layout of physical objects and their sonic behavior drive interaction, while visual display is used for feedback, sometimes anticipatory of the audible result.

Another context where tabletops or showcases are largely used is in exhibits. In traditional settings the visitor is not allowed to touch the objects, thus preventing a full experience of their tactile or acoustics properties. Headsets are often used to accompany visitors along the exhibit with spoken comments and non-speech sounds, but they typically prevent freedom of choice and active exploration. In the exhibit "Re-Tracing the Past" at the Hunt Museum in Limerick (Ferris et al. 2004; Ottaviani 2004), sounds have been used to partially overcome this limitation by means of virtual tapping: the visitor can tap a virtual rendering of the object and get sonic feedback (see Figure 5). Since the sound is generated in real-time according to gestural parameters, the overall impression is of direct manipulation rather than simple triggering of pre-recorded audio snapshots.

4.4   Response from the Public

Audio research is having a big impact in everyday life. One example is the popularity reached by compressed sound file formats such as mp3 that was also ranked in the top 10 of Google popular queries for year 2004. Portable devices for playing music in compressed formats are widely used, and manufacturers have equipped some of these players with very large memories that allow for the storage of up to 10000 songs ore more. Problems arise when users have to browse their music database using small displays and button-based interfaces. Aware of these problems researchers have started to design tools for gesture control of portable devices. Research on the perception of basic sound qualities and on the interactive sonification of gestures may help in this direction.

In the framework of the Sounding Object project different psychophysical experiments have been conducted. Responses from the subjects indicate, among other things, that humans are able (1) to identify gross-material categories of a sounding object and paradoxically make finer distinctions (e.g. metal vs. glass) on the basis of its size, (2) to estimate the hardness both of a struck object and of its striker (Giordano 2003), (3) to perceive a sequence of sounds as walking steps or running steps depending on their temporal organization (Bresin and Dahl 2003), (4) to control the position of an object using continuous sound feedback (Rath and Rocchesso 2005).

These results should be taken into account when designing applications involving sound and gesture. In particular, among main fields of application for sound models reacting to gesture are foreseen to be the therapy/rehabilitation field and the entertainment/leisure industry. Both fields can take great advantage if direct coupling between sound and gesture is considered. In the field of therapy, continuous sonification of gestures can make a person aware of own body movements and help her in controlling them. The same kind of application has been used in the training of sport professionals. Athletes had first to listen to the sonification of the "perfect" movement and than to train it by listening to the real-time sonification of their own movements (Effenberg 2004).

In the entertainment field, multisensory applications involving sound, gesture and vision have resulted to be more interesting, funny, enjoyable, and engaging if user's body gestures have a clear connection to acoustic and visual feedback and if the user is more actively engaged (Lindström et al. 2005). Applications with real-time communication of expressive and emotional content are foreseen as promising in social, artistic, and communicative entertainment. In this perspective, sound models that react to gestures in a meaningful way will enhance activities such as dance, interactive sonification, human-computer interaction, and computer games.

An example of application in the entertainment/leisure field is the already mentioned ZiZi couch, a two and a half meter length couch that "purrs when touched, growls when sat on and can become aroused if stroked. Left all alone, Zizi mews for attention". In this application sound is used for both capturing the attention of potential user and for giving her feedback once sitting on it. Feedback is both acoustic and haptic via the vibrations caused by the large sub-woofers placed under the couch. Reaction from the public visiting the various exhibitions at which Zizi was presented can be summarized with the following report from the exhibition at the Heide Museum of Contemporary Art: "Love at first sight of the colour and fabric, followed by delighted surprise when they sat down and heard and felt Zizi being affectionate"[7].

Acknowledgement

The Sounding Object project was financed by the European Commission under contract IST-2000-25287. We acknowledge the contribution of all participant of the consortium. In particular, we would like to thank Matthias Rath, Federico Fontana, Federico Avanzini,

Laura Ottaviani, Nicola Bernardini, Gianpaolo Borin, Sofia Dahl, Kjetil Falkenberg Hansen, Giovanni Bruno Vicario, Bruno Giordano, Massimo Grassi, Roberto Burro, Aleardo Maestrini, Mikael Fernström, Eoin Brazil, Bridget Moynihan, Mark Marshall.

References

Avanzini, F., Rocchesso, D.: Controlling material properties in physical models of sounding objects. In: Schloss, A., Dannenberg, R., Driessen, P. (eds.) Proceedings International Computer Music Conference. ICMA, San Francisco, pp. 91–94. Instituto Cubano de la Musica, La Habana (2001)
Avanzini, F., Rath, M., Rocchesso, D., Ottavini, L.: Low-level models: resonators, interactions, and surface textures. In: Rocchesso, D., Fontana, F. (eds.) The Sounding Object, pp. 137–171. Mondo Estremo, Florence (2003)

---

[7] http://www.twenty121.com

Avanzini, F., Serafin, S., Rocchesso, D.: Friction sounds for sensory substitution. In: Barrass, S., Vickers, P. (eds.) Proceedings International Conference Auditory Display. ICAD, Sydney (July 2004)

Accot, J., Zhai, S.: Performance evaluation of input devices in trajectory-based tasks: An application of steering law. In: Proceedings of the SIGCHI conference on Human factors in computing systems. CHI '99, Pittsburgh, PA, pp. 466–472. ACM Press, New York (1999)

Barrass, S.: Sonification design patterns. In: Brazil, E., Shinn-Cunningham, B. (eds.) Proceedings International Conference Auditory Display, Boston, MA, pp. 170–175 (2003)

Bresin, R., Dahl, S.: Experiments on gestures: walking, running, and hitting. In: Rocchesso, D., Fontana, F. (eds.) The Sounding Object, pp. 111–136. Mondo Estremo, Florence (2003)

Bresin, R., Friberg, A.: Emotional coloring of computer-controlled music performances. Computer Music Journal 24(4), 44–63 (2000)

Bresin, R., Friberg, A.: Expressive musical icons. In: Hiipakka, J., Zacharov, N., Takala, T. (eds.) Proceedings International Conference Auditory Display, Espoo, Finland, pp. 141–143 (2001)

Bregman, A.S.: Auditory scene analysis: the perceptual organization of sound. MIT Press, Cambridge (1990)

Brodsky, W.: The effects of music tempo on simulated driving performance and vehicular control. Transportation Research, Part F. Traffic Psychology and Behavior 4, 219–241 (2002)

Dahl, S.: Playing the accent - comparing striking velocity and timing in an ostinato rhythm performed by four drummers. Acta. Acustica united with Acustica 90(4), 762–776 (2004)

Dourish, P.: Where the action is: the foundations of embodied interaction. MIT Press, Cambridge (2001)

Dent, M.L., Tollin, D.J., Yin, T.C.T.: Cats exhibit the Franssen effect illusion. Journal of the Acoustical Society of America 116(6), 3070–3074 (2004)

Effenberg, A.: Using sonification to enhance perception and reproduction accuracy of human movement patterns. In: Hunt, A., Hermann, T. (eds.) Proceedings of International Workshop on Interactive Sonification (Human Interaction with Auditory Displays), CD-ROM. Bielefeld University, Germany (2004)

Eriksson, S., Fjellström, O., Grahn, J., Lundholm, P., Nilbrink, F., Shalit, T.: Gesture recorder demonstration (Paper presented at the Gesture Workshop 2003. Genoa, Italy, http://www.dh.umu.se/fprw/files/OSKAR/GestRecDemo.pdf) (2003)

Fallman, D.: Wear, point, and tilt: Designing support for mobile service and maintenance in industrial settings. In: Proceedings of the conference on Designing interactive systems: processes, practices, methods, and techniques, London, UK, pp. 239–302. ACM Press, New York (2002)

Fernström, M., Brazil, E., Bannon, L.: Human-computer interaction design and interactive sonification an interface for fingers and ears. IEEE Multimedia 12(2) (2005)

Ferris, K., Bannon, L., Ciolfi, L., Gallagher, P., Hall, T., Lennon, M.: Shaping experiences in the Hunt museum: a design case study. In: Proceedings of the 2004 conference on Designing interactive systems: processes, practices, methods, and techniques, Cambridge, MA, pp. 205–214. ACM Press, New York (2004)

Fishkin, K.P., Gujar, A., Harrison, B.L., Moran, T.P., Want, R.: Embodied user interfaces for really direct manipulation. Communications of the ACM 43(9), 75–80 (2000)

Franssen, N.V.: Stereophony, (English Trans. 1964). Philips Tech. Library, Eindhoven, The Netherlands (1963)

Fajen, B.R., Warren, W.H.: Behavioral dynamics of steering, obstacle avoidance, and route selection. Journal of Experimental Psychology: Human. Perception and Performance 29(2), 343–362 (2003)

Gaver, W.W.: How do we hear in the world? Explorations in ecological acoustics. Ecological Psychology 5(4), 285–313 (1993a)

Gaver, W.W.: What in the world do we hear? An ecological approach to auditory event perception. Ecological Psychology 5(1), 1–29 (1993b)

Gaver, W.W.: Using and creating auditory icons. In: Kremer, G. (ed.) Auditory Display: Sonification, Audification, and Auditory Interfaces, pp. 417–446. Addison-Wesley, Reading (1994)

Gutwin, C., Greenberg, S.: A descriptive framework of workspace awareness for real-time groupware. Computer Supported Cooperative Work. 11(3), 411–446 (2002)

Gibson, J.J.: The Ecological Approach to Visual Perception. Lawrence Erlbaum Associates, Cambridge (1979)

Giordano, B.: Material categorization and hardness scaling in real and synthetic impact sounds. In: Rocchesso, D., Fontana, F. (eds.) The Sounding Object, pp. 73–93. Mondo Estremo, Florence (2003)

Giordano, B., Bresin, R.: Walking and playing: What's the origin of emotional expressiveness in music? In: Baroni, M., Addessi, A.R., Caterina, R., Costa, M. (eds.) 9th International Conference on Music Perception and Cognition, ICMPC9, Bologna, Italy, p. 149 (Aug. 2006)

Gye, L.: Future longing. Real Time 58, 47–54 (Jan. 2004), http://www.realtimearts.net

Hansen, K.F., Bresin, R.: Analysis of a genuine scratch performance. In: Camurri, A., Volpe, G. (eds.) GW 2003. LNCS (LNAI), vol. 2915, pp. 519–528. Springer, Heidelberg (2004)

Hermann, T., Höner, O., Ritter, H.: AcouMotion - An Interactive Sonification System for Acoustic Motion Control. In: Gibet, S., Courty, N., Kamp, J.-F. (eds.) GW 2005. LNCS (LNAI), vol. 3881, pp. 18–20. Springer, Heidelberg (2006)

Hunt, A., Hermann, T.: Special issue on Interactive Sonification. IEEE Multimedia 12(2) (2005)

Juslin, P.N., Laukka, P.: Communication of emotions in vocal expression and music performance: Different channels, same code? Psychological Bulletin 129(5), 770–814 (2003)

Johansson, G.: Visual perception of biological motion and a model for its analysis. Perception and Psychophysics 14, 201–211 (1973)

Kaltenbrunner, M., Geiger, G., Jorda, S.: Dynamic patches for live musical performance. In: Proceedings of the 4th Conference on New Interfaces for Musical Expression. NIME 04, Hamamatsu, Japan, pp. 19–22 (2004)

Klatzky RL, Lederman SJ (2002) Touch. In: Healy AF, Proctor RW (eds) Experimental Psychology. Wiley, New York, pp 147-176

Krumhansl, C.L.: An exploratory study of musical emotions and psychophysiology. Canadian Journal of Experimental Psychology 51(4), 336–352 (1997)

Kubovy, M., van Valkenburg, D.: Auditory and visual objects. Cognition 80, 97–126 (2001)

Lindström, E., Camurri, A., Friberg, A., Volpe, G., Rinman, M.-L.: Affect, attitude and evaluation of multi-sensory performances. Journal of New. Music. Research 34(1), 69–86 (2005)

Lécuyer, A., Coquillart, S., Kheddar, A., Richard, P., Coiffet, P.: Pseudo-haptic feedback: Can isometric input devices simulate force feedback? In: VR '00 Proceedings of the IEEE Virtual Reality 2000 Conference, New Brunswick, US, pp. 83–90. IEEE Computer Society, Washington (2000)

Lindblom, B.: Explaining phonetic variation: a sketch of the H&H theory. In: Hardcastle, W.J., Marchal, A. (eds.) Speech production and speech modeling, pp. 403–439. Kluwer, Dordrecht (1990)

Li, X., Logan, R.J., Pastore, R.E.: Perception of acoustic source characteristics: Walking sounds. Journal of the Acoustical Society of America 90(6), 3036–3049 (1991)

Martin, S.: Theremin, an electronic odissey (Documentary on DVD). MGM (2001)

Michotte, A.: The perception of causality. (Orig., La perception de la causalité, 1946). Basic Books, New York (1963)

Massimino, M.J., Sheridan, T.B.: Sensory substitution for force feedback in teleoperation. Presence 2(4), 344–352 (1993)

van Mensvoort, K.: What you see is what you feel. In: DIS '02: Proceedings of the conference on Designing interactive systems, London, UK, pp. 345–348. ACM Press, New York (2002)

Müller-Tomfelde, C., Streitz, N.A., Steinmetz, R.: Sounds@work - auditory displays for inter-action in cooperative and hybrid environments. In: Stephanidis, C., Jacko, J. (eds.) Human-Computer Interaction: Theory and Practice (Part II), pp. 751–755. Lawrence Erlbaum Publishers, Mahwah (2003)

Ottavini, L.: Representation of Multi-Dimensional Data through Auditory Display. Ph.D. thesis, Università di Verona, Italy (2004)

Prante, T., Streitz, N.A., Tandler, P.: Roomware: Computers disappear and interaction evolves. IEEE Computer 37(12), 47–54 (2004)

Rasch, R.A.: Timing and synchronization in ensemble performance. In: Sloboda, J. (ed.) Generative processes in music: The psychology of performance, improvization, and composition, pp. 70–90. Oxford University Press, Oxford (1988)

Rath, M., Rocchesso, D.: Continuous sonic feedback from a rolling ball. IEEE Multimedia 12(2) (2005)

Schafer, R.M.: The Tuning of the World. McClelland and Stewart Limited, Toronto (1977)

Schaeffer, P.: Traité des Objets Musicaux. Éditions du Seuil, Paris, France (1966)

Schelleng, J.C.: The bowed string and the player. Journal of the Acoustical Society of America 53(1), 26–41 (1973)

Scherer, K.R., Banse, R., Wallbott, H.G.: Emotion inferences from vocal expression correlate across languages and cultures. Journal of Cross.-Cultural Psychology 32(1), 76–92 (2001)

Scheuren, J., Martner, O., Zerbs, C.: Practical aspects of product sound quality design. In: Proceedings Les Journés du Design Sonore, Paris, France (2004), http://www.design-sonore.org

Thomas, B.H., Calder, P.: Applying Cartoon Animation Techniques to Graphical User Interfaces. ACM Trans. on Computer-Human Interaction 8(3), 198–222 (2001)

Vicario, G.B.: On experimental phenomenology. In: Masin, S.C. (ed.) Foundations of Perceptual Theory, pp. 197–219. Elsevier Science Publishers, Amsterdam (1993)

Wilkie, R.M., Wann, J.P.: Controlling steering and judging heading: retinal flow, visual direction and extra-retinal information. Journal of Experimental Psychology: Human. Perception and Performance 29(2), 363–378 (2003)

Electronically Functional Fibre Technology Development for Ambient Intelligence

Thomas Healy[1], Constantin Papadas[2], Nikos Venios[2], Frank Clemens[4],
Markus Wegmann[4], Doerte Winkler[3], Astrid Ullsperger[3], Wolf Hartmann[3],
Brendan O'Neill[1], Julie Donnelly[1], Anne-Marie Kelleher[1], John Alderman[1],
and Alan Mathewson[1]

[1] National Microelectronics Research Centre (NMRC), Cork, Ireland
[2] Integrated Systems Development (ISD), Athens, Greece
[3] Klaus Steilmann Institute (KSI), Cottbus, Germany
[4] Swiss Federal Laboratories for Materials Testing and Research (EMPA),
Duebendorf, Switzerland

1 Introduction

Most of everyday clothing consists of textile fibres woven together to produce a fabric. Their primary purpose is structural and aesthetic. Fibres can have added functionality by the integration of computing power into the material that forms them. The purpose of the "fibre computing" concept is to integrate this new dimension of functionality into fibres, thus turning everyday objects into intelligent artefacts. The objective is to make large flexible integrated systems for wearable applications and high-tech-textile products by building functional fibres with single crystal silicon transistors at its core. The concept of wearable computing opens entirely new possibilities in areas such as medical monitoring and telemedicine, sports and athletics, entertainment and expressive musical/dance performance (Gemperle 1998). It offers the potential of harnessing a very high degree of applicable functional processing power for the user in a particularly convenient manner through the placement of non-invasive sensors around the body. However, a key barrier to this are the challenges associated with the unobtrusive deployment of effective sensors. Even current state of the art (VivoMetrics), in integrating electronics into wearable systems comprises of previously packaged integrated electronic components, interconnected with each other by means of conductive fibres and enclosed by protective material/casing. An approach more conducive to everyday living, which would enable this technology to recede even further into the background is required. The solution is the development of a novel technology for creating intelligent fibres.

There are two approaches to fibre technology development investigated in this paper. The first approach is a novel technology that enables the fabrication of silicon orientated electronically functional fibres. The concept involves building a circuit in silicon on insulator material (SOI), laying it out in such a way that its topography is linear and constrained in the direction of the wafer diameter and releasing the circuit by under-cutting the silicon dioxide layer using a combination of isotropic and anisotropic plasma etch processes, see Figure 1. Some of the difficulties encountered including fibre release, handling and fibre interconnection, along with the different scenarios investigated to overcome them are presented throughout the paper.

N. Streitz, A. Kameas, and I. Mavrommati (Eds.): The Disappearing Computer, LNCS 4500, pp. 255–274, 2007.
© Springer-Verlag Berlin Heidelberg 2007

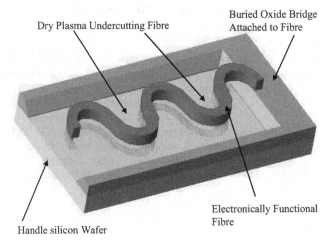

Dry Plasma Undercutting Fibre

Buried Oxide Bridge
Attached to Fibre

Electronically Functional
Fibre

Handle silicon Wafer

Fig. 1. SOI Fibre Approach

The other method for creating functional fibres is a much more speculative approach which investigates the possibility of building electronics onto three-dimensional extruded fibres, see Figure 2. In this instance, an experimentally based programme evaluated the production of individual transistors on different cross section shaped (square, circular, elliptical etc.) fibres of different length and major axis dimension.

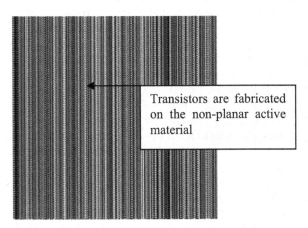

Transistors are fabricated on the non-planar active material

Fig. 2. Extruded Fibre Approach

From the point of view of the textile industry, the general idea of fibre computing constitutes a major innovation that has not been achieved since the invention of the first man made fibres. The concept merges two industries that until today have been separate even to the extent of using diverse vocabularies. This interfacial concept offers completely new applications and markets for the textile industry and advances with the growing importance of technical textiles in many markets. Items of clothing are only one of many textile products to be revolutionized by computing fibres. A few scenarios will be described in order to demonstrate the manifold application possibilities and to give an impression of the advantage of embedding high-tech-technologies into fibres instead of attaching these devices to the fabric.

A system specification based upon the applications considered to be most useful was developed, along with identifying the prospective most successful applications, not only focussed on textile and clothes but also Ambient Intelligence Solutions. It has been established that Fibre Computing will emulate a network of basic functions (named "System on a Fibre" (SoF)) connected with a simple serial bus (named SoF-Bus).

2   Application Areas for Wearable and Ambient Electronics

Before a detailed overview over the technological challenges of electronically functional fibres is given, some areas of applications should be highlighted that are emerging out of current market needs, as well as out of the general technological development of wearable and ubiquitous computing.

2.1   Health and Well-Being Applications

Health and Well-being are part of the great future markets for almost all branches. Currently, this market is gaining relevance in the textile industry. The core areas of this new market are innovative fibres and finishing technologies that enable the integration of new functions into clothes and other textile products. These fibres can act as a substrate with specialised functions, from anti-bacterial functions and aromatherapy to vitamins or medicine. There are also new application fields involving microsystems, nanochemicals and biotechnologies.

Electronic functions, to date, are not performed by these fibres. Until now, discrete elements are still integrated into clothes for such functions, like for example sensors for vital sign monitoring and health.

Pioneering work in this field is the "sensate liner" (Lind et al. 1998), developed at the Georgia Institute of Technology. However, this smart shirt does not have the technology embedded in the fibre but creates a network of optical and conductive fibres with interface facilities for active components. This work does not only give a good example of how useful the integration of computing power into fibres could be but also how they may be interlinked into an intelligent network of microelectronic components.

On a global platform, discussions have started to bring new intelligent functions not only into the second skin but also under the first skin, in connection with the body using biomedical sensors.

Thus ambient intelligence objects with the facility to monitor and improve our health are one big field of application for the outlined technology.

2.2   Security Applications

The demographical factor of the industrial states in the European Union has reached a highly important factor. Against the background of these fact the future standard cost estimate for health systems will be exploding through the next decades. The benefit of modern health systems based on new communication and interaction systems, will be provide an intense help function. That means i.e. for the nursing staff to get an opportunity to have more time for individual care for elderly person.

Another huge development of security applications in our modern society is a growing demand for individual safety. The mobility of humans and the daily dangers are versatile. The security of children and/or elderly persons should be guaranteed anyway which place they are. As our market research showed personal security and the security of close family members, children or the elderly are a great concern for many potential customers.

That is why security and safety functions are seen as an important field of application for wearable electronics. This includes:

- Emergency call functions

- Location and navigation facilities

- Simple communication facilities

- Special circumstances emergency facilities like for instance avalanche beeper

- Visibility in the dark

Such kinds of security applications form the second big area of applications.

2.3 Special Target Groups for Smart Clothes

In the field of smart clothes, a significant market potential lies in special target groups; for smart work-wear, teaching and learning helps, functional sports, hobbies and fun including computer game extensions through smart clothes.

One of these new groups is formed by e-sport community members and teams. These, mainly, young people have a high affinity towards new technology and technological gimmicks and could become a leading group in the dissemination of smart clothes functions.

Other special target groups are different professionals. Work-wear for different branches and companies could supply professionals with exactly the mobile functions they need. Relevant functions for this target group are for instance communication, security and sensing functions.

2.4 Technical Textiles

For the core area of this work, the main focus of application lay in the field of clothes, mainly because the real advantage of fibre computing impacts mostly in the perspective of the clothes people are wearing.

However, as market studies show, technical textiles offer a huge potential of applications for fibre computing.

Technical textiles are used for instance in:

Home textiles,	Industry textiles,
Mobile textiles,	Military textiles,
Sport textiles,	Geo textiles,
Building and construction textiles,	Packaging industry
Medical textiles,	Protection textiles.

Compared to all other textile branches the technical textile industry is the only one that is constantly growing. Additionally, the innovation potential and resources for innovation in these companies are much higher than in the average textile and clothing industry. Industry and the mobile textiles areas hold the highest market share in this field. The markets for geo and protection textiles are growing. Application possibilities for these product fields are exhaustive, reaching from sensing networks to interaction with the surrounding environment.

2.5 Systematisation of Ambient Intelligence Applications for Electronically Functional Fibres

For the systematisation of the applications and the definition of interfaces a classification system had to be found. Therefore a classification system called "7 skin model" (Figure 3) with the following levels of computing fibre integration has been developed:

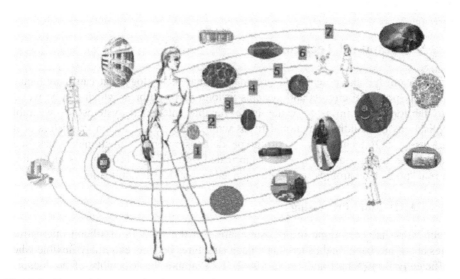

Fig. 3. 7 skin model *Personal Fibres:* 1. Fibres under the skin (implants), 2. Fibres on the skin (like hair), 3. Fibres next to the skin (underwear), 4. Fibres loose to the skin (clothes); *Group Specified Fibres:* 5. Permanent outer skin (houses, office), 6. Mobile outer skin (cars, trains); *Shared Fibres:* 7. Environmental Fibres (Ambient general)

This model can be used in defining intelligent objects for electronically functional fibres.

2.6 Comparison with Current Wearable Systems

Today there are 3 main approaches to embed technology into textiles and other everyday objects:

1. The simplest approach: To embed existing technologies into clothes and other products in a way that it can be removed or exchanged if necessary (for instance for washing, battery exchange etc.)

2. In the two dimensional format, existing technology is adopted to be embedded into textile products with special textile interfaces.

3. In the three dimensional format, new technology is developed, which small enough to be embedded comfortably into textiles and interconnected via textile interfaces (i.e. conductive yarns and ribbons).

The most promising approaches in bringing electronic functions into textiles are research activities based upon conductive fibres, yarns and coatings and the interconnection scenarios involved with hermetically packaged active and passive components (VivoMetrics).

The research involved in electronically functional fibres goes far beyond these current approaches, by making the technology recede seamlessly into the fabric that makes up the garment. The electronically functional components would no longer be separate entities to the garment, but will make the basic building block of any textile, the fibre, an intelligent and autonomous unit.

3   SOI Float off Technology

This concept has the potential to provide a planar technology that can manufacture extremely powerful circuits and systems in long narrow fibres, which can be woven into fabrics. The aim is to make large flexible integrated systems for wearable applications by building functional fibres with single crystal silicon transistors at its core using SOI technology. A prototype demonstration of functionality has been realised i.e. a p-n junction has been fabricated on a fibre. Through this technology current "pocket electronics" could be replaced by real textile applications.

3.1   CMOS Fibre Processing

Much work has been done in the examination of the strength of silicon microstructures and it has been established that silicon structures become extremely flexible when sufficiently thin (Najafi and Hetke 1990). To examine the feasibility of producing a functional silicon fiber that could be implemented into any everyday object and to investigate the influence of the mechanical strength of a silicon fibre shape, a number of different structures of varying length, width and shape were designed

Silicon on Insulator (SOI) type structure wafers (Kou and Ker-Wei 1998) were chosed because of their suitability to the release process, which is explained in more detail later in the text. The structure of the SOI wafer consists of a a 525 µm thick Si handle layer covered with a 1µm thick buried SiO_2 layer and finally a 3400Angs top silicon device layer . Initially, a prototype structure was developed in the form of a PN Diode fibre by patterning the top silicon device layer in the desired shape of the fiber, then subjecting the devices to diffusion doping with phosphorous (5e15@00KeV) and boron (5e13@5KeV) to   create the necessary metallurgical junction. Figure 4 shows a free standing functional PN diode fiber after the release process being threaded through the eye of a needle.

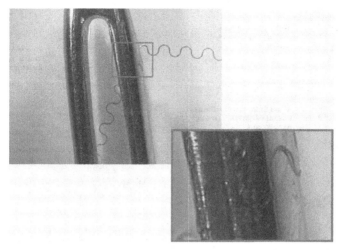

Fig. 4. Free standing PN diode fiber after the release process being threaded through the eye of a needle

3.2   Active Device Circuit Fabrication

After demonstrating the feasability of creating a diode in fibre form, a more complex demonstration of functionality was developed. The ring oscillator, which is a standard circuit for delay measurement was developed in fibre form. This circuit was chosen to investigate possible influences external mechanical stressing would have on a circuit in a wearable environment. With the ring oscillator, an inital frequency measurement could be obtained with no stress applied. The mechanical influences on the circuit can then be evaluated by performing subsequent frequency measurements, while the circuit is under stress.

The mechanical flexibility required to integrate the circuit into a wearable artefact is also a key issue. By using polyimide (Stieglitz et al. 2000) as a passivation layer covering the circuit, it also acts as a support structure maintaining the physical integrity of the silicon fibre after release from the handle wafer.

The fabrication process for the device uses conventional planar processing techniques and is illustrated in Figure 5. Firstly, the top silicon device layer of an SOI structured wafer is patterned by means of plasma etch process to create the active silicon islands. The N and P well implants are split into two with the N well having a deep phosphorous implant (3e12@90KeV) and a top boron implant (2e12@20KeV). The P well implant is split between a deep boron implant (2e11@70KeV) and a top boron implant (1.1e12@20KeV). A 3500A layer of polysilicon is deposited and patterned to create the gate. This is followed by source/drain implants of phosphorous (5e14@60KeV) and boron (2e11@70K   eV). The contact stage is a 3μm patterned layer of polyamide used to increase the flexibility of the circuit after release from the handle wafer. A 6000A layer of Al1%Si metal is deposited and patterned to create the interconnect between silicon islands. Finally a polyamide passivation layer is deposited and patterned over the circuit to increase the flexibility and overall mechanical robustness of the circuit.

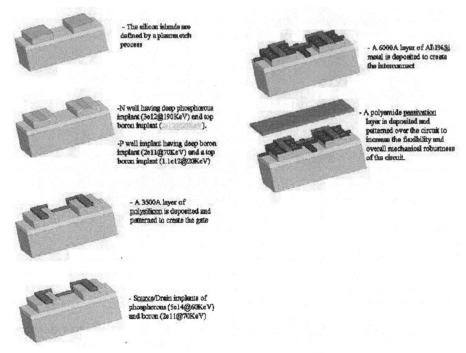

- The silicon islands are defined by a plasma etch process

-N well having deep phosphorous implant (3e12@190KeV) and top boron implant (2e12@20KeV).

-P well implant having deep boron implant (2e11@70KeV) and a top boron implant (1.1e12@20KeV)

- A 3500A layer of polysilicon is deposited and patterned to create the gate

- Source/Drain implants of phosphorous (5e14@60KeV) and boron (2e11@70KeV)

- A 6000A layer of Al1%Si metal is deposited to create the interconnect

- A polyamide passivation layer is deposited and patterned over the circuit to increase the flexibility and overall mechanical robustness of the circuit.

Fig. 5. Active Device Circuit Process Flow

3.3   SOI Fibre Release Process

One of the most critical aspects of realising a flexible electronically functional fibre is the release mechanism. This is the process in which the silicon fibres removed. It is one of the most challenging aspects of the electronically functional fibre concept.

Two different approaches for removing the fibres from the wafer, a back etch approach and a front etch approach were investigated, while observing the issue of maintaining the structural integrity of the membrane and the wafer as a whole during and after the etch process. The front or back etch terms correspond to which side of the wafer in relation to the devices, is being etched.

A number of processing experiments were designed to evaluate the best approach to maintain the structural integrity of the wafer and the devices before and after the etch processes. The front etch mechanism proved to be the most reliable while observing critical structural integrity issues.

The front etch approach is a combination isotropic and anisotropic etch processes. An isotropic etch is one that etches the silicon in all-crystallographic directions at the same rate, while anisotropic etching is is in a lateral direction only . The concept involves patterning the device side of the wafer with a photo resist material and anisotropically etching the buried oxide layer. The patterned oxide and the resist material over the devices act as an etch mask for the isotropic etch of the handle wafer silicon, please refer back to Figure 1 for an illustration of the release approach. This process avoids any problems associated with the wafer and device integrity. Figure 6 shows a free standing ring oscillator in fibre form.

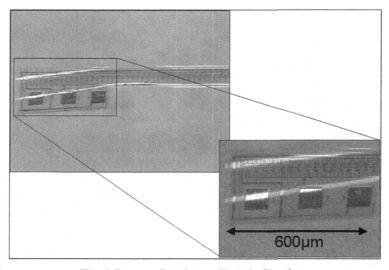

Fig. 6. Free standing ring oscillator in fibre form

3.4 Electrical Evaluation

Electrical testing of both devices proved to be extremely difficult due to the flexible nature of the unconfined fiber. However, the first electrical device on a semi-conducting fiber was produced and its diode characteristics before and after release are illustrated in Figure 7.

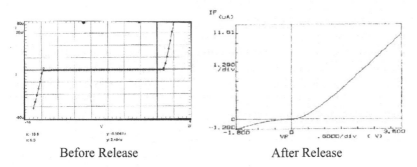

Before Release   After Release

Fig. 7. Fiber diode characteristics before and after the release process

The lack of continuity between the curves for before and after release could be related to the release mechanism. No formal investigions were performed.

After establishing the concept for flexible active devices a more complex demonstration of functionality was investigated. Subsequent active device circuits were evaluated.

Figure 8 illustrates the waveform of a single strip 679-stage ring oscillator at wafer level. As can be seen the period of oscillation is approximately 25μ, which is equivalent to a frequency of 40 kHz.

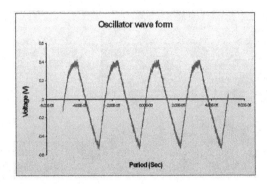

Fig. 8. Waveform of a 679-stage ring oscillator

4   Fibre Interconnection

One of the key initial considerations in integrating this technology into a wearable format is the interconnection between the individual fibres. This section discusses the concept and the initial prototype demonstrator of a flexible light emitting diode (LED) structure interconnecting the individual silicon fibres by means of a conductive adhesive paste, along designated landing sites on the flexible printed circuit board (PCB).

Flexible LED Circuit Design and Fabrication

For the initial concept demonstrator, an LED circuit was selected to demonstrate the electrical connectivity. The prototype is fabricated using the electronically functional fibres (EFF) as the resistors in the circuit, which are interconnected using a conductive adhesive paste and a flex PCB substrate. The flex PCB structure consists of a patterned copper (Cu) layer on a thin film of polyimide, which is also patterned to create channels for the EFF. The conductive adhesive paste is the interface between the EFF and the Cu track, while the patterned Cu layer acts as the metal interconnect between the LED's and the silicon fibres. The LEDs are then situated along designated landing sites on the polyimide.

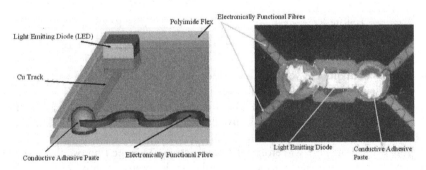

Fig. 9. Flex PCB structure   **Fig. 10.** Flexible active LED circuit

Figure 9 illusrates the layout for the Cu tracks, the position of each LED and the designated landing site for each EFF. The EFF selected for this demonstrator are 1 mm in length and 35 ɲm in diameter.

Figure 10 shows the active circuit with a 5 V power supply attached and the light from the LED is clearly visible, demonstrating the electrical connectivity between the fibres and the LEDs. There were no formal stress tests performed on the circuit, however, there appeared to be no visible changes in the luminosity of the LEDs due to manual stressing.

5   Extruded Fibre Fabrication

The substrate fibers for this application had to be made from an active semiconductor material, or from a passive material onto which an active coating or device is applied, the raw materials and the production processes would be different from those targeted for the traditional textile industry.

Material Selection

Regarding semiconducting materials, the conventional industrial choice for high-performance electronics is silicon (Si). As can be seen in Table 4.1, Si can be obtained in fiber form, however, the resulting fibers are either not sufficiently flexible or cannot be made in lengths suitable for integration into textiles.

Polymers, which are both flexible and can be easily shaped into fibers, can in certain cases also be processed to exhibit semiconducting properties (Vollmer 2001) and thus they are also candidates for active fiber substrates. Integrated circuits based on polymers (so-called polytronics) exist (Drury et al 1998; Gelinck et al. 2000; Lange 2001), however, the circuits are many hundreds of microns wide while drawn polymer fibers are generally less than 10 mm in diameter (Table 4.1). Due to this size incompatibility, polytronics were not considered for the current work.

Another possible choice was silicon carbide (SiC), which under high-temperature, high-power, and/or high-radiation conditions shows better semiconducting device performance than conventional semiconductors (Choyke and Pensl 1997; Itoh 1997; Siergiej et al. 1999). Doping of SiC to create semiconducting devices is achieved by selected-area ion implantation techniques and annealing at temperatures in excess of 1700℃. SiC can also be fabricated in the form of long and flexible continuous fibers (Table 4.1), and on this basis (proven semiconducting performance and ability to be formed into fibers), SiC was initially selected as the active substrate material for this work.

Regarding passive substrate materials, flat sheets of silicon dioxide (SiO_2, quartz) glass are widely used in the microelectronics industry as substrates for thin film amorphous and polycrystalline integrated circuits. Fibers of SiO_2-based glasses and pure SiO_2 glasses can and are being manufactured in bulk by a variety of methods (Table 4.1), and as in the case of SiC above, SiO_2 was selected for its role as a passive fiber substrate for this work on the basis of its proven performance as a passive substrate in the semiconducting industry and the ability to form the material into fibers.

Table 1. Fiber substrate processing methods for materials suitable for semiconductor applications

Fiber material	Technology	Dimensions	Remarks
Si-fiber	Micro-Pulling-Down	>120 µm	Insufficient flexibility
	Silicon-on-Insulator	<30 µm	Short fiber length
SiC-fiber	Extrusion	>50 µm	polycrystalline microstructure
	Sol-Gel	<10 µm	Free carbon present
	Precursor	<10 µm	Free carbon present
Polymer fiber	Drawing	<10 µm	Polytronic devices too big for fibers
SiO₂-fiber	Melt Spinning	<10 µm	Not pure silicon oxide
	Drawing	<10 µm	Method for optical fiber
	Extrusion	>50 µm	Nanoparticles essential
	Sol-Gel	<10 µm	Si-precursors essential

In general any polymer fiber can be used as a passive substrate material too. For example for a first study polyethylene (PE) was chosen as the base polymer because of its suitable electrical, mechanical and chemical resistance properties.

Polyethylene (PE) was also chosen as the base polymer because of its suitable electrical, mechanical and chemical resistance properties.

6   Fiber Fabrication Process Description

6.1   Extrusion

The principle of inorganic powder extrusion can be explained in conjunction with Figure 11. An inorganic powder (in this case SiC or SiO_2), is first compounded at elevated temperature with a thermoplastic binder (i.e. polyethylene) and other organic additives (i.e. wax, surfactants). The binder and the organic additives are necessary to provide the powder with good extrusion behaviour and plasticity and the extruded fiber with sufficient mechanical strength. The additives specifically act to plasticize the binder (i.e. reduce its viscosity) and to provide surface active molecular groups which adsorb to the powder surface and thereby form a "chemical bridge" between the inorganic powder and the purely organic binder. After compounding the irregularly-shaped material to be extruded (feedstock, or extrusion paste) is fed into the rear of the extruder and transported along the barrel either by a screw (screw extruder), as shown, or by the axial motion of a piston (ram extruder). The feedstock is plastically deformed and compressed at elevated temperature, flows into a die, which imparts a desired cross-section on the flow, and is granulated upon exiting the die to yield regularly-shaped feedstock granules which pack and flow well. The extrusion process is then repeated with this granulated feedstock, but now using a die with the cross-section of the desired fiber.

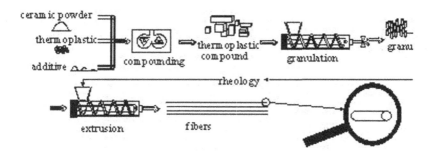

Fig. 11. Fiber extrusion schematic

6.2   Preform Drawing

A bulk preform made of the desired material (in this case amorphous SiO_2) is ground and polished to give it the cross-section desired for the final fiber. The preform is then held into the hot-zone of a vertical tube furnace and heated above the softening point of the glass. The final cross-sectional dimensions of the fiber and the retention of the cross-sectional profile depend on the initial preform dimensions, the viscosity of the glass (and hence the temperature in the hot-zone), the speed with which the preform is fed into the hot-zone, and the speed with which the fiber is drawn off onto the take-up drum.

The fibre is simply pulled through a coating applicator where surface tension causes a thin layer of sizing liquid to be deposited on the fibre surface. Depending on the sizing type (i.e. aqueous- or organic-based), the sizing either solidifies by evaporation of the solvent phase (water or organic solvent), or a reaction in the organic phase (e.g. cross-linking of a polymer under a UV-light source placed after the coating applicator).

Using the technology outlined abovePolymer, ceramic-polymer composite and ceramic fibres with the following properties were developed as the initial test vehicles.

- Equilateral triangular, 260μm edge

- Rectangular, 350 μm x 115 μm.

The technology can easily be adapted to extrude other non-circular cross-sections, requiring only the design and manufacture of new extrusion dies with the appropriately-designed die lands.

A number of other protoype fibres including Extruded SiC fibres, Extruded SiO_2 glass, and Drawn SiO_2 glass fibres which can be used as a substrate material for the flexible SOI active integrated circuits were also developed.

6.3   Fibre Coatings

Using the extrusion technology it's also possible to coat the fibres outlined above with a protective polymer coating (UV-hardening acrylate, commercial product).

The process involves coating the fibres with a fluid sizing compound. The "wet" fibres were then either air-dried (solvent-based size) or exposed to ultraviolet radiation under a protective nitrogen atmosphere (UV-curing size).

SiO$_2$ glass and the ceramic-polymer composite fibres, proved to be the most suitable for incorporation into textile fabrics. Figure 12 shows a woven fabric with extruded fibres.

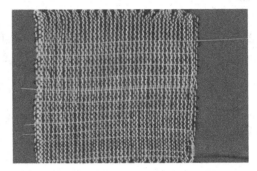

Fig. 12. Woven fabric with extruded fibres

The colorless fibres in the Figure 12 are the ceramic-polymer composite fibres with a triangular shape, which were produced by using extrusion process.

7   Definition of Transistors on Extruded Fibres

The work to be addressed in this section is primarily one of determining how to use conventional planar processing technologies to fabricate transistors on extruded fibres, which consist of a passive core (SiO$_2$) coated with an active silicon layer (see Figure 13).

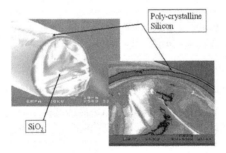

Fig. 13. Extruded fibre with active outer layer

Fibre Fixing

Securing the circular shaped fibre in order to perform the conventional planar processing techniques was the initial issue that had to be investigated. After various attempts at securing the fibre, an anodic bonding approach (Figure 14) proved to be the most effective. This process involved etching a V-groove on a single wafer and then anodic bonding to a Pyrex wafer. The fibre is secured within the groove and the front of the silicon wafer is back etched to the v-groove while exposing the fibre within for subsequent processing. Figure 14 gives an illustration of the holder structure.

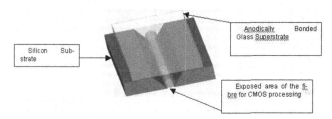

Fig. 14. Holder mechanism for planar processing of extruded fibres

Using the approach illustrated above, a primitive demonstration was developed in the form of metal patterning on a 3-D fiber. Unfortunately, more complicated patterning of these types of fibers was not possible due to a number of different issues such as the alignment of various constituent layers involved in fabricating transistors. After various approaches were attempted, fabricating active devices on these extruded fibers was abandoned and it was decided they would be developed primarily as a support structure for the SOI float off substrates.

8   System on a Fibre Design

As well as the fabrication and interconnection issues involved with fibre computing, a completely new design protocol needed to be developed. The constraints imposed by the fibre structure on the design process were one of the primary issues involved with bringing this technology to fruition. Initial considerations for the development of a system in fibre form raised two pertinent questions:

i)   How the final electronically functional fiber will look?

and

ii) How to re-use the available HW blocks that the IC industry has validated in advanced CMOS/BiCMOS processes, for making electronically functional fibers?

Regarding the first question, it has been concluded that the initial fiber will look like a network of basic functions connected by a simple serial bus. The interfacing with the external world will be achieved via an external interface (most likely wireless; i.e. Bluetooth or 802.xx). Such architecture has been named "System on a Fiber" (SoF) and the interconnecting bus SoF-Bus (see Figure 15).

Regarding the second question it has been assumed that the SOI fiber technology outlined earlier has a viable future and that it will follow soon the scaling down Moore's law. If this will be the case, then the HW cores (called hereafter IPs) that have already been validated by the IC industry in advanced processes can be used as is, provided that only the interface with the SoF bus has been properly engineered (Figure 16).

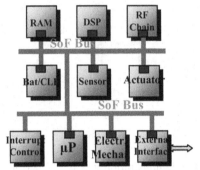

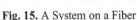

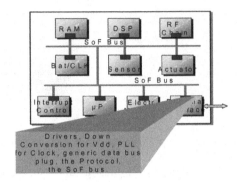

Fig. 15. A System on a Fiber   **Fig. 16.** Interfacing with the SoF bus

After Fig. 4.17, the major blocks of the SoF bus interface are:

- **Drivers for driving high capacitive loads:** The SoF bus could be as long as 1m and hence the parasitic capacitance of such a cable could be quite high.

- **PLL for clock generation:** The clock of the SoF bus should be quite low (order of kHz). However, each node of the SoF network could run at much higher internal clock frequency necessitating the existence of a PLL at the interface.

- **Generic bus plug:** In order to dissociate completely the internal IP world that runs in a high clock frequency with wide internal data buses from the SoF bus world that runs at a low frequency clock and very narrow data bus, a generic bus plug is needed.

- **Vdd Distribution:** The Vdd will be distributed from a central battery to the nodes of the SoF via dedicated power lines in the bus. Since the SoF bus will run over a high distance, it has been decided that an up-conversion/down-conversion scheme should be used to minimize power losses.

- **EMC/EMI/ESD Protection:** Taking into account that the SoF will run over a human body and that other electronic devices can operate in parallel, it is obvious that it will be vulnerable to electrostatic stress.
  Echo Canceller, etc

Generic Bus Plug

The Generic Bus Plug block is designed to facilitate the communication of each IP on the SoF network with the SoF bus. It acts as an intermediate between each specific IP and the bus, with the following benefits:

- Simplifies the IP bus-control part to a strictly minimum set of control signals.

- Handles the clock-conversion problem in the most efficient manner, allowing each IP to have its own clock.

- Permits complex underlying bus protocols to be used easily on the system.

- Hides big bus latencies through programmable FIFO storage.

- It is completely parametrizable in terms of storage, data width, address width etc.

- It is completely reusable in all parts of the system (no differentiation between targets & initiators, masters & slaves etc.)

A view of the Generic Bus Plug positioning in a SoF is shown in Figure 17. Each IP is connected to the SoF bus using a Generic Bus Plug interface. Moreover, the IP interfaces the plug to its own clock domain, and possibly using different generic parameters (datapath width etc.).

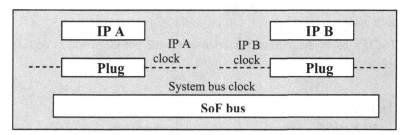

Fig. 4.17 Generic Bus Plug positioning in a SoF

The Generic Bus Plug was implemented in synthesizable VHDL code. Testing environment was created and the block was debugged. Following that, a bus-heavy existing application (a 2D DMA engine) was modified to be connected to the Generic Bus Plug. The validation procedure proved that the DMA block was capable of functioning perfectly through our plug.

The final design was synthesized, placed and routed in CMOS 0.18 μm^2 technology. The final circuit, parameterized to 16-bit wide system interface and 100 kbits total memory size, produced a 3.5 mm^2 silicon area with a 1:5 aspect ratio (700 μm x 3500 μm).

9   ALERT_SCU

The ALERTSCU was developed as an IP app lication for the SoF. It is a full custom 4-bit system control engine that retrieves a sensor measurement such as temperature, or poisonous gas concentration in surrounding area. Depending on the value levels, two warning flags are managed.

This circuit provides an indication of the challenges that would arise in the design of a circuit targeted for the wearable and ambient application fields. Such challenges are propagation, delay of long interconnected wire busses and the constraints set by the textile industry: the circuit should be 150 um wide.

It has a reasonably restricted interface and comprises of only basic logic elements such as registers, comparator logic macros, multiplexers and an adder/counter. It will also provide a first level indication of how the aspect ratio of the circuit periphery affects the efficiency of the layout, the compromises that need to be made, as well as its effect on the fabrication yield of such an integrated circuit.

Key Points

- The input data (data_in) is the measurement value issued by the sensor.

- The constraint level indicates the safety limits to be followed. Two levels are available provided with hardwired thresholds.

- The enable safety system flag (safety_sy st_en) indicates that the lower threshold has been reached and informs the application layer.

- The alert flag indicates that the safety system has either failed to act upon the emergency or its response has been too slow. This is manifested by a violation of the higher threshold or staying above the lower threshold for more than 63 clock cycles.

ALERTSCU's block diagram and interface with the outside world is depicted in Figure 18.

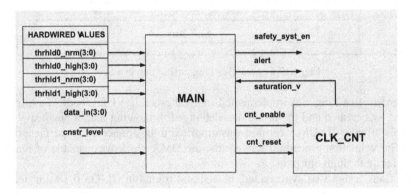

Fig. 17. ALERTSCU Block Diagram

Targeting an operating frequency of 100KHz, several attempts have been made to map the ALERTSCU circuit on a 150um wide Si strip, using 1.5um CMOS technology and a validated standard cell library for the design compiler. Although several aspect ratios have been simulated, the narrowest physical mapping that made the timing constraints is 370um.

Since it has not been possible to make a synthesis that respects both the timing and layout constraints alternative scenarios were investigated to:

i)   to use for the design compiler a custom-made cell library with reduced height and

ii) to make a full custom design.

Both approaches have been studied and in conclusion the most adequate approach is to perform a full custom design. Hence it has been proven that design of ICs fulfilling timing criteria and layout constraints imposed by the textile industry is almost impossible using standard cell library validated by the IC industry. It is anticipated that if the SOI electronically functional fibre concept proves viable beyond the 0.5um CMOS generation, then 150um wide circuits suitable for the textile industry will be synthesised automatically from a standard cell library.

10   Conclusion

A number of issues have emerged over the development of this technology. It is clear that there are barriers to overcome in relation to the basic requirements between the different disciplines involved.

Both approaches for creating flexible electronically functional fibres have been presented in this paper. The more speculative of the two, which involved the fabrication of IC's on three-dimensional extruded fibres proved to be too ambitious for the conventional planar processing technology currently available. This technology will be developed further in the form of a flexible substrate for the SOI active fibres.

The SOI approach to realizing this novel technology and the issues involved have also been explained in detail. A detailed description of the market areas involved with this type of technology has been investigated, along with a system specification based upon the applications considered to be most useful. The issues involved with the development of a system on a fibre (SOF) in terms of the textile industry have been exhaustively investigated and this paper illustrates a merging between a number of different technologies.

The challenge required to implement electronically functional fibres is significant, and while the current focus on software innovation in necessary, the level of research required in order to implement effective hardware is very high. Silicon-based systems will be at the heart of this research, and there will be a requirement, in particular, for new forms of silicon substrates to be developed in order that electronically functional fibres may ultimately be realized in a ubiquitous environment.

Acknowledgement

The work presented in this chapter was funded by the European Commission as part of "The Disappearing Computer" initiative in the IST-FET programme (contract number IST-2000-25247).

References

Choyke, W.J., Pensl, G.: Physical properties of SiC. Mrs Bulletin β] pp. 25–29 (1997)

Drury, C.J., Mutsaers, C.M.J., Hart, C.M., Matters, M., de Leeuw, D.M.: Low-cost all-polymer integrated circuits. Applied Physics Letters 73(1), 108–110 (1998)

Gelinck, G.H., Geuns, T.C.T., de Leeuw, D.M.: High-performance all-polymer integrated circuits. Applied Physics Letters 77(10), 1487–1489 (2000)

Gemperle, F. et al.: Design for Wearability. In: Proceedings Second International Symposium on Wearable Computers, Pittsburgh, PA (1998)

Itoh, A.: Single crystal growth of SiC and electronic devices. Solid State and Materials Sciences 22(2), 111–197 (1997)

Kou, J.B., Ker-Wei, S.: Cmos Vlsi Engineering Silicon on Insulator (SOI), pp. 15–59. Kluwer Academic Publishers, Dordrecht (1998)

Lange, E.: Chips von der Rolle. VDI Nachrichten 13, 24 (2001)

Lind, J., Jayaraman, S., Park, S., Rajamanickam, R., Eisler, Mckee, T., Burghart, G: A Sensate Liner for Personnel Monitoring Applications. In: Proceedings Second International Symposium on Wearable Computers, Pittsburgh, PA (1998)

Muhlsteff, J., Such, O.: Dry Electrodes for monitoring of vital signs in functional textiles. In: 26th Annual International Conference of the IEEE, EMBS, pp. 2212–2215 (2004)

Najafi, K., Hetke, J.F.: Strength Characterisation of Silicon Microprobes in Neurophysiological Tissues. IEEE Transaction on BiomedicalEngineering 37, 474–481 (1990)

Siergiej, R.R., Clarke, R.C., Sriram, S. et al.: Advances in SiC materials and devices: an industrial point of view. MAT. SCI. ENG. B61-62, 9–17 (1999)

Stieglitz, T. et al.: Micromachined, Polyimide-Based Devices for Flexible Neural Interfaces, pp. 283–284. Kluwer Academic Publishers, Dordrecht (2000)

VivoMetrics Life Vest, http://www.vivometrics.com/site/pressmediaarticles.html

Vollmer, A.: RFID-Tags aus Polymerelektonik. Elektronik Industrie 9, 42 (2001)

Augmented Paper: Developing Relationships Between Digital Content and Paper

Paul Luff[1], Guy Adams[2], Wolfgang Bock[3], Adam Drazin[4], David Frohlich[5],
Christian Heath[1], Peter Herdman[6], Heather King[7], Nadja Linketscher[8],
Rachel Murphy[9], Moira Norrie[10], Abigail Sellen[11], Beat Signer[10],
Ella Tallyn[12], and Emil Zeller[13]

[1] Department of Management, King's College, London, UK
[2] Hewlett Packard Laboratories, Bristol, UK
[3] Anitra Medienprojekte, Germany
[4] Department of Sociology, Trinity College, Dublin, Ireland
[5] Digital World Research Centre, University of Surrey, UK
[6] Arjo Wiggins, UK
[7] Department of Education and Professional Studies, King's College,
London, UK
[8] Siemens, Germany
[9] Rudegirl Designs, UK
[10] Institute for Information Systems, ETH Zurich, Switzerland
[11] Microsoft Research, Cambridge, UK
[12] London College of Communication, University of the Arts, UK
[13] MCT Lab GmbH, Switzerland

1 Introduction

Some of the most interesting developments within computer system design in recent years have emerged from an exploration of the ways everyday objects and artefacts can be augmented with computational resources. Often under the rubric of "ubiquitous computing", research programmes in Europe, North America and Japan have directed substantial funding towards these initiatives, and leading industrial and academic research laboratories have developed a diverse range of ubiquitous computing "solutions". These developments mark an important shift in system design, a shift that is having a corresponding impact on social science research. Surprisingly though, given the growing commitment to the ubiquitous and the tangible, there is a mundane, even humble artefact that pervades our ordinary lives that has received less attention than one might imagine. This artefact is paper.

In this chapter, we discuss a solution that enables people to create dynamic associations between paper and digital resources. The solution does not rest upon replacing paper with technology, nor with transforming the character of paper, but rather with augmenting paper to support systematic links with digital content. Our approach was not primarily concerned with the capture and enhancement of writing and note-taking (as with other developments), but rather was primarily concerned with reading, and enabling people to access, or create connections between paper documents and digital resources. As an example, consider how one might link an educational book with a television series. Such a book could be augmented to enable the reader to point to pictures or text on the page and instantly view associated video clips on a workstation, a

N. Streitz, A. Kameas, and I. Mavrommati (Eds.): The Disappearing Computer, LNCS 4500, pp. 275–297, 2007.

PDA or television set. Pointing to the paper document might also allow readers to access and play interactive games, listen to associated audio clips or seek out other kinds of related information.

In this chapter, we discuss the three year development of an augmented paper solution as part of "Paper ++", a pan-European project funded by the Disappearing Computer Programme. This project focused on the potential for augmented paper within a particular broad domain – learning environments – ranging from more "formal" educational settings such as classrooms through to more "informal" settings such as museums and galleries. We discuss the emergence of a technical system and the ways in which it resonates with observations and findings from empirical research, both our own and studies by others (Luff and Heath 1998; Heath and Luff 1996; Heath et al. 1994; Suchman 2000; Harper et al. 1989; Sellen and Harper 2002). We chart how it rests upon developments in inks, printing, electronics and software, developments that appeared to provide a simple and cheap solution to a pervasive human problem. We discuss the ways in which the solution emerged through a series of empirical studies, simulation studies and conceptual design exercises. Finally, we describe a "naturalistic experiment" in which school children used the prototype system during their visit to a museum. In the course of this project, difficulties emerged that required reconsideration of the approach - both in terms of the technology and how it could be exploited. These raised questions regarding our understandings not only of an everyday object and how it figures in collaboration and interaction, but also of the development of augmented everyday objects.

2   Background and Reqirements

One of the developments within areas such as Human-Computer Interaction (HCI) and Computer-Supported Collaborative Work (CSCW) has been the emergence of a substantial body of naturalistic research concerned with human conduct, communication and collaboration in everyday settings. These studies have provided empirical findings that have allowed us to reconsider and even re-specify many of the more traditional ideas concerning the ways in which tools and technologies, objects and artefacts feature in action and interaction (e.g. Sellen and Harper 2002; Bannon 2000; Schmidt 2000). Many of our earlier studies focused on complex organisational environments, environments that were subject to the deployment of a range of sophisticated tools and technologies. Ironically perhaps, these studies discovered over and over again one remarkable fact: despite the pervasiveness of new technologies, paper remained and remains a critical feature of work and collaboration. Many of the examples are well known - flight strips in air traffic control (Harper et al. 1989); the paper timetable in London Underground (Heath and Luff 1992); the traditional medical record in primary health care (Heath and Luff 1996); the tickets in financial dealing rooms (Heath et al. 1994); the documents reviewed by lawyers (Suchman 2000); and so on. The significance and purpose of paper within these domains and many others has been drawn together in Sellen and Harper's book - The Myth of the Paperless Office (Sellen and Harper 2002).

In the rest of this section we review how and why paper has remained such a resilient and useful resource for information and collaboration alongside newer digital technologies. This draws on insights from a number of observational studies of reading from paper and screen conducted within the project in educational settings as well as on previously published studies. We do this in order to identify requirements for augmenting the functionality of paper in an environment where paper and digital resources co-exist.

2.1 The Affordances of Paper

In schools, colleges and universities, as elsewhere, we find the persistence of paper. In schools, for example, papers and books are taken home for homework, books and worksheets are taken to the teacher to be marked, and paper materials are used as the focus for discussion. Similarly in museums and science centres, paper provides resources for visitors throughout their visit around the setting. These materials range from simple brochures and maps through to catalogues that provide detailed information concerning particular exhibits. Amongst many other activities, such resources allow visitors to carry the information to particular exhibits and delicately juxtapose reading the document with inspection of the exhibit.

It is clear that one of the reasons paper excels in these roles is because it is easily manoeuvred. However, we can see that it is not just that paper is easy to carry around, or easy to pass from one person to another, but it also affords tiny shifts in position or orientation, which plays a vital role both in configuring materials for the activity at hand, and also in directing attention in collaborative activities – a property we have previously characterised as "micro-mobility" (Luff and Heath 1998).

Previous studies in a number of workplaces have also highlighted how the flexible nature of paper supports a range of activities. For example, the discrete and lightweight properties of paper mean that it can easily be passed around in an office environment, and also moved in the local area of a desk, for example to configure related

Fig. 1. Two children manipulating a book at the same time

sets of documents for a particular activity (Luff and Heath 1998). Furthermore, individual papers can be literally flexed for example, when comparing information on one part of a page to another. The ability to lay information out in space using paper has also been found to be of vital importance in many key kinds of reading activities (Sellen and Harper 2002).

These properties not only support the individual but also support the way in which participants collaborate over documents together. In an example taken from one of our studies, two children (Figure 1) are using an encyclopaedia to find out information about a particular animal. They use the book together, bending the pages enabling them to undertake distinct but related activities with the book. For example, one child can look at one part of the book whilst the other is reading an earlier section, bending the page of the book to get a better angle to view the page. The children also can mark out particular areas in the book when they are both viewing the same page, for example by placing their hands or fingers in the book as the pages bend around them.

The mobility of paper also supports collaboration. For example, in reading, a document can be tilted towards the reader or a document can be slid across the desk for another participant to see. The manoeuvrability of paper can also support transitions between different kinds of collaborative activity. Paper is often shifted or moved to encourage participation or invite a response from another person by, for example, rotating or sliding the paper to provide the other person with better access. There are many ways, therefore, we see children make use of the properties of paper to support delicate shifts in orientation and access to materials at hand. In developing augmented paper, it was a goal of the project to ensure that such properties could be preserved as much as possible.

2.2   Embodied Writing

Paper is rarely used in isolation from other artefacts. Most often it is used as part of a collection of various paper documents, writing devices, and other information sources, even digital displays (O'Hara et al. 2002).

Pens are probably the most obvious common implements that we see used in conjunction with paper. But pens are not just used for writing, they are often used to point, delineate, and mark items or pages. However, from our empirical materials, it is apparent that writing is an embodied activity that involves more than the fingers of the writing hand holding the pen. Indeed it often requires the whole of the body and may involve the second hand to steady the paper as the writing takes place. Further, writing, and the ways in which it is produced, can also be as a resource for collaborative activities. In the course of writing, boundaries or junctures in the writing activity are visible to others. The position and orientation of a pen can be used as a resource to assess the current activity of the writer. From whether it is raised above the page, held above an item, or moved down to the edge of page, the activity of writing can serve as a resource for assessing the ongoing activities of another person. Moreover, the position of the pen in relation to the geography of the page allows one to determine another person's location within an activity. This can then be a resource for others to coordinate their own activities.

All of this points to the fact that in addition to paying careful attention to the particular affordances of paper within our domains of interest, so too do we need to consider the details of the activities within these contexts. Writing, and more particularly the use of pens, can be seen to be a key part of the activities with which we are concerned. Therefore we have to consider how the design of the system can be sensitive to how paper is used in combination with other mundane artefacts like pens and pencils.

2.3   Interrelating Paper and Digital Displays

Novel augmented paper technologies may provide quite innovative resources for relating paper and digital materials. However, it should not be overlooked that in a number of domains, particularly educational settings, paper is already commonly used alongside electronic materials and devices. Examples include using a computer to search for information that is then written into a paper document, or, transferring and comparing information across documents.

One typical difficulty faced by people we observed in school settings is actually physically getting both paper and digital sources close enough together to be able to interrelate information from one to the other, as illustrated in Figure 2. Here, two children are in the classroom working with a CD-ROM and a book (which comes with the CD). In this example, the boy has to move the book around for the different activities involved. It is awkward for him to position the book so that he can, for example, look from the information on the screen to information in the book, discuss the information with the girl next to him, and type in answers using the book. The book has to be positioned not only so the girl with whom he is working can see it, but also in relation to the other artifacts he needs in order to complete the task (i.e. the monitor and the keyboard). It is hard to configure the computer technology and the book in the environment to support collaboration between the participants.

The foregoing observations may seem quite mundane, focusing as they do on slight movements of paper across the desk, the turning of a page, the holding of a pen or

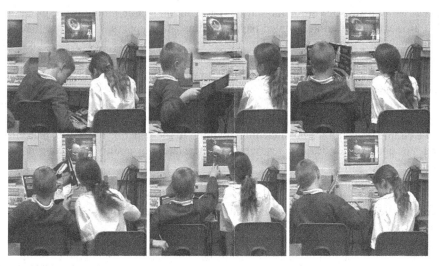

Fig. 2. Children in a classroom using a conventional book alongside a computer which presents related materials

efforts to see how a paper print-out relates to its computer-based counterpart. However, these kinds of properties are critical to how activities are accomplished from moment-to-moment in interactions with others. Studies of the domestic environment, classrooms, museums and galleries, and a range of workplaces reveal many examples of how paper is used within and alongside digital technologies. Students, teachers, journalists and the like edit text on paper and transpose those corrections to digital copy, architects modify paper plans and integrate those changes in a CAD system, administrators litter their workstations with reminders, diary notes and other pieces of paper, and booking clerks labouriously write down the details of travel arrangements before trying to enter the information into a system.

All of this shows that paper is not just an independent resource that somehow has continued to survive despite attempts to remove it, but rather is an integral feature of using new technologies. Enhancing the relationship between paper and the digital realm therefore has the potential to deepen and enrich existing practices.

2.4 Requirements

Coupled with our previous studies of the uses of paper and specific studies of educational settings, these new insights suggested some preliminary requirements for interweaving paper and digital documents.

At the highest level, the co-existence of paper and digital technologies, and especially the pervasiveness of reading from screen and paper together, reveal both the value and limitations of each media form. Paper is useful for information and collaboration, but is no longer sufficient alone. Digital information already supplements paper-based information, but has not replaced it. This leads us to the obvious conclusion of connecting paper and digital resources in more intimate ways, to support and extend the kind of movements people are already making between them.

Furthermore, studies of the mobility of paper in interaction point toward properties that are required of an augmented paper substrate. It is apparent that more than one individual often needs to read, and in other ways use, the same document at the same time. This suggests the kind of reading angles and visibility required of the paper document, the kinds of flexibility required, how roughly paper is sometimes handled, and the kinds of actions performed on paper by pens and other devices. To be mobile, not only does paper have to be light, but it also needs to be malleable. Following on from this, it is important that any augmentation not interfere or degrade this mobility. For example, this implies not attaching anything to the paper or forcing its placement under or above other devices, restricting its orientation or unduly increasing its friction over other surfaces.

Our observational studies also suggest some less definite criteria. For example, for the sake of application and media design it may be preferable not to pre-define the way that the design of a paper document should be linked to digital resources. Given the potentially wide range of uses or applications, and the legacy of existing documents in these settings, it may not be desirable to constrain how parts of a page should be used. Hence, the whole surface of the paper should have the potential of being 'active'. Unlike other approaches (such as barcodes which encode information about a link directly), the Paper++ solution requires only indirect encoding of locations, the associated information, link and 'response' being defined by the software.

3   Interrelating Paperwork and Screenwork

3.1   Previous Approaches

A number of researchers in ubiquitous computing have developed their own techno-logical solutions to exploit or capture some of the affordances of paper. They have tried to replicate some of the paper document's capabilities, for example by making applications more portable or mobile. These include *electronic books* which provide searchable, dynamic or multimedia texts, as well as *context-sensitive appliances* which adjust media content in response to other triggers in the environment (e.g. Kindberg et al. 2002; Aoki et al. 2002; Fagrell et al. 1999). The limited flexibility of mobile devices and screens have led other researchers to look for alternative kinds of displays. Considerable attention is now being devoted to developing *plastic displays* that are extremely thin and flexible, and offer paper-like viewing experiences (e.g. Gyricon LLC; Dymetman and Copperman 1998; E Ink Corporation; Lamble 2003; Remonen 2003; Wood 2003; Philips Research; Seyrat and Hayes 2001). However, none of the above technologies is even close to being as cheap as paper; so they are competing with LCD technology rather than with paper (Herdman 2004). They also tend to overlook the interaction between electronic material or appliances and paper itself.

Other approaches have considered using paper as an input device. For example, the *DigitalDesk* used video-capture, where a camera above a desk was used to track the position of the pen and paper (Wellner 1991) or where a camera was placed above a pen to 'capture' images (Arai et al. 1997). Other approaches such as SMARTBoards or graphics tablets (like the Cross Computing iPen) have used alternative techniques to capture marks, annotations and even handwriting to be transferred to the digital domain (Mackay et al. 2002; McGee et al. 2000; Yeh et al. 2006). A device that uses a similar approach to Paper++ is the "LeapPad", a robust touch sensitive tablet on which paper books are overlaid. Designed for children, the LeapPad is now a highly successful educational product, but relies on a substantial casing to hold the paper books.

More recently, devices have become commercially available that use ultrasonic tri-angulation to capture the motion of special pens on A4 pads, such as Seiko's Ink Link, or Mimio for use on flip-charts. While these techniques begin to bridge the divide between the paper and electronic domains, all of these solutions typically require some external device to detect interaction, detracting from the portability and flexibility of paper. A more direct pen and paper paradigm would seem to be required to link the position of a pen on a writing surface (Herdman 2004).

Another approach has been to link paper and digital materials through the use of visible marks on paper, the most familiar of which are barcodes (Johnson et al. 1993; Siio et al. 1999). More sophisticated methods encode linking information within locations on the paper. This may be by printing visible patterns such as Xerox glyphs or CyberCodes on a page and detecting these from cameras (Koike et al. 2001; Hecht 2001; Wiziway; Nelson et al. 1999) or some other reading device such as the emerging popularity of RFID tags (Harrison et al. 2001). Relying on barcodes or other visible marks does reveal the augmented functionality to the user, but it can be quite disruptive of the look and layout of the paper document.

Alternative approaches track the position of a pen or reader over the paper surface using invisible or unobtrusive encoding techniques – techniques which do not interfere with the design of the paper document. One such method has been developed by Anoto (Silberman 2001) which forms the basis of commercially available products such as Nokia's Digital Pen, Logitech's IO, Sony Ericsson's Chatpen and Maxell's PenIt. These devices capture handwriting so notes can be sent via e-mail or downloaded to a computer and then converted to text. The Anoto technology relies on an almost invisible pattern of pre-printed dots on the paper and sophisticated electronics built into the pen. Instead of scanning and recognizing single lines of text, the Anoto pen uses a built-in CCD camera to view the infrared-absorbing dots, each of which is slightly misplaced from a square array. The relative positions of dots in a six-by-six array maps to a unique x-y position in a vast possible address space. Images are recorded and analysed in real time to give up to 100 x-y positions per second, which is fast enough and of sufficient resolution to capture a good representation of all handwriting. The equivalent of around 50 A4 pages can be recorded and stored in the pen before being transmitted to a PC.

The Anoto technology, which has now been used in a number of research investigations (Mackay et al. 2002; Yeh et al. 2006) offers one way of interlinking paper and digital resources. This technology does, however, focus on the capture of handwriting through fairly sophisticated technology – cameras, processors and mobile transmitters. In addition, although with Anoto the paper is not significantly transformed, the use of the Anoto pen, like most augmented devices, transforms the activity of writing. As well as requiring additional explicit activities of the user (e.g. ticking boxes when pages should be transmitted), in current implementations, it requires users to consider when pages are complete and 'done'.

3.2 The Paper++ Approach

In the Paper++ project we explored a different approach to augmenting paper by considering what seemed the simplest way of interlinking paper and digital resources, namely, by pointing to paper documents. Our observations that individuals often use pre-established texts alongside computer systems also suggested, at first, a focus on support for augmented reading rather than writing.

The underlying technical approach taken by Paper++ is quite simple. As with Anoto, this uses both a paper substrate and a non-obtrusive pattern on the page. However, this approach focuses on the circumstances where users interact with pre-printed documents, where the paper could be a single sheet, a booklet, a pack, or a printed book. These documents would be overprinted with a non-obtrusive pattern that uniquely encodes the x-y (and page) location on the document. This code would then be interpreted by a pen when it comes in contact with the paper. To do this, the pen would need to convert the code into a signal that could be an input to a PC, or another digital device. When a location is selected, supported by a software infrastructure, an appropriate action in the digital domain would be initiated – this could be playing a sound, the display of some text or web page or activating a video clip of some animation. The paper then operates like a touch-screen, only encoding information about location, all other relationships being defined through software by a content provider. This would be easier to update or tailor for particular users. Given a pre-printed paper product, like a text book, one could envisage applications where updates, additional resources and customised information would be provided in the digital domain.

Obviously this approach relies on some way of establishing a relationship between the paper and the electronic. Similar to Anoto, the Paper++ solution relies on a non-obtrusive pattern, but the process for this is quite different. Rather than using a pattern that can be detected optically, as by Anoto, we use inks that can be detected conductively. Conductive inks have been developed that have electrical properties which have been used in some security applications (e.g. banknotes) and more notably for reducing static on films where the inks used had to be transparent. It seemed feasible that sophisticated invisible and conductive inks could serve as a foundation for a simple way of encoding non-obtrusive patterns on paper. A detector could be developed requiring just two electrodes that could convert the code into a frequency-modulated signal. This solution also has the potential of being very cheap.

This choice implies challenges that differ from many recent attempts at developing ubiquitous or augmented applications. In particular, it requires technological developments in a number of diverse disciplines: organic chemistry for the inks, electronics for the pen, signal processing and mathematics for the encoding and information architectures for the software infrastructure. This technical choice means that there are few components commercially available that we could integrate. The technical challenges of identifying an appropriate conductive ink and paper combination, designing an encoding pattern and developing a robust reader are considerable.

3.3 Refining the Approach Through Simulation Studies

One way of short-circuiting some of these technical challenges is to simulate a solution with more readily available technology. Hence, as well as observations of the use of paper in everyday settings, we also have undertaken a number of 'simulation studies'. As their name suggests, these aim at simulating certain aspects of the technology and assessing how users engage with it.

For example, in a first simulation study we used conventional barcode technology to connect a commercially available printed encyclopedia to a companion CD-ROM. For this study we designed a six-page augmented paper booklet, based on the 'Prehistoric Life' section of the *Encyclopedia of Nature* by Dorling Kindersley (with permission). Barcode stickers were laminated onto each page and associated with a range of video, audio, graphic and textual information from the corresponding CD-ROM. An example page is shown in Figure 3. Pairs of 9 and 10 year olds used the booklet in conjunction with a Windows laptop, fitted with a barcode reader. They were asked to work together to answer a series of questions on the material, before discussing their experience with us and going on to design their own augmented page. For comparison, half the pairs also performed a similar exercise on 'Seabirds', using either the printed textbook or CD-ROM alone. This allowed us to examine the usability and value of augmented paper, and its relationship to conventional and computer-based reading.

The studies suggested that children could use an augmented paper interface to search effectively for information in paper *and* digital form. Furthermore, users expressed a preference for augmented paper over the use of paper alone. This was despite of a number of difficulties that seemed to hamper information retrieval. For example, the children were initially confused about what kind of content they were

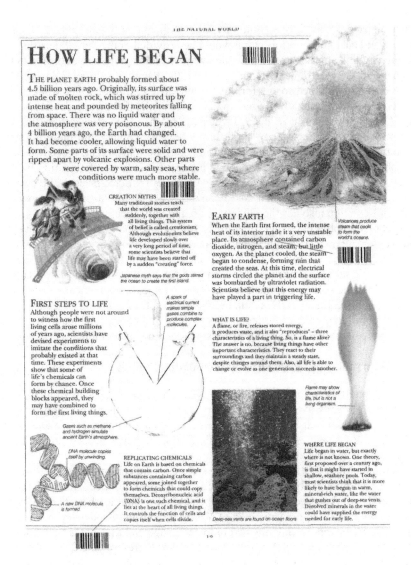

THE NATURAL WORLD

HOW LIFE BEGAN

THE PLANET EARTH probably formed about 4.5 billion years ago. Originally, its surface was made of molten rock, which was stirred up by intense heat and pounded by meteorites falling from space. There was no liquid water and the atmosphere was very poisonous. By about 4 billion years ago, the Earth had changed. It had become cooler, allowing liquid water to form. Some parts of its surface were solid and were ripped apart by volcanic explosions. Other parts were covered by warm, salty seas, where conditions were much more stable.

CREATION MYTHS
Many traditional stories teach that the world was created suddenly, together with all living things. This system of belief is called creationism. Although evolutionists believe life developed slowly over a very long period of time, some scientists believe that life may have been started off by a sudden "creating" force.

Japanese myth says that the gods stirred the ocean to create the first island.

FIRST STEPS TO LIFE
Although people were not around to witness how the first living cells arose millions of years ago, scientists have devised experiments to imitate the conditions that probably existed at that time. These experiments show that some of life's chemicals can form by chance. Once these chemical building blocks appeared, they may have combined to form the first living things.

A spark of electrical current makes simple gases combine to produce complex molecules.

Gases such as methane and hydrogen simulate ancient Earth's atmosphere.

DNA molecule copies itself by unwinding.

A new DNA molecule is formed.

REPLICATING CHEMICALS
Life on Earth is based on chemicals that contain carbon. Once simple substances containing carbon appeared, some joined together themselves. Deoxyribonucleic acid (DNA) is one such chemical, and it lies at the heart of all living things. It controls the function of cells and copies itself when cells divide.

EARLY EARTH
When the Earth first formed, the intense heat of its interior made it a very unstable place. Its atmosphere contained carbon dioxide, nitrogen, and steam, but little oxygen. As the planet cooled, the steam began to condense, forming rain that created the seas. At this time, electrical storms circled the planet and the surface was bombarded by ultraviolet radiation. Scientists believe that this energy may have played a part in triggering life.

Volcanoes produce steam that cools to form the world's oceans.

WHAT IS LIFE?
A flame, or fire, releases stored energy, it produces waste, and it also "reproduces" – three characteristics of a living thing. So, is a flame alive? The answer is no, because living things have other important characteristics. They react to their surroundings and they maintain a steady state, despite changes around them. Also, all life is able to change or evolve as one generation succeeds another.

Flame may show characteristics of life, but is not a living organism.

WHERE LIFE BEGAN
Life began in water, but exactly where is not known. One theory, first proposed over a century ago, is that it might have started in shallow, seashore pools. Today, most scientists think that it is more likely to have begun in warm, mineral-rich water, like the water that gushes out of deep-sea vents. Dissolved minerals in the water could have supplied the energy needed for early life.

Deep-sea vents are found on ocean floors

Fig. 3. An example page from a barcode-augmented booklet on prehistoric life

going to encounter from any barcode in the booklet. Without any printed clues, and because of the fun and novelty of revealing hidden information, they tended to swipe barcodes almost randomly at first to see what lay behind them. In the simulation there were no pause, rewind and volume controls for time-based clips. This made discussing or writing down awkward and time-consuming. A final issue, identified by children themselves, was that they could not interact directly with screen-displayed content. The approach of triggering a single instance of screen-displayed content from paper appeared to be too constraining for children who are used to interacting with multiple levels of information through a screen-based interface. It also led to a style of use which involved the constant shifting of attention between the paper and the laptop screen.

We also found that the children enjoyed a range of multimedia enhancements to traditional textbook material. They particularly liked those enhancements which appeared to bring the text to life such as readings, narration, sound effects and video. However, the means by which the children preferred to access these enhancements, all other things being equal, was through the traditional CD-ROM computer application rather than through the augmented paper booklet. This was partly due to the problems with the augmented booklet mentioned above. However, it also had to do with the design of the associations between the booklet and the CD-ROM in comparison to the internal associations built into the CD-ROM alone. The augmented paper links were effectively 'reversed engineered' from the seeming overlap between content originally designed for paper *or* screen. Conceptually, these links did not always make sense. This meant that they were not as informative as the links built into the CD-ROM and the children noticed this.

These insights have a number of implications for re-designing the augmented paper solution, affecting both its content and the interface. Augmented paper needs to be considered as a new medium in its own right, rather than a vehicle for connecting two existing media. The original design of paper content was not ideal for an augmented paper solution such as Paper++. This means that the original content needs to be transformed for reading paper alongside a screen. As for the interface, the first simulation study suggested incorporating multimedia controls for time-based media on-screen, and consistent labelling of active areas of paper to help indicate what lies behind them.

To explore a richer situation, using more abundant media resources and information content we undertook a second simulation study in collaboration with the Open University. This was based on a set of course materials which employed both video footage from the BBC's ground-breaking Blue Planet documentary series, as well as multimedia resources. The Blue Planet reviews life in the oceans over six one-hour episodes, and the Open University's first year Biology course made reference to these episodes in its coursebook while supplying students with the video cassettes.

For this second study we redesigned the original Open University materials in augmented paper format and used a specially revised version of the Anoto technology to simulate the Paper++ approach. The format of the text was redesigned, with wider spaces between lines to enable better targeting of 'active' areas, denoted as blue text visually comparable to internet hyperlinks, and wider margins to contain icons. An example page is shown in Figure 4. When students tapped the blue text or icons with a pen, the corresponding videoclips or interactive diagrams were triggered on a tablet computer. The tablet computer facilitated more manipulation than the desktop screens of the first study, and could be laid flat alongside the augmented paper.

In order to test these materials, we recruited science students at an educational level appropriate to a first year course, that is either already at university or else doing science at school with a view to university. Half of the students were observed using the augmented paper materials (booklet and tablet), and the other half used the original analogue materials as a student would receive them (a comparable booklet, a video, CD-ROM and glossary). Both groups of students were asked to read through the materials and then take a short quiz. After doing the exercise, they were interviewed about their perceptions of the task and the technology.

The experience with the Paper++ simulation seemed to be more consistent, more assured, and also suited different types of student. Some students expressed a preference

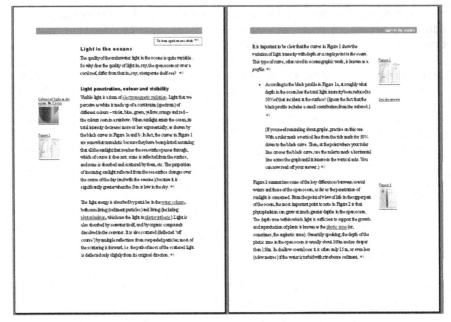

Fig. 4. An example page from an augmented booklet on biology

for book-learning, some for screen-learning. With the analogue materials therefore, these different students would tend to find themselves protractedly watching the video and superficially skimming the booklet, or vice-versa. With Paper++, both types of learner developed a similar learning rhythm, alternating between using paper and screen. For people who preferred screens, the paper was the means to access and control the screen; for expressed paper-learners, the screen was integrated into the activity of reading. It also seemed that those students using the conventional media were also more inclined to look for guidance, feedback and reassurance that they were doing the exercise correctly. They had to feel their way to making their own connections between information in different formats.

Contrary to expectations, the experience of using the simulated Paper++ technology appears comparable to browsing through a book, more than "surfing" a purely digital domain, because it has more structure. As an illustration, with the analogue materials, several students browsed back and forth, interleaving a thumb in the text while reading so as to look back at a useful diagram. The equivalent with the augmented paper was to click an icon and turn to the screen, but never needing to turn back a page. The simulated Paper++ therefore gave the benefit of a pre-planned structure to the exercise, proceeding from beginning to end, and with the constant option of choosing to browse "sideways" into and out of the digital.

The two simulation studies produced materials illustrating the challenges and work required in designing materials for an augmented paper approach. They were, however, simulations, although successfully incorporating many of the functions we wanted, they also demonstrated some of the unique technological and content design requirements for a Paper++ solution.

4   An Augmented Paper Technology

4.1   The Hardware Solution

In trying to preserve the features of paper that afford collaboration, the Paper++ project chose to try and maintain the use of a conventional mass-produced paper product. The principal hardware innovations required the development of conductive inks, the design of a pattern that could encode locations and a reader to detect these locations from the surface of the paper.

This approach relies upon developments in conductive inks which emerged from innovations in conductive polymers in the 1970s, in particular the efforts to print electronics and to produce plastic conductors and related developments. At the commencement of the project, it appeared that invisible conductive inks were available, at least in trial quantities. However, although having good conductive properties, the inks available were not robust and failed abrasion tests. They required another coating (or substrate) and thus transformed the flexibility of the material or reduced the visibility of any printed artwork (i.e. they appeared black or an opaque blue). A solution that appears at first glace to be a simple deployment and adaptation of existing technologies and techniques is later found to be more complex.

It emerged that research undertaken on derivatives of a conductive polymer called Pedot (Poly(3 4)-ethylenedioxythiophene) might be of direct relevance to a solution but would require further investigation (Braun and Heeger 1991). Indeed this required a separate 12 month Disappearing Computer project called Superinks, the primary goal being to produce the printed conductive solution that met the Paper++ requirements. This mini project was successful printing a pale blue/grey Pedot pattern of reasonable conductivity over the artwork. Even after this activity the printing was visible but not obtrusive.

The Paper++ approach requires an encoding for several A4 pages to a resolution of a few millimetres. In our investigations we encoded 8 A4 pages, each divided into 16 columns and 32 rows. In each cell we printed a code comprising a start sequence, a 3 bit address for the page, a 4 bit address for the column and a 5 bit address for the row. The resulting pattern resembled a complete tiling of very pale bar codes 8 mm high and 13 mm wide. Each bar code represented a unique address of page, row and column. A simple software method to interpolate horizontal position to 1/10 of a code cell gave the final resolution of position to 1.3mm by 8mm.

With regard to the detector, we needed a completely ambidextrous solution for all users which prevented abrasion of the conductive ink. The resulting solution was a symmetric tip resembling a retractable ball point pen. The outer casing had a large radius of curvature outer electrode that only applied a low force per unit area on the artwork. The second electrode had a small radius central spring-loaded contact that applies a constant low force on the artwork. The resistance between these two electrodes depended on the conductivity of the surface and these changed as the user "swiped" across the surface. The change in resistance was then converted into a frequency modulated signal that could be readily decoded by interfacing through a PC sound card. Thus the solution comprised a coaxial swipe reader that was stroked across small conductive, Pedot, bar codes printed over artwork (see Figure 5).

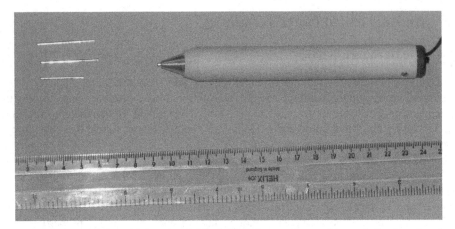

Fig. 5. The co-axial pen with 3 optional nibs (left). Below a ruler provides an indication of scale

As can be gathered what seemed like a simple and straightforward solution for linking a physical artefact, paper, to electronic resources required significant effort and extensive work. It also depended on considerable knowledge and expertise in organic chemistry, paper and printing, electronic design, mathematics and system integration.

4.2   The Software Solution

For many software applications, the ways you might link paper and electronic resources could be quite simple. It is easy to envisage a straightforward linking mechanism that ties locations generated from the pen-paper interface to simple actions. This could be accomplished in much the same way as links on web pages, for example tying a paper resource to a particular document and application so that audio, video and animation files could easily be invoked in the electronic domain. A designer could then just associate locations on the paper pages with particular electronic resources when required. These could be updated and amended when required. It could also be straightforward to develop authoring tools to support the creation of such links.

This was an approach we undertook in the initial phases of Paper++. However, this simple model provided only a one-to-one correspondence between locations on a page and electronic resources. We realized there were applications where it might be useful for different actions to be invoked depending on the context of use. Responses by the system could depend, for example, on the particular user or on other actions the user has previously accomplished. Although the pattern was printed on the page it did not have to be tied to fixed actions or indeed simple shapes. As well as allowing for flexibility in the objects that were linked together we could also could allow flexible ways of managing the links. There could be applications where links could be generated on the fly or produced in some form of collaborative activity amongst users.

In order to allow for the possibility of more general and flexible solutions we developed an open hypermedia system, called iServer, based on a generic cross-media link framework (Norrie and Signer 2003, 2005; Signer 2006). This allowed specific media types to be integrated through a plug-in mechanism as indicated in Figure 6 which shows the main components of the iServer core and those of the plug-in developed for

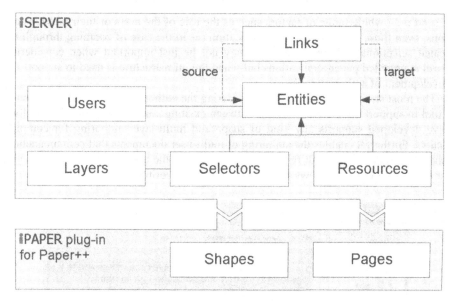

Fig. 6. Generic Cross-Media Link Server

Paper++. Links are first-class objects which can have any number of sources and targets. By introducing a general concept of entities that may be sources or targets of links and then making links a subset of entities, we achieve full generality of allowing links to any types of entity, including links themselves.

The plug-in for a specific media type must provide implementations for selectors and resources. In the case of Paper++, selectors are active areas within a page defined by arbitrarily complex shapes and resources are pages. To date, we have also developed plug-ins for XHTML, images, audio and video.

The iServer framework was implemented using the OMS database management system developed at ETH Zurich (Kobler and Norrie 2002). In OMS, both data and metadata are represented as objects and handled uniformly. By using expressions of the OMS query language (AQL) as selectors on OMS database resources, we are also able to create links to and from objects of a database where these objects may either represent application concepts (metadata) or instances of those concepts (data).

The approach that we have taken provides us with a very flexible means of integrating printed information with digital information. We can dynamically map not only document positions to information objects but also information objects to documents positions and it is therefore possible to find references to digital objects within a collection of paper documents. The infrastructure also supports the layering of information in different ways, allowing single points on the paper surface to be related to different kinds of resources (Norrie and Signer 2003, 2005; Signer 2006). A resource may have any number of virtual layers and a selector is associated with exactly one layer. Layers are ordered and may be re-ordered, activated and deactivated dynamically by the application.

A user management component is also integrated into the iServer core and in combination with the layering mechanism this offers the potential for link activation to depend on a whole range of factors such as the role of the users or their previous actions, even those made over the same location (as in the case of zooming through repeated selections). These capabilities may not be just important when considering novel augmented paper applications but when the infrastructure is used to support the development of authoring tools.

The most straightforward way of considering the authoring of links was to provide a tool to support the creation of links between existing content elements. The tool we have developed supports any kind of shape and multi-layer authoring for complex figures. Further, it enables the authoring of multi-user documents that contain anchors (shapes) linking to different resources determined by the user currently working with the document. Figure 7 shows a screen shot of the authoring tool.

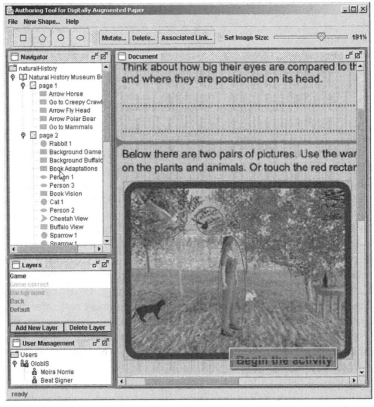

Fig. 7. The authoring tool using material developed by the project. It is also possible to see the positions of the coding scheme in the figure (right hand window)

5   An Integrated Demonstrator

In order to consider the integration of the various hardware components with the software infrastructure and to assess our initial concepts of linking and authoring, we developed an integrated demonstrator in Paper++. Keeping to our theme of educational settings, this was undertaken in the domain of museums. In collaboration with the Natural History Museum London (NHM), we designed an augmented paper worksheet for use in various galleries in the museum. The primary aim of the worksheet was to tie together the gallery experience with focused activities that take place in the "Investigate Area" – a work space for children to handle and explore real museum exhibits and access digital media.

In collaboration with museum educators and designers, we developed a worksheet on ocular adaptation in animals. Children could use the worksheet alongside the exhibits and then, when in the Investigate Area, they could examine the digital content, and explore further information in a selection of reference books, to complete the tasks on the worksheet.

The worksheet was a two-sided page (European A3 in size, but folded to A4 in Portrait format), one of the sides having the conductive pattern. The worksheet was printed on thick (card-like) paper (250 g/m^2) for ease of use around the museum (see Figure 8). The participants used the co-axial pen developed in the project to trigger digital media from the worksheet, the results presented via a computer system on a flat screen. They also had a keyboard and mouse through which they could explore the electronic domain if they chose to.

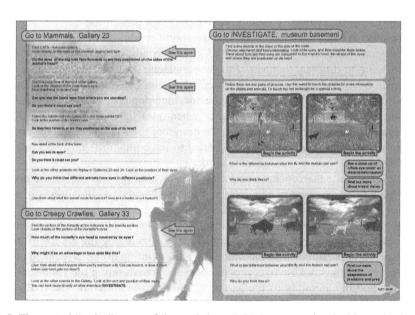

Fig. 8. The central "active" pages of the worksheet (left). Layers are invoked by activating the pictures on the right hand side.

Figure 8 shows the worksheet. Active areas on the worksheet are indicated by darker blue boxes. On the left page there are several links to digital images of relevant gallery exhibits so that children could view these again without having to revisit the gallery itself. On the right side there are a series of images which can be used in two different modes. In the default mode, touching on the animals in the images shows video footage of them in their natural environment involved in activities which demonstrate reasons for their particular ocular adaptations. Touching on the "Begin the activity" area triggers a game mode. This game enables them to test their understanding of the concepts of ocular adaptation explored so far. The game is comprised of audio instructions and feedback, but is played out on the paper. This interactive element required the use of complex shapes defined by the designer, and a basic use of multiple layers.

Once the paper worksheet and digital content were designed and produced, we used the authoring tool to assemble the digital content and create the links with the paper sheet.

The principal achievement of the trial was the production and demonstration of a complete chain of the technology involving participation from seven organisations and collaboration between museum professionals, educators, social scientists, designers, engineers, chemists and computer scientists. Over 20 users (aged 9 – 14) tried the Paper++ technology as well as numerous museum professionals, educators, parents, teachers and other members of the general public. All considered this to be a technology that could enhance visits to the museum, including general visits and those undertaken by school groups. Although the code was visible, from the recordings we made of the users carrying out the task, it did not seem to detract from the artwork or become obtrusive. Indeed many thought the coding was part of the design. The sheet could be used in many locations with varied lighting conditions in the museum. Children read and wrote on it whilst supported in their hands, on their knee, by cabinets and in relation to different features of the environment. As expected, the sheet, when either open or folded, was a resource for collaboration between two or three participants. Groups of two or three could read the document together in a variety of orientations, one could read and another write, or when on a flat surface two could write and/or draw at the same time. Moreover, the design of the worksheet and the configuration of the pen also meant that users seemed to have little difficulty understanding the technology and how it was meant to work.

However, despite the concept being clear, the technology was still at too preliminary a stage to be assessed in any detail with respect to its use. Even though laboratory experiments showed a "hit-rate" for selecting an active paper region of 80%-90%, in a museum setting the rate was much lower (nearer 20%). Technical investigations pointed to a number of explanations for this including the choice of the paper (being a Xerox paper it had too much salt), the printing of the associated content on the covers of the book (a laser process possibly transforming the conductivity of the paper) and the humidity of the basement room in the museum. The trial engendered a number of technical activities to be undertaken, including investigation of different printing processes, consideration of other factors in the choice of papers and inks and a re-design of the circuitry and nib of the pen. The demonstration provided evidence that such an approach was feasible and that elements of the technical chain could be integrated.

6   Discussion

Paper ++ reflects the growing commitment in system development to augment every-day physical artefacts with associated computational resources. It has been an attempt to preserve the integrity of paper whilst enabling complex and systematic links to digital materials. While there are other existing solutions, these have largely focused on enhancing writing or have radically transformed the material qualities and characteristics of paper.

Although, the project focused on exploring applications in educational domains, Paper++ technology could be applied to numerous other settings associated with either work or domestic settings. For example, one could envisage applications for medical environments where standard documents or bespoke materials produced by professionals, practitioners or even patients are associated with electronic resources. As another example, one could envisage the production of augmented paper materials for the design professions, particularly in cases where additional computational resources can support different ways of interacting with texts and diagrams, for example in showing details, other forms of visualisations or calculations.

In developing an augmented paper solution, however, we have found many complex issues that need to be considered and worked through, ranging from technical issues right through to the practicalities of designing content and supporting the larger scale production of hybrid paper and digital documents. Many of the technical and design issues we have already discussed. However, there are other lessons that we have learned following our efforts to augment an everyday physical artefact.

For example, Paper++ technology requires that we rethink and reconsider a long-standing and well-known process, namely printing inks on paper. Over the centuries, printers have progressively refined the process to enable inks to provide quick drying, clear images. Paper is optimised to give good wear resistance and strong visual effect. The refractive index creates considerable light scattering that gives inks added clarity. Printers describe this as "snap", and the paper as having low "holdout". These qualities are enhanced by giving paper a rough porous surface at the micron scale; papers with high holdout tend to produce very poor printed images. To successfully print conductive inks we require very different qualities. We need to lay down a continuous, transparent film over the printed area; a film that requires a smooth surface with high holdout. The requirements for the continuity of the film and the invisibility of the layer stand in strong contrast to the aims of conventional image printing. This has led us to radically reconsider the printing approaches by which we lay down conductive patterns on the page.

Another set of lessons concern the design of content for hybrid paper-digital documents. Our initial conception of how the paper and digital could be interrelated was by simple linking – an action on a page would invoke related responses via a computer system. Nevertheless, this seemingly simple relationship between the paper and digital resources involved considerable effort to produce even the limited materials for the trial in the Natural History Museum. This included identifying, collecting, re-editing and re-segmenting existing materials, collecting new materials and assembling these together in a coherent design. We were informed that conventional activity sheets designed by the museum typically undergo ten iterations of design and assessment. However, even in our single iteration it was apparent that an augmented paper solution adds additional complexity for the work of content providers.

This reflects the findings from our studies of content providers, which represented another strand of work within the project (Luff et al. 2000). These revealed that many conventional publishers (of educational text books, for example) are wary of new electronic means of production. This is partly due to previous problems they have had when developing related CD-ROMs, Web and eBook materials. It is also in part because of the extensive work required to author content, even when this is available and not subject to copyright or other license arrangements. Those publishers who already produce across different media have related concerns. In order to design integrated augmented paper solutions it seems necessary that at best some redesign of the content is necessary. Even in the case of linking paper to video fragments, a technology like Paper++ seems to require considerable work. At the very least, it requires editing clips so that they are coherent and consistent with the associated paper content. From our experiments, it is apparent that it may not be straightforward to transform such materials simply by trimming. It is more likely that there would have to be significant alterations to the original content and the way these materials are gathered. It may require, for example, a number of different versions of the same digital material if that material is to be varied depending on the what the user does or has done on the paper document. Therefore a great deal of additional authoring work may be required and new sets of skills necessary to support the development of augmented paper documents. As with many technologies that seek to augment existing media, the potential of re-use of existing content may not be so great as first hoped. This has longer term implications for the kinds of organizational processes needed to support the creation of augmented paper within publishing.

This also has implications for the kinds of authoring tools that need to be provided for the creation of Paper++ documents both for content providers and for end users. The explicit authoring of links can be time-consuming and it may be that sophisticated tools are required not just to support the authoring of content, but also of links, perhaps even to support the automatic production of links. It may be that models of the process of authoring links could be reconsidered. Rather than this being the sole responsibility of a publisher or a designer, these may be produced by "users", for example, commencing from a simple foundation, more links may emerge through authoring by communities of users, and making use of existing links by others in other media. Indeed, it may be that publishers may not be the only providers of content for augmented paper solutions. There may also be applications of augmented paper for bespoke publishers. Even in educational settings there are already individuals who have the responsibility for assembling content for ad hoc publications or packages of content, whether these are curators, educationalists, teachers, parents or even school groups. If users can author their own links, then through a more open link authoring scheme, users could produce links above and beyond those provided by a single publisher. Clearly, the ability to freely create links between arbitrary printed materials implies a major shift in the consideration of augmented paper. Such capabilities require a sophisticated information infrastructure that can manage emerging links and interconnections in a coherent way. Perhaps unusually in developments of this kind, this has required drawing on expertise in database design and required significant innovations in database architectures. It also requires detailed consideration of the needs, resources and practices of various "content providers" rather than just on the usual focus on "end users."

All of this shows that although the concept of augmenting reading seems simple and straightforward, developing a pervasive and resilient artefact may not be enough. Drawing together the many elements of the Paper++ project has shown that we need also to consider the requirements and demands of others in the production of such a solution, particularly those which have to produce and transform content for augmented technologies. All of this only serves to highlight the fact that our studies have only begun to touch the surface. Yet, despite the complex sets of issues that have emerged throughout the course of the project, this kind of attempt to bridge the paper-digital divide should, we believe, be at the heart of an agenda to consider how the disappearing computer integrates with the real world.

Acknowledgements

Our thanks to colleagues on the projects, particularly: Lars-Olov Hennerdal and Tommi Remonen. We are also grateful to the EU Commission (funding by the IST-FET initiative "The Disappearing Computer" under contract IST-2000-26130), the participating organisations and associated institutions for all their help and support in the undertaking the project, in particular, Loretta Anania of the IST programme and Dan Wormald of the Natural History Museum.

References

Aoki, P., Grinter, R., Hurst, A., Szymanski, M., Thornton, J., Woodruff, A.: Sotto Voce Exploring the interplay of conversation and mobile audio spaces. In: CHI, pp. 431–438 (2002)

Arai, T., Aust, D., Hudson, S.: PaperLink: a technique for hyperlinking from real paper to electronic content. In: Proceedings of CHI, pp. 327–333 (1997)

Bannon, L.: Situating workplace studies within the human-computer interaction field. In: Luff, P., Hindmarsh, J., Heath, C. (eds.) Workplace Studies, pp. 230–241. Cambridge University Press, Cambridge (2000)

Braun, D., Heeger, A.: Visible Light emission from semi-conducting polymer diodes. Applied Physics Letters 58(18), 1982–1984 (1991)

Dymetman, M., Copperman, M.: Intelligent Paper. In: Porto, V.W., Waagen, D. (eds.) Evolutionary Programming VII. LNCS, vol. 1447, pp. 392–405. Springer, Heidelberg (1998)

E Ink Corporation, http://www.eink.com

Fagrell, H., Ljungberg, F., Kristofforsen, S.: Exploring Support for Knowledge Management in Mobile Work. In: Proceedings of ECSCW, pp. 259–275. Kluwer Academic Publishers, Dordrecht (1999)

Gyricon LLC, http://www.gyriconmedia.com

Harper, R., Hughes, J., Shapiro, D.: Harmonious Working and CSCW: Computer Technology and Air Traffic Control. In: ECSCW, pp. 73–86. North-Holland, Amsterdam (1989)

Harrison, S., Minneman, S., Back, M., Balsamo, A., Chow, M., Gold, R., Gorbet, M., MacDonald, D.: The what of XFR: eXperiments in the future of reading. Interactions 8(3) (2001)

Heath, C., Luff, P.: Collaboration and Control: Crisis Management and Multimedia Technology in LU Line Control Rooms. CSCW 1, 1–2 (1992)

Heath C and Luff P (1996) Documents and Professional Practice: "bad" organisational reasons for "good" clinical records. In: Proceedings of CSCW. ACM, pp 354-63

Heath, C., Jirotka, M., Luff, P., Hindmarsh, J.: Unpacking Collaboration: the Interactional Organisation of Trading in a Dealing Room. CSCW 3(2), 147–165 (1994)

Hecht, D.: Printed Embedded Data Graphical User Interfaces. IEEE Computer 34(3), 47–55 (2001)

Herdman, P.T.: A reading and writing revolution in Physics World, pp. 18–19 (2004)

Johnson, W., Jellinek, H., Klotz, L., Rao, R., Card, S.: Bridging the paper and electronic worlds: the paper user interface. In: Proceedings of INTERCHI, pp. 507–512 (1993)

Kindberg, T., Barton, J., Morgan, J., Becke, G., Caswell, D., Debaty, P., Gopal, G., Frid, M., Krishinan, V., Morris, H., Schettino, J., Serra, B., Spasojevic, M.: People, Places, Things: Web Presence in The Real World. In: Proceedings of MONET, pp. 365–376 (2002)

Kobler, A., Norrie, M.: MS Java: A Persistent Object Management Framework, in Java & Databases. Kogan Page Science, London (2002)

Koike, H., Sato, Y., Kobayashi, Y.: Integrating paper and digital information on Enhanced-Desk: a method for realtime finger tracking on an augmented desk system. TOCHI 8(4), 307–322 (2001)

Lamble, C.: Active Matrix Electronic Paper Displays. In: Proceedings of Reforming Paper: Dissolving the paper-digital divide, Beaconsfield, UK (2003)

Luff, P., Heath, C., Norrie, M., Signer, B., Herdman, P.: Only Touching the Surface: Creating Affinities Between Digital Content and Paper. In: Proceedings of CSCW, Chicago, 8th - 10th November, pp. 523–532 (2004)

Luff, P., Heath, C.: Mobility in Collaboration. In: Proceedings of CSCW, pp. 305–314. ACM Press, New York (1998)

Luff, P., Tallyn, E., Sellen, A., Heath, C., Frohlich, D., Murphy, R.: User Studies, Content Provider Studies and Design Concepts (IST-2000-26130/D4 & 5) (25th Jan. 2000)

Mackay, W.E., Pothier, G., Letondal, C., Bøegh, K., Sørensen, H.E.: The Missing Link: Augmenting Biology Laboratory Notebooks. In: Proceedings of UIST, pp. 41–50. ACM Press, New York (2002)

McGee, D., Cohen, P., Wu, L.: Something from nothing: Augmenting a paper-based work practice with multimodal interaction. In: Proceedings of DARE, pp. 71–78. ACM Press, New York (2000)

Nelson, L., Ichimura, S., Rønby Pedersen, E., Adams, L.: Palette: a paper interface for giving presentations. In: Proceedings of CHI, pp. 354–361 (1999)

Norrie, M., Signer, B.: Switching over to Paper: A New Web Channel. In: Proceedings of WISE, pp. 209–218. IEEE Computer Society Press, Los Alamitos (2003)

O'Hara, K., Taylor, A., Newman, W., Sellen, A.: Understanding the Materiality of Writing from Multiple Sources. International Journal of Human-Computer Studies 56(3), 269–305 (2002)

Philips Research, http://www.research.philips.com

Remonen, T.: Paper as an Active Display. In: Proceedings of Reforming Paper. Beaconsfield, UK (2003)

Schmidt, K.: The critical role of workplace studies in CSCW. In: Luff, P., Hindmarsh, J., Heath, C. (eds.) Workplace Studies, pp. 141–149. CUP (2000)

Sellen, A., Harper, R.H.R.: The Myth of the Paperless Office. MIT Press, Cambridge (2002)

Seyrat, E., Hayes, R.A.: Amorphous fluoropolymers as insulators for reversible low-voltage electrowetting. J. Appl. Phys. 90(3), 1383–1386 (2001)

Signer, B.: Fundamental Concepts for Interactive Paper and Cross-Media Information Spaces. PhD Thesis ETH No. 16218, Zurich, Switzerland (2006)

Signer, B., Norrie, M.: Multi-Layered Cross-Media Linking. In: Proceedings of Hypertext, pp. 106–107. ACM Press, New York (2003)

Signer, B., Norrie, M.: A Framework for Cross-Media Information Management. In: Proceedings of EuroIMSA, International Conference on Internet and Multimedia Systems and Applications, Grindelwald, Switzerland (Feb. 2005)

Siio, I., Masui, T., Fukuchi, K.: Real-world Interaction using the FieldMouse. In: Proceedings of UIST, pp. 113–199 (1999)

Silberman, S.: The Hot New Medium: Paper How the oldest interface in the book is redrawing the map of the networked world. In: Wired, pp. 184–191 (2001)

Suchman, L.: Making a Case: "Knowledge" and "Routine" Work in Document Production. In: Luff, P., Hindmarsh, J., Heath, C. (eds.) Workplace Studies, pp. 29–45. CUP (2000)

Wellner, P.: The DigitalDesk Calculator: Tactile Manipulation on a Desk Top Display. In: Proceedings of UIST, pp. 27–33 (1991)

Wiziway, http://www.new.wiziway.com

Wood, D.: NanoChromics – how like paper can it get? In: Proceedings of Reforming Paper, Beaconsfield, UK (2003)

Yeh, R.B., Liao, C., Klemmer, S.: ButterflyNet: A Mobile Capture and Access System for Field Biology Research. In: Proceedings of CHI, ACM, New York (2006)

Author Index

Subject Index

Lecture Notes in Computer Science

For information about Vols. 1–4395

please contact your bookseller or Springer

Vol. 4448: M. Giacobini et al. (Ed.), Applications of Evolutionary Computing. XXIII, 755 pages. 2007.

Vol. 4447: E. Marchiori, J.H. Moore, J.C. Rajapakse (Eds.), Evolutionary Computation,Machine Learning and Data Mining in Bioinformatics. XI, 302 pages. 2007.

Vol. 4446: C. Cotta, J. van Hemert (Eds.), Evolutionary Computation in Combinatorial Optimization. XII, 241 pages. 2007.

Vol. 4445: M. Ebner, M. O'Neill, A. Ekárt, L. Vanneschi, A.I. Esparcia-Alcázar (Eds.), Genetic Programming. XI, 382 pages. 2007.

Vol. 4444: T. Reps, M. Sagiv, J. Bauer (Eds.), Program Analysis and Compilation, Theory and Practice. X, 361 pages. 2007.

Vol. 4443: R. Kotagiri, P.R. Krishna, M. Mohania, E. Nantajeewarawat (Eds.), Advances in Databases: Concepts, Systems and Applications. XXI, 1126 pages. 2007.

Vol. 4440: B. Liblit, Cooperative Bug Isolation. XV, 101 pages. 2007.

Vol. 4439: W. Abramowicz (Ed.), Business Information Systems. XV, 654 pages. 2007.

Vol. 4438: L. Maicher, A. Sigel, L.M. Garshol (Eds.), Leveraging the Semantics of Topic Maps. X, 257 pages. 2007. (Sublibrary LNAI).

Vol. 4433: E. Şahin, W.M. Spears, A.F.T. Winfield (Eds.), Swarm Robotics. XII, 221 pages. 2007.

Vol. 4432: B. Beliczynski, A. Dzielinski, M. Iwanowski, B. Ribeiro (Eds.), Adaptive and Natural Computing Algorithms, Part II. XXVI, 761 pages. 2007.

Vol. 4431: B. Beliczynski, A. Dzielinski, M. Iwanowski, B. Ribeiro (Eds.), Adaptive and Natural Computing Algorithms, Part I. XXV, 851 pages. 2007.

Vol. 4430: C.C. Yang, D. Zeng, M. Chau, K. Chang, Q. Yang, X. Cheng, J. Wang, F.-Y. Wang, H. Chen (Eds.), Intelligence and Security Informatics. XII, 330 pages. 2007.

Vol. 4429: R. Lu, J.H. Siekmann, C. Ullrich (Eds.), Cognitive Systems. X, 161 pages. 2007. (Sublibrary LNAI).

Vol. 4427: S. Uhlig, K. Papagiannaki, O. Bonaventure (Eds.), Passive and Active Network Measurement. XI, 274 pages. 2007.

Vol. 4426: Z.-H. Zhou, H. Li, Q. Yang (Eds.), Advances in Knowledge Discovery and Data Mining. XXV, 1161 pages. 2007. (Sublibrary LNAI).

Vol. 4425: G. Amati, C. Carpineto, G. Romano (Eds.), Advances in Information Retrieval. XIX, 759 pages. 2007.

Vol. 4424: O. Grumberg, M. Huth (Eds.), Tools and Algorithms for the Construction and Analysis of Systems. XX, 738 pages. 2007.

Vol. 4423: H. Seidl (Ed.), Foundations of Software Science and Computational Structures. XVI, 379 pages. 2007.

Vol. 4422: M.B. Dwyer, A. Lopes (Eds.), Fundamental Approaches to Software Engineering. XV, 440 pages. 2007.

Vol. 4421: R. De Nicola (Ed.), Programming Languages and Systems. XVII, 538 pages. 2007.

Vol. 4420: S. Krishnamurthi, M. Odersky (Eds.), Compiler Construction. XIV, 233 pages. 2007.

Vol. 4419: P.C. Diniz, E. Marques, K. Bertels, M.M. Fernandes, J.M.P. Cardoso (Eds.), Reconfigurable Computing: Architectures, Tools and Applications. XIV, 391 pages. 2007.

Vol. 4418: A. Gagalowicz, W. Philips (Eds.), Computer Vision/Computer Graphics Collaboration Techniques. XV, 620 pages. 2007.

Vol. 4416: A. Bemporad, A. Bicchi, G. Buttazzo (Eds.), Hybrid Systems: Computation and Control. XVII, 797 pages. 2007.

Vol. 4415: P. Lukowicz, L. Thiele, G. Tröster (Eds.), Architecture of Computing Systems - ARCS 2007. X, 297 pages. 2007.

Vol. 4414: S. Hochreiter, R. Wagner (Eds.), Bioinformatics Research and Development. XVI, 482 pages. 2007. (Sublibrary LNBI).

Vol. 4412: F. Stajano, H.J. Kim, J.-S. Chae, S.-D. Kim (Eds.), Ubiquitous Convergence Technology. XI, 302 pages. 2007.

Vol. 4411: R.H. Bordini, M. Dastani, J. Dix, A.E.F. Seghrouchni (Eds.), Programming Multi-Agent Systems. XIV, 249 pages. 2007. (Sublibrary LNAI).

Vol. 4410: A. Branco (Ed.), Anaphora: Analysis, Algorithms and Applications. X, 191 pages. 2007. (Sublibrary LNAI).

Vol. 4409: J.L. Fiadeiro, P.-Y. Schobbens (Eds.), Recent Trends in Algebraic Development Techniques. VII, 171 pages. 2007.

Vol. 4407: G. Puebla (Ed.), Logic-Based Program Synthesis and Transformation. VIII, 237 pages. 2007.

Vol. 4406: W. De Meuter (Ed.), Advances in Smalltalk. VII, 157 pages. 2007.

Vol. 4405: L. Padgham, F. Zambonelli (Eds.), Agent-Oriented Software Engineering VII. XII, 225 pages. 2007.

Vol. 4403: S. Obayashi, K. Deb, C. Poloni, T. Hiroyasu, T. Murata (Eds.), Evolutionary Multi-Criterion Optimization. XIX, 954 pages. 2007.

Vol. 4401: N. Guelfi, D. Buchs (Eds.), Rapid Integration of Software Engineering Techniques. IX, 177 pages. 2007.

Vol. 4400: J.F. Peters, A. Skowron, V.W. Marek, E. Orłowska, R. Słowiński, W. Ziarko (Eds.), Transactions on Rough Sets VII, Part II. X, 381 pages. 2007.

Vol. 4399: T. Kovacs, X. Llorà, K. Takadama, P.L. Lanzi, W. Stolzmann, S.W. Wilson (Eds.), Learning Classifier Systems. XII, 345 pages. 2007. (Sublibrary LNAI).

Vol. 4398: S. Marchand-Maillet, E. Bruno, A. Nürnberger, M. Detyniecki (Eds.), Adaptive Multimedia Retrieval: User, Context, and Feedback. XI, 269 pages. 2007.

Vol. 4397: C. Stephanidis, M. Pieper (Eds.), Universal Access in Ambient Intelligence Environments. XV, 467 pages. 2007.

Vol. 4396: J. García-Vidal, L. Cerdà-Alabern (Eds.), Wireless Systems and Mobility in Next Generation Internet. IX, 271 pages. 2007.